George F. Cram Company

Unrivaled Atlas of the World

indexed

George F. Cram Company

Unrivaled Atlas of the World
indexed

ISBN/EAN: 9783337293772

Printed in Europe, USA, Canada, Australia, Japan

Cover: Foto ©Andreas Hilbeck / pixelio.de

More available books at **www.hansebooks.com**

GEORGE F. CRAM,

415 Dearborn Street, CHICAGO, ILL.

AND

113 Nassau Street, NEW YORK CITY.

Address Office Nearest To You

TABLE OF CONTENTS.

MAPS OF THE STATES AND TERRITORIES OF THE UNITED STATES.

MAPS OF CONTINENTS, FOREIGN COUNTRIES, ETC.

TABLE OF CONTENTS.

MAPS OF CITIES.

HISTORY AND HISTORICAL MAPS

DIAGRAMS AND ILLUSTRATIONS.

STATISTICS.

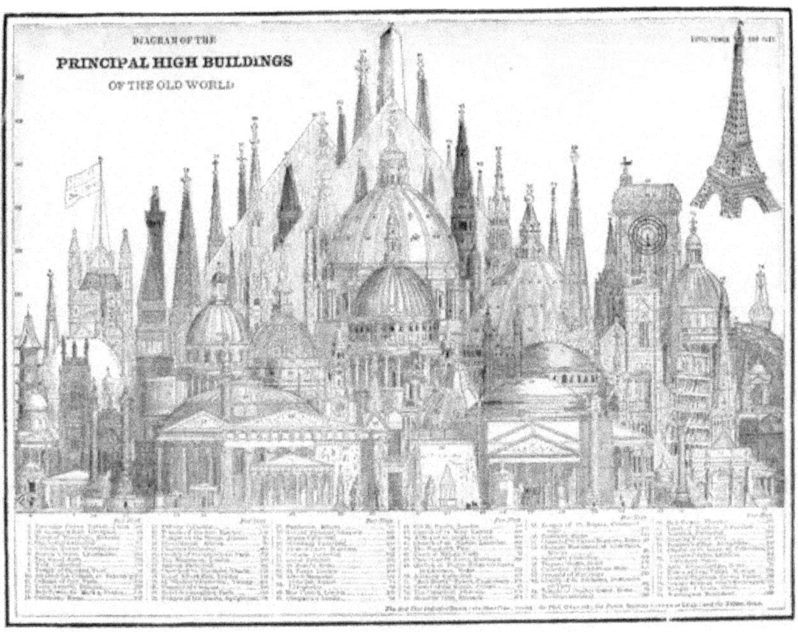
DIAGRAM OF THE
PRINCIPAL HIGH BUILDINGS
OF THE OLD WORLD

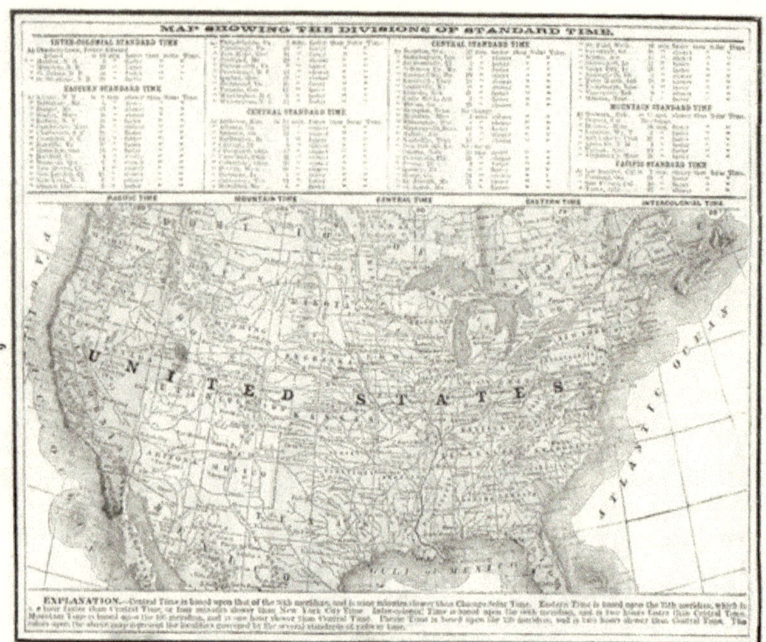
MAP SHOWING THE DIVISIONS OF STANDARD TIME.
INTER-COLONIAL STANDARD TIME
EASTERN STANDARD TIME
CENTRAL STANDARD TIME
CENTRAL STANDARD TIME
MOUNTAIN STANDARD TIME
PACIFIC STANDARD TIME
PACIFIC TIME
MOUNTAIN TIME
CENTRAL TIME
EASTERN TIME
INTERCOLONIAL TIME
UNITED STATES
ATLANTIC OCEAN
GULF of MEXICO
EXPLANATION.

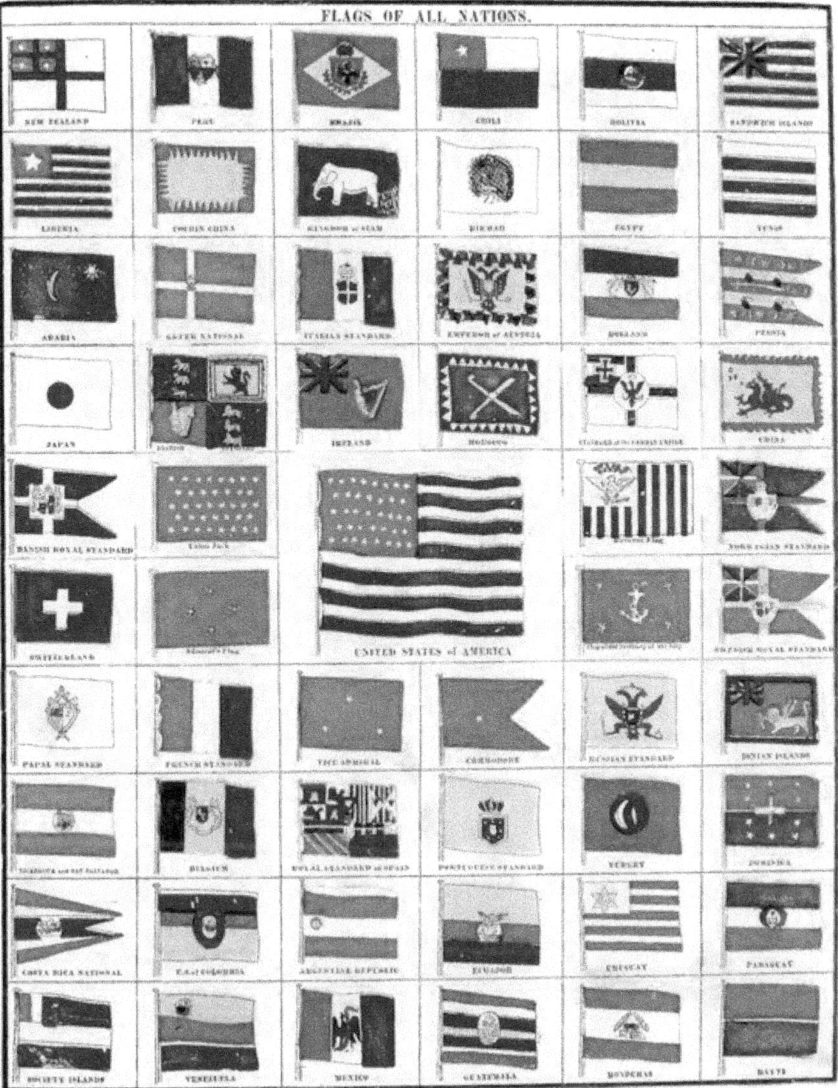
FLAGS OF ALL NATIONS.
UNITED STATES of AMERICA

ARMS OF VARIOUS NATIONS.
UNITED STATES
GREAT BRITAIN
GERMANY
FRANCE
AUSTRIA
RUSSIA
CANADA
ITALY
BELGIUM
NETHERLANDS
SPAIN
TURKEY
AUSTRALIA
CHINA
EGYPT
NORWAY
SWEDEN
IRELAND
HAYTI
SIAM
TUNIS
SCOTLAND
SWITZERLAND
PORTUGAL
JAPAN
MEXICO
PARAGUAY
BRAZIL
GREECE
HONDURAS
U. S. OF COLUMBIA
GUATEMALA
PERSIA
SAN SALVADOR
CUBA
TUSCANY
LIBERIA
HAWAIIAN IS.
PERU
IONIAN IS.
DENMARK
URUGUAY
LUXEMBURG
ORANGE FREE STATE
ARGENTINE REPUBLIC
CHILI
ECUADOR
VENEZUELA

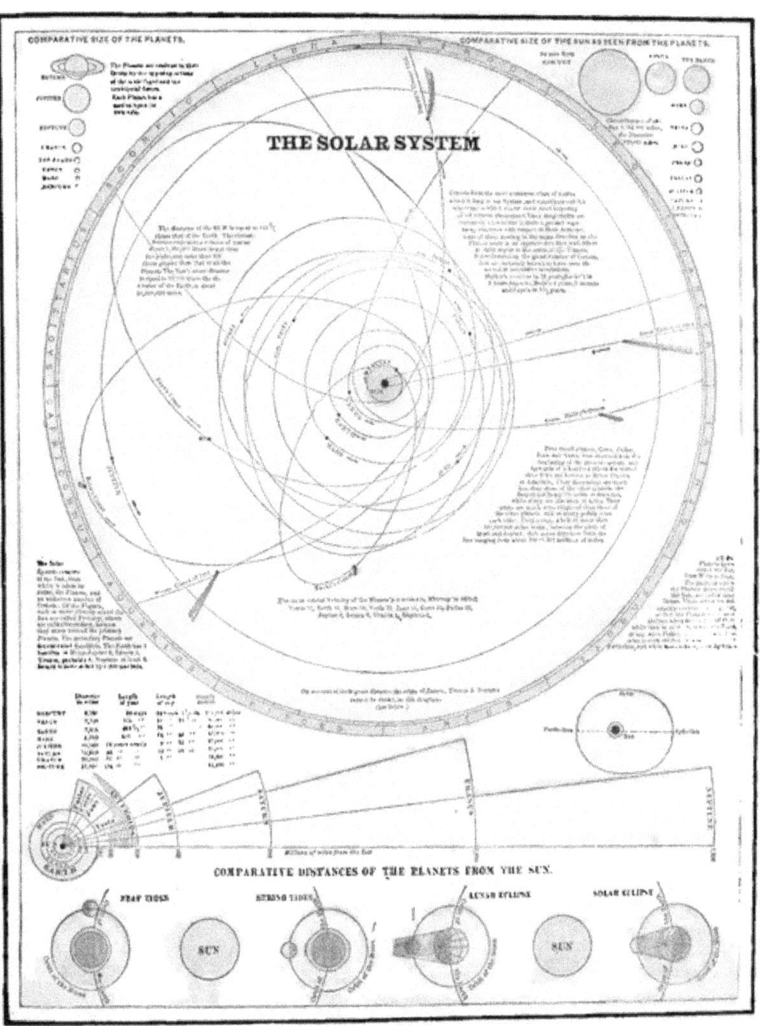
COMPARATIVE SIZE OF THE PLANETS.
COMPARATIVE SIZE OF THE SUN AS SEEN FROM THE PLANETS.
THE SOLAR SYSTEM
COMPARATIVE DISTANCES OF THE PLANETS FROM THE SUN.
SUN
SUN

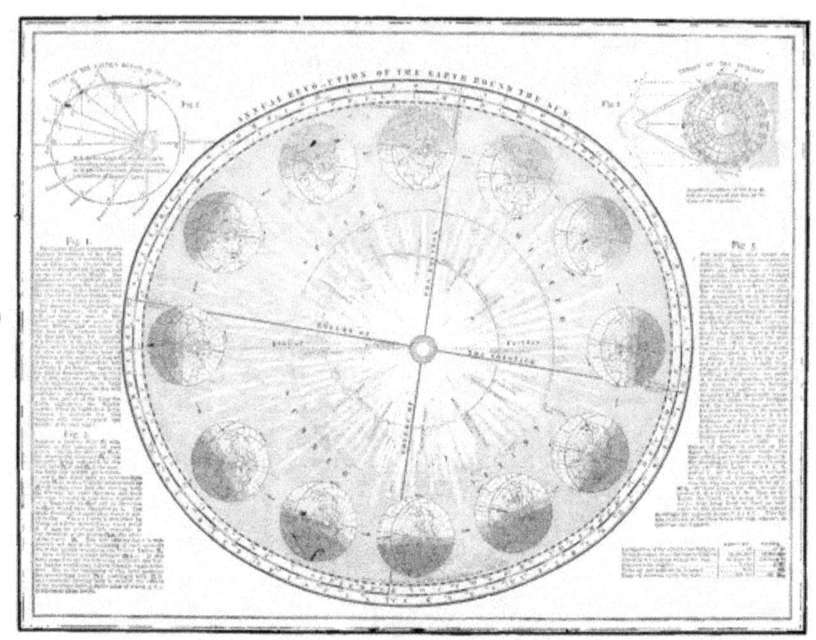
ANNUAL REVOLUTION OF THE EARTH ROUND THE SUN
Fig. 1
Fig. 2
Fig. 3

THE EARTH

THE origin of the earth is an unsolved, if not an insolvable mystery. Ingenious theories on this subject have been elaborated, but none of them have been actually verified. Kant, Laplace, and others, have devoted a good deal of study to the birth of the earth. Their ideas are interesting without being satisfactory, or worthy of more than mere reference in this connection. We know that it was a slow development. That much is certain. The records of geology show that "in the beginning" must have been millions, and probably billions, of ages ago, and that the present life, animal and vegetable, of the world, including man, must be of comparatively recent date. The commonly received opinion is that originally the planets were sparks from the sun, vast gaseous or liquid matter, and that, by a process of cooling and solidifying, was brought into existence the rocks, soil, and various transmutations which make up a habitable world. It is supposed that some planets are now going through the process of preparation for utility, and perhaps others, again, have literally outlived their usefulness.

Earth history is written in the strata or crust of the earth. Each stratum represents and records a vast and distinct formative period. Geological scientists class the strata into five distinct geological periods—these consist of the silurian, the carboniferous, the cretaceous, the tertiary and the alluvial. The latter period is subdivided into the eocene, miocene, pliocene, and the diluvian, man first appearing in the latter. Other scientists divide the earth's history into seven ages, as follows: First, archæan, or before that of mollusks; second, age of mollusks; third, age of fishes; fourth, age of frogs and relative animals; fifth, age of true reptiles; sixth, age of mammals; seventh, age of man.

GEOGRAPHY is a description of the earth. The term is derived from two Greek words signifying "the earth" and "to describe." It may be divided into three departments—mathematical, physical or natural, and political geography.

Mathematical geography treats of the form, size and motions of the earth; of its division by circles, and of the representation of its surface upon globes, maps and charts. The earth is nearly round. Its curvature is not that of an exact sphere, but the form is that of an oblate spheroid "flattened at the poles." The polar diameter is 7,899 miles, and the equatorial, 7,925½, a difference of about 26½ miles. The calculations of scientists vary somewhat. Airy computed the polar diameter at 7,899.17 miles, equatorial, 7,925.64 miles, and the compression at the poles, 26.47 miles; Bessel computed the polar at 7,899.11, equatorial, 7,925.60, and the compression, 26.4 miles.

For convenience of reference the earth is divided by imaginary lines called the great and small circles. Great circles divide it into two equal parts—the equator is a great circle, the boundary between the Northern and Southern Hemispheres. Circles, for convenience of measurement, are divided into 360 degrees. A degree is 1-360 part of a circle, the length of the degree varying with the size of the circle. A degree on the equator is about 69½ English or American miles. As the circles of latitude grow smaller as their distance from the equator increases, the length of each degree lessens.

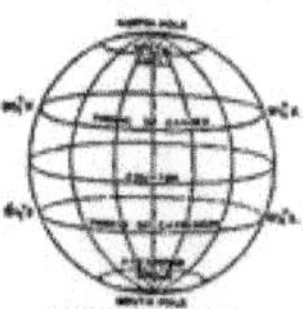
THE CIRCLES OF THE EARTH.

The Meridian circles are those great circles which pass through the poles. Each divides the earth into an Eastern and Western Hemisphere. A meridian is a half of a meridian circle and extends from pole to pole. Parallels are small circles parallel to the equator; the principal ones being the two tropics and the polar circles.

LATITUDE is distance north or south from the Equator. It is measured, in degrees, on a meridian. Places between the Equator and the North Pole are in north latitude; those between the Equator and the South Pole are in south latitude; those on the Equator have no latitude. The poles have the greatest possible latitude, which is 90 degrees.

LONGITUDE is distance east or west from a selected meridian. It is measured, in degrees, on the Equator or any parallel. The selected meridian is called the first meridian. The meridian in most common use is that which passes through Greenwich Observatory, near London. In the United States the meridian of Washington is sometimes used; places on the first meridian have no longitude. The greatest longitude is 180 degrees, east or west. A degree of any great circle measures 60 geographical miles, or about 69½ statute miles of the United States. A degree on the parallel of 60° is just half as long.

ZONES are broad belts or divisions of the earth's surface parallel to the Equator. They are bounded by the tropics and the polar circles. They are five in number: The Torrid, the North and South Temperate, and the North and South Frigid.

William Swinton in his excellent work presents in the following table a view of the several zones, with important particulars under the various topics of climate, vegetation, products of cultivation, animals, and population:

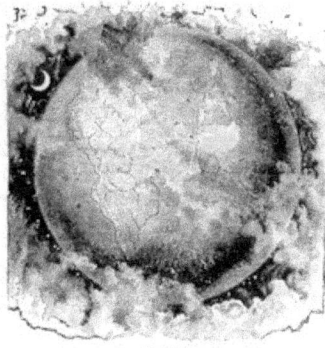

	Climate.	Vegetation.	Products of Cultivation.	Animals.	Population.
Torrid Zone.	Marked by great and uniform heat, with two seasons,—the rainy and the dry; snow never seen except on high mountain-tops; days and nights of little variation in length.	Marked by a very great luxuriance; characteristic trees are palms and tree ferns, mahogany, sandal-wood, cinchona, etc.	Cotton, coffee, sugar, rice, spices, oranges, bananas, etc.	Noted for their largeness, fierceness, and strength; characteristic types are the elephant, lion, camel-leopard, rhinoceros, tiger, gorilla, crocodile, ostrich.	Generally of a dark complexion, and with few exceptions, not progressive or highly civilized; in some cases savages.
Temperate Zones.	Marked by the four seasons, with hot summers and cold winters, and days and nights varying more in length than in Torrid Zone.	Oak, laurel, olive, etc., in the warm regions; maple, elm, beech, ash, walnut, chestnut, etc., in the middle regions; pine, fir, in the cold regions.	Grains, potatoes, peas, beans, flax, hemp, the apple, the pear, rice, tobacco, cotton.	The domestic animals, as the horse, ox, sheep, camel, etc.; also deer, wolves, bears, etc.	The superior races of the world, noted for their great progress in wealth, intelligence, and enterprise.
Frigid Zones.	Marked by a long and intensely cold winter, and by a short but comparatively warm summer, with days lengthening toward the Poles, where day and night are each six months long.	Exceedingly scanty, being almost confined to mosses and lichens.	Neither grain nor excellent fruits can be grown.	White bear, reindeer, and fur-bearing animals, with the whale, walrus, seal and sea-birds.	Scanty in numbers, and showing a low type of civilization.

PHYSICAL GEOGRAPHY.—Treats of the land and water into which the earth's surface is divided; of the atmosphere which surrounds the earth, and of the animals and plants which live upon it. A little more than one-fourth of the surface of the earth is land, about 52,158,000 square miles, and the remainder water, 147,000,000 square miles. The Eastern Hemisphere contains more than twice as much land as the Western, the Northern nearly three times as much land as the Southern. At no point on the earth's surface is the great body of water entirely separated by land. It extends from pole to pole, and entirely encompasses each of the large masses of land on the surface of the earth.

The principal natural divisions of the land are continents and islands. Continents are large bodies of land. They are six in number: Europe, Asia, Africa and Australia in the Eastern Hemisphere, and North and South America in the Western Hemisphere. Islands are a body of land entirely surrounded by water. The chief distinction between a continent and an island is the difference in size.

The Continents comprise more than five-sixths of the land surface of the earth. They are often divided into two—the Eastern and Western Continents. The Eastern Continent is broad and compact in shape, and its greatest extent is from east to west. The Western is long and narrow and its greatest extent is from north to south.

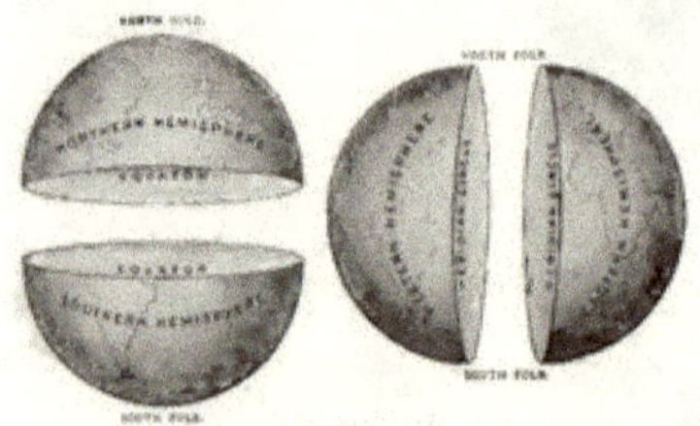

THE HEMISPHERES.

The chief elevations of the land surface are mountains, table lands, or plateaus, and lowland plains. A mountain is a tract of land which rises considerably above the general surface.

Mountains are seldom found single, but are generally in groups or chains. A mountain chain is an irregular mass of elevated land, which is sometimes several thousand miles long and more than a hundred wide. A chain of mountains is also called a ridge, or range. A number of chains, extending in the same general direction, constitute what is called a mountain system. The highest point on the earth's surface is a mountain lately discovered in the Island of New Guinea, named Mt. Hercules. The greatest depression of the land surface is at the Dead Sea, 1,300 feet below the level of the ocean.

A volcano is a mountain which sends forth flames, melted rocks, clouds of steam, ashes, or other heated substance, from an opening called a crater. A table land or plateau is a broad extent of high land. Table lands are often crossed or bordered by mountain ranges. The breadth of a mountain is generally less than that of a plateau. A lowland plain is

ZONES OF ANIMAL LIFE.

a broad extent of land not much above the level of the sea. A valley is land between hills or mountains. A desert is a barren tract of land. An oasis is a low, fertile spot in a desert.

The principal natural divisions of the water are divided into ocean water and drainage waters. The former are the great bodies of salt water that surround all the continents. Its five principal divisions are the Atlantic, the Pacific, the Indian, the Arctic and Antarctic oceans. A sea, gulf, bay, strait or channel are portions or arms of the ocean. The Drainage waters are rivers and lakes. A river is a large stream of fresh water. A lake is a body of water surrounded by land. The color of the ocean is generally a deep blue, but toward the coast it turns to a bluish green. The Pacific ocean has the greatest area. (See colored diagram, page 18.) The depth of the ocean varies from 1,000 to 30,000 feet. Its greatest depth is in the North Atlantic. Ocean currents are extensive and regular movements flowing through the ocean. They are caused by the winds and tides, the earth's rotation on its axis, and the heat of the sun. They may be constant or periodical. The former arises from permanent causes, as the earth's rotation and constant winds; the latter from periodical causes, as the tides, shifting winds, etc. The most extensive of the constant currents is the Equatorial current, caused by the earth's rotation. Other important currents are the Gulf Stream, the Japan stream, the Antarctic and Arctic, the East Greenland and the South Atlantic.

The Atmosphere covers the earth to a height of about fifty miles. The upper portions press upon the lower and make them denser. Nearly all the moisture and all animal and vegetable life are found within three and a half miles of the level of the sea. Heat causes air first to expand and become lighter, and second to absorb and render invisible large quantities of water. Cold produces opposite effect. The heat of the sun produces ascending currents of hot air, other air flows in to fill the space, hence we have winds or currents of air.

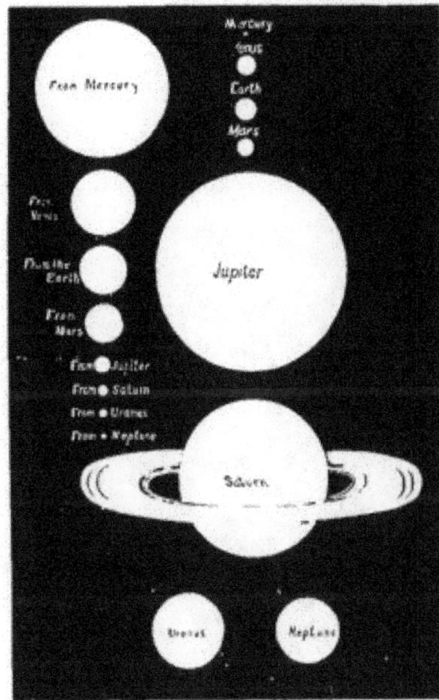
Mercury
Venus
Earth
Mars
From Mercury
From Venus
From the Earth
From Mars
From Jupiter
From Saturn
From Uranus
From Neptune
Jupiter
Saturn
Uranus
Neptune

MALAYAN
MONGOLIAN
CAUCASIAN
AFRICAN
AMERICAN

chronology with exactness, nor do they present to the mind individual types and details; they simply show us the stages by which the savage became a man capable of historic achievements. Horace, the Roman poet, was prophetic of what would be discovered centuries after him when he wrote: "When these brutes, now called men, first crawled out of the ground, a dumb and dirty lot, they fought for nuts and sheltering spots, with nail and fist; then with sticks; later with arms forged of metal. Then they invented names and words. With language and thought came cities, and some relief from strife." In the days of the mammoth man lived in caves—feeding on fruits, nuts and roots, on fish and flesh, by slow and gradual steps he emerged from the cavern of darkest savagery, he was still a hunter living by the chase, or a fisher as circumstances might determine. From hunting to pastoral life was the natural gradation; each of these were necessarily a migratory life. Pastoral life is succeeded by the agricultural. It is only when a people have so far progressed that they are tillers of the soil that permanent habitations are built, and stable institutions are formed.

Man was early endowed with a strong predilection for some sort of implement. Hence we have the stone and bronze age. The researches of archæology have traced out five distinct stages of the stone age. First came the rudest flints, mere chunks of stone. Next came flakes clipped from the rock, showing the dawn of creative or fashioning faculty. The third stage indicates some skill and art in the fashioning of the flint. The fourth age was the beginning of grinding or rubbing. The points are made sharp by attrition. The fifth stage brings the perfectly polished and quite artistic flint implements, which show constructive invention. Between the fifth or stone age and the bronze age intervened a sixth stage, transitional in character, in which copper, cold and crude, was hammered into shape. It was used like a stone, and not fused and fashioned in conformity to the peculiar properties of metals. It was treated as a kind of malleable stone. Very little creative progress was made anywhere during this stage.

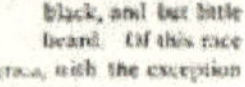

PRIMITIVE MAN AND ANIMAL LIFE.

The seventh stage opens to view the bronze age proper. Then began the fusing of metals. The soft copper and hard tin were blended into the bronze of the prehistoric age.

Sir John Lubbock remarks that "the use of bronze weapons is characteristic of a particular phase in the history of civilization and one which was anterior to the discovery, or, at least, to the general use of iron. Soon after iron came pottery. Man found, not only the advantage of softening metals with fire, but of hardening clay with it. A mass of evidence proves that a stone age prevailed in every great district of the inhabited world, followed, as general progress was made, by the other ages named." As Figuier observes, "The development of man must have been doubtless the same in all parts of the earth, and in whatever country we may consider him, man must have passed through the same phases in order to arrive at his present state. He must have had everywhere his age of stone, his epoch of bronze, and his epoch of iron, in orderly succession."

The human race, found in nearly every part of the world, and adapted to nearly every variety of climate and soil, may be arranged into five general classes or races, namely:

1. The Caucasian, or White. 2. The Mongolian, or Yellow. 3. The Ethiopian, or Negro. 4. The Malay. 5. The American, or Indian.

I. The *Caucasians* take their name from the Caucasus, between the Black and Caspian Seas, where the people are noted for their great beauty; complexion fair, forehead full, hair soft, beard heavy. They are inhabitants of Southwestern Asia, Europe, America, and parts of Africa. They are noted for civilization and great intellect; said to number 600,000,000.

II. The *Mongolians* have a yellow complexion, a flat face, prominent cheek bones, oblique eyes, and coarse, straight black hair. They inhabit Asia, Arctic America, and Northeastern Europe. Their number is estimated at 589,000,000.

III. The *Ethiopians*, or *Negroes*, are quite black; forehead receding, nose flat, lips thick, jaw-bones prominent, hair black and woolly. They number about 185,000,000 and inhabit Africa.

IV. The *Malays* are of different shades of brown with head narrow, forehead low and broad, mouth large, hair and beard abundant, black and curly. They inhabit the Malay peninsula and the islands of Oceanica. Estimated number, 55,000,000.

V. The *Americans*, or *Indians*, are copper colored; broad face, prominent features, forehead low, cheek-bones high, hair straight, close, and black, and but little beard. Of this race are the native tribes of North and South America, with the exception of the inhabitants on the Arctic coasts. Estimated number, 11,000,000.

POLITICAL GEOGRAPHY treats of the division of the world into various Countries or States, and of the state of society, government, religion and occupation of the inhabitants. Nations are divided in respect to their social condition into four classes: 1. Savage. 2. Barbarous. 3. Half civilized. 4. Civilized or enlightened. Savages are those who live in tribes and are the lowest and most degraded class; they obtain their food by hunting and fishing. Barbarians are somewhat more advanced than the savage; they live in tents, possess flocks and herds, and practice a rude agriculture. Half-civilized nations carry on agriculture—have made considerable advance in mechanic arts; have towns and cities, but hold very little communication with foreign countries. Civilized nations are engaged in agriculture, manufactures, commerce—possessing a thorough division of labor, have established systems of education, and have reached the highest perfection. The civilized nations are nearly all Caucasian.

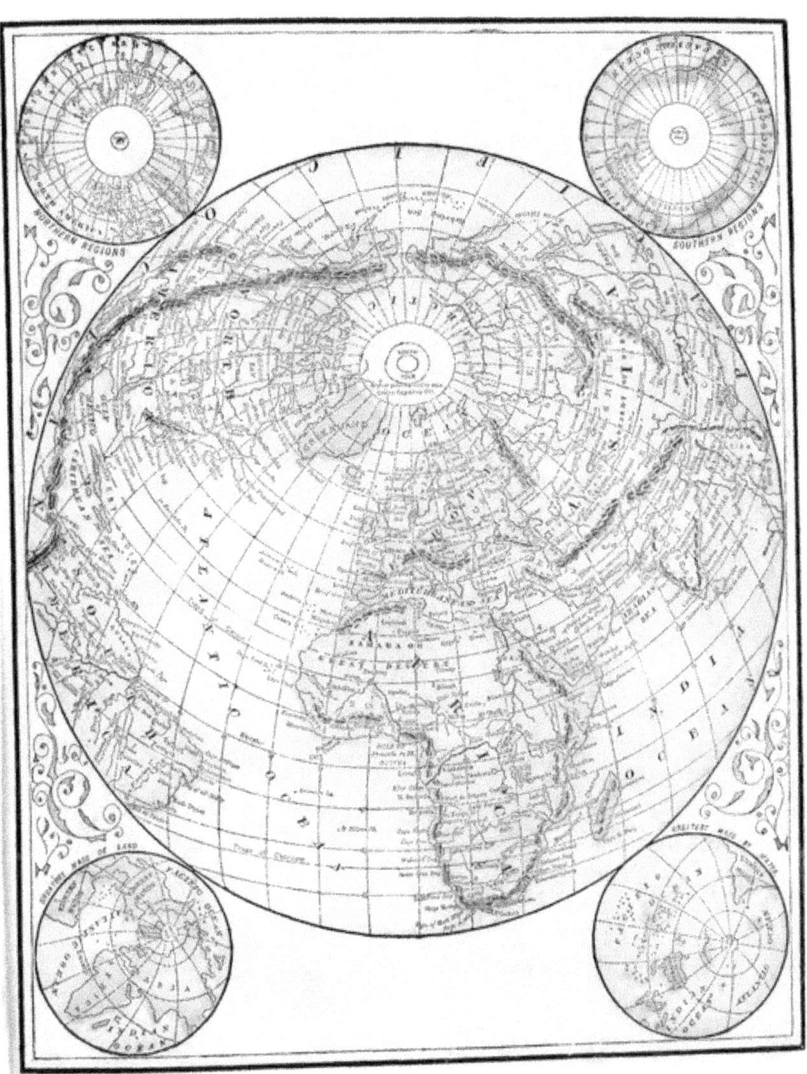
SOUTHERN REGIONS
SOUTHERN REGIONS
INDIAN OCEAN
GREATEST MASS OF WATER
INDIAN OCEAN
MEDITERRANEAN SEA
ARABIAN SEA
SAHARA OR GREAT DESERT
ATLANTIC OCEAN
AFRICA

WESTERN HEMISPHERE

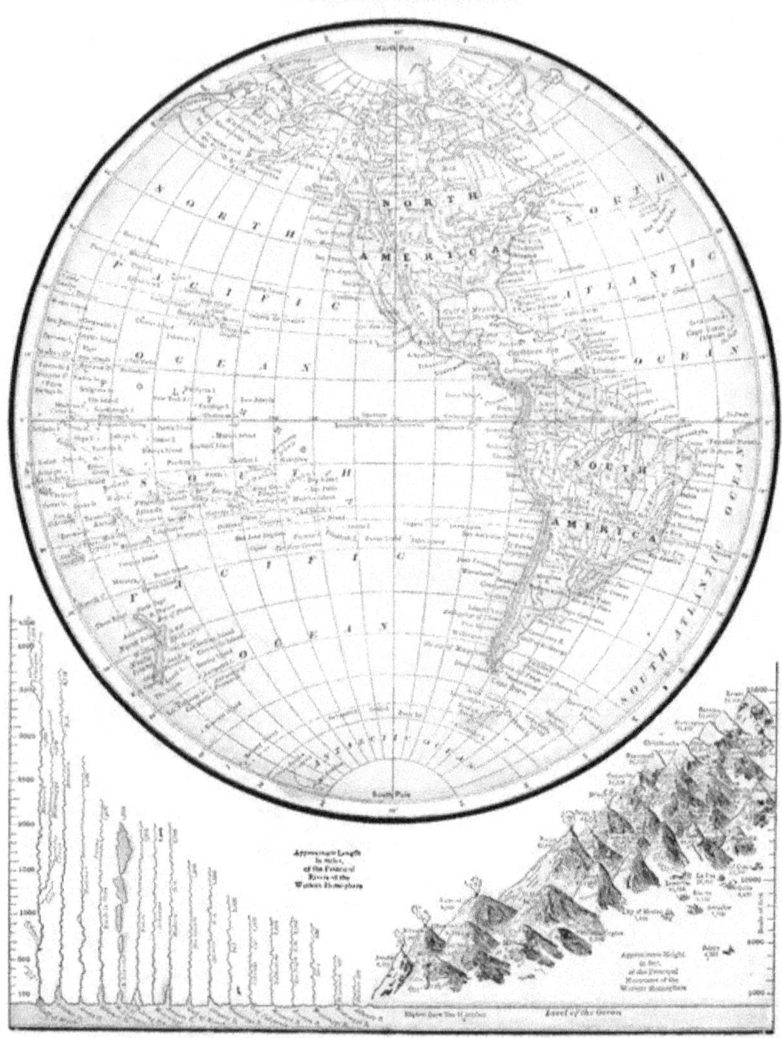

EASTERN HEMISPHERE

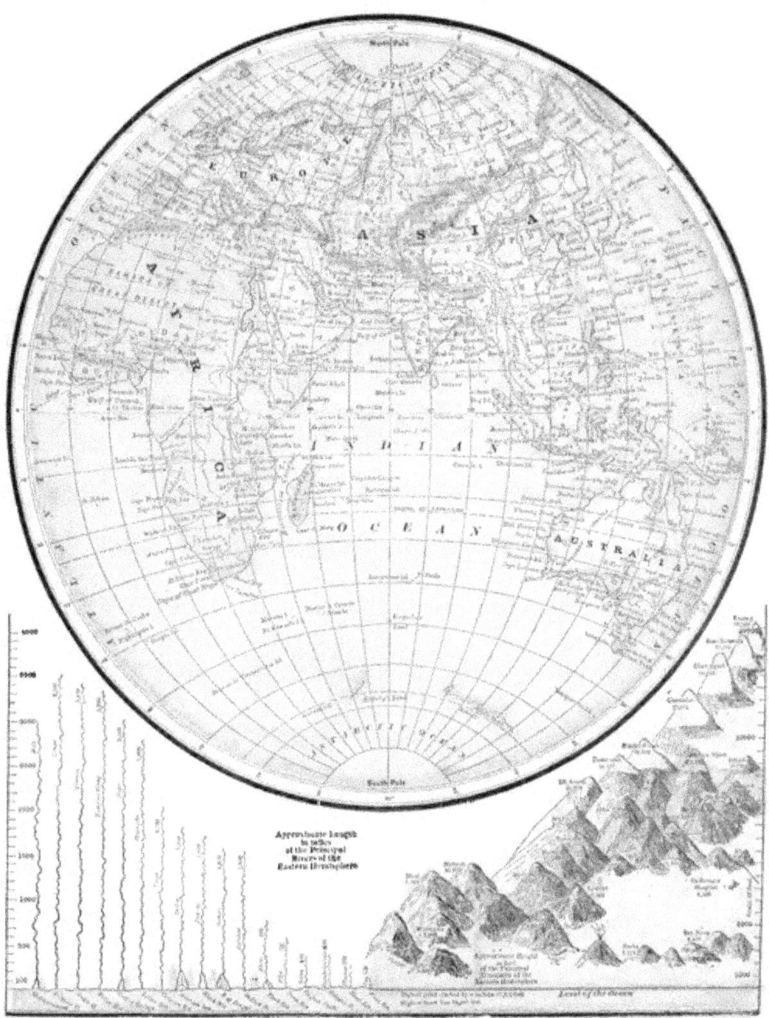

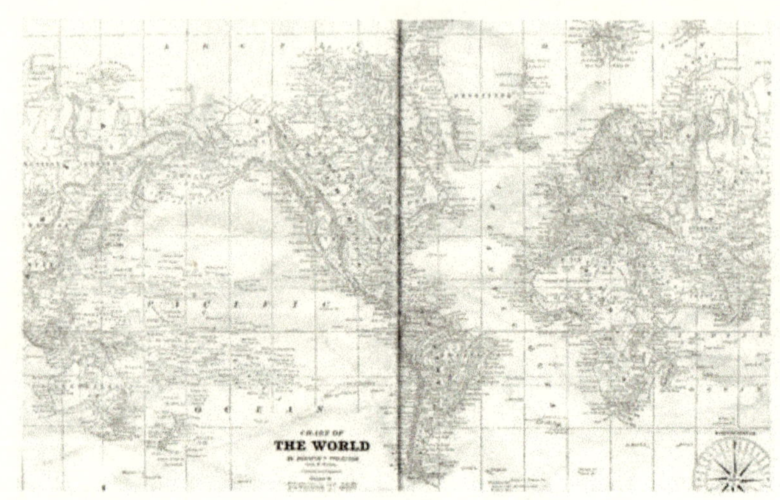
CHART OF
THE WORLD

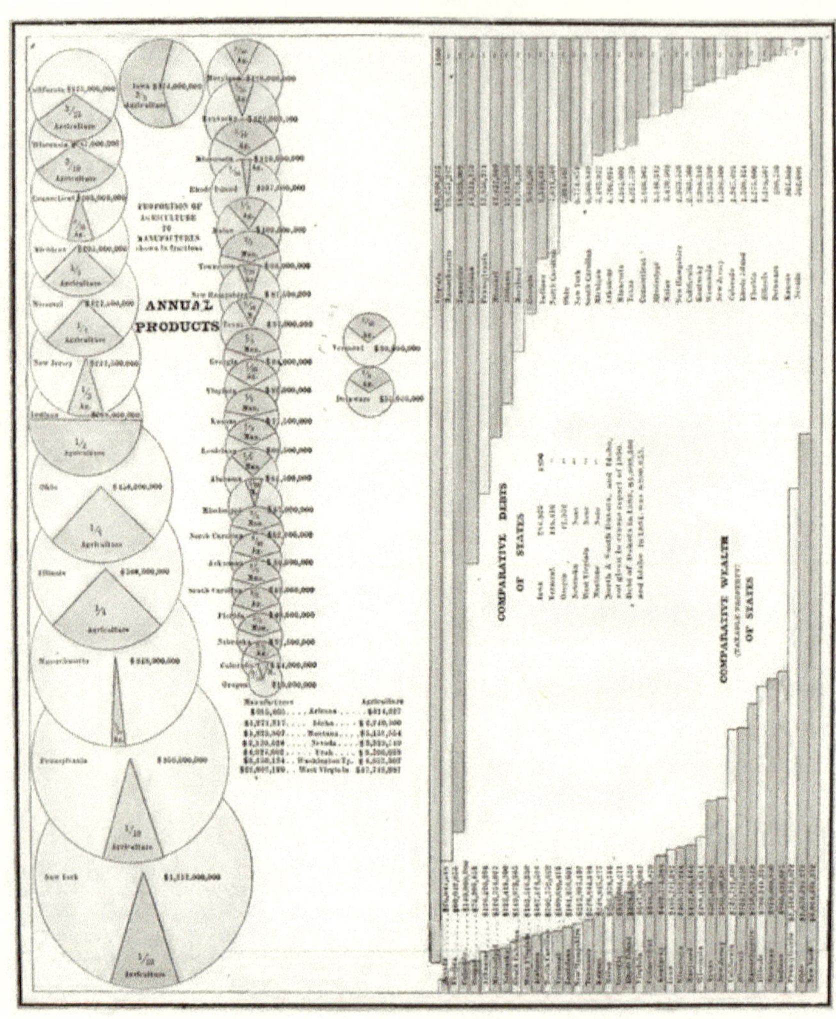
ANNUAL
PRODUCTS
COMPARATIVE DEBTS
OF STATES
COMPARATIVE WEALTH
OF STATES

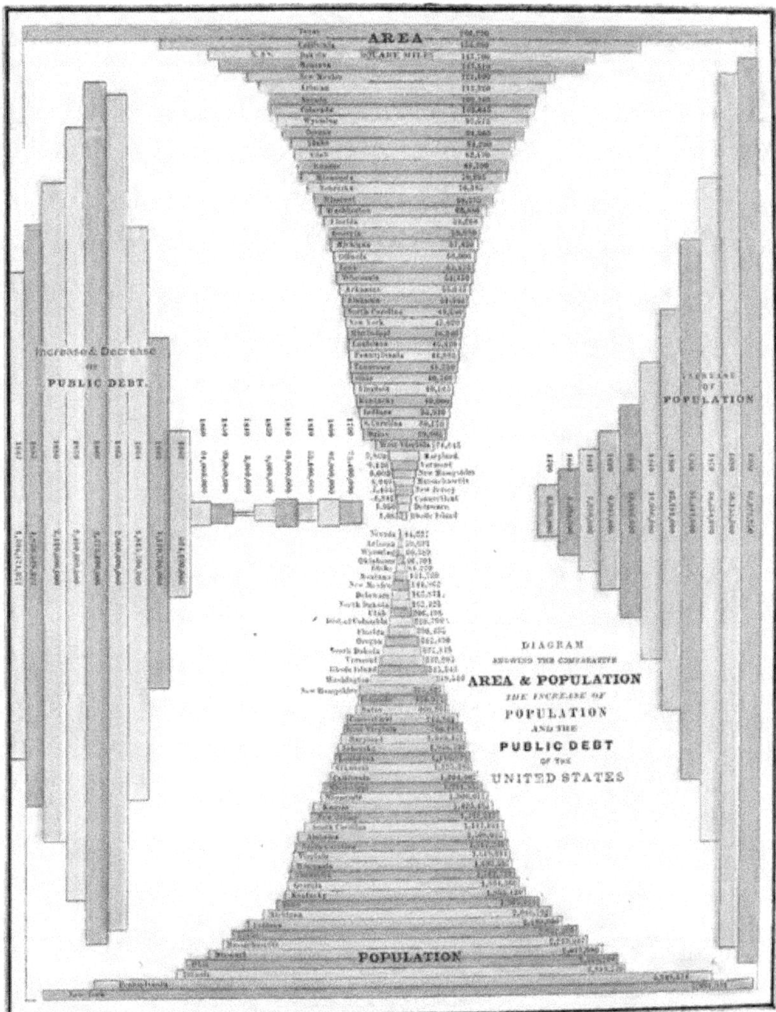
AREA
SQUARE MILES
Increase & Decrease
of
PUBLIC DEBT.
INCREASE
OF
POPULATION
DIAGRAM
SHOWING THE COMPARATIVE
AREA & POPULATION
THE INCREASE OF
POPULATION
AND THE
PUBLIC DEBT
OF THE
UNITED STATES
POPULATION

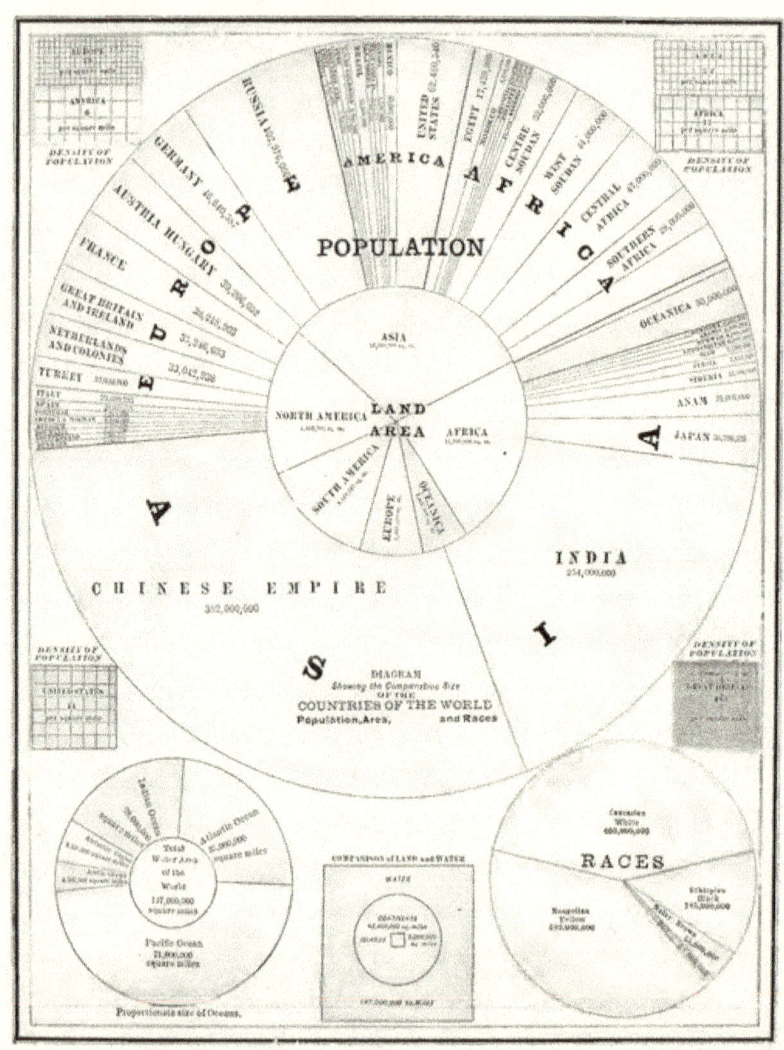

POPULATION
EUROPE
AMERICA
AFRICA
ASIA
RUSSIA
GERMANY
AUSTRIA HUNGARY
FRANCE
GREAT BRITAIN AND IRELAND
NETHERLANDS AND COLONIES
TURKEY
UNITED STATES
EGYPT
CENTRE SOUDAN
WEST SOUDAN
CENTRAL AFRICA
SOUTHERN AFRICA
OCEANICA
ANAM
JAPAN
INDIA
254,000,000
CHINESE EMPIRE
382,000,000
LAND AREA
ASIA
NORTH AMERICA
SOUTH AMERICA
EUROPE
OCEANICA
AFRICA
DENSITY OF POPULATION
DIAGRAM
Showing the Comparative Size
OF THE
COUNTRIES OF THE WORLD
Population, Area, and Races
RACES
Caucasian
White
Mongolian
Yellow
Ethiopian
Black
Total
Water Area
of the
World
Atlantic Ocean
Indian Ocean
Pacific Ocean
square miles
Proportionate size of Oceans.
COMPARISON of LAND and WATER

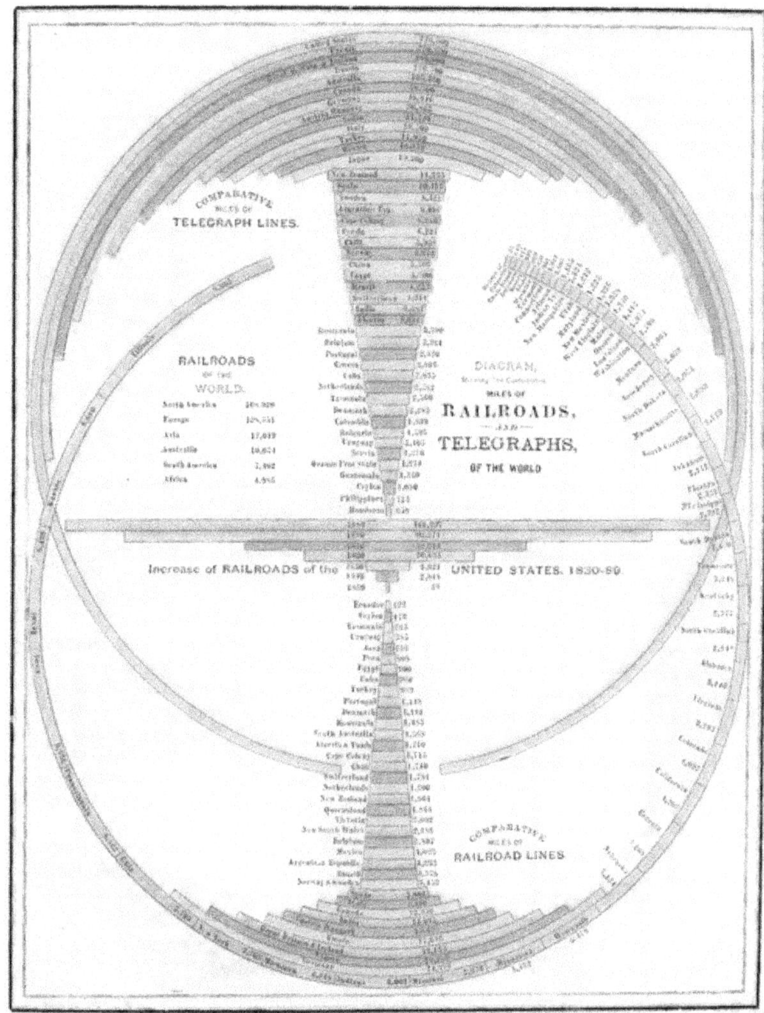
COMPARATIVE MILES OF TELEGRAPH LINES.
RAILROADS OF THE WORLD.
DIAGRAM,
RAILROADS, AND TELEGRAPHS, OF THE WORLD
Increase of RAILROADS of the UNITED STATES. 1830-89
COMPARATIVE MILES OF RAILROAD LINES

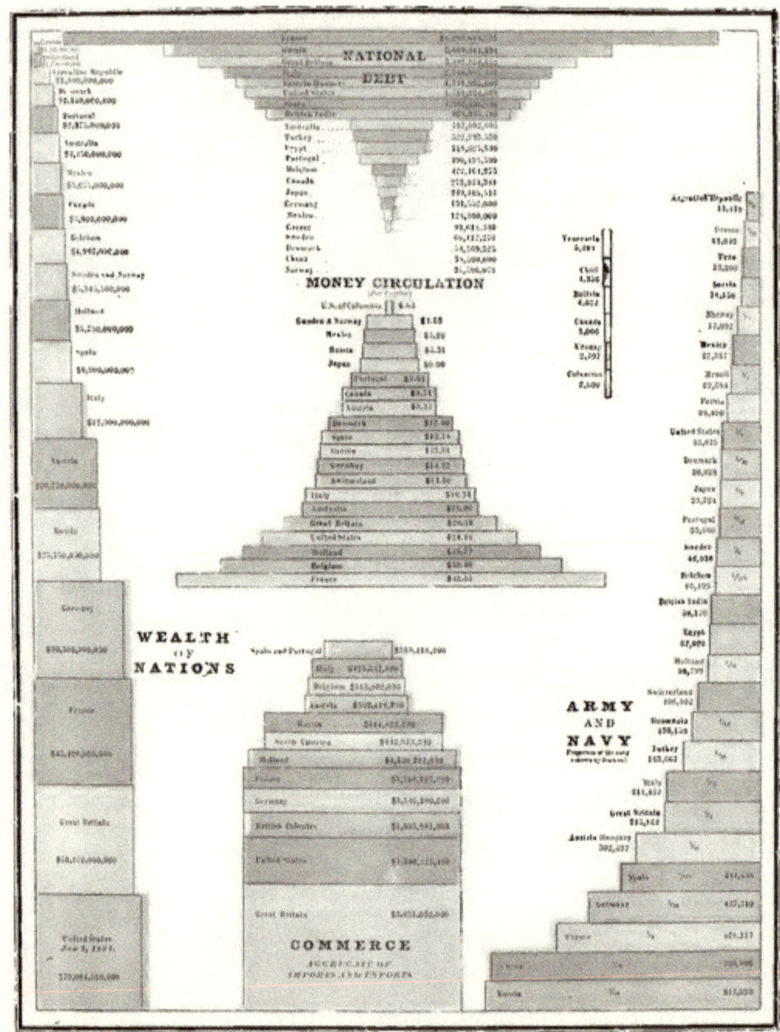
NATIONAL
DEBT
MONEY CIRCULATION
WEALTH
OF
NATIONS
ARMY
AND
NAVY
COMMERCE
AGGREGATE OF
IMPORTS AND EXPORTS

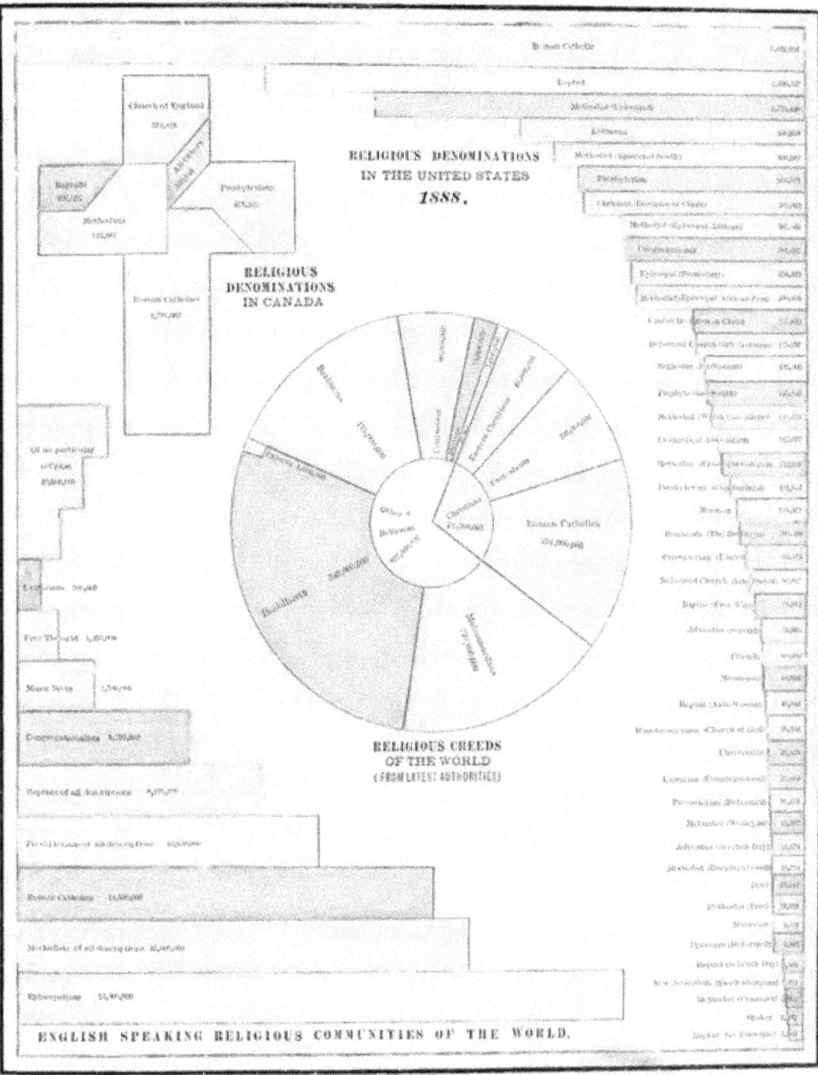
RELIGIOUS DENOMINATIONS
IN THE UNITED STATES
1888.
RELIGIOUS
DENOMINATIONS
IN CANADA
Roman Catholics
Buddhists
Christians
RELIGIOUS CREEDS
OF THE WORLD
(FROM LATEST AUTHORITIES)
ENGLISH SPEAKING RELIGIOUS COMMUNITIES OF THE WORLD.

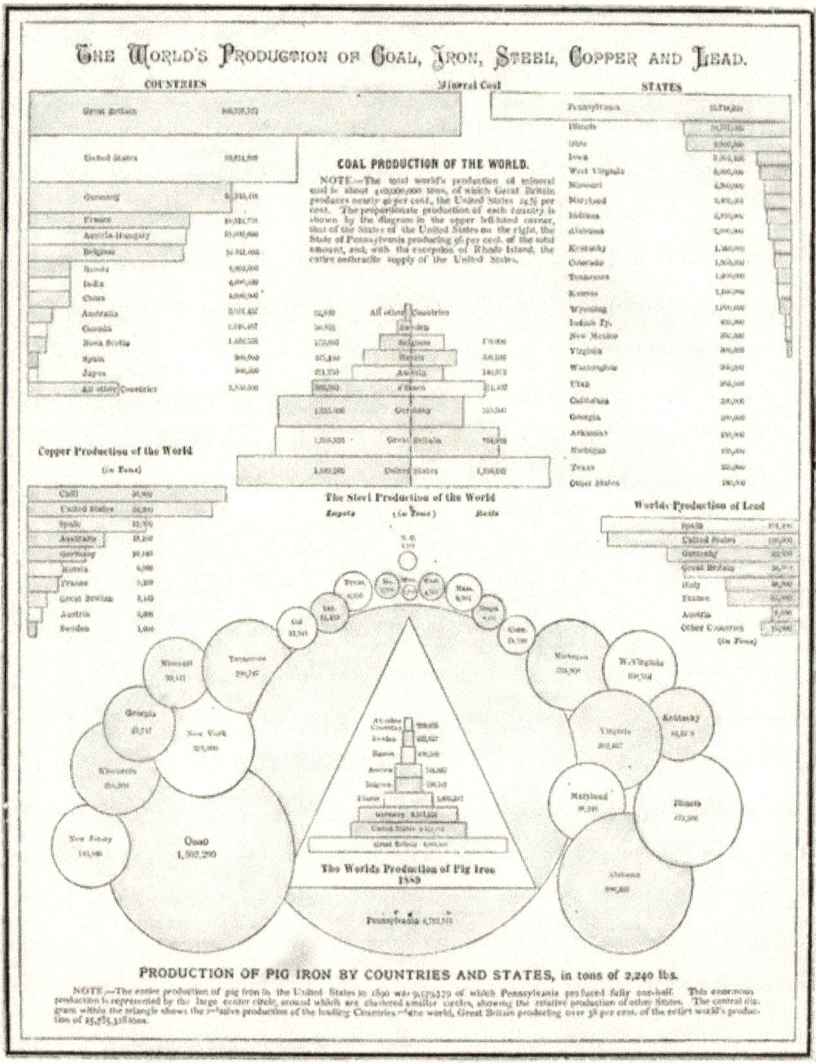
The World's Production of Coal, Iron, Steel, Copper and Lead.
COUNTRIES
Mineral Coal
STATES
Great Britain
United States
Germany
France
Austria-Hungary
Belgium
Russia
India
China
Australia
Canada
Nova Scotia
Spain
Japan
All other Countries
Pennsylvania
Illinois
Ohio
Iowa
West Virginia
Missouri
Maryland
Indiana
Alabama
Kentucky
Colorado
Tennessee
Kansas
Wyoming
Indian Ty.
New Mexico
Virginia
Washington
Utah
California
Georgia
Arkansas
Michigan
Texas
Other States
COAL PRODUCTION OF THE WORLD.
All other Countries
Sweden
Belgium
Russia
Austria
France
Germany
Great Britain
United States
The Steel Production of the World
Ingots
(in Tons)
Rails
Copper Production of the World
(in Tons)
Chili
United States
Spain
Australia
Germany
Russia
France
Great Britain
Austria
Sweden
Worlds Production of Lead
Spain
United States
Germany
Great Britain
Italy
France
Austria
Other Countries
(in Tons)
Texas
Ind.
Col
Missouri
Tennessee
Georgia
New York
Wisconsin
New Jersey
Ohio
1,562,290
Mass.
Conn.
Michigan
W. Virginia
Kentucky
Virginia
Maryland
Illinois
Alabama
All other Countries
Sweden
Russia
Austria
Belgium
France
Germany
United States
Great Britain
The Worlds Production of Pig Iron
1889
Pennsylvania
PRODUCTION OF PIG IRON BY COUNTRIES AND STATES, in tons of 2,240 lbs.

AGRICULTURE

AGRICULTURAL AND PASTORAL PRODUCTS

HORSE POWER

OF NATIONS

U. Kingdom

Germany

Russia 2,545

United States 3,020

STEAM POWER

OF NATIONS

U. States

Germany

HOUSES OF THE WORLD

(VALUE IN MILLION DOLLARS)

United States

France

Germany

Austria

Italy

CATTLE OF THE WORLD

United States

Russia

Germany

Austria

France

Spain

Italy

RAILWAYS OF THE WORLD

Germany

France

United States

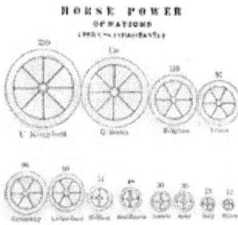

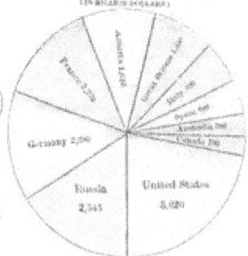

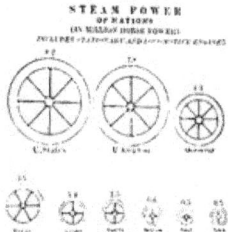

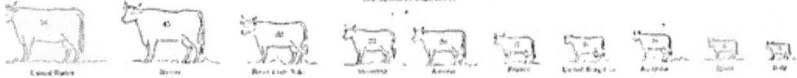

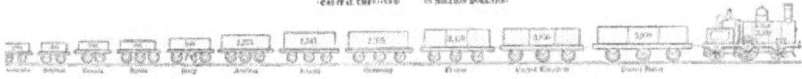

OCCUPATIONS OF THE UNITED STATES

Female 15,234,476

Male

Under 10 years of age 13,394,176

Occupations

Manufactures

Trades

Professions

Agricultural

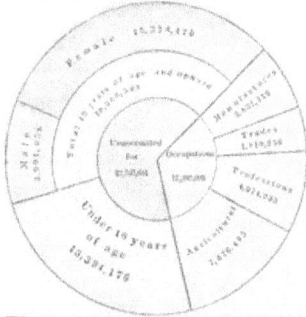

POPULATION OF THE UNITED STATES

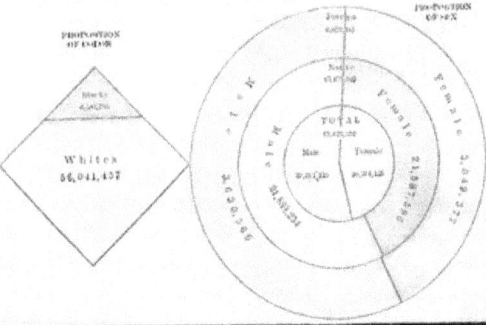

Whites 56,041,437

TOTAL

Male

Female

CHRONOLOGICAL OUTLINE OF AMERICAN HISTORY FROM 986 TO 1891.

PERIOD OF VOYAGE AND DISCOVERY.

COLONIAL PERIOD, 1607 TO 1789.

NATIONAL PERIOD, 1789 TO 1890.

PRESIDENTS OF THE UNITED STATES WITH THEIR CABINETS FROM 1789 TO 1889

Presidents	Elected	Vice-Presidents	Inaug.	Sec'y of State	Appointed	Sec'y of Treas'y	Appointed	Sec'y of War	Appointed	Sec'y of Navy	Appointed	Sec'y of Interior	Appointed	Postmaster Gen.	Appointed	Attorney Gen.	Appointed
George Washington George Washington	1789 1793	John Adams John Adams	1789 1793	Thomas Jefferson Edm. Randolph Tim. Pickering	1789 1794 1795	Alex. Hamilton Oliver Wolcott	1789 1795	Henry Knox T. Pickering J. McHenry	1789 1795 1796			Interior Dept. created 1849		Samuel Osgood T. Pickering Jos. Habersham	[illegible]	E. Randolph Wm. Bradford Charles Lee	[illegible]
John Adams	1797	Thomas Jefferson	1797	Tim. Pickering John Marshall	[illegible]	Oliver Wolcott S. Dexter	[illegible]	J. McHenry S. Dexter John Marshall Roger Griswold	[illegible]	George Cabot B. Stoddert	[illegible]			Jos. Habersham	[illegible]	Charles Lee	[illegible]
Thomas Jefferson Thomas Jefferson	1801 1805	Aaron Burr George Clinton	1801 1805	James Madison	1801	S. Dexter Albert Gallatin	[illegible]	H. Dearborn	1801	B. Stoddert Robert Smith J. Crowninshield	[illegible]			Jos. Habersham Gideon Granger	[illegible]	Levi Lincoln Robert Smith J. Breckinridge C. A. Rodney	[illegible]
James Madison James Madison	1809 1813	George Clinton Elbridge Gerry	1809 1813	Robert Smith James Monroe	[illegible]	Albert Gallatin G. W. Campbell Alex. J. Dallas	[illegible]	William Eustis J. Armstrong James Monroe W. H. Crawford	[illegible]	Paul Hamilton William Jones B. W. Crowninshield	[illegible]			Gideon Granger R. J. Meigs	[illegible]	C. A. Rodney W. Pinckney Richard Rush	[illegible]
James Monroe James Monroe	1817 1821	Dan. D. Tompkins	1817	John Q. Adams	1817	W. H. Crawford	1817	Isaac Shelby J. C. Calhoun	[illegible]	B. W. Crowninshield S. Thompson John Rodgers S. L. Southard	[illegible]			R. J. Meigs John McLean	[illegible]	William Wirt	[illegible]
John Q. Adams	1825	John C. Calhoun	1825	Henry Clay	1825	Richard Rush	1825	James Barbour P. B. Porter	[illegible]	S. L. Southard	[illegible]			John McLean	[illegible]	William Wirt	[illegible]
Andrew Jackson Andrew Jackson	1829 1833	John C. Calhoun Martin VanBuren	1829 1833	Martin VanBuren Ed. Livingston Louis McLane John Forsyth	[illegible]	Samuel D. Ingham Louis McLane William J. Duane Roger B. Taney Levi Woodbury	[illegible]	John H. Eaton Lewis Cass	[illegible]	John Branch L. Woodbury M. Dickerson	[illegible]			W. T. Barry Amos Kendall	[illegible]	J. M. Berrien R. B. Taney B. F. Butler	[illegible]
Martin VanBuren	1837	R. M. Johnson	1837	John Forsyth	1837	Levi Woodbury	1837	J. R. Poinsett	1837	M. Dickerson J. K. Paulding	[illegible]			Amos Kendall John M. Niles	[illegible]	B. F. Butler Felix Grundy H. D. Gilpin	[illegible]
Wm. H. Harrison John Tyler	1841 1841	John Tyler	1841	Daniel Webster Hugh S. Legare Abel P. Upshur John Nelson John C. Calhoun	[illegible]	Thomas Ewing Walter Forward John C. Spencer George M. Bibb	[illegible]	John Bell John C. Spencer James M. Porter Wm. Wilkins	[illegible]	Geo. E. Badger Abel P. Upshur David Henshaw T. W. Gilmer John Y. Mason	[illegible]			Francis Granger C. A. Wickliffe	[illegible]	J. J. Crittenden H. S. Legare John Nelson	[illegible]
James Knox Polk	1845	George M. Dallas	1845	James Buchanan	1845	Robt. J. Walker	1845	W. L. Marcy	1845	Geo. Bancroft John Y. Mason	[illegible]			Cave Johnson	[illegible]	J. Y. Mason N. Clifford Isaac Toucey	[illegible]
Zachary Taylor Millard Fillmore	1849 1850	Millard Fillmore	1849	John M. Clayton Daniel Webster Edward Everett	[illegible]	W. M. Meredith Thomas Corwin	[illegible]	G. W. Crawford Winfield Scott Chas. M. Conrad	[illegible]	Wm. B. Preston Wm. A. Graham J. P. Kennedy	[illegible]	Thomas Ewing A. H. H. Stuart	[illegible]	Jacob Collamer Nathan K. Hall S. D. Hubbard	[illegible]	R. Johnson J. J. Crittenden	[illegible]
Franklin Pierce	1853	Wm. R. King	1853	William L. Marcy	1853	James Guthrie	1853	Jefferson Davis	1853	James C. Dobbin	1853	R. McClelland	1853	James Campbell	1853	Caleb Cushing	1853
James Buchanan	1857	J. C. Breckenridge	1857	Lewis Cass Jeremiah S. Black	[illegible]	Howell Cobb Philip F. Thomas John A. Dix	[illegible]	John B. Floyd Joseph Holt	[illegible]	Isaac Toucey	1857	J. Thompson	1857	Aaron V. Brown Joseph Holt Horatio King	[illegible]	J. S. Black E. M. Stanton	[illegible]
Abraham Lincoln	1861	Hannibal Hamlin	1861	Wm. H. Seward	1861	Salmon P. Chase W. P. Fessenden Hugh McCulloch	[illegible]	S. Cameron E. M. Stanton	[illegible]	Gideon Welles	1861	Caleb B. Smith John P. Usher James Harlan	[illegible]	Montg. Blair Wm. Dennison	[illegible]	Edw. Bates James Speed	[illegible]
Abraham Lincoln Andrew Johnson	1865 1865	Andrew Johnson	1865					Ulysses S. Grant Lorenzo Thomas J. M. Schofield	[illegible]			O. H. Browning	[illegible]	A. W. Randall	[illegible]	H. Stanbery W. M. Evarts	[illegible]
Ulysses S. Grant Ulysses S. Grant	1869 1873	Schuyler Colfax Henry Wilson	1869 1873	E. B. Washburne Hamilton Fish	1869 1869	Geo. S. Boutwell W. A. Richardson Benj. H. Bristow L. M. Morrill	[illegible]	J. M. Schofield J. A. Rawlins W. W. Belknap Jas. D. Cameron	[illegible]	Adolph E. Borie G. M. Robeson	[illegible]	J. D. Cox C. Delano Zach. Chandler	[illegible]	J. A. J. Creswell Jas. W. Marshall Marshall Jewell Jas. N. Tyner	[illegible]	E. R. Hoar A. T. Akerman G. H. Williams E. Pierrepont A. Taft	[illegible]
Rutherford B. Hayes	1877	Wm. A. Wheeler	1877	Wm. M. Evarts	1877	John Sherman	1877	G. W. McCrary Alex. Ramsey	[illegible]	R. W. Thompson Nathan Goff, Jr.	[illegible]	Carl Schurz	1877	D. M. Key Horace Maynard	[illegible]	C. Devens	1877
James A. Garfield Chester A. Arthur	1881 1881	Chester A. Arthur	1881	James G. Blaine F. T. Frelinghuysen	[illegible]	William Windom Charles J. Folger Hugh McCulloch	[illegible]	Robt. T. Lincoln	1881	Wm. H. Hunt Wm. E. Chandler	[illegible]	S. J. Kirkwood Henry M. Teller	[illegible]	Thomas L. James Timothy O. Howe Walter Q. Gresham	[illegible]	Wayne MacVeagh B. H. Brewster	[illegible]
Grover Cleveland	1885	T. A. Hendricks	1885	T. F. Bayard	1885	Dan'l Manning C. S. Fairchild	[illegible]	W. C. Endicott	1885	W. C. Whitney	1885	L. Q. C. Lamar W. F. Vilas	[illegible]	Wm. F. Vilas Don M. Dickinson	[illegible]	A. H. Garland	1885
Benjamin Harrison	1889	Levi P. Morton	1889	Jas. G. Blaine	1889	Wm. Windom	1889	R. Proctor	1889	Benj. F. Tracy	1889	J. W. Noble	1889	J. Wanamaker	1889	W. H. H. Miller	1889

Jeremiah Rusk Sec'y of Agriculture

THE U. S. HOUSE OF REPRESENTATIVES ACCORDING TO THE APPORTIONMENT UNDER EACH CENSUS FROM 1789–1883.

(The last Apportionment Bill was passed February 25, 1882.)

*These States admitted subsequent to the apportionment.

Capitals, Temperature, Settlement, &c., of the United States.

*The thirteen original States.

TIME OF RESIDENCE REQUIRED IN STATE, COUNTY AND PRECINCT BEFORE VOTING.

	STATE.	COUNTY.	TOWN.	WARD OR PRECINCT.
Alabama	1 year	3 months		30 days
Arizona	1 year	30 days		
Arkansas	1 year	6 months		30 days
California	1 year	90 days		30 days
Colorado	6 months	90 days		10 days
Connecticut	1 year		6 months	
Delaware	1 year	1 month		
Florida	1 year	6 months		
Georgia	1 year	6 months		
Idaho	6 months	30 days		
Illinois	1 year	90 days		30 days
Indiana	6 months		60 days	30 days
Iowa	6 months	60 days		
Kansas	6 months			30 days
Kentucky	2 years	1 year		60 days
Louisiana	1 year	6 months		30 days
Maine	3 months	3 months	3 months	
Maryland	1 year	6 months		1 day
Massachusetts	1 year			6 months
Michigan	3 months	10 days		10 days
Minnesota	6 months	10 days		10 days
Mississippi	2 years	1 month		
Missouri	1 year	60 days	60 days	60 days
Montana	1 year			
Nebraska	6 months	40 days		10 days
Nevada	6 months	30 days		
New Hampshire	6 months		6 months	
New Jersey	1 year	5 months		
New Mexico	6 months	3 months		30 days
New York	1 year	4 months		30 days
North Carolina	1 year	90 days		
North Dakota	1 year	6 months		90 days
Ohio	1 year	30 days		20 days
Oregon	6 months	30 days		
Pennsylvania	1 year			2 months
Rhode Island	1 year		6 months	
South Carolina	1 year	60 days		
South Dakota	1 year	6 months		30 days
Tennessee	1 year	6 months		
Texas	1 year	6 months		
Utah	6 months			
Vermont	1 year			
Virginia	1 year	3 months	3 months	
Washington	1 year	90 days		30 days
West Virginia	1 year	60 days		
Wisconsin	1 year			
Wyoming	90 days			

IMPORTANT INVENTIONS, WITH NAME OF INVENTOR AND DATE OF INVENTION.

NAME OF INVENTION.	NAME OF INVENTOR.	DATE.
Air Gun	Marin	[illegible]
Air Pump	Otto von Guericke	1654
Anastatic Printing	Baldermus	1841
Anchor	Anacharsis	594 B.C.
Anemometer	Wolfius	1709
Balloon	Montgolfier	1783
Barometer	Evangelista Torricelli	1643
Bellows	Anacharsis the Scythian	592 B.C.
Camel (Docking)	Meurs Meinderts Bakker	1688
Camera Lucida	Dr. Hooke	[illegible]
Camera Obscura	Roger Bacon	1297
Cannon	Chinese (Some credit to John Owen)	About [illegible] B.C.
Chronoscope	Wheatstone	1840
Clock	First one erected in Padua	13th Century
Compass	Chinese	1115 B.C.
Cotton Gin	Eli Whitney	1793
Dial	Anaximander	550 B.C.
Diving Bell	Unknown	1538
Electric Clock	Wheatstone	1840
Electric Light	Sir Humphrey Davy	1814
Electrotype	Spencer and Jacobi	1837
Engraving	Chinese	[illegible] B.C.
Fire Arms	Unknown	1364
Fire Engine	Hautsch	1657
Gas	Van Helmont	[illegible]
Gas Meter	Clegg	1814
Geographical Maps	Anaximander	[illegible] B.C.
Glass	Phoenicians	
Gunpowder	Berthold Schwartz	1320
Hydraulic Press	Joseph Bramah	1796
Hydraulic Ram	Montgolfier	1796
Kaleidoscope	David Brewster	1814
Lightning Conductor	Benjamin Franklin	1752
Lithography	Alois Senefelder	1798
Locomotive	Watt	[illegible]
Matches	Walker	1827
Microscope	Zackarias Jansen	1590
Organ	Archimedes and Ctesibius	[illegible] B.C.
Phonograph	Thomas A. Edison	1877
Photography	Thomas Wedgwood	1802
Piano-Forte	Bartolommeo Christofali	1714
Pneumatic Railway	Henry Pinkus	[illegible]
Stocking Frame	William Lee	1589
Printing	Johann Gutenberg	1438
[illegible]	[illegible]	[illegible]
[illegible] Machine	By a Hollander; subsequently improved by Payne, Woodhouse and Brown	[illegible]
Sewing Machine	Elias Howe	[illegible]
Steamboat	Robert Fulton	[illegible]
Steam Engine	James Watt	[illegible]
Telegraph	Samuel F. B. Morse	1837
Torpedo	David Bushnell	1775
Telephone	Elisha Gray, A. Graham Bell, A. C. Dolbear, and Thomas A. Edison	1877
Telescope	Hans Lippershein, Jacob Adriaans	1608
Thermometer	Drebbel, Sanctorius	1609
Watch	Said to have been first invented at Nuremberg, 1477, although it is affirmed that Robert King, of Scotland, had a watch about 1310. Spring watches have been ascribed to Dr. Hooke, and by some to Huyghens, about 1658; the anchor arrangement, by Clement, 1680; the horizontal watch by Graham, 1724; repeating watches by Barlow, in 1676.	1477

EXEMPTION LAWS OF UNITED STATES AND TERRITORIES.

	VALUE OF PERSONAL PROPERTY.	ACRES OF LAND.	VALUE OF HOMESTEAD.
Alabama	$1,000	160	$2,000
Arizona	500		4,000
Arkansas	500	160	2,500
California	500		5,000
Colorado	1,000	Any number.	2,000
Connecticut	300		*
Dakota	1,500	160	*
Delaware	100		‡
District of Columbia	300		*
Florida	1,000 No acres	160	
Georgia	300	50	1,600
Idaho	300		5,000
Illinois	300		1,000
Indiana	600		*
Iowa	300	40	No limit
Kansas	600	160	No limit
Kentucky	300		1,000
Louisiana	†	160	*
Maine	About 300		500
Maryland	100		*
Massachusetts	About 400		800
Michigan	400	40	1,500
Minnesota	500	80	
Mississippi	500	80	2,000
Missouri	300	160	1,500
Montana	900		2,500
Nebraska		160	2,000
Nevada	300		5,000
New Hampshire	About 400		500
New Jersey	200		1,000
New Mexico	200		5,000
New York	250		1,000
North Carolina	500		1,000
Ohio	400		1,000
Oregon	500		*
Pennsylvania	300		*
Rhode Island	500		*
South Carolina	500		1,000
Tennessee	1,300		1,000
Texas		200	5,000
Utah			1,000
Vermont	200		500
Washington Territory	‡	‡	‡
West Virginia	200		1,000
Wisconsin	400	40	
Wyoming	500		2,000

* No Homestead Law. † The homestead, land and personal property not to exceed $2,000. ‡ Similar to California.

A TABLE EXHIBITING THE DIFFERENCE OF TIME BETWEEN WASHINGTON AND THE PLACES NAMED.

When the clock is at 12, noon, at Washington, it is at

Philadelphia	12.07 p.m.
Baltimore	12.01 "
Wilmington, Del.	12.06 "
Jersey City, N. J.	12.12 "
New York City	12.12 "
[illegible]	[illegible]

COMPOUND INTEREST TABLE.

[illegible]

INTEREST LAWS IN THE UNITED STATES.

[illegible]

Ratio of Persons Engaged in Manufactures and Mechanical and Mining Industries to Total Persons 10 years of age and over, by States, 1890.

[illegible]

POSTAL INFORMATION.

DOMESTIC POSTAGE RATES.

[illegible]

Domestic Money Orders.

[illegible]

Foreign Postage.

[illegible]

Foreign Money Orders.

GERMAN RATES.

[illegible]

BRITISH, SWISS AND AUSTRIAN RATES.

[illegible]

FEES FOR FRANCE AND ALGERIA.

[illegible]

FEES FOR ITALIAN MONEY ORDERS.

[illegible]

FEES FOR CANADA MONEY ORDERS.

[illegible]

Foreign Postage for Newspapers and Other Printed Matter.

[illegible]

Population, Capitals and Public Debt of the Principal Countries of the World.

[illegible]

Table Showing Growth of Large American Cities, from 1840 to 1890.

Cities.	1840.	1850.	1860.	1870.	1880.	1890.
[illegible]	[illegible]	[illegible]	[illegible]	[illegible]	[illegible]	[illegible]

UNITED STATES POST-OFFICE STATISTICS.

Years.	No. of Post-Offices.	Extent of Post Routes in Miles.	Revenue of the Department.	Expenditures of the Department.	Amount Paid for Salaries of Postmasters.	Amount Paid for Transportation of the Mail.
[illegible]	[illegible]	[illegible]	[illegible]	[illegible]	[illegible]	[illegible]

* Includes steam, messenger and special office service.

Table Showing Area and Early Settlements of the States and Territories.

States and Territories.	Area Square Miles.	First Settled. When.	First Settled. Where.	Admitted to the Union.
[illegible]	[illegible]	[illegible]	[illegible]	[illegible]

STATES AND TERRITORIES: THEIR CAPITALS AND GOVERNORS IN 1890.

Republicans are designated by R; Democrats by D.

STATE.	CAPITAL.	GOVERNOR.	STATE.	CAPITAL.	GOVERNOR.
[illegible]	[illegible]	[illegible]	[illegible]	[illegible]	[illegible]

Table Showing the Religious Divisions of the World for 1870.

Christians—viz.	Roman Catholic / Protestants / Eastern Churches	[illegible]
[illegible]	[illegible]	[illegible]

	Whole Population.	Roman Catholics.	Protestants.	Eastern Churches.
America	[illegible]	[illegible]	[illegible]	[illegible]
Europe	[illegible]	[illegible]	[illegible]	[illegible]
Asia	[illegible]	[illegible]	[illegible]	[illegible]
Africa	[illegible]	[illegible]	[illegible]	[illegible]
[illegible]	[illegible]	[illegible]	[illegible]	[illegible]
Total	[illegible]	[illegible]	[illegible]	[illegible]

THE ELECTORAL VOTE.

The Presidential Electoral Vote of the States for 1888 was as follows:

[illegible]	[illegible]
Total	[illegible]

RELIGIOUS DENOMINATIONS

OF THE

UNITED STATES.

Denominations.	Churches.	Ministers.	Members.	Denominations.	Churches.	Ministers.	Members.
[illegible]	[illegible]	[illegible]	[illegible]	[illegible]	[illegible]	[illegible]	[illegible]

[illegible]

VALUE OF LANDS IN THE UNITED STATES.

The following Table shows the average value per acre of Improved and Timber Lands, throughout the United States.

States.	Av. Value per acre of cleared lands in 1882.	Av. Value per acre of timber lands in 1882.	Per cent increase in one year.
Maine	$12.87	$22.86	.05
New Hampshire	[illegible]	[illegible]	[illegible]
Vermont	[illegible]	[illegible]	[illegible]
Massachusetts	[illegible]	[illegible]	[illegible]
Rhode Island	[illegible]	Not reported.	[illegible]
Connecticut	[illegible]	[illegible]	[illegible]
New York	[illegible]	[illegible]	[illegible]
New Jersey	[illegible]	[illegible]	[illegible]
Pennsylvania	[illegible]	[illegible]	[illegible]
Delaware	[illegible]	[illegible]	[illegible]
Maryland	[illegible]	[illegible]	[illegible]
Virginia	[illegible]	[illegible]	[illegible]
North Carolina	[illegible]	[illegible]	[illegible]
South Carolina	[illegible]	[illegible]	[illegible]
Georgia	[illegible]	[illegible]	[illegible]
Florida	[illegible]	[illegible]	[illegible]
Alabama	[illegible]	[illegible]	[illegible]
Mississippi	[illegible]	[illegible]	[illegible]
Louisiana	[illegible]	[illegible]	[illegible]
Texas	[illegible]	[illegible]	[illegible]
Arkansas	[illegible]	[illegible]	[illegible]
Tennessee	[illegible]	[illegible]	[illegible]
West Virginia	[illegible]	[illegible]	[illegible]
Kentucky	[illegible]	[illegible]	[illegible]
Ohio	[illegible]	[illegible]	[illegible]
Michigan	[illegible]	[illegible]	[illegible]
Indiana	[illegible]	[illegible]	[illegible]
Illinois	[illegible]	[illegible]	[illegible]
Wisconsin	[illegible]	[illegible]	[illegible]
Minnesota	[illegible]	[illegible]	[illegible]
Iowa	[illegible]	[illegible]	[illegible]
Missouri	[illegible]	[illegible]	[illegible]
Kansas	[illegible]	[illegible]	[illegible]
Nebraska	[illegible]	[illegible]	[illegible]
California	[illegible]	[illegible]	[illegible]
Oregon	[illegible]	[illegible]	[illegible]

The following Table shows the Expectation of Life at different years, as computed by Dr. Wm. Farr.

Age.	Male.	Fem.	Age.	Male.	Fem.	Age.	Male.	Fem.
[illegible]	[illegible]	[illegible]	[illegible]	[illegible]	[illegible]	[illegible]	[illegible]	[illegible]

RAILROAD MILEAGE IN THE UNITED STATES.

Statement showing the number of miles of railroad constructed and in operation each year in the United States, from 1830 to 1885 inclusive.

Year.	Miles in Operation.	Annual increase of Mileage.	Year.	Miles in Operation.	Annual increase of Mileage.
[illegible]	[illegible]	[illegible]	[illegible]	[illegible]	[illegible]

RAILROAD MILEAGE IN THE UNITED STATES.

(Continued.)

Year.	Miles in Operation.	Annual increase of Mileage.	Year.	Miles in Operation.	Annual increase of Mileage.
[illegible]	[illegible]	[illegible]	[illegible]	[illegible]	[illegible]

Cotton Crop of the United States for 60 Years.

Years Ending September 1.

From the Commercial and Financial Chronicle.

Year.	Bales.	Year.	Bales.	Year.	Bales.
[illegible]	[illegible]	[illegible]	[illegible]	[illegible]	[illegible]

Note.—The average net weight per bale is [illegible] lbs.

Sugar Product of Louisiana, 1840-1883. (Bouchereau's Statement.)

Year.	Hogsheads.	Year.	Hogsheads.	Year.	Hogsheads.
[illegible]	[illegible]	[illegible]	[illegible]	[illegible]	[illegible]

The average weight of the hogshead is reckoned at [illegible] lbs. net.

TOBACCO PRODUCTION OF THE UNITED STATES.

From the Tenth Census, 1880.

States and Territories.	Acres.	Pounds.
Alabama	[illegible]	[illegible]
Arizona	[illegible]	[illegible]
Arkansas	[illegible]	[illegible]
California	[illegible]	[illegible]
Connecticut	[illegible]	[illegible]
Dakota	[illegible]	[illegible]
Delaware	[illegible]	[illegible]
District of Columbia	[illegible]	[illegible]
Florida	[illegible]	[illegible]
Georgia	[illegible]	[illegible]
Idaho	[illegible]	[illegible]
Illinois	[illegible]	[illegible]
Indiana	[illegible]	[illegible]
Iowa	[illegible]	[illegible]
Kansas	[illegible]	[illegible]
Kentucky	[illegible]	[illegible]
Louisiana	[illegible]	[illegible]
Maine	[illegible]	[illegible]
Maryland	[illegible]	[illegible]
Massachusetts	[illegible]	[illegible]
Michigan	[illegible]	[illegible]
Minnesota	[illegible]	[illegible]
Mississippi	[illegible]	[illegible]
Missouri	[illegible]	[illegible]
Nebraska	[illegible]	[illegible]
Nevada	[illegible]	[illegible]
New Hampshire	[illegible]	[illegible]
New Jersey	[illegible]	[illegible]
New Mexico	[illegible]	[illegible]
New York	[illegible]	[illegible]
North Carolina	[illegible]	[illegible]
Ohio	[illegible]	[illegible]
Oregon	[illegible]	[illegible]
Pennsylvania	[illegible]	[illegible]
Rhode Island	[illegible]	[illegible]
South Carolina	[illegible]	[illegible]
Tennessee	[illegible]	[illegible]
Texas	[illegible]	[illegible]
Vermont	[illegible]	[illegible]
Virginia	[illegible]	[illegible]
Washington	[illegible]	[illegible]
West Virginia	[illegible]	[illegible]
Wisconsin	[illegible]	[illegible]
Total United States	[illegible]	[illegible]

WHEAT CROPS OF THE PRINCIPAL GRAIN-GROWING NATIONS.

Estimated by the Department of Agriculture.

Countries.	Period.	Average Annual Yield.
		Bushels.
U. S.	[illegible]	[illegible]
France	[illegible]	[illegible]
India	[illegible]	[illegible]
Russia	[illegible]	[illegible]
Italy	[illegible]	[illegible]
Germany	[illegible]	[illegible]
Austria-Hungary	[illegible]	[illegible]
Spain	[illegible]	[illegible]
Great Britain	[illegible]	[illegible]
Australia	[illegible]	[illegible]
Belgium	[illegible]	[illegible]
Turkey	[illegible]	[illegible]
Roumania	[illegible]	[illegible]
Mexico	[illegible]	[illegible]
Netherlands	[illegible]	[illegible]
Portugal	[illegible]	[illegible]
Greece	[illegible]	[illegible]
Sweden	[illegible]	[illegible]
Servia	[illegible]	[illegible]
Norway	[illegible]	[illegible]
Denmark	[illegible]	[illegible]
Switzerland	[illegible]	[illegible]

WHERE OUR GOLD AND SILVER COME FROM.

Gold and Silver of Domestic Production, Deposited at the Mints and Assay Offices, from their organization, in 1793, to the close of the Fiscal Year, ended June 30th, 1884.

From the Annual Report of the Director of the Mint, November, 1884.

Locality.	Gold.	Silver.	Total.
	Dollars.	Dollars.	Dollars.
Alabama	[illegible]	[illegible]	[illegible]
Alaska	[illegible]	[illegible]	[illegible]
Arizona	[illegible]	[illegible]	[illegible]
California	[illegible]	[illegible]	[illegible]
Colorado	[illegible]	[illegible]	[illegible]
Dakota, North and South	[illegible]	[illegible]	[illegible]
Georgia	[illegible]	[illegible]	[illegible]
Idaho	[illegible]	[illegible]	[illegible]
Indiana	[illegible]		[illegible]
Maine	[illegible]	[illegible]	[illegible]
Maryland	[illegible]	[illegible]	[illegible]
Massachusetts		[illegible]	[illegible]
Michigan	[illegible]	[illegible]	[illegible]
Montana	[illegible]	[illegible]	[illegible]
Nebraska	[illegible]	[illegible]	[illegible]
Nevada	[illegible]	[illegible]	[illegible]
New Hampshire	[illegible]	[illegible]	[illegible]
New Mexico	[illegible]	[illegible]	[illegible]
North Carolina	[illegible]	[illegible]	[illegible]
Oregon	[illegible]	[illegible]	[illegible]
Pennsylvania	[illegible]	[illegible]	[illegible]
South Carolina	[illegible]	[illegible]	[illegible]
Tennessee	[illegible]	[illegible]	[illegible]
Texas	[illegible]	[illegible]	[illegible]
Utah	[illegible]	[illegible]	[illegible]
Vermont	[illegible]	[illegible]	[illegible]
Virginia	[illegible]	[illegible]	[illegible]
Washington	[illegible]	[illegible]	[illegible]
Wyoming	[illegible]	[illegible]	[illegible]
Refined Bullion	[illegible]	[illegible]	[illegible]
Other Sources	[illegible]	[illegible]	[illegible]
Total unrefined	[illegible]	[illegible]	[illegible]
Total	[illegible]	[illegible]	[illegible]

GEOGRAPHICAL TABLES.

Highest Mountains.

Longest Rivers.

(APPROXIMATED.)

Oceans.

Largest Lakes.

Population of the Principal Cities of the Old World.

(According to the Latest Census or Estimate.)

The Presidents of the United States.

HEADS OF THE PRINCIPAL NATIONS OF THE WORLD.

Governments.	Rulers.	Titles.	Year of Birth.	Date of Accession.
Argentine Republic	Dr. Miguel Juarez Celman	President		Oct. 12, 1886
Austria-Hungary	Franz Joseph I	Emperor	1830	Dec. 2, 1848
Belgium	Leopold II	King	1835	Dec. 10, 1865
Bolivia	Aniceto Arce	President		[illegible]
Brazil	Marshal M. D. Da Fonseca	President		[illegible]
Chili	Don José Man'l Balmaceda	President		[illegible]
China	Kuang Hsu	Emperor	[illegible]	[illegible]
Colombia	R. Nunez	President		[illegible]
Costa Rica	Gen. Don Bernardo Soto	President		[illegible]
Denmark	Christian IX	King	[illegible]	[illegible]
Ecuador	Antonio Flores	President		[illegible]
France	Sadi-Carnot	President	[illegible]	[illegible]
Germany	William II	Emperor	[illegible]	[illegible]
Alsace-Lorraine	F. H. Baron Manteuffel	Statthalter	[illegible]	[illegible]
Anhalt	Frederick	Duke	[illegible]	[illegible]
Baden	Frederick I	Grand Duke	[illegible]	[illegible]
Bavaria	Otto	King	[illegible]	[illegible]
Bremen		Burgomasters		
Brunswick	Prince Albrecht	Regent	[illegible]	[illegible]
Hamburg		Burgomasters		
Hesse	Louis IV	Grand Duke	[illegible]	[illegible]
Lippe	G. F. Waldemar	Prince	[illegible]	[illegible]
Lübeck		Burgomasters		
Mecklenburg-Schwerin	Frederick Francis III	Grand Duke	[illegible]	[illegible]
Mecklenburg-Strelitz	Frederick William I	Grand Duke	[illegible]	[illegible]
Oldenburg	Peter I	Grand Duke	[illegible]	[illegible]
Prussia	William II	King	[illegible]	[illegible]
[illegible]	[illegible]	[illegible]	[illegible]	[illegible]

CAPACITY OF NOTED PUBLIC BUILDINGS.

Building.	City.	Capacity.	Building.	City.	Capacity.
[illegible]	[illegible]	[illegible]	[illegible]	[illegible]	[illegible]

LIVE-STOCK STATISTICS OF THE UNITED STATES.

States.	Horses.			Milch Cows.			Oxen and Other Cattle.			Sheep.			Hogs.		
	Number.	Average Price.	Value.	Number.	Average Price.	Value.	Number.	Average Price.	Value.	Number.	Average Price.	Value.	Number.	Average Price.	Value.
[illegible]	[illegible]	[illegible]	[illegible]	[illegible]	[illegible]	[illegible]	[illegible]	[illegible]	[illegible]	[illegible]	[illegible]	[illegible]	[illegible]	[illegible]	[illegible]

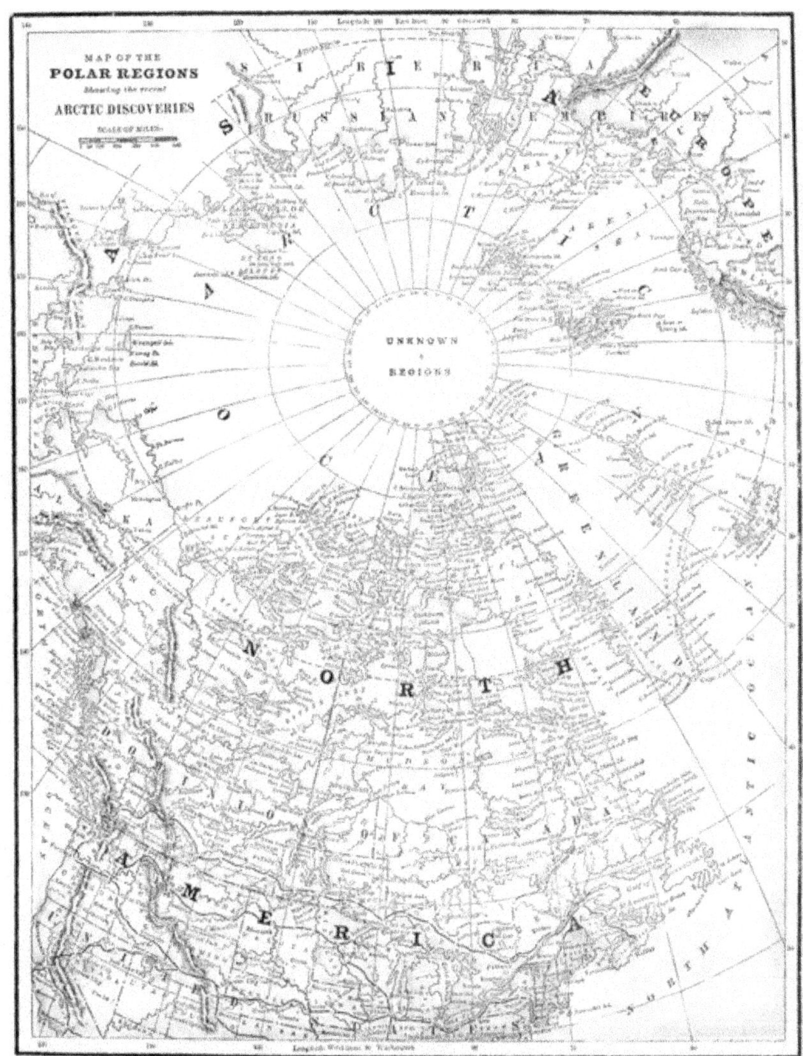
MAP OF THE
POLAR REGIONS
Showing the recent
ARCTIC DISCOVERIES
UNKNOWN
REGIONS

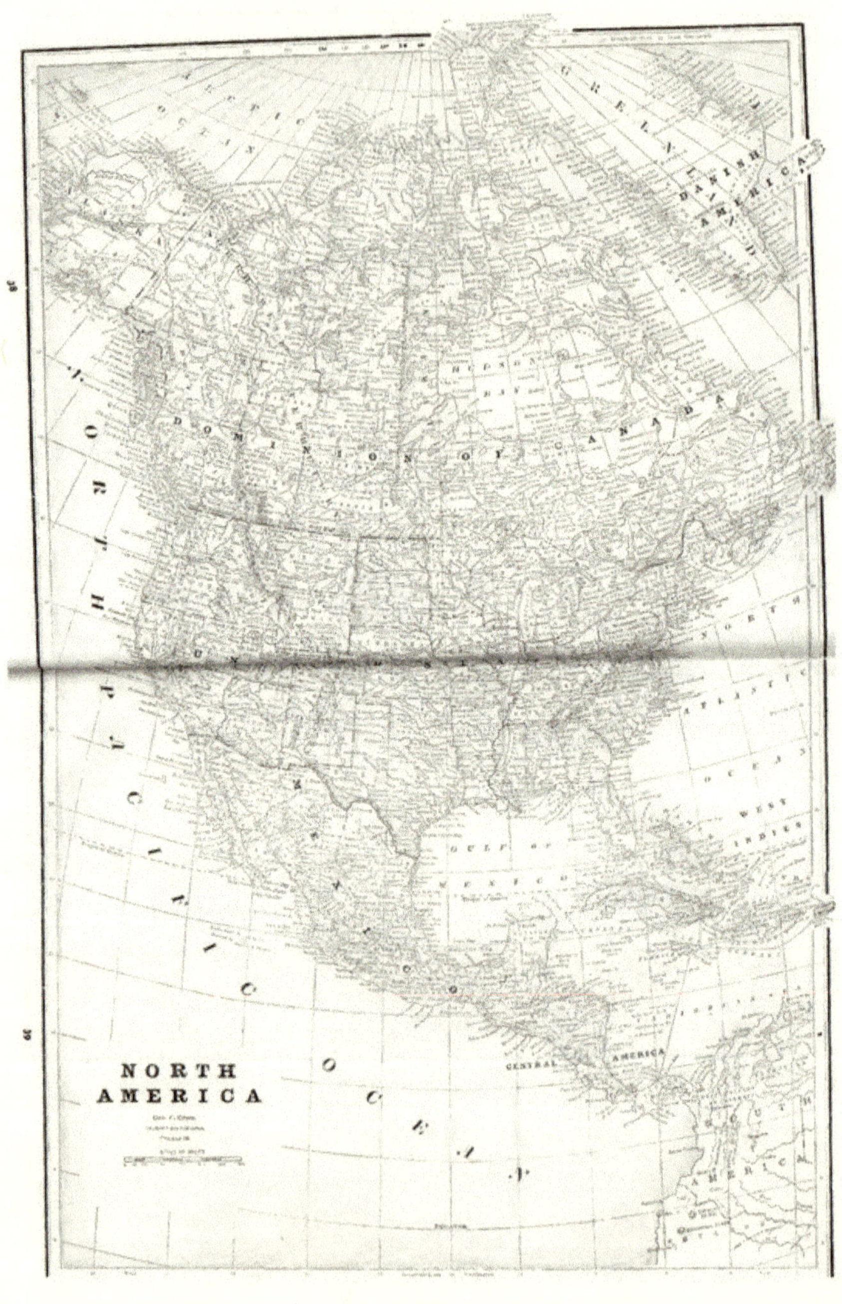
NORTH
AMERICA
DOMINION OF CANADA
HUDSON BAY
GREENLAND
DANISH AMERICA
NORTH PACIFIC OCEAN
NORTH ATLANTIC OCEAN
GULF OF MEXICO
MEXICO
WEST INDIES
CENTRAL AMERICA
SOUTH AMERICA

ALASKA
EASTERN
NORTH
PACIFIC OCEAN

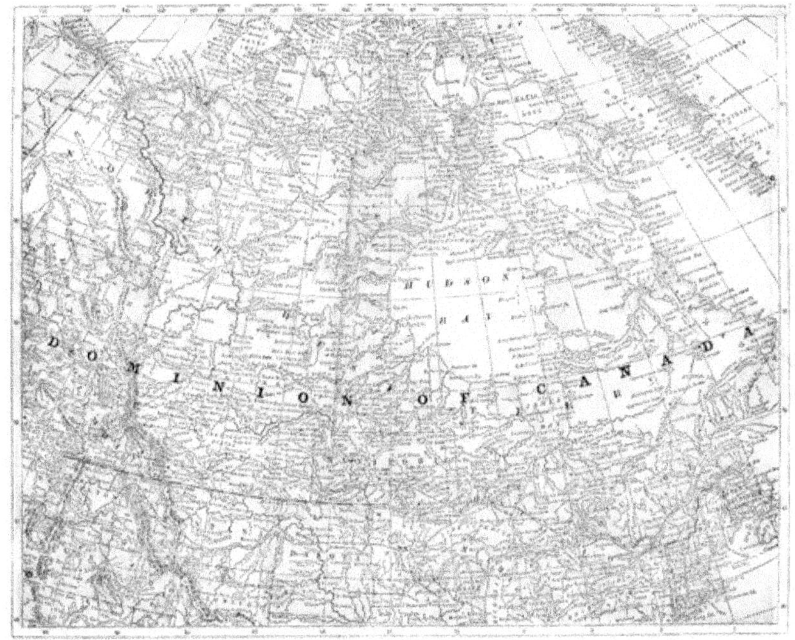
HUDSON
BAY
DOMINION OF CANADA

GULF OF
ST. LAWRENCE
NEW BRUNSWICK &
NOVA SCOTIA

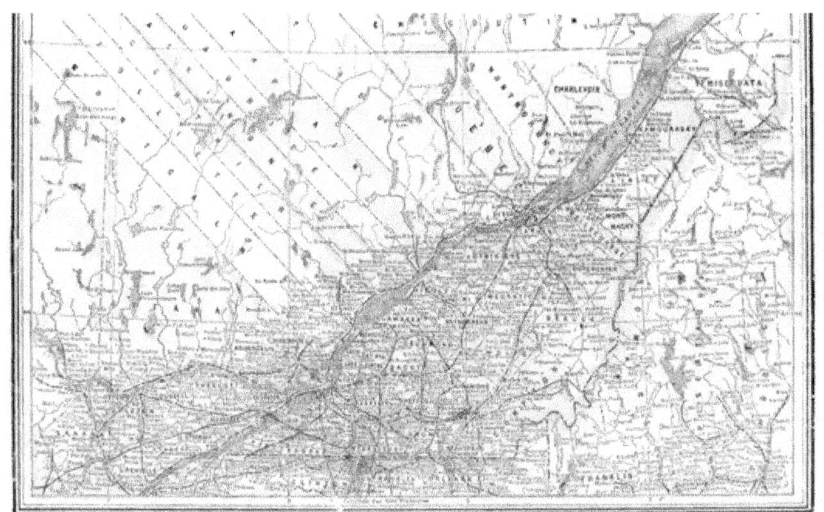
CHARLEVOIX
TEMISCOUATA
KAMOURASKA
FRANKLIN

ONTARIO

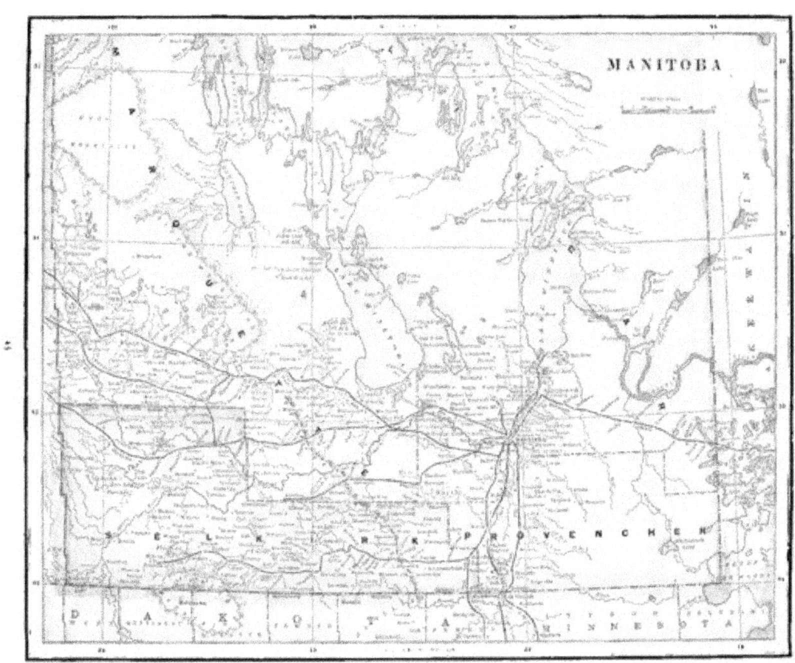
MANITOBA
SELKIRK
PROVENCHER
DAKOTA
MINNESOTA

UNITED STATES
ATLANTIC OCEAN
GULF OF MEXICO
DOMINION
CANADA

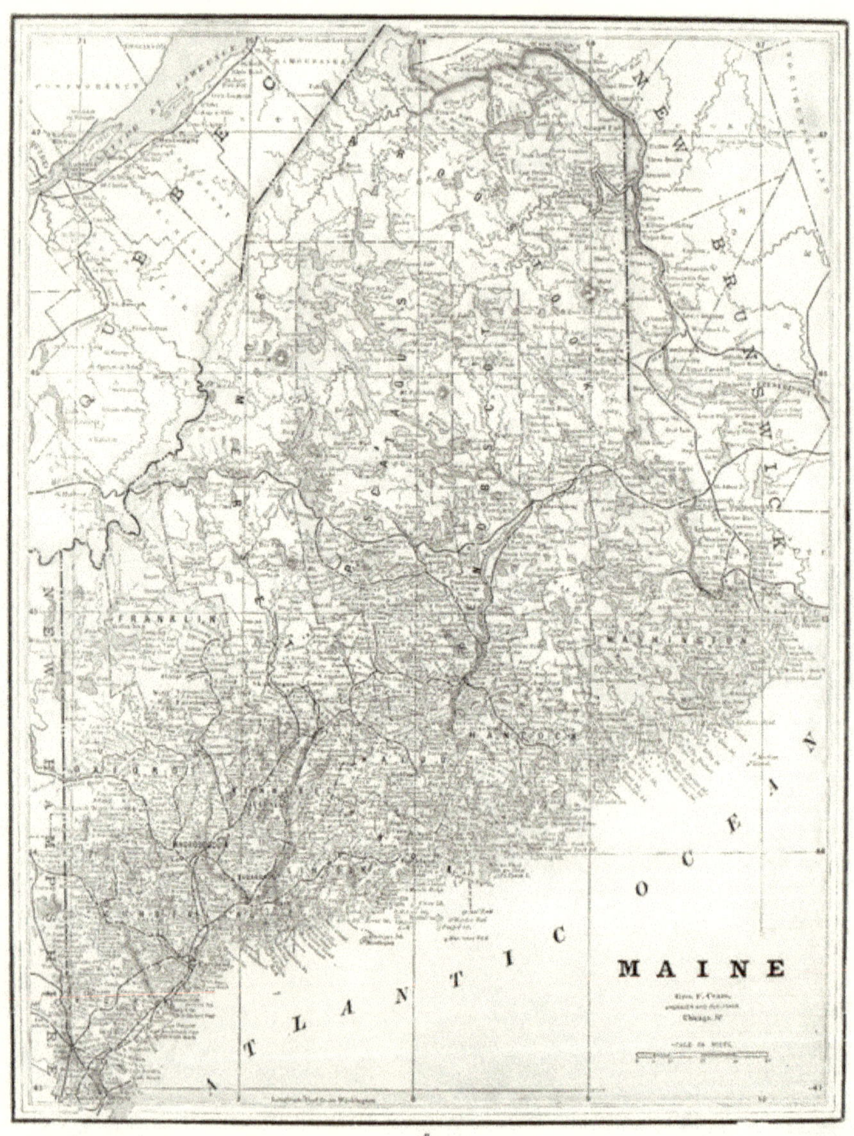
MAINE
ATLANTIC OCEAN
NEW BRUNSWICK
QUEBEC
FRANKLIN
WASHINGTON
HANCOCK

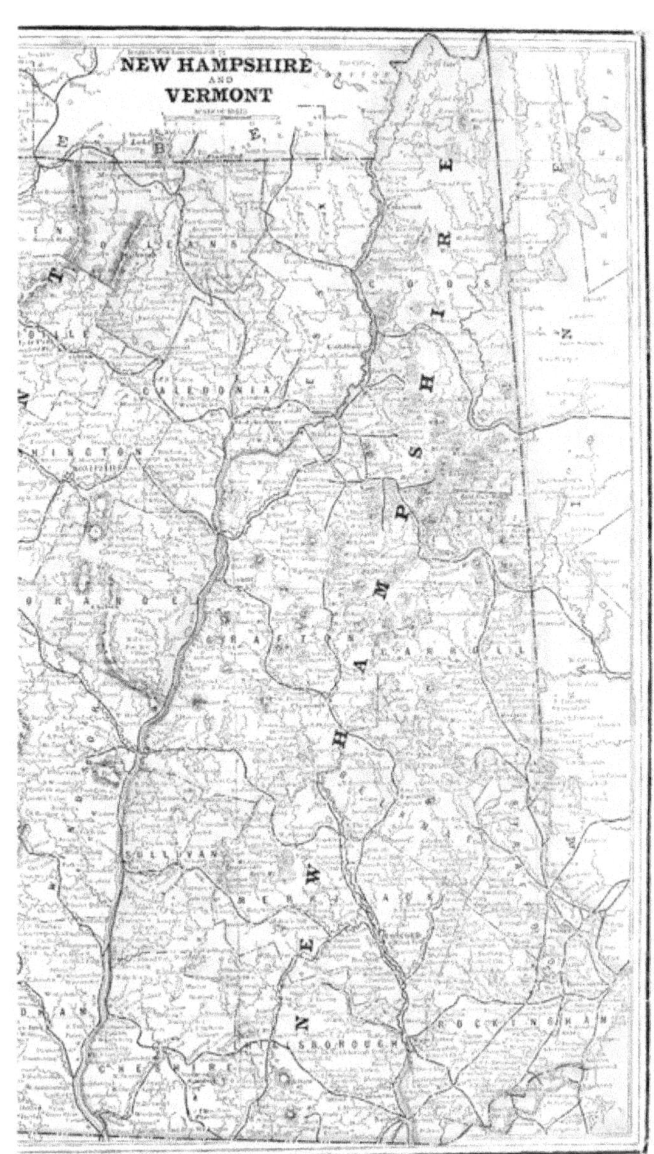
NEW HAMPSHIRE
AND
VERMONT
CALEDONIA
GRAFTON
CARROLL
SULLIVAN
ROCKINGHAM
HILLSBOROUGH
NEW HAMPSHIRE

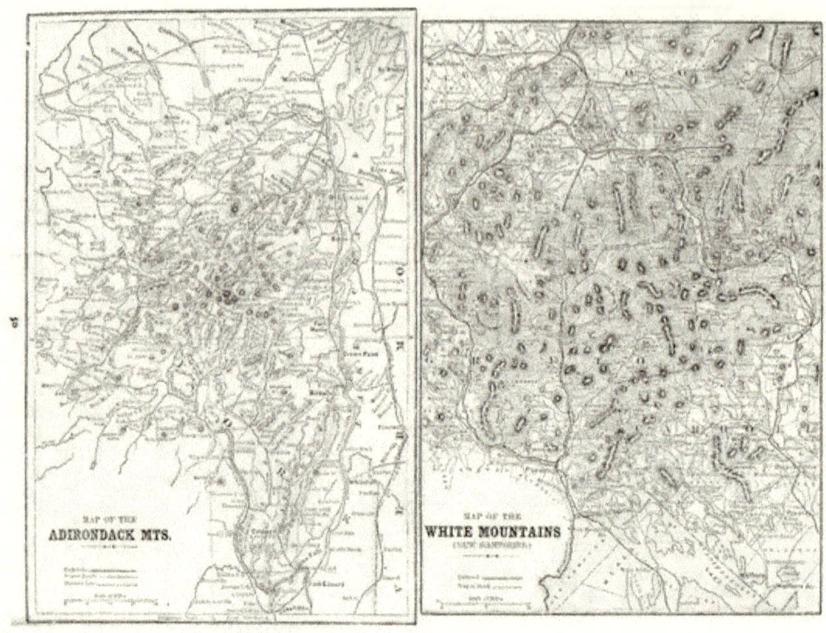
MAP OF THE
ADIRONDACK MTS.
MAP OF THE
WHITE MOUNTAINS

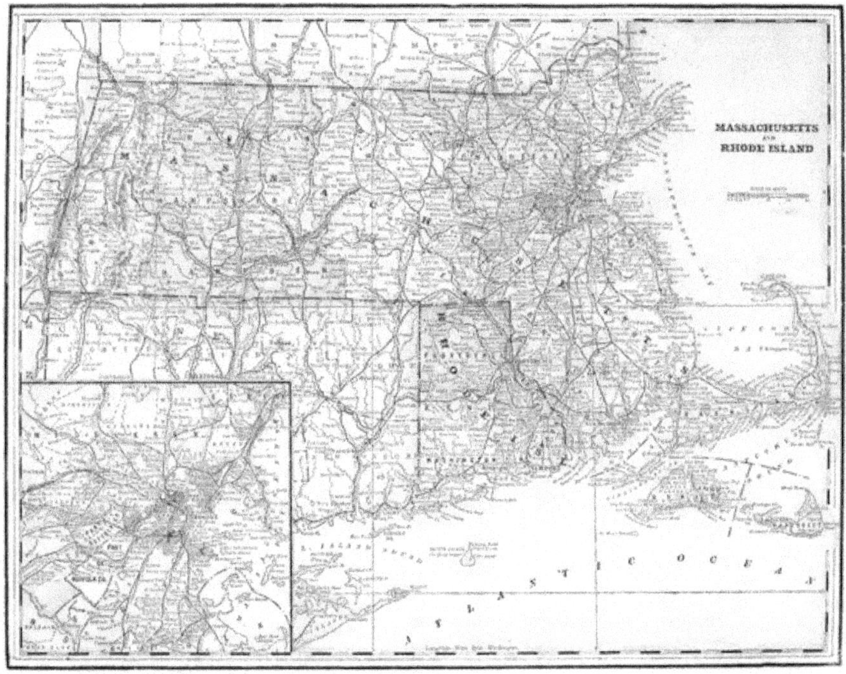
MASSACHUSETTS
AND
RHODE ISLAND

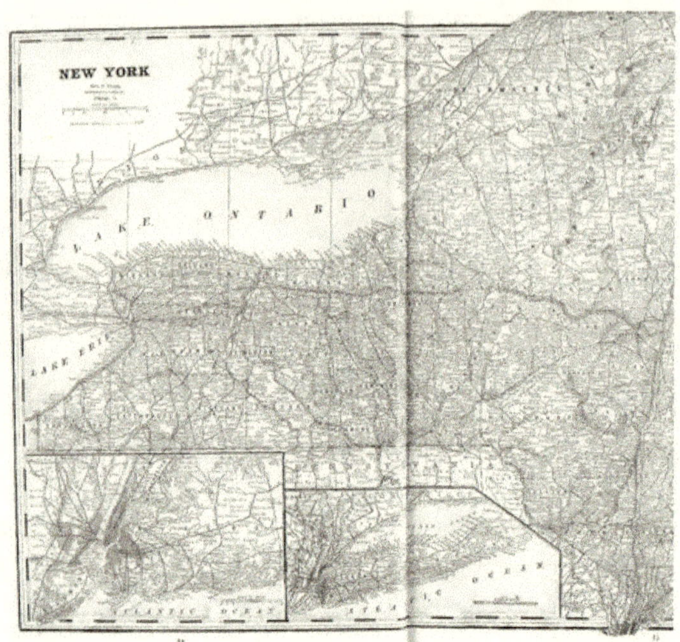
NEW YORK
LAKE ONTARIO
ATLANTIC OCEAN

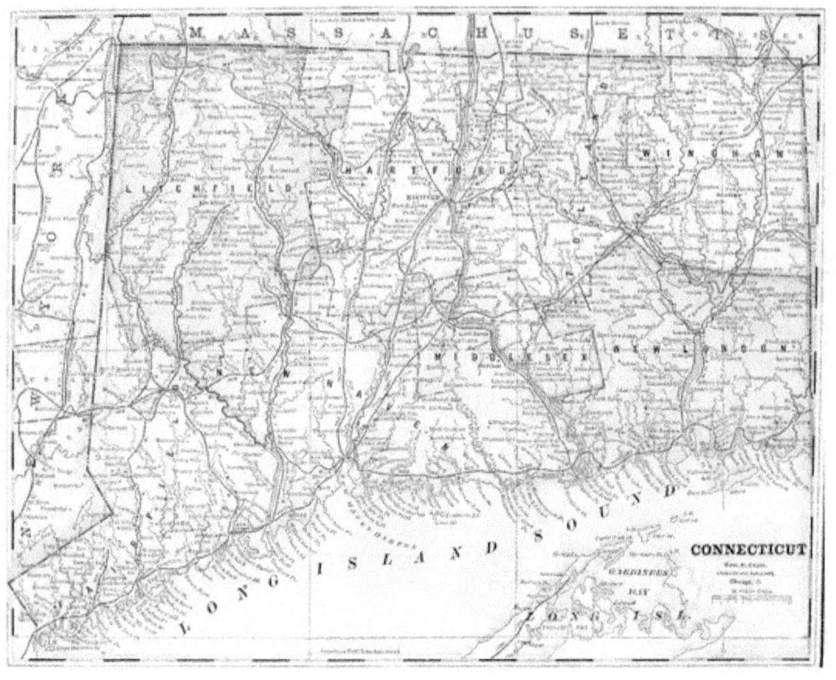

MASSACHUSETTS
LITCHFIELD
HARTFORD
WINDHAM
MIDDLESEX
NEW LONDON
LONG ISLAND SOUND
GARDINERS BAY
CONNECTICUT

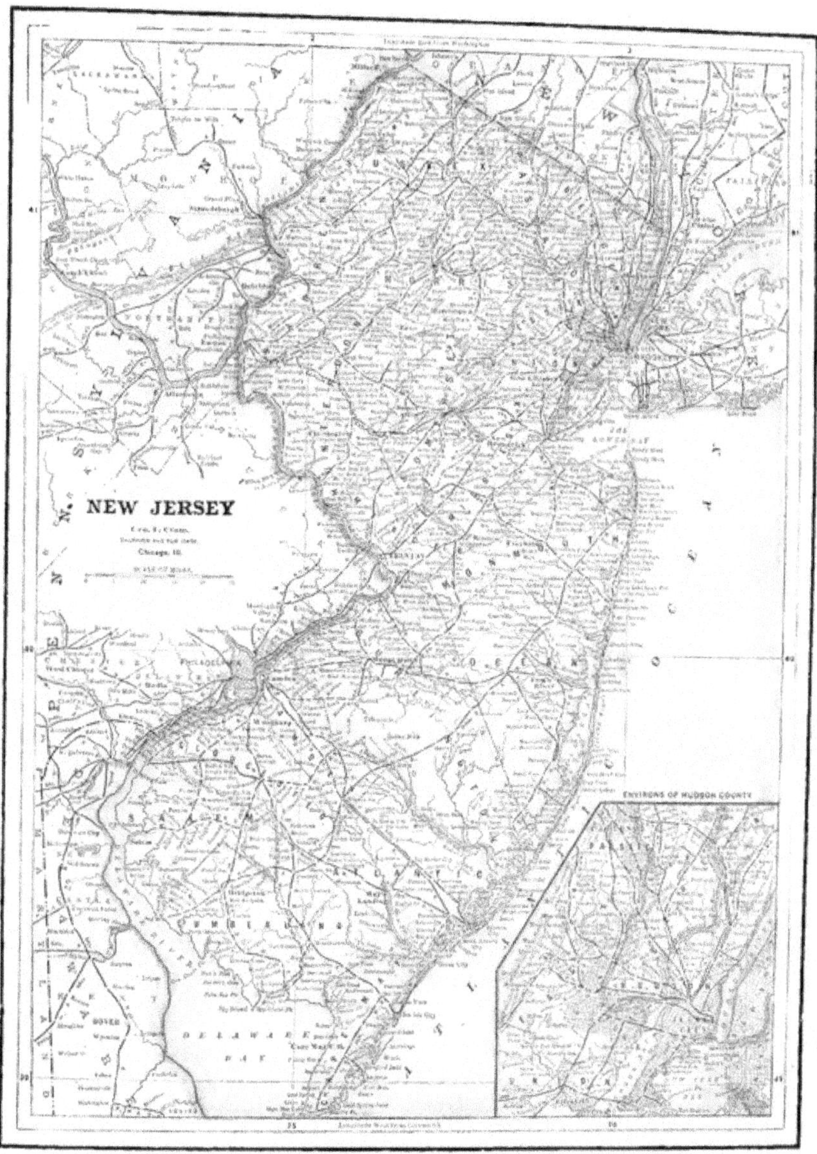
NEW JERSEY
ENVIRONS OF HUDSON COUNTY
PHILADELPHIA
DELAWARE
BAY
DOVER

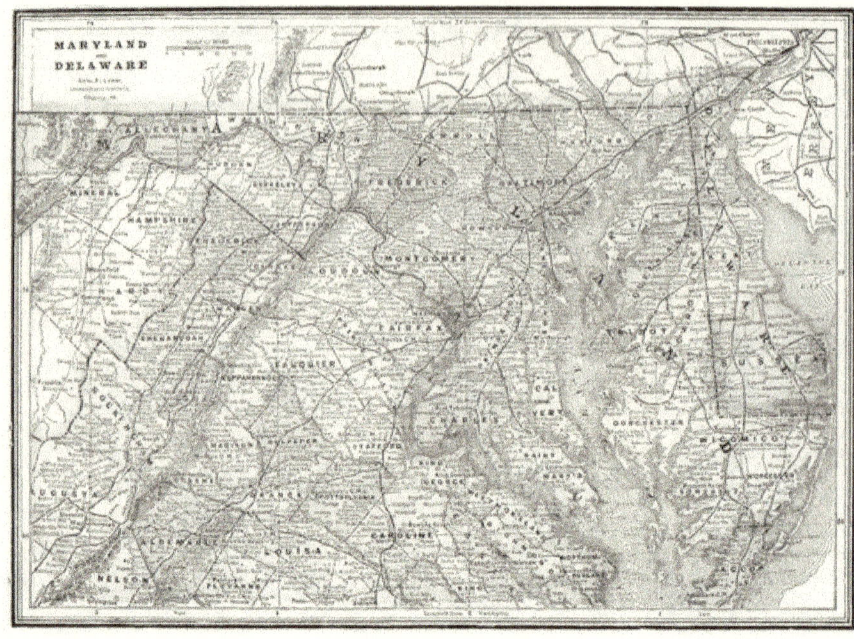
MARYLAND
and
DELAWARE
FREDERICK
BALTIMORE
MONTGOMERY
LOUDOUN
FAIRFAX
FAUQUIER
CULPEPER
MADISON
ORANGE
ALBEMARLE
LOUISA
CAROLINE
NELSON
AUGUSTA
SHENANDOAH
HAMPSHIRE
MINERAL
CHARLES
STAFFORD
TALBOT
DORCHESTER
KENT
SUSSEX
WORCESTER
SOMERSET

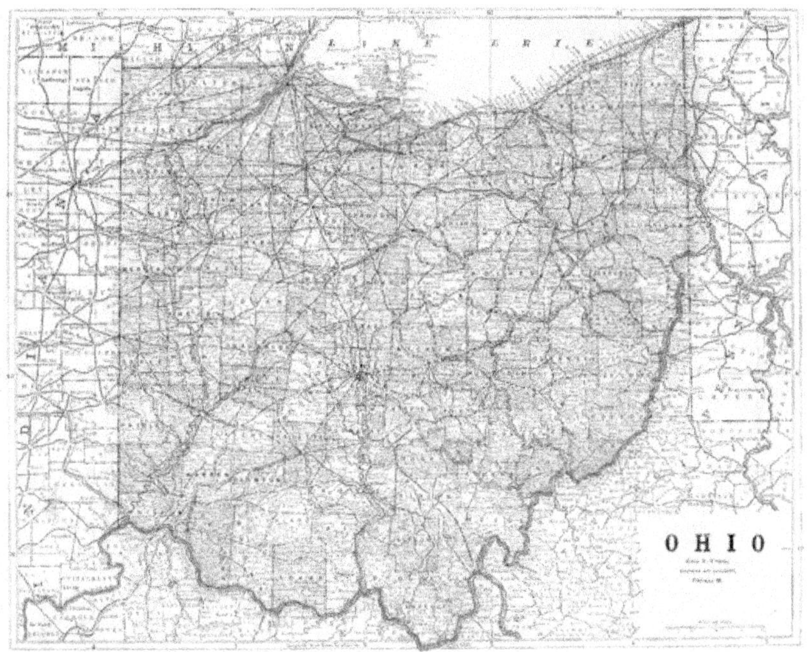
OHIO

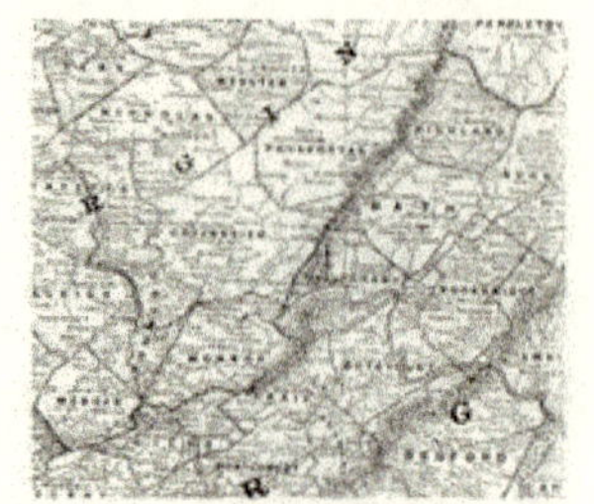
BEDFORD

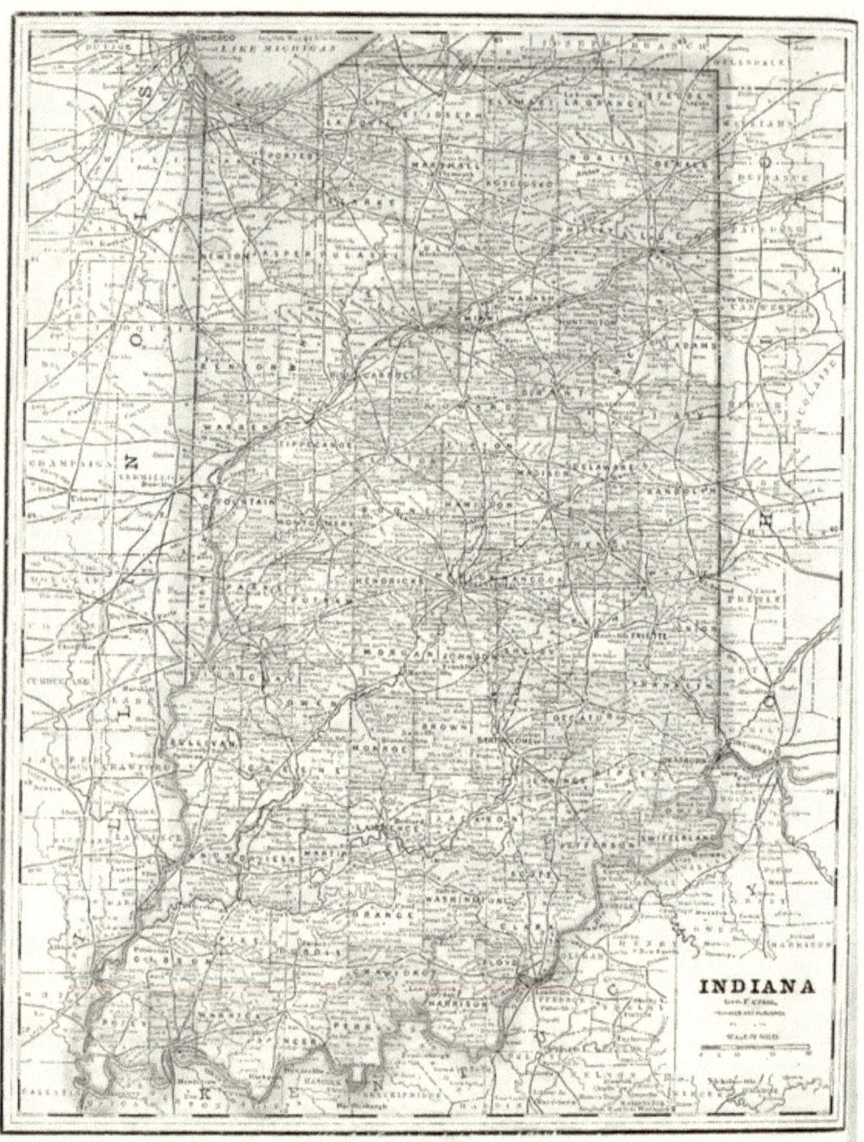
INDIANA

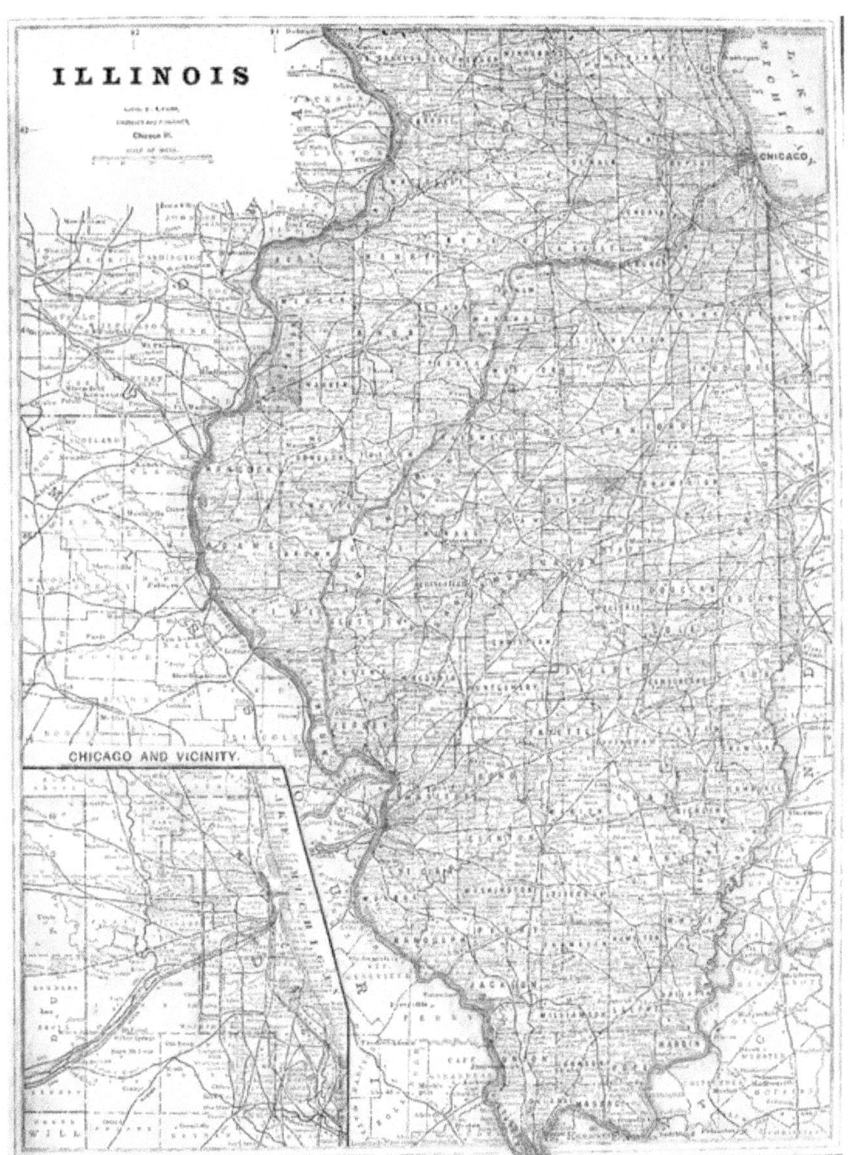
ILLINOIS
CHICAGO
CHICAGO AND VICINITY.

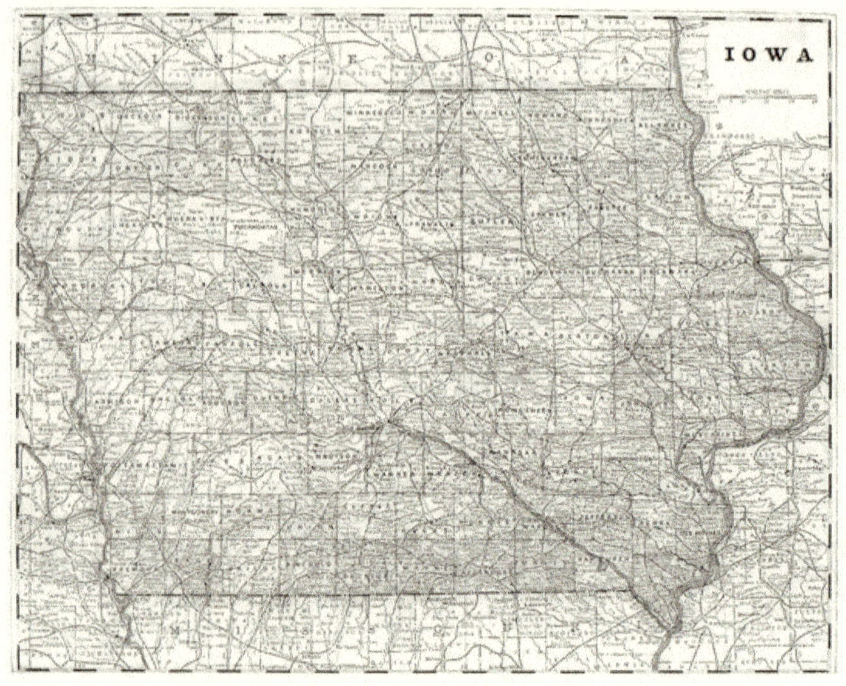
IOWA

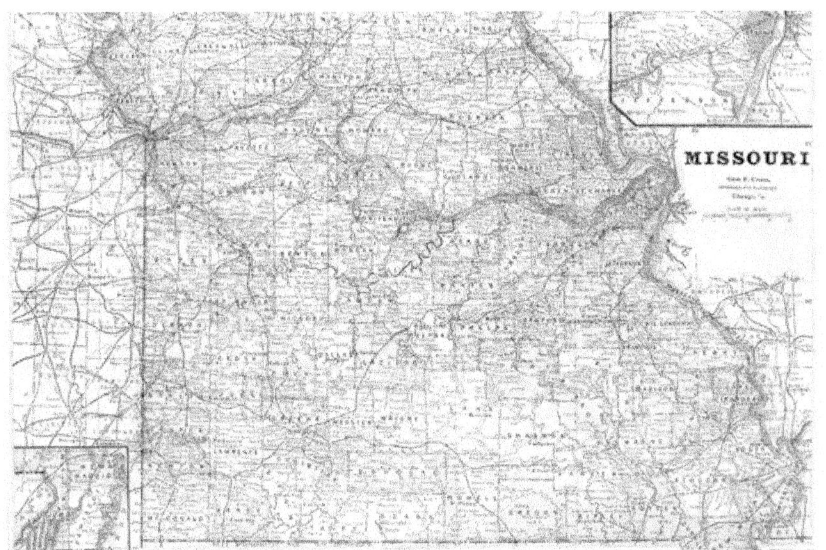
MISSOURI

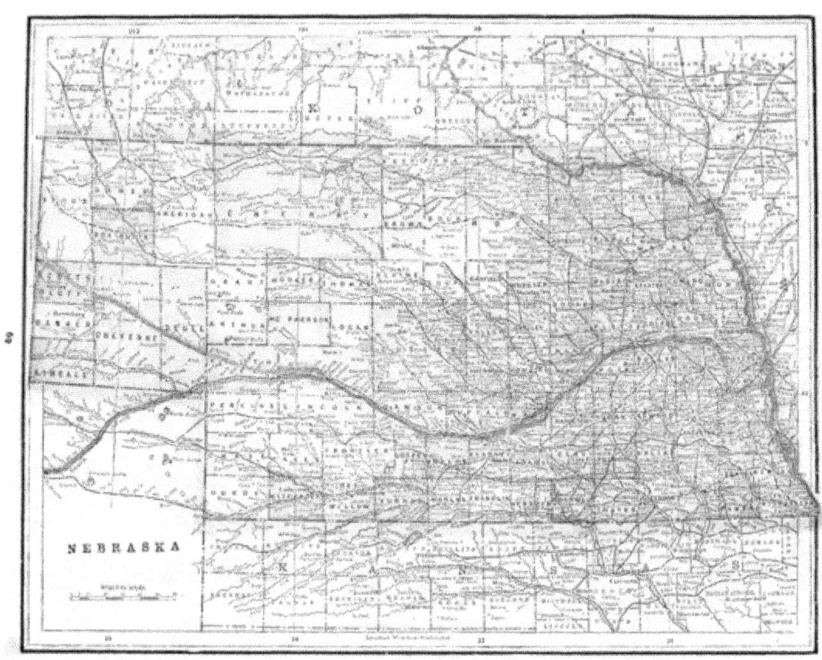
NEBRASKA

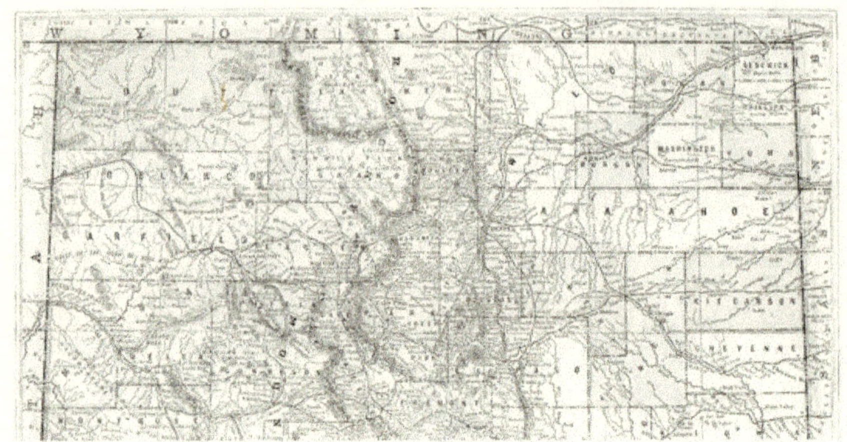

W Y O M I N G
A R A P A H O E
KIT CARSON

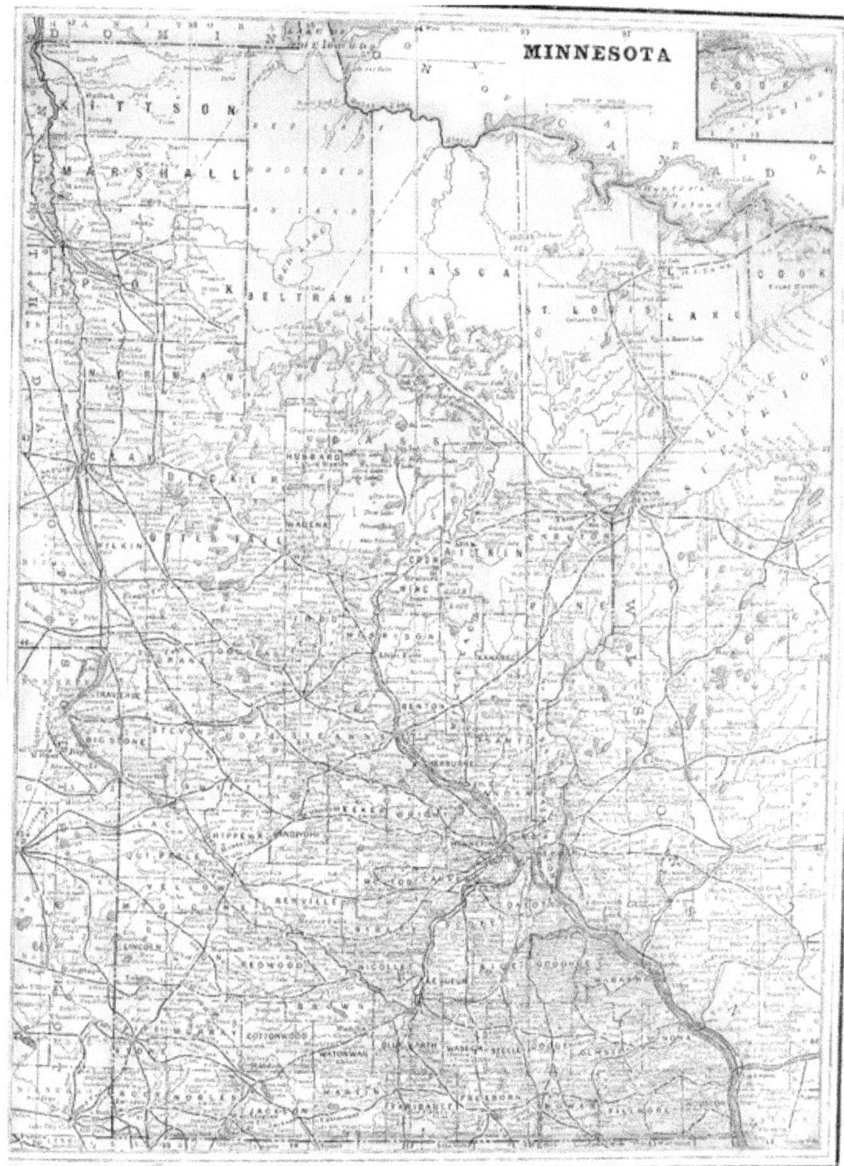
MINNESOTA
KITTSON
MARSHALL
POLK
NORMAN
CLAY
BECKER
BELTRAMI
ITASCA
ST. LOUIS
LAKE
COOK
CASS
HUBBARD
WADENA
WILKIN
AITKIN
CARLTON
PINE
MORRISON
TODD
DOUGLAS
TRAVERSE
BIG STONE
STEVENS
BENTON
KANABEC
SHERBURNE
WRIGHT
CHIPPEWA
LINCOLN
REDWOOD
RENVILLE
DAKOTA
GOODHUE
WABASHA
NICOLLET
COTTONWOOD
WATONWAN
BLUE EARTH
WASECA
STEELE
DODGE
OLMSTED
MARTIN
FARIBAULT
FREEBORN
MOWER
FILLMORE
JACKSON
NOBLES

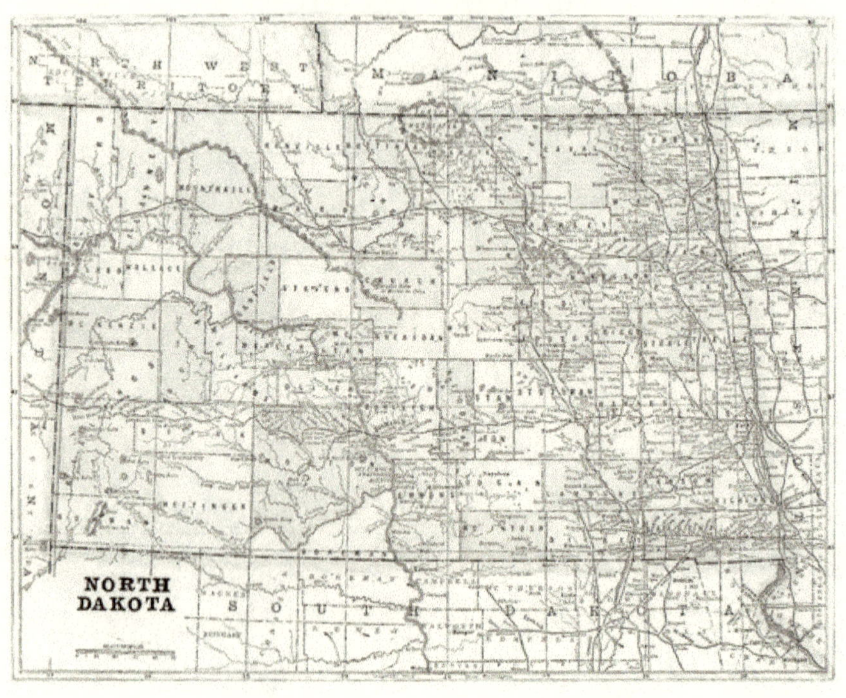
NORTH WEST TERRITORY
MANITOBA
NORTH DAKOTA
SOUTH DAKOTA

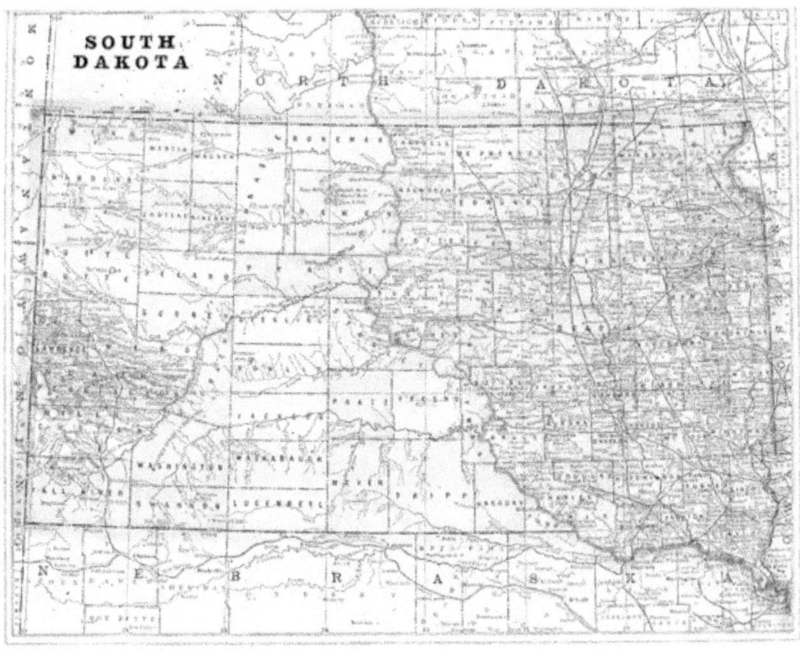
SOUTH DAKOTA
NORTH DAKOTA
NEBRASKA

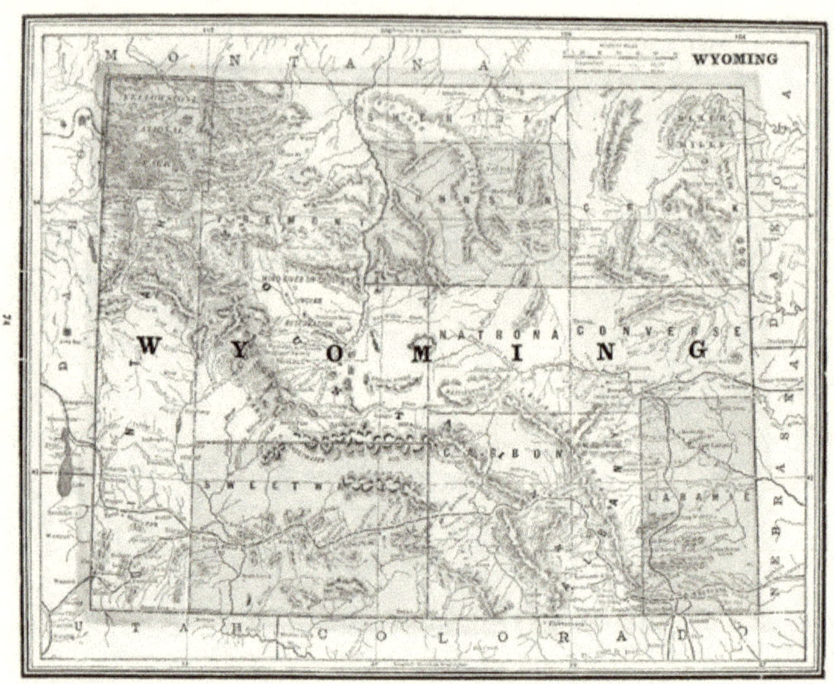
WYOMING
M O N T A N A
W Y O M I N G
NATRONA
C O N V E R S E
L A R A M I E
U T A H
C O L O R A D O

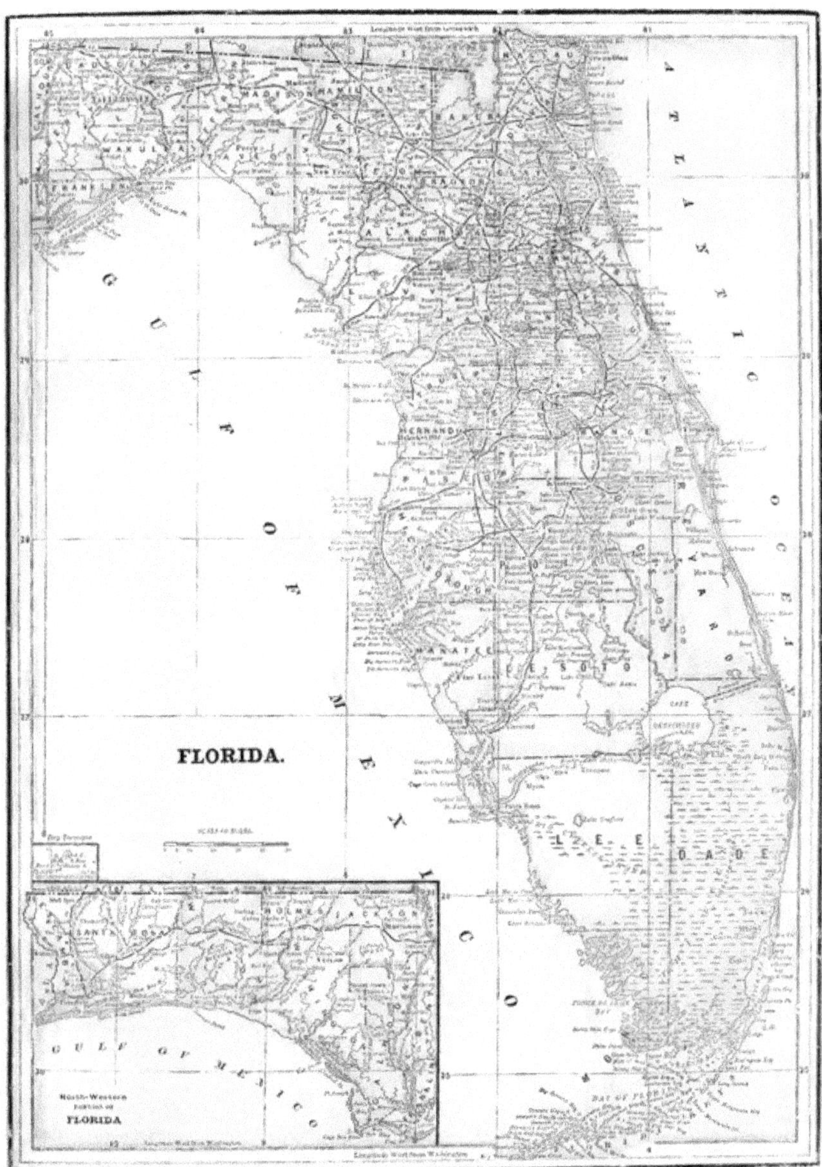
FLORIDA.
GULF OF MEXICO
ATLANTIC OCEAN
FRANKLIN
WAKULLA
MADISON
HAMILTON
NASSAU
BAKER
ALACHUA
HERNANDO
PASCO
MANATEE
DE SOTO
LEE
DADE
LAKE OKEECHOBEE
HOLMES
JACKSON
SANTA ROSA
GULF OF MEXICO
North-Western Portion of FLORIDA

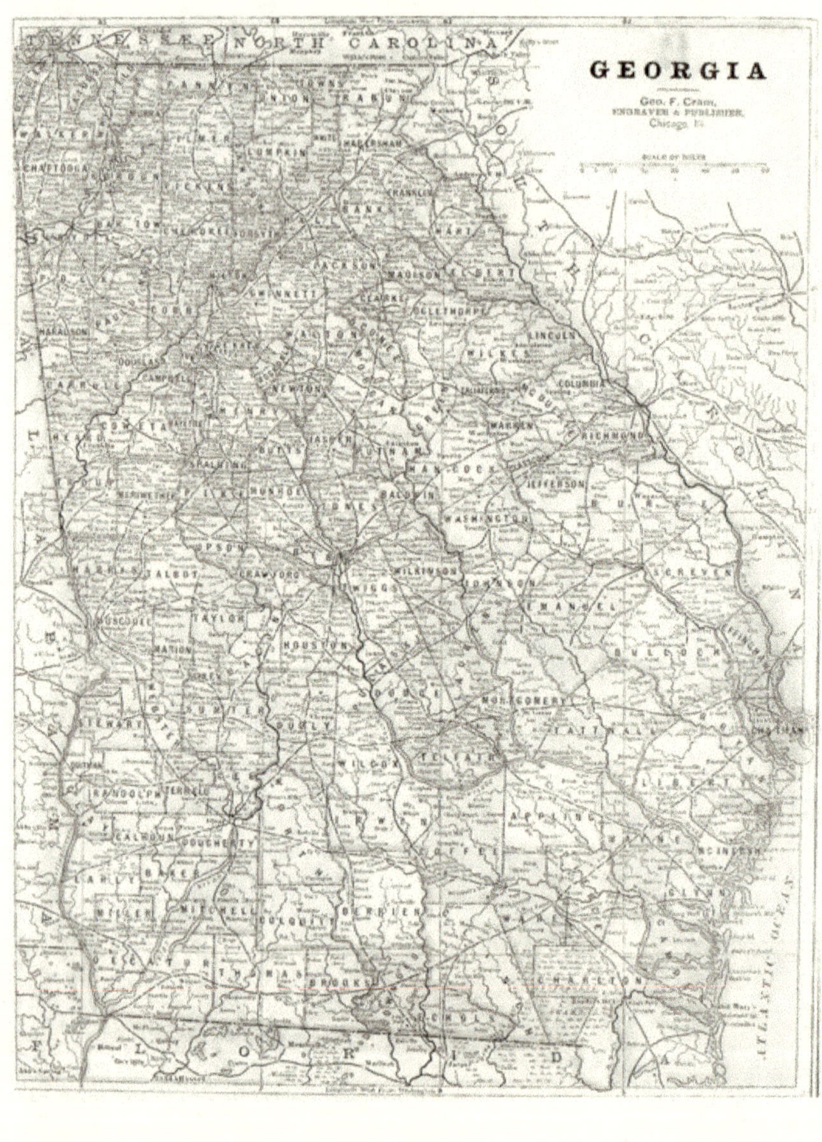
GEORGIA
Geo. F. Cram,
ENGRAVER & PUBLISHER,
Chicago, Ill.
SCALE OF MILES
TENNESSEE
NORTH CAROLINA
SOUTH CAROLINA
FLORIDA
ALABAMA
ATLANTIC OCEAN

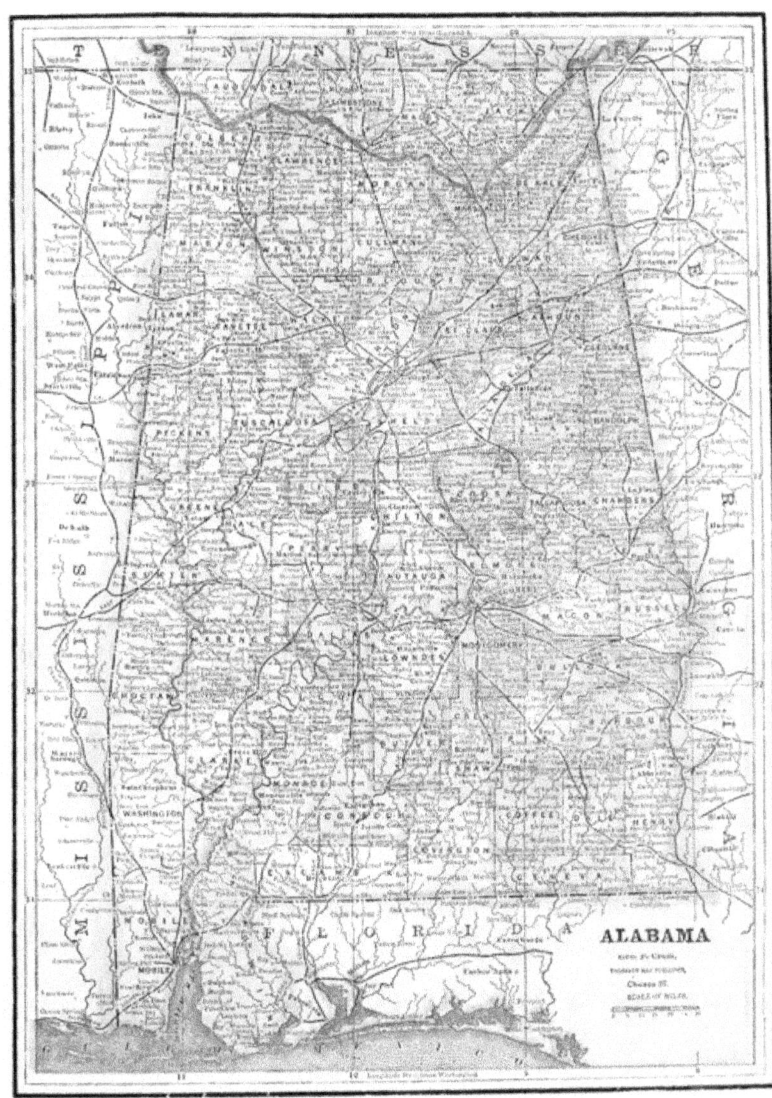
ALABAMA

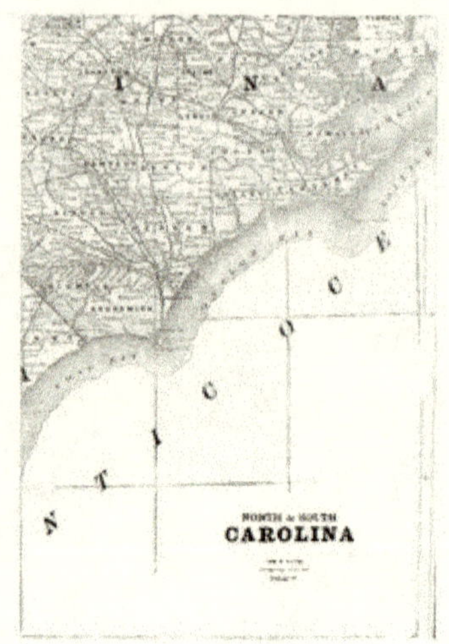
NORTH & SOUTH
CAROLINA

MISSISSIPPI
DE SOTO
MARSHALL
TIPPAH
ALCORN
TATE
PRENTISS
PANOLA
LA FAYETTE
UNION
PONTOTOC
ITAWAMBA
COAHOMA
TALLAHATCHIE
YALOBUSHA
CALHOUN
CHICKASAW
MONROE
GRENADA
WEBSTER
CARROLL
CHOCTAW
WASHINGTON
HOLMES
ATTALA
WINSTON
NOXUBEE
LEAKE
NESHOBA
KEMPER
MADISON
SCOTT
NEWTON
HINDS
SMITH
JASPER
CLARKE
SIMPSON
COPIAH
JEFFERSON
LINCOLN
LAWRENCE
COVINGTON
JONES
WAYNE
ADAMS
FRANKLIN
WILKINSON
AMITE
PIKE
MARION
PERRY
GREENE
PEARL RIVER
HARRISON
JACKSON
HANCOCK
GULF OF MEXICO

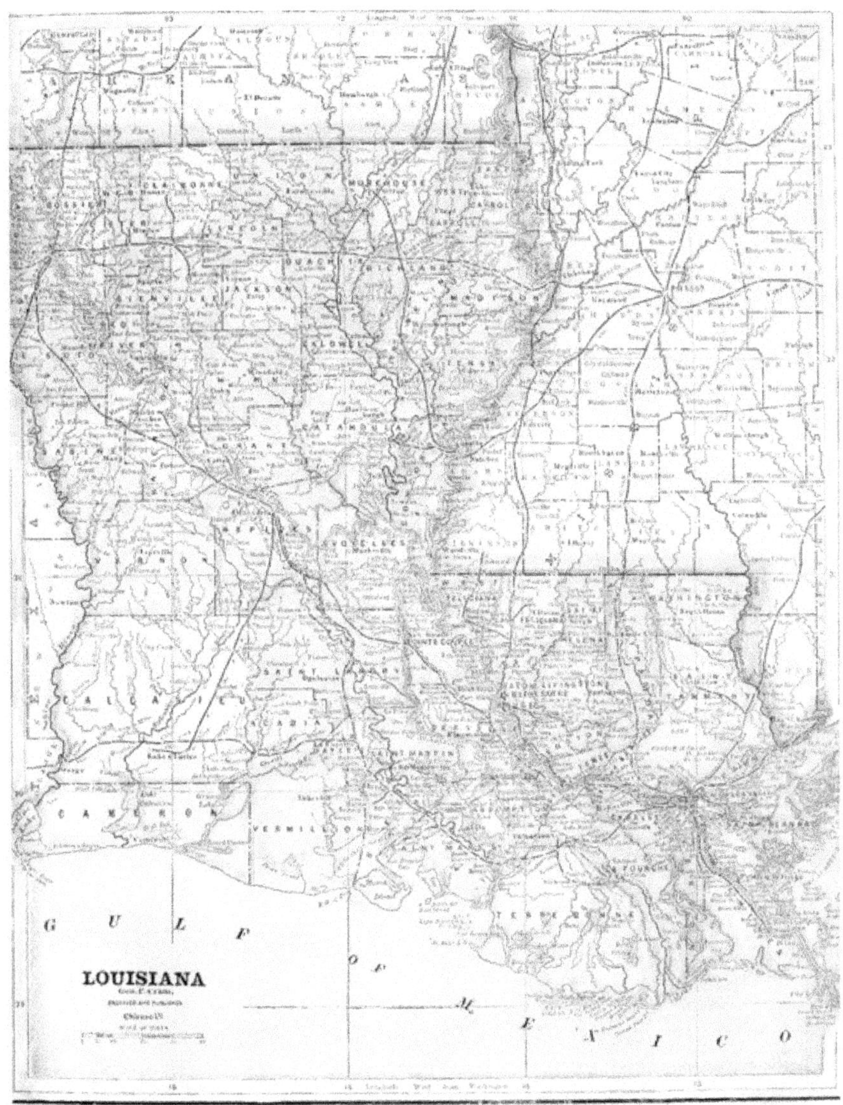
G U L F
O F
M E X I C O
LOUISIANA

ARKANSAS

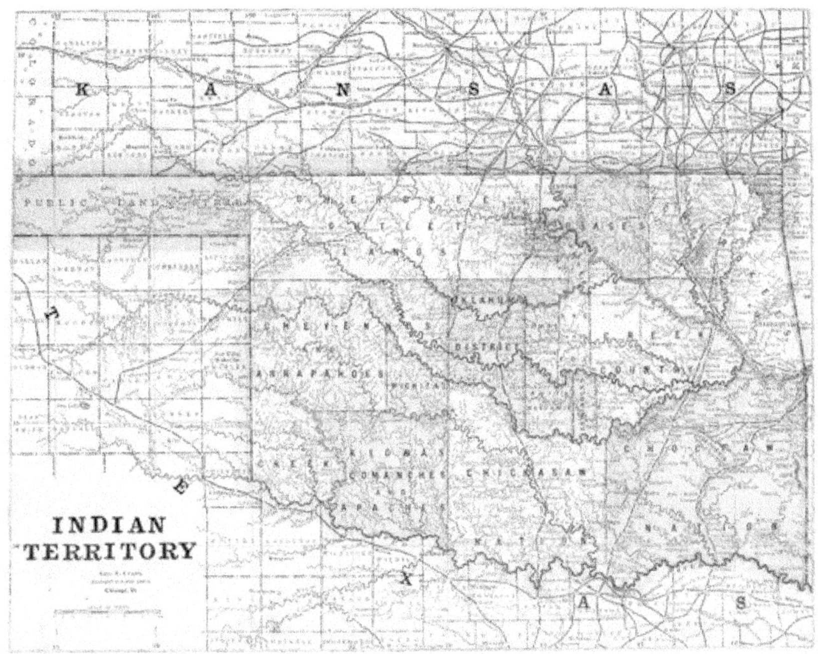
K A N S A S
PUBLIC LAND STRIP
CHEROKEE OUTLET LANDS
OSAGES
OKLAHOMA DISTRICT
CHEYENNES AND ARAPAHOES
CREEK COUNTRY
KIOWAS COMANCHES AND APACHES
CHICKASAW NATION
CHOCTAW NATION
INDIAN TERRITORY

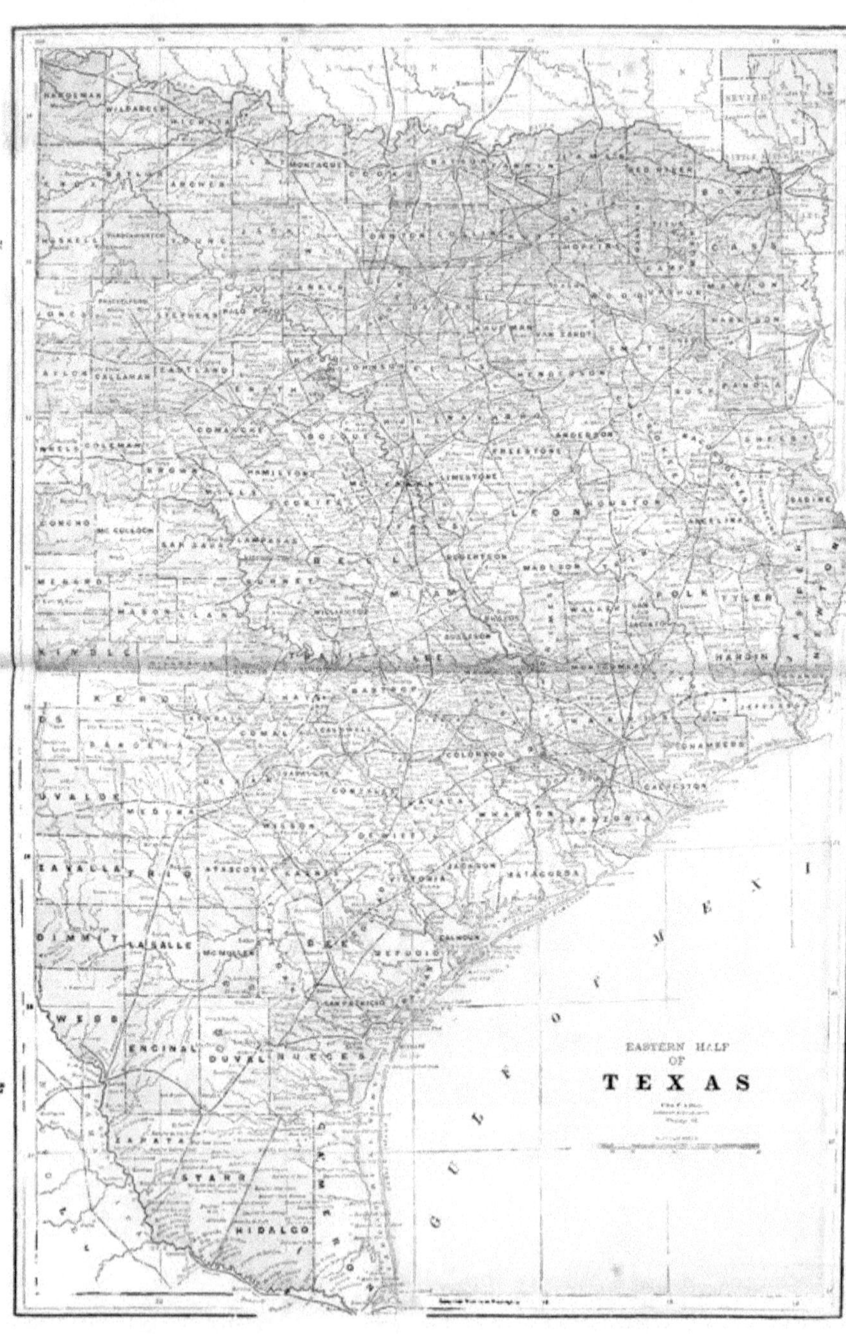
EASTERN HALF
OF
TEXAS
HARDEMAN
WILBARGER
WICHITA
MONTAGUE
COOKE
GRAYSON
FANNIN
LAMAR
RED RIVER
BOWIE
KNOX
BAYLOR
ARCHER
HASKELL
THROCKMORTON
YOUNG
JACK
DENTON
COLLIN
HOPKINS
CASS
SHACKELFORD
STEPHENS
PALO PINTO
PARKER
DALLAS
KAUFMAN
VAN ZANDT
UPSHUR
MARION
HARRISON
CALLAHAN
EASTLAND
ERATH
JOHNSON
ELLIS
HENDERSON
SMITH
RUSK
PANOLA
COMANCHE
BOSQUE
NAVARRO
ANDERSON
FREESTONE
SHELBY
COLEMAN
BROWN
HAMILTON
LIMESTONE
McLENNAN
CORYELL
LEON
HOUSTON
SABINE
CONCHO
McCULLOCH
SAN SABA
LAMPASAS
BELL
ROBERTSON
MADISON
ANGELINA
MENARD
BURNET
MILAM
WALKER
POLK
TYLER
MASON
WILLIAMSON
BURLESON
SAN JACINTO
KIMBLE
TRAVIS
LEE
MONTGOMERY
HARDIN
KERR
HAYS
BASTROP
JEFFERSON
BANDERA
COMAL
CALDWELL
COLORADO
CHAMBERS
UVALDE
MEDINA
GONZALES
LAVACA
GALVESTON
WILSON
WHARTON
BRAZORIA
DE WITT
ZAVALLA
FRIO
ATASCOSA
KARNES
VICTORIA
JACKSON
MATAGORDA
DIMMIT
LASALLE
McMULLEN
BEE
REFUGIO
CALHOUN
SAN PATRICIO
WEBB
ENCINAL
DUVAL
NUECES
ZAPATA
STARR
HIDALGO
SEVIER
GULF OF MEXICO

M E X I
S O C O R R O
D O N A

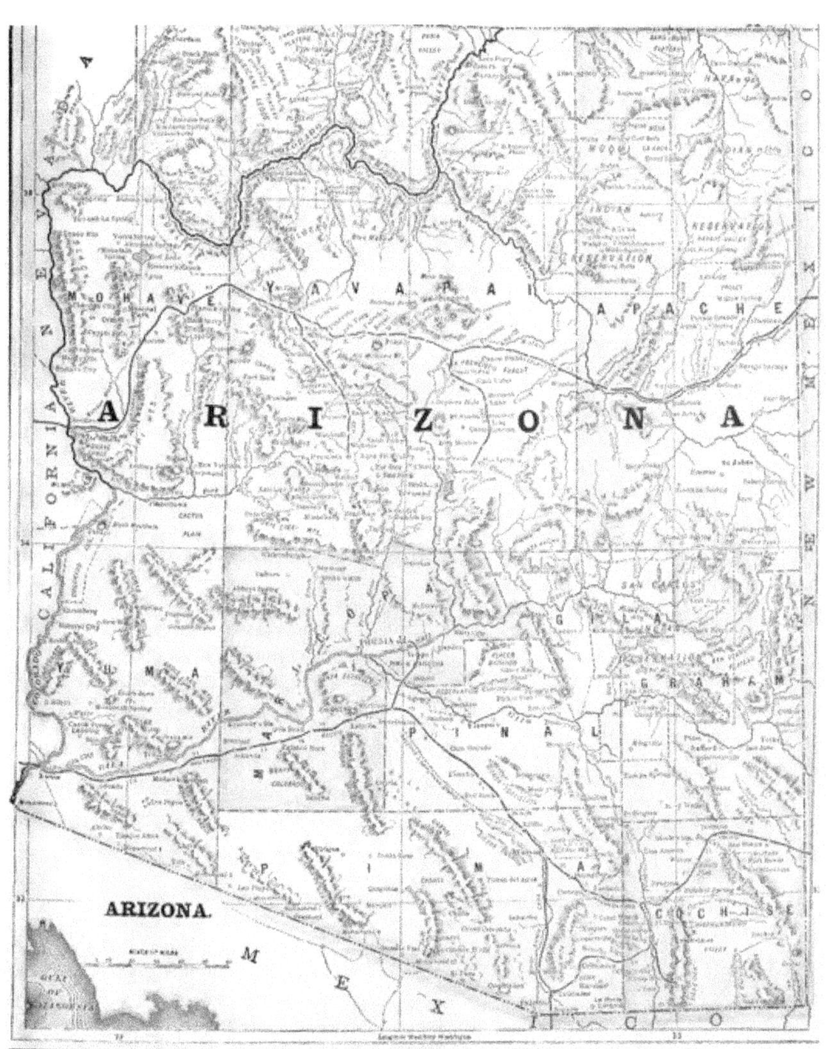
ARIZONA.
A R I Z O N A
M O H A V E
Y A V A P A I
A P A C H E
Y U M A
P I N A L
P I M A
G I L A
G R A H A M
C O C H I S E
C A L I F O R N I A
N E W M E X I C O
M E X I C O

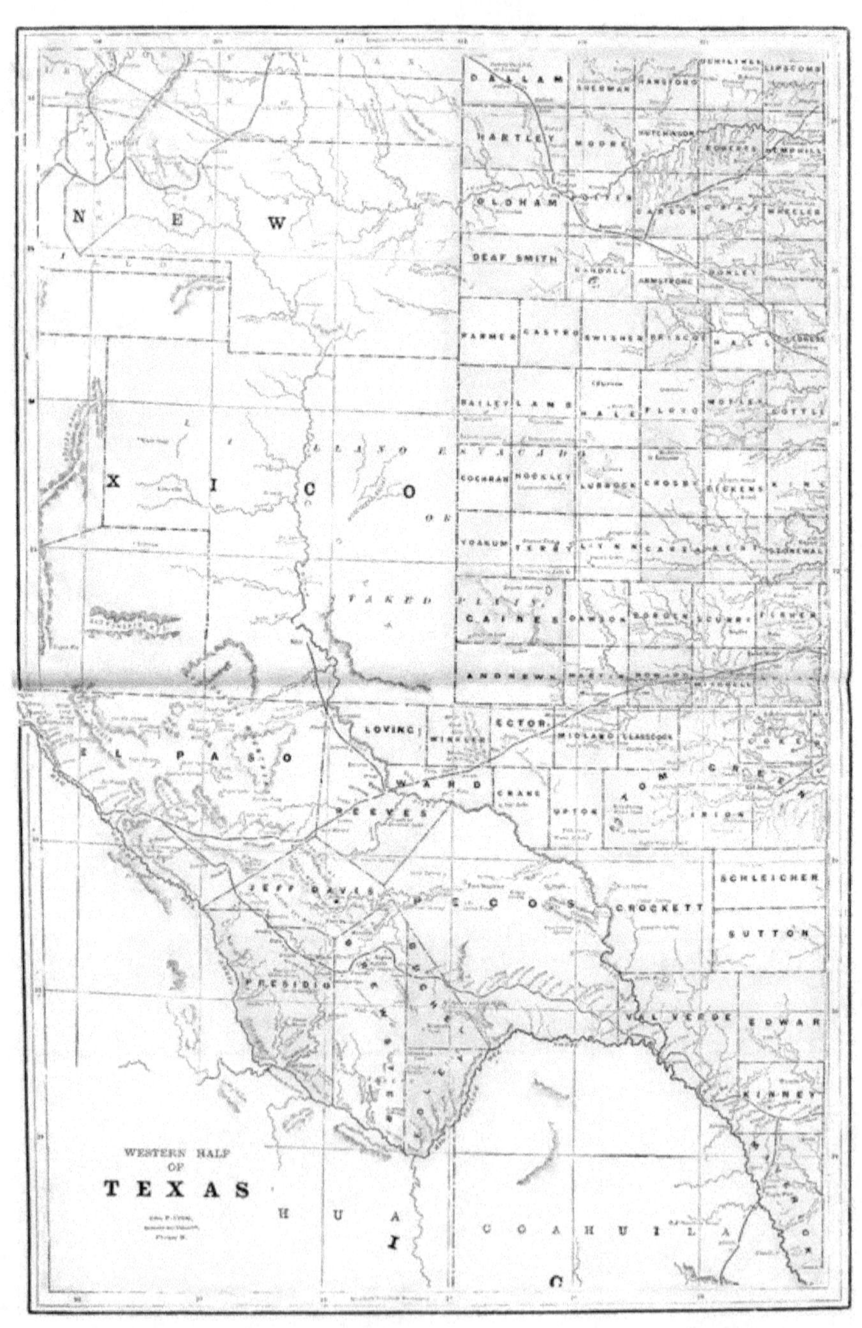

WESTERN HALF
OF
TEXAS
DALLAM
SHERMAN
HANSFORD
LIPSCOMB
HARTLEY
MOORE
HUTCHINSON
HEMPHILL
OLDHAM
CARSON
WHEELER
DEAF SMITH
RANDALL
ARMSTRONG
DONLEY
FARMER
CASTRO
SWISHER
BRISCOE
HALL
BAILEY
LAMB
HALE
FLOYD
MOTLEY
COTTLE
COCHRAN
HOCKLEY
LUBBOCK
CROSBY
DICKENS
YOAKUM
TERRY
LYNN
GAINES
DAWSON
BORDEN
SCURRY
FISHER
ANDREWS
MARTIN
HOWARD
MITCHELL
LOVING
WINKLER
ECTOR
MIDLAND
GLASSCOCK
COKE
WARD
CRANE
UPTON
IRION
REEVES
JEFF DAVIS
PECOS
CROCKETT
SCHLEICHER
SUTTON
PRESIDIO
VAL VERDE
KINNEY
EL PASO
N E W
X I C O
LLANO ESTACADO
OR
STAKED PLAIN
C O A H U I L A

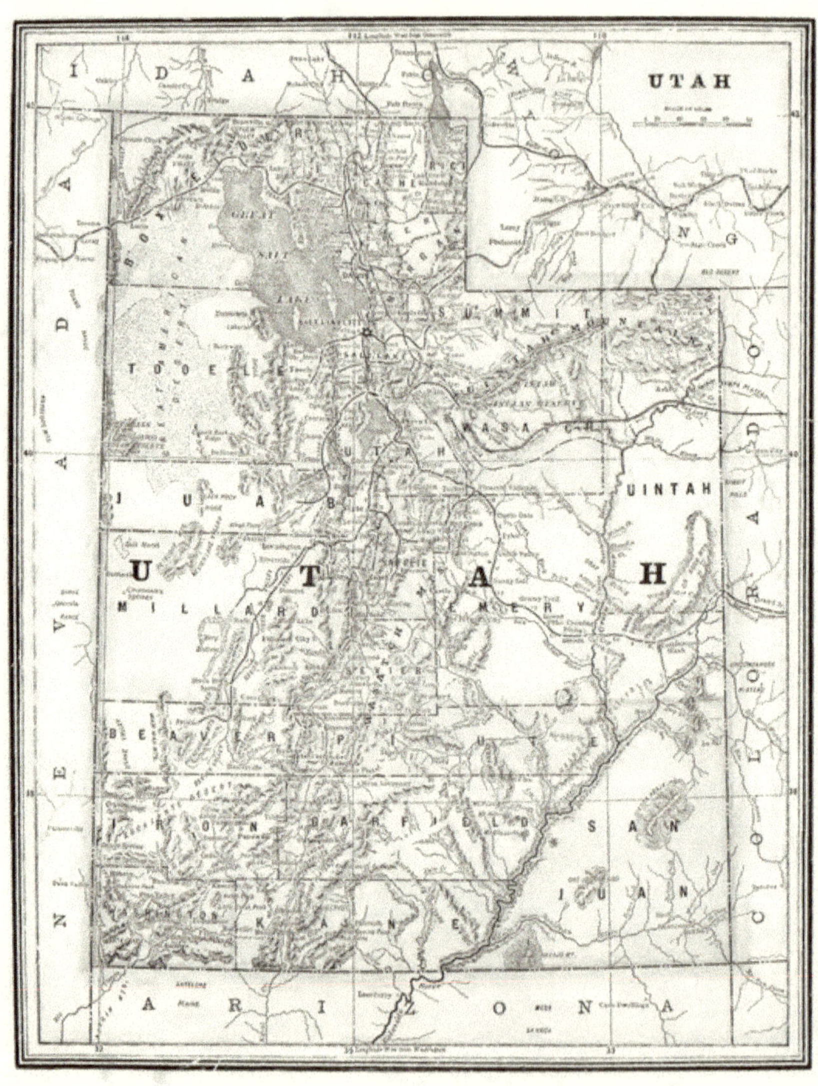
UTAH
I D A H O
W Y O M I N G
N E V A D A
C O L O R A D O
A R I Z O N A
U T A H
TOOELE
JUAB
MILLARD
BEAVER
IRON
KANE
GARFIELD
PIUTE
SEVIER
EMERY
UINTAH
SAN JUAN
SUMMIT
WASATCH
GREAT SALT LAKE

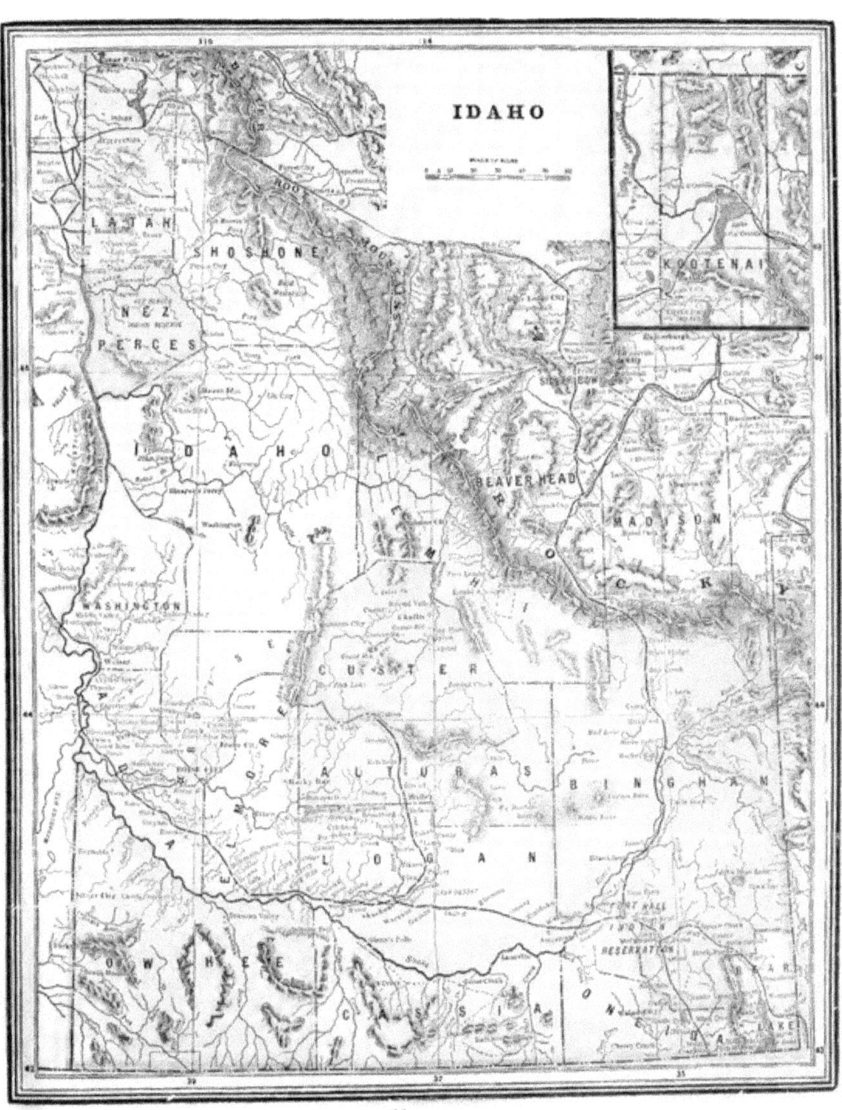
IDAHO
LATAH
SHOSHONE
NEZ PERCES
IDAHO
WASHINGTON
BEAVER HEAD
MADISON
CUSTER
ALTURAS
BINGHAM
LOGAN
CASSIA
KOOTENAI
FORT HALL
INDIAN
RESERVATION
BEAR
LAKE

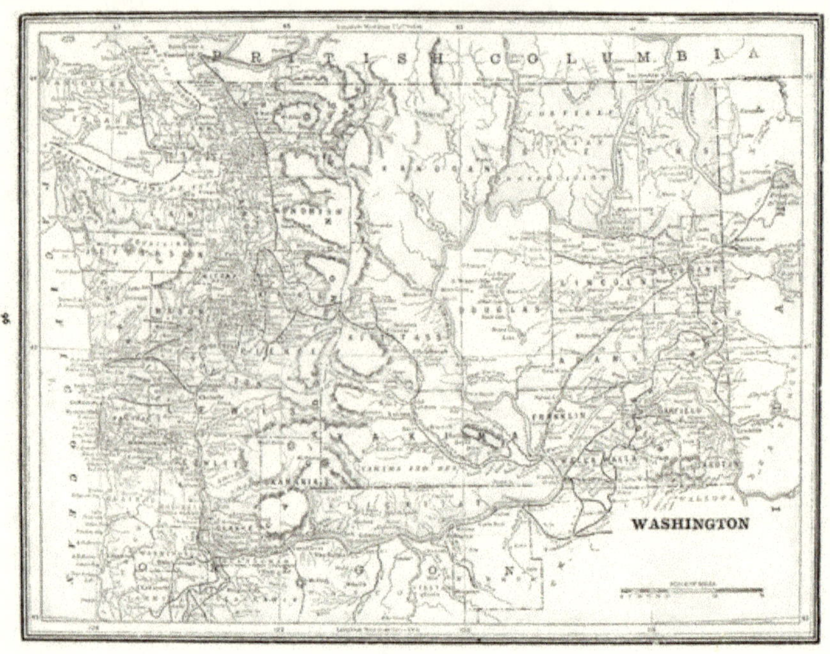
BRITISH COLUMBIA
WASHINGTON
OREGON

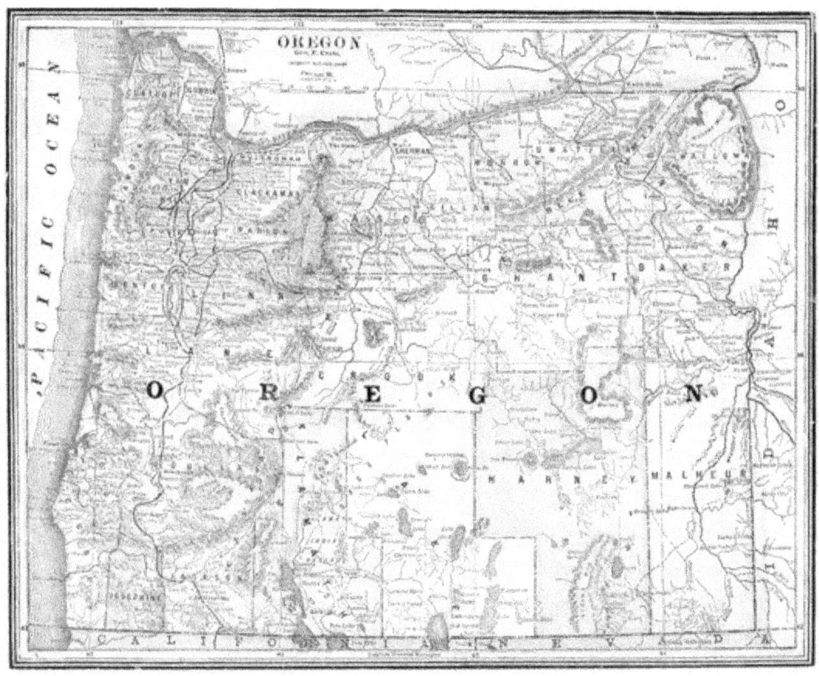
OREGON
PACIFIC OCEAN
O R E G O N
MULTNOMAH
CLACKAMAS
SHERMAN
MORROW
GRANT
BAKER
HARNEY
MALHEUR
JOSEPHINE
CALIFORNIA
NEVADA
IDAHO

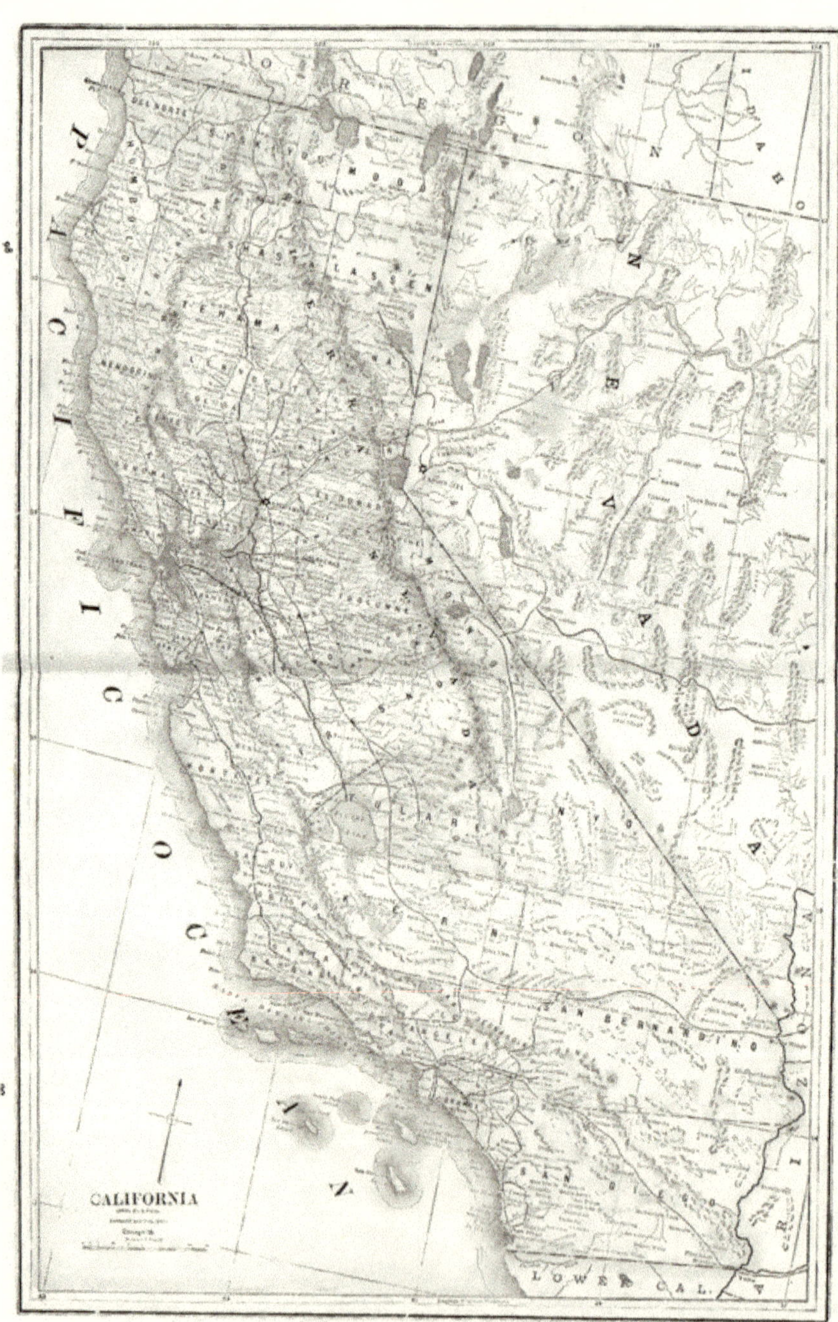
CALIFORNIA
PACIFIC OCEAN
OREGON
IDAHO
NEVADA
ARIZONA
LOWER CAL.
DEL NORTE
SISKIYOU
MODOC
SHASTA
LASSEN
TEHAMA
MENDOCINO
TULARE
KERN
INYO
SAN BERNARDINO
SAN DIEGO

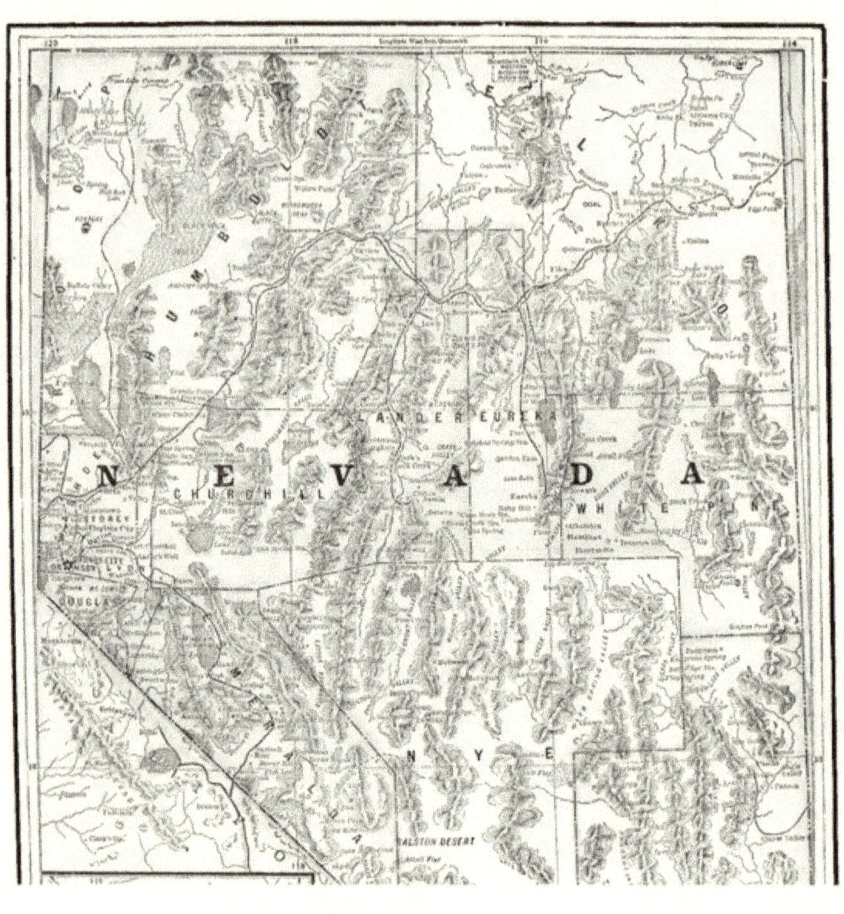

N E V A D A
LANDER
EUREKA
CHURCHILL
WHITE PINE
STOREY
DOUGLAS
N Y E
RALSTON DESERT

YELLOWSTONE NATIONAL PARK

WYOMING

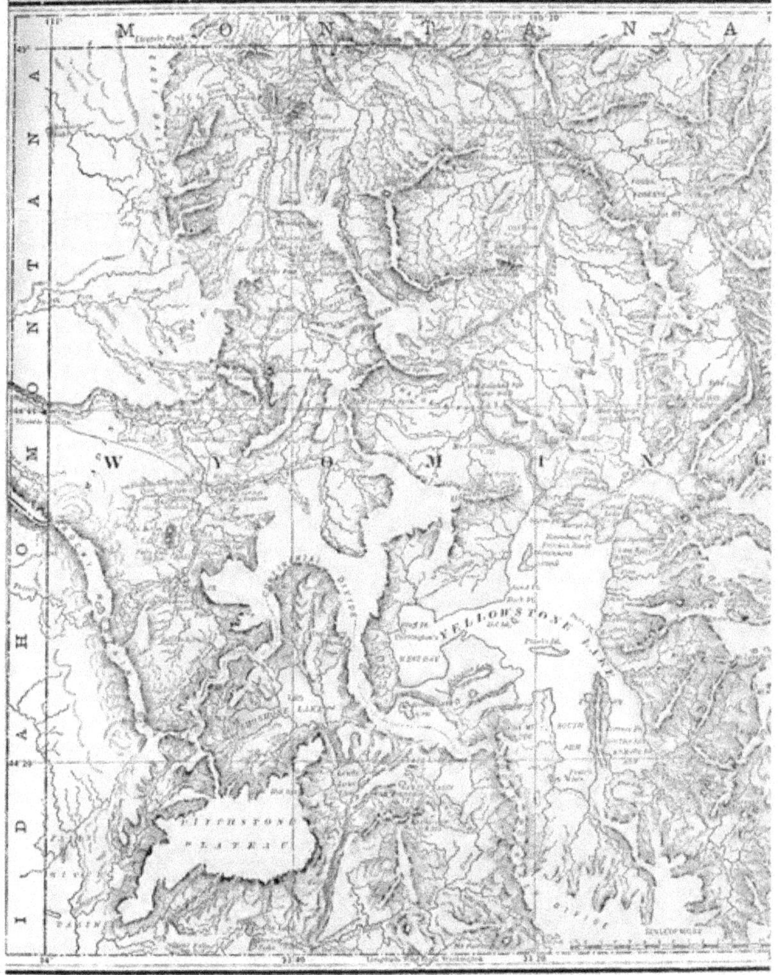

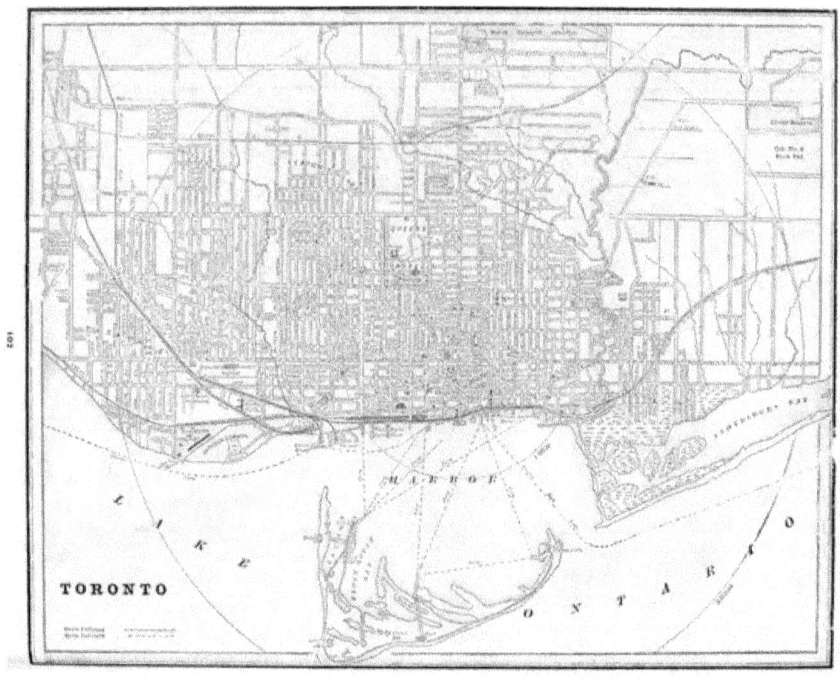
TORONTO
L A K E
O N T A R I O

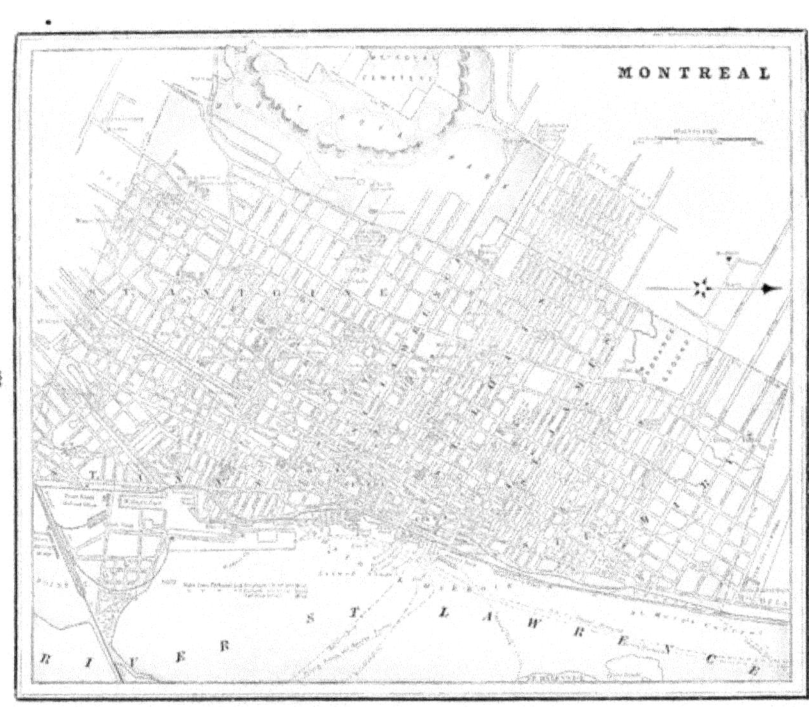
MONTREAL
S T. L A W R E N C E
R I V E R

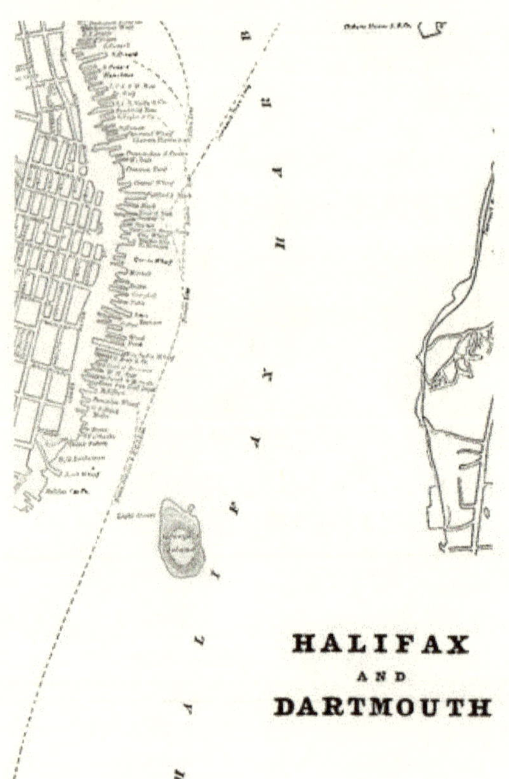

H A L I F A X H A R B
HALIFAX
AND
DARTMOUTH

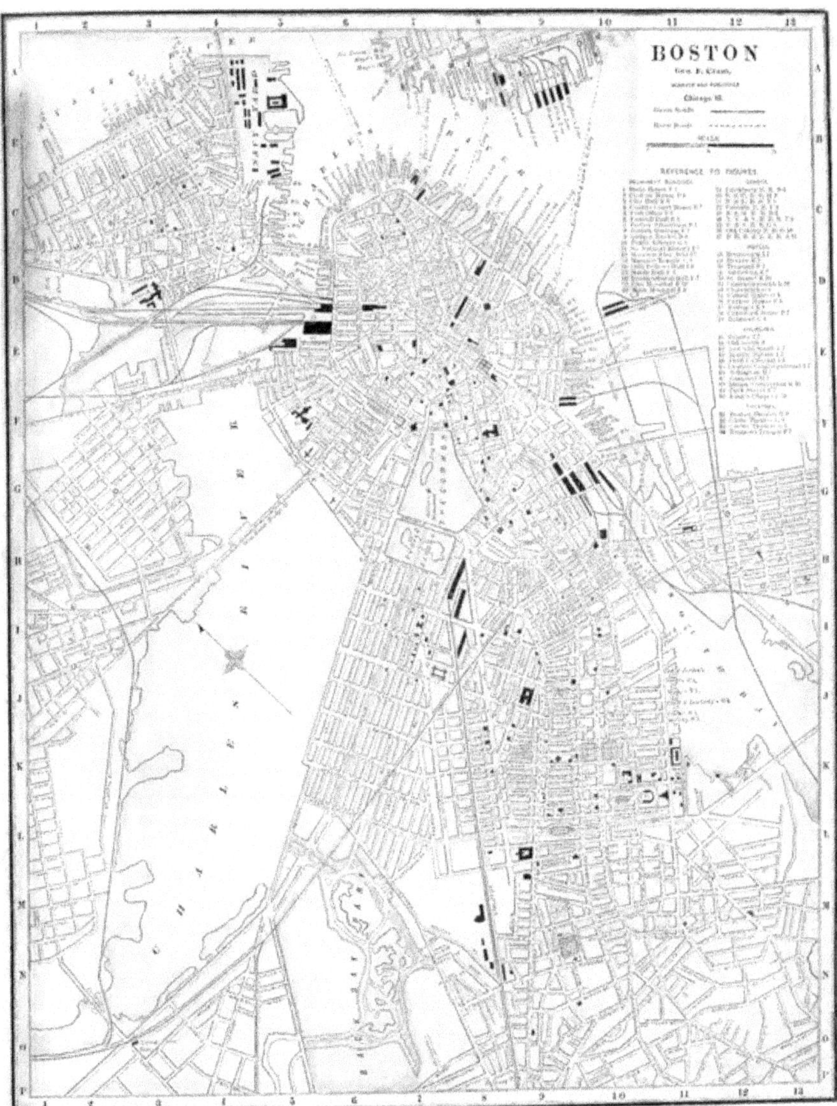
BOSTON
REFERENCE TO FIGURES

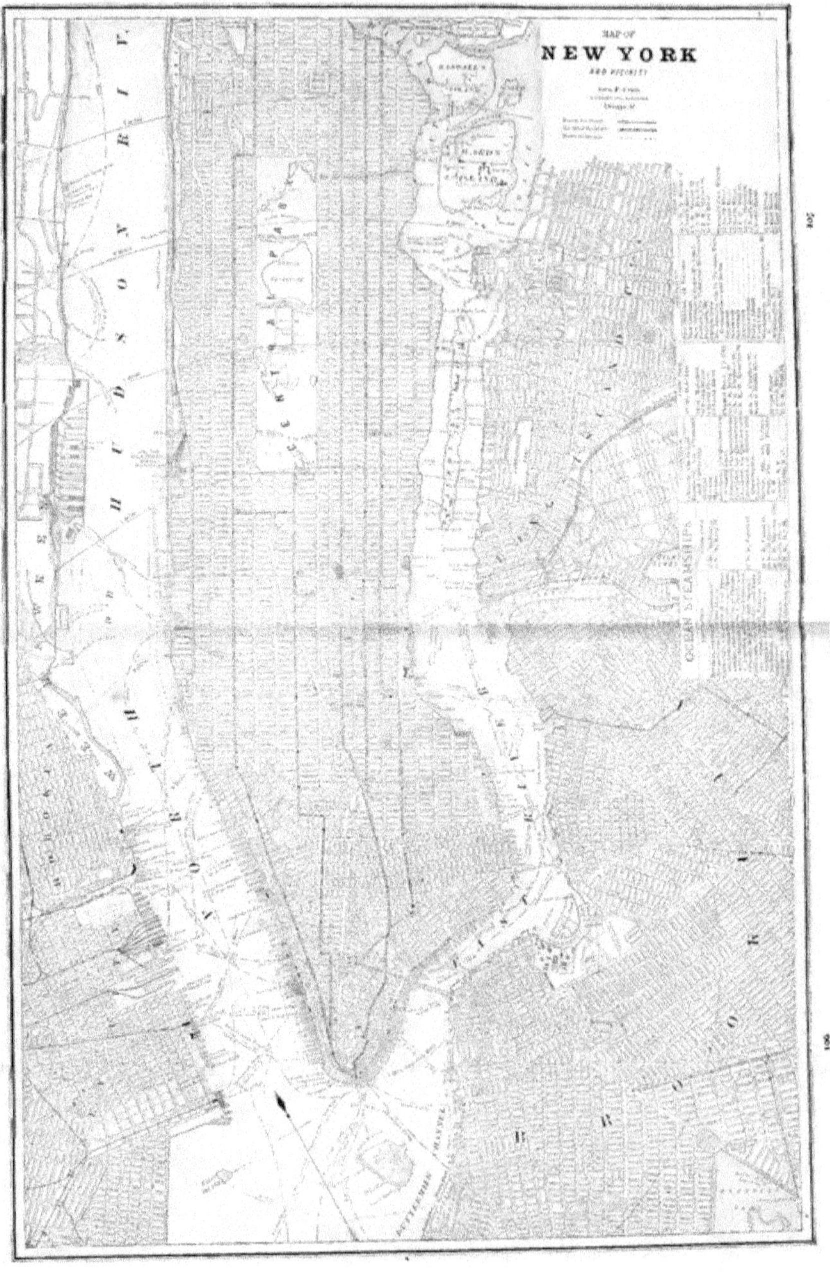

MAP OF
NEW YORK
AND VICINITY
CENTRAL PARK
OCEAN STEAMSHIPS

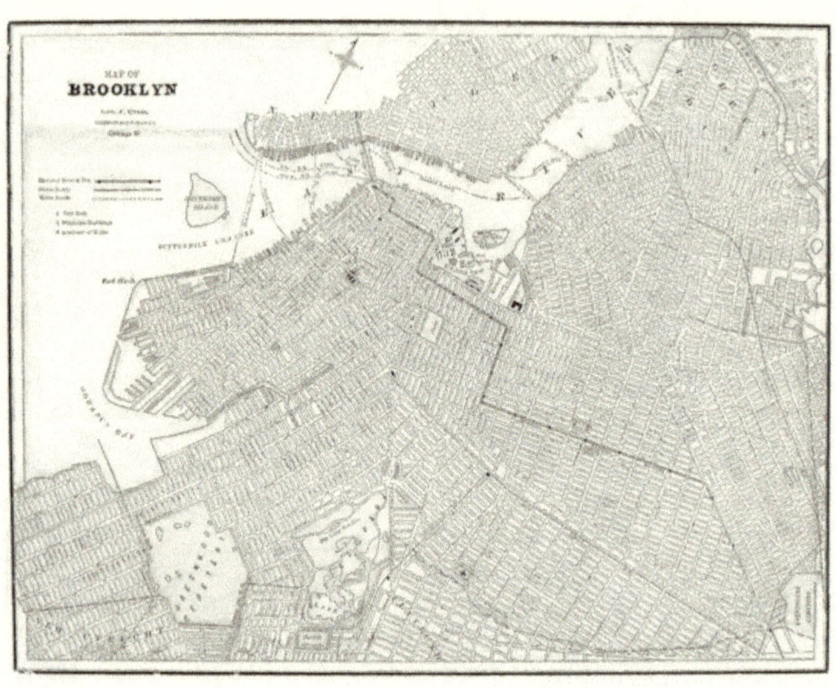
MAP OF
BROOKLYN

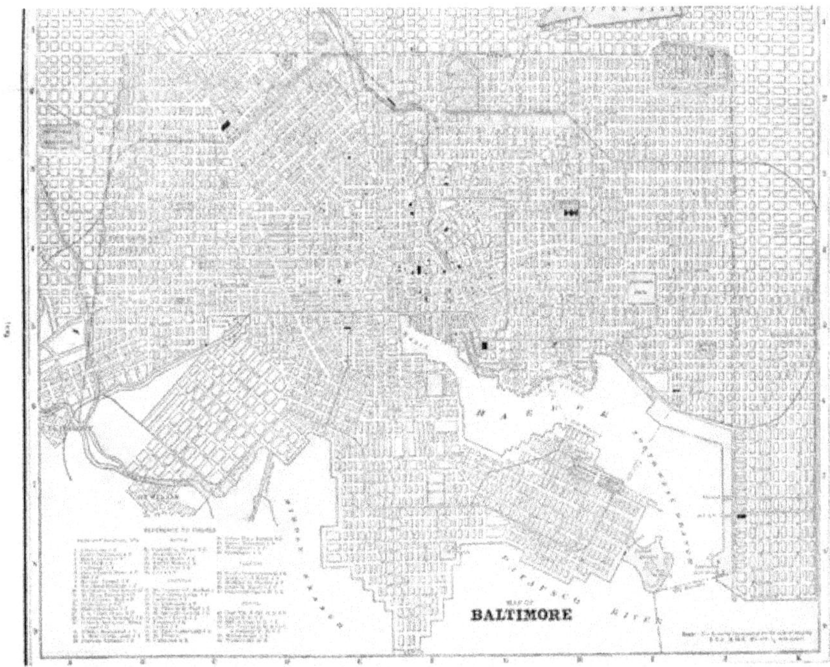
MAP OF
BALTIMORE

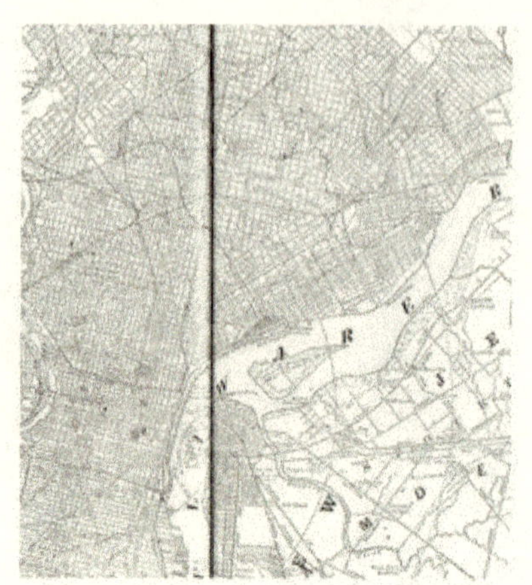

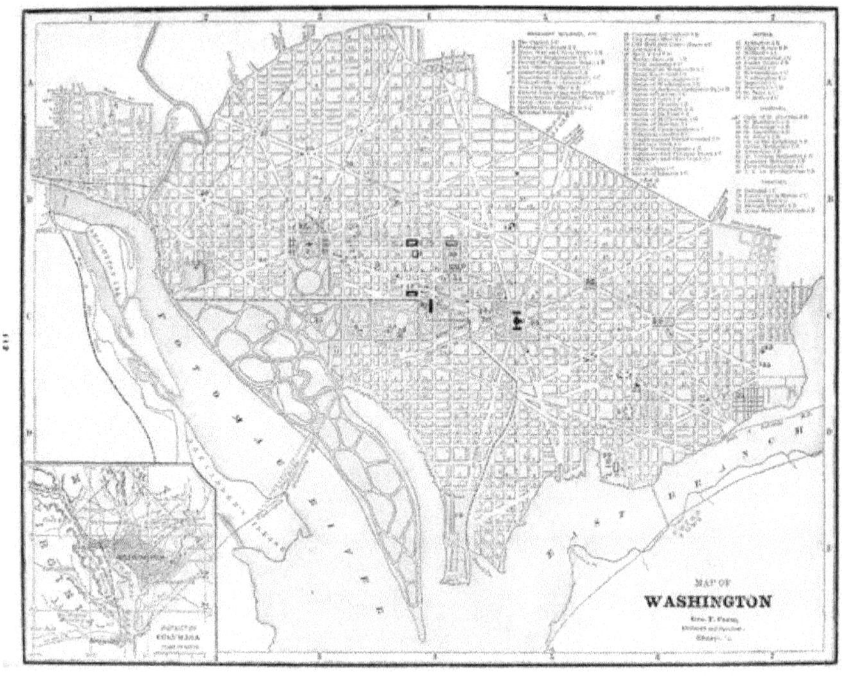
MAP OF
WASHINGTON

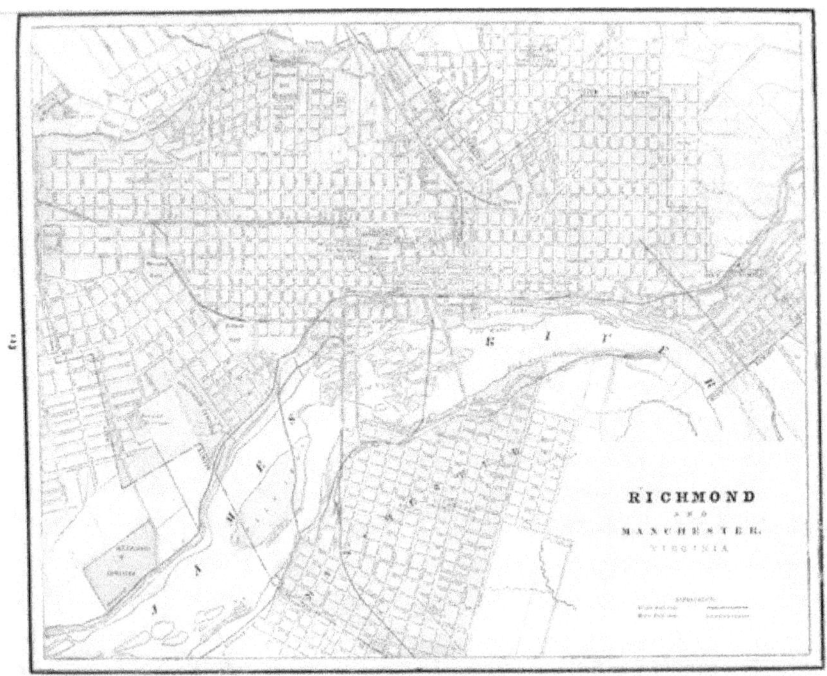
RICHMOND
AND
MANCHESTER,
VIRGINIA.
JAMES RIVER

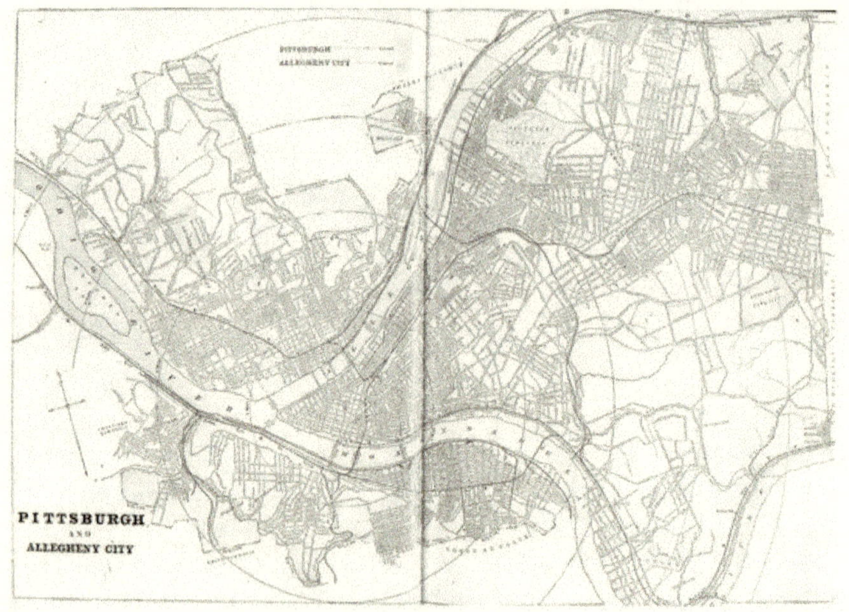
PITTSBURGH
AND
ALLEGHENY CITY

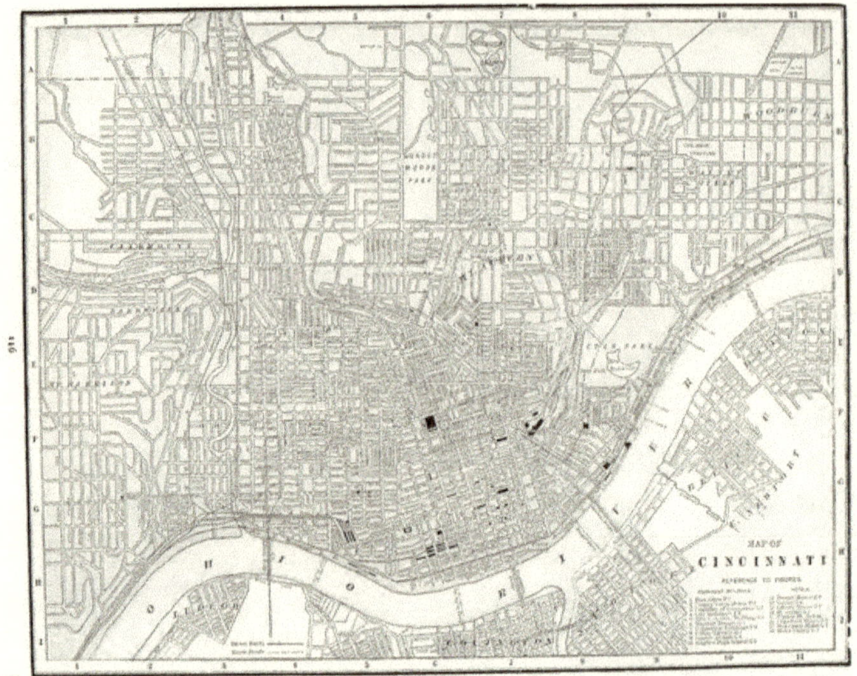
MAP OF
CINCINNATI
REFERENCE TO FIGURES

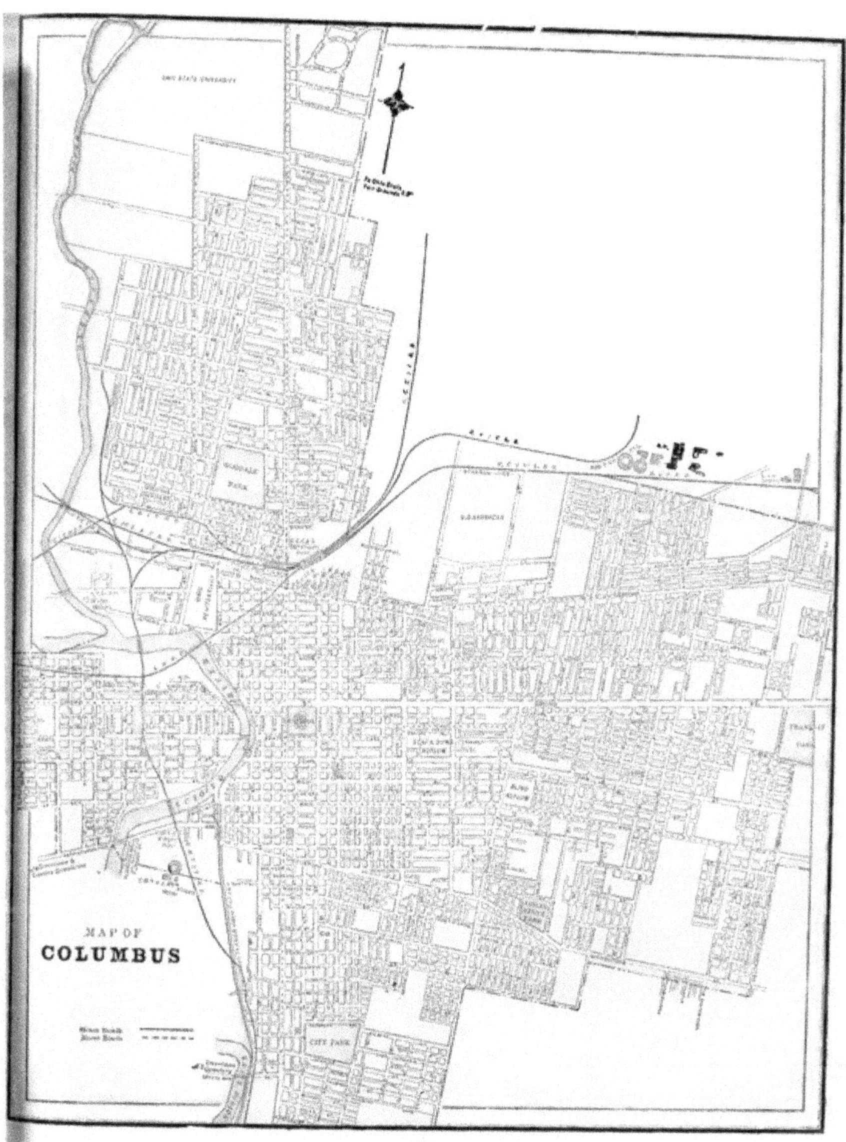
MAP OF
COLUMBUS

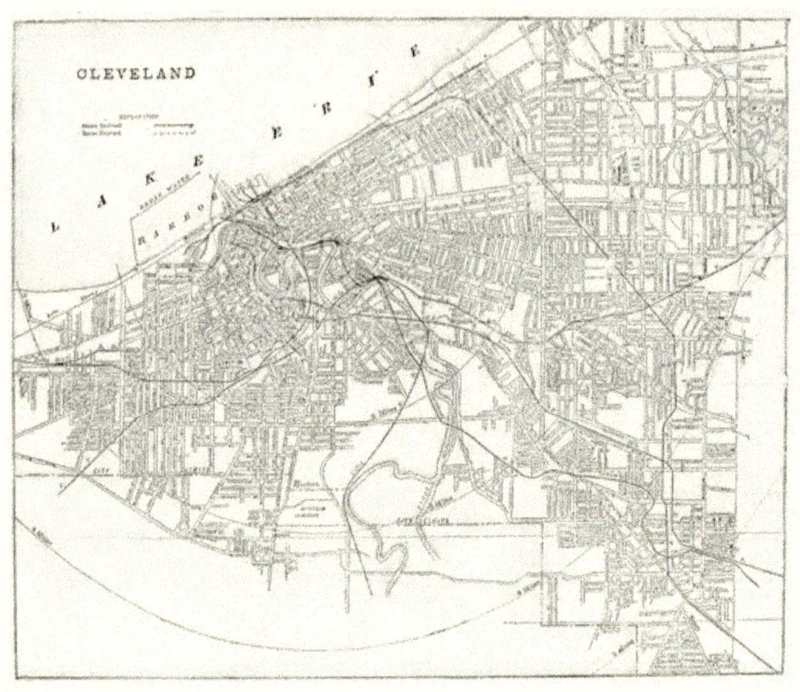
CLEVELAND
LAKE ERIE
HARBOR

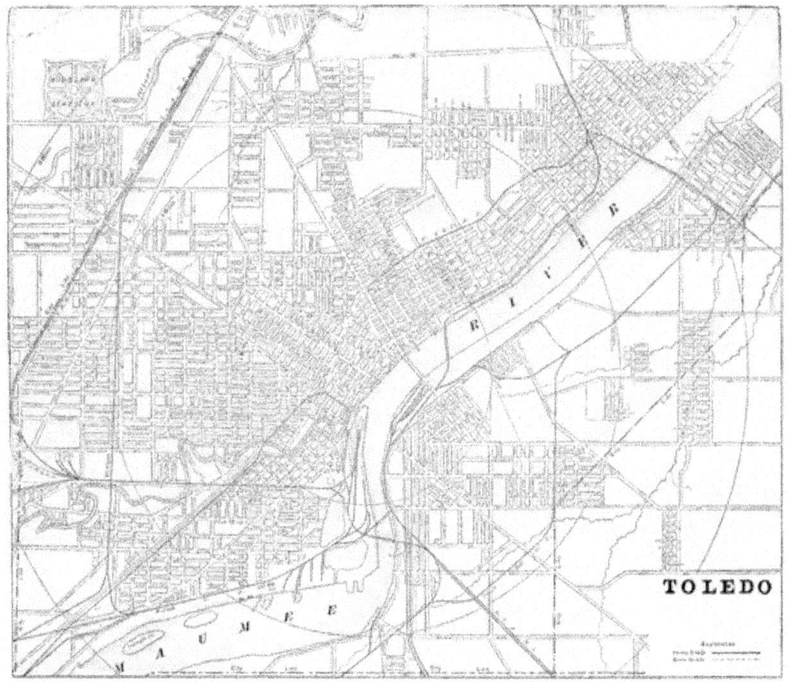

TOLEDO
MAUMEE
RIVER

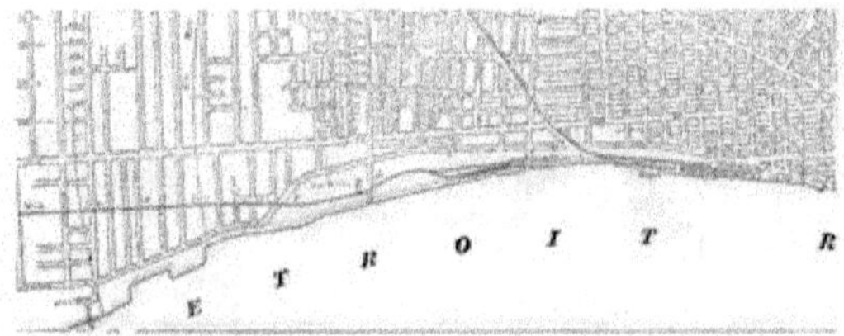

CHICAGO
REFERENCE TO FIGURES.
OUTER HARBOR
LAKE MICHIGAN
A
B
C
D
E
F
G
H
I
J
K

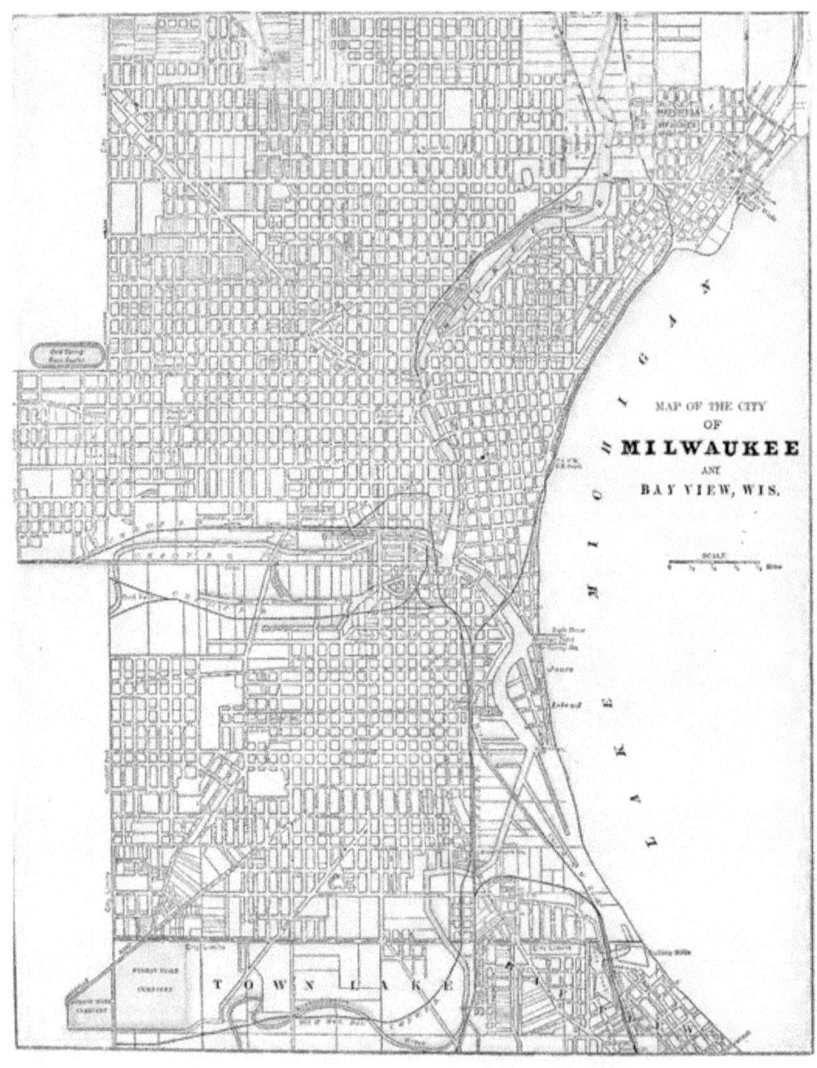
MAP OF THE CITY
OF
MILWAUKEE
AND
BAY VIEW, WIS.
LAKE MICHIGAN
TOWN LAKE
SCALE

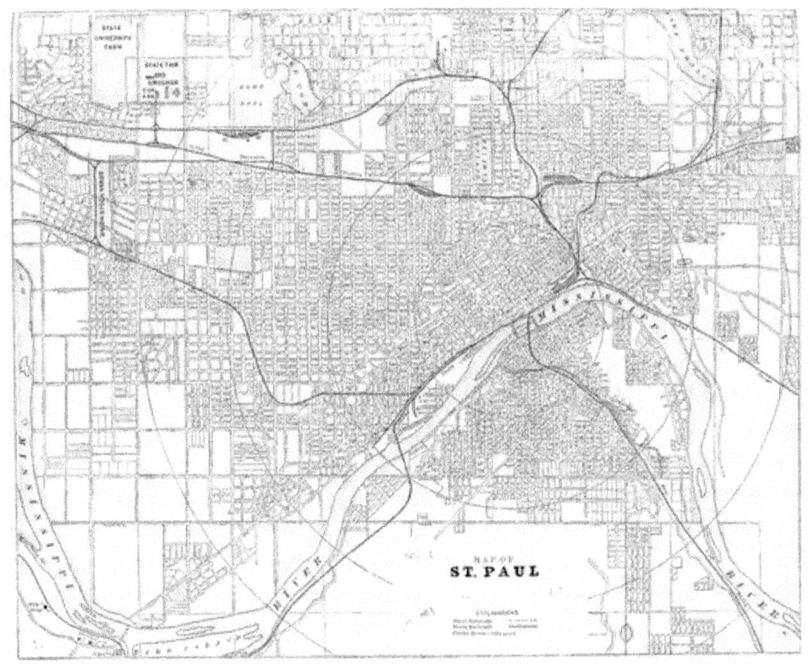
MAP OF
ST. PAUL
MISSISSIPPI
MISSISSIPPI
MISSISSIPPI
RIVER
RIVER

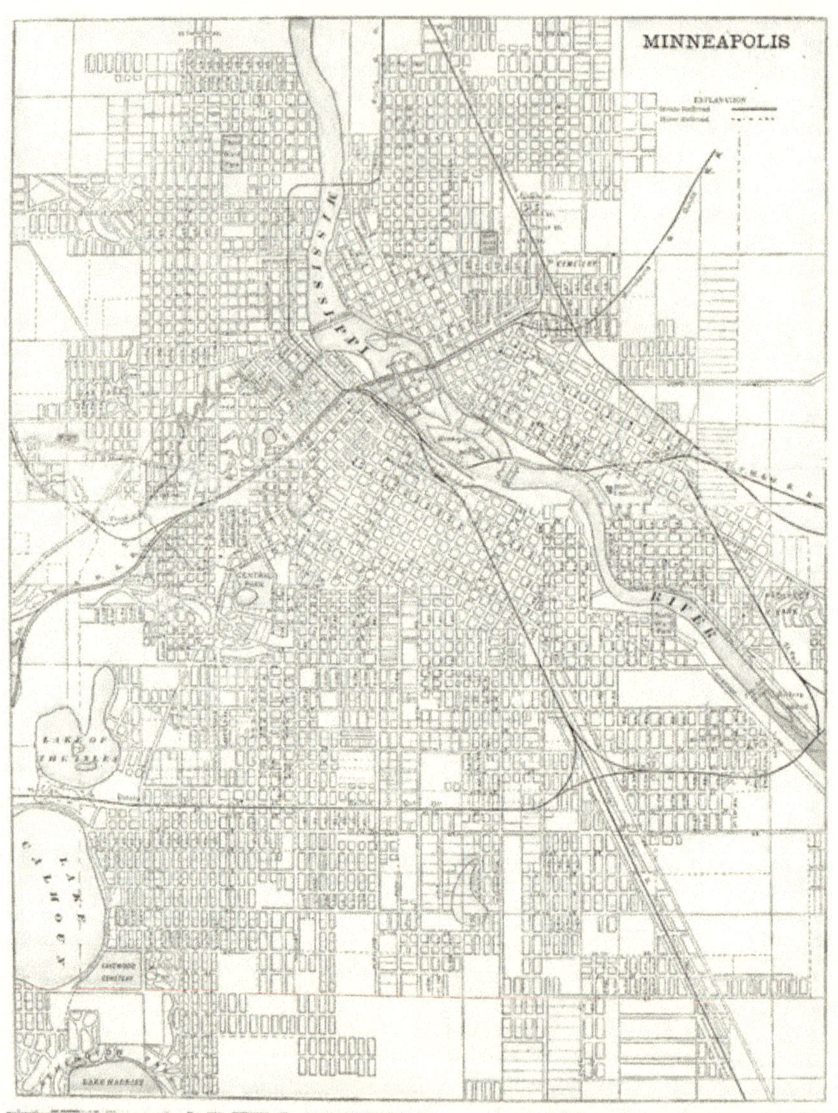
MINNEAPOLIS
MISSISSIPPI
RIVER
LAKE OF THE ISLES
LAKE CALHOUN
LAKE HARRIET

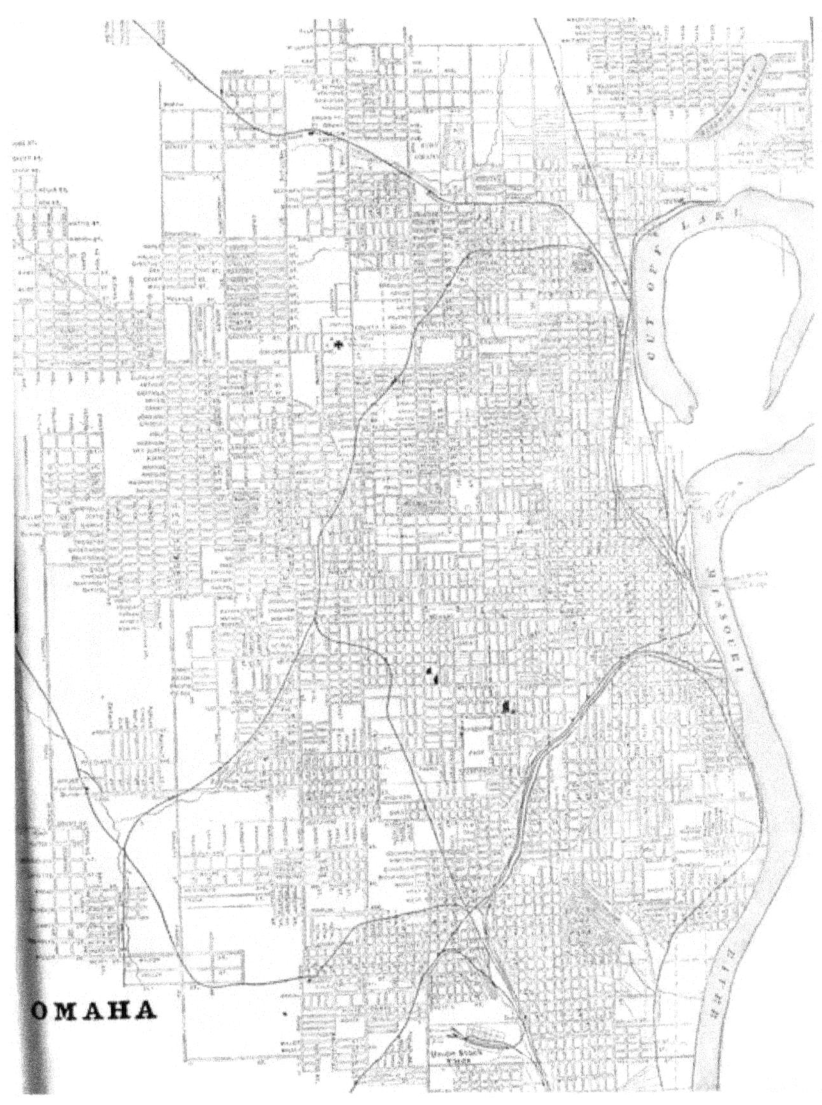
CUT OFF LAKE
MISSOURI
RIVER
OMAHA

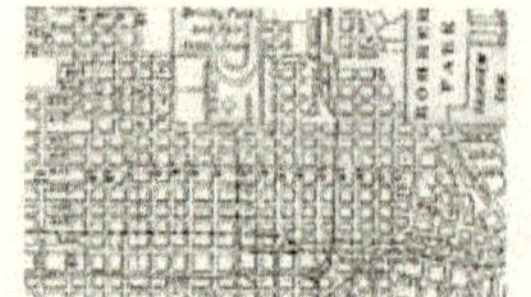
PARK

MAP OF
ST. LOUIS
BELLEFONTAINE CEMETERY
O'FALLON'S PARK
FOREST PARK
TOWER GROVE PARK
REFERENCE TO FIGURES.

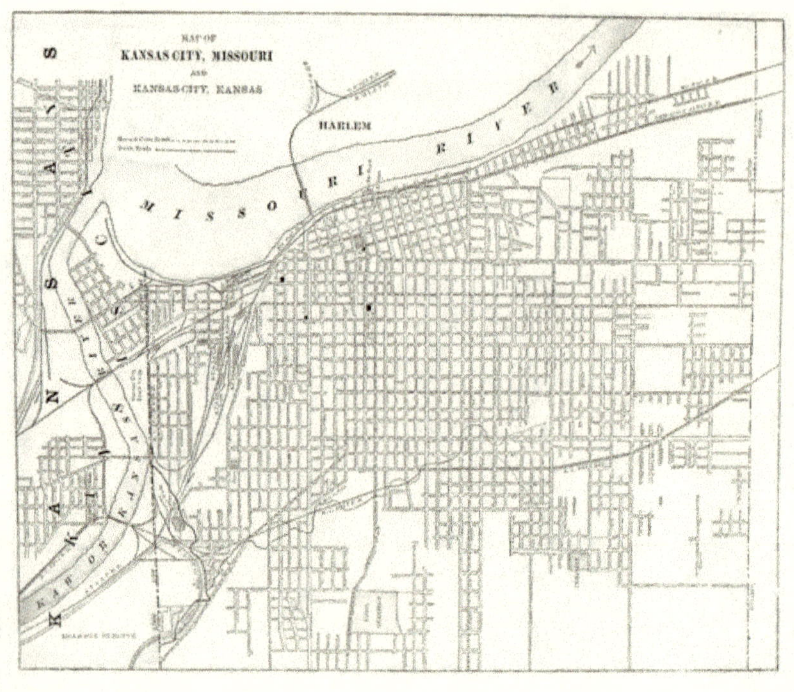

MAP OF
KANSAS CITY, MISSOURI
AND
KANSAS CITY, KANSAS
HARLEM
MISSOURI RIVER
KANSAS CITY
KANSAS
KAW OR KANSAS

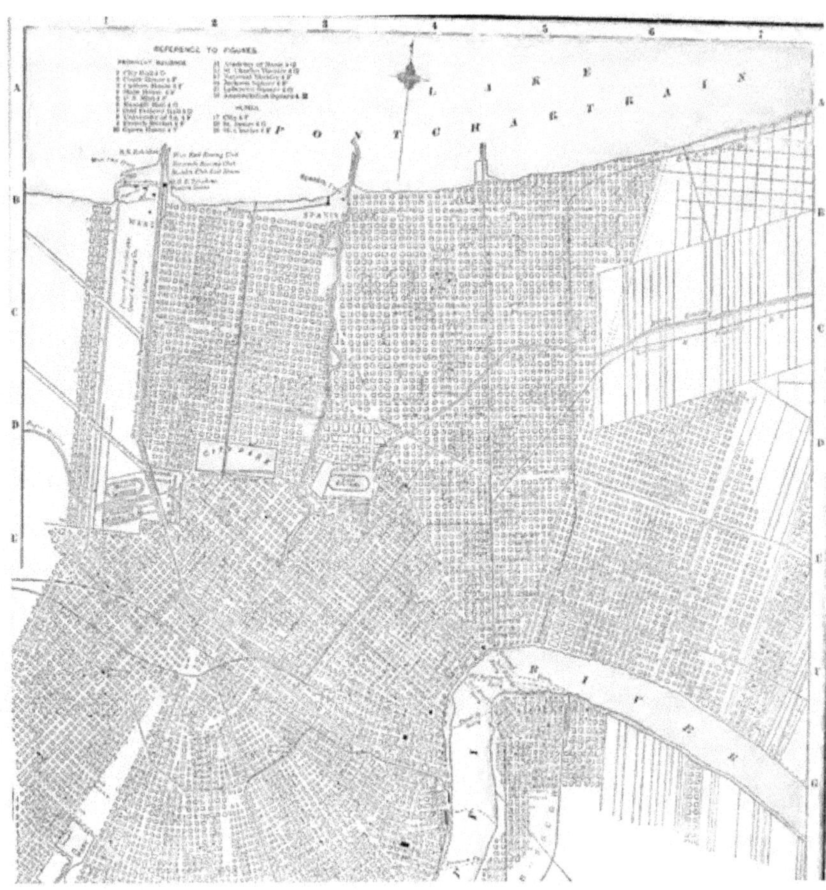

REFERENCE TO FIGURES
L A K E
P O N T C H A R T R A I N
CITY PARK
R I V E R

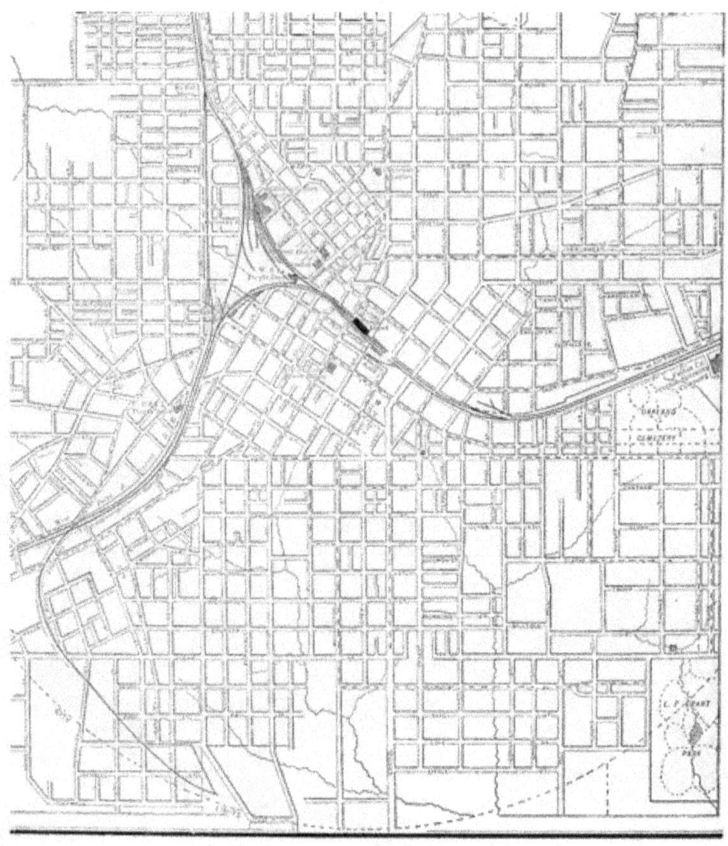
CEMETERY
L. P. GRANT
PARK

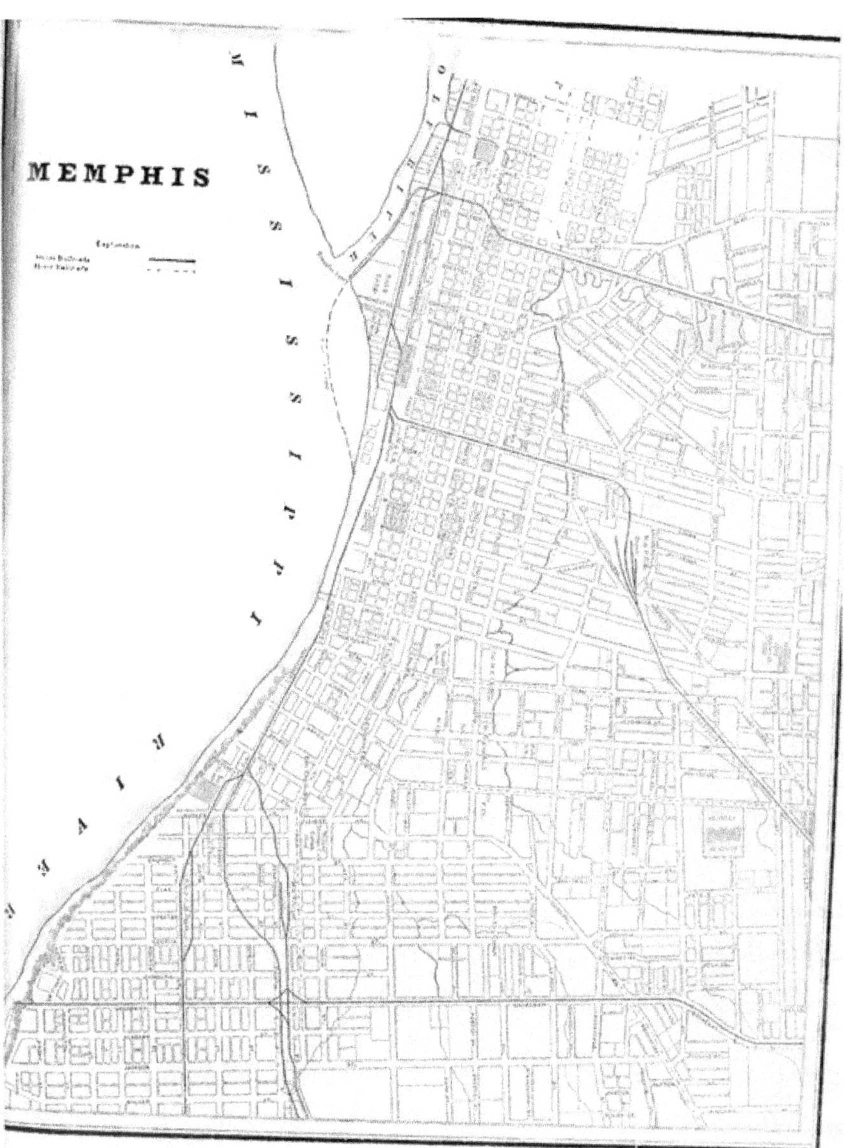
MEMPHIS
MISSISSIPPI

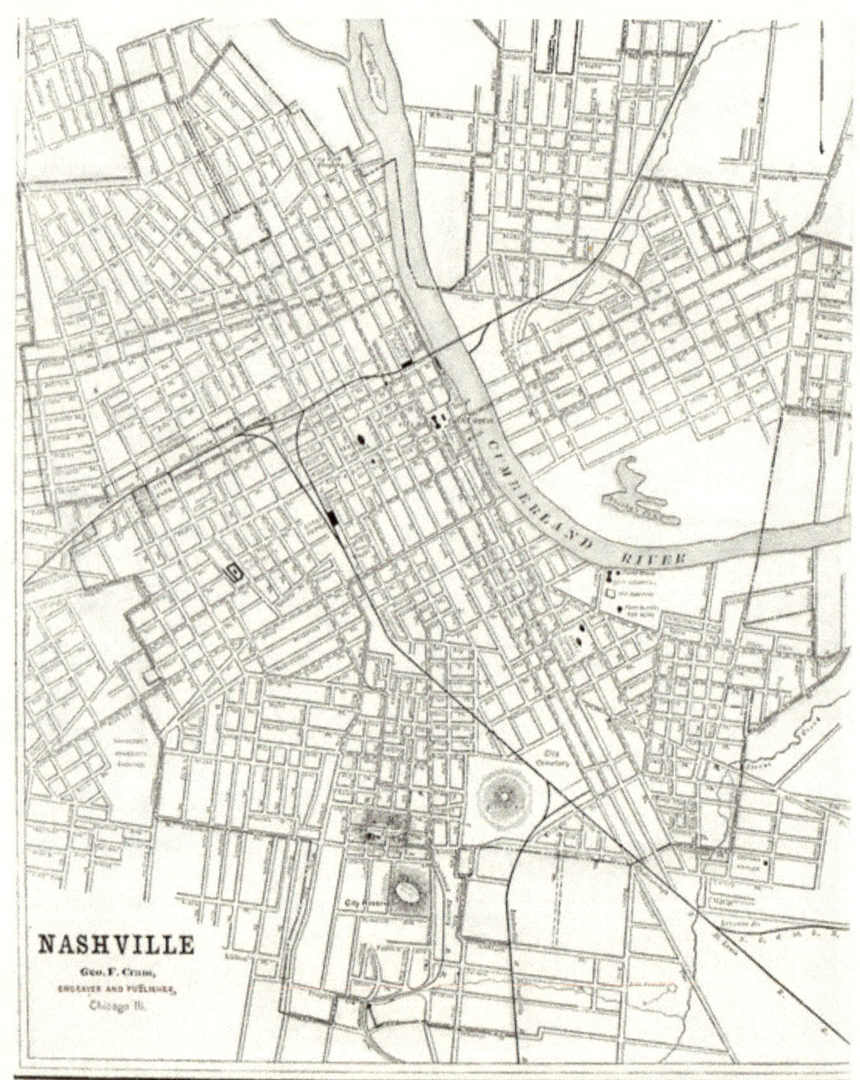
NASHVILLE
Geo. F. Cram,
ENGRAVER AND PUBLISHER,
Chicago Ill.
CUMBERLAND RIVER
City Cemetery

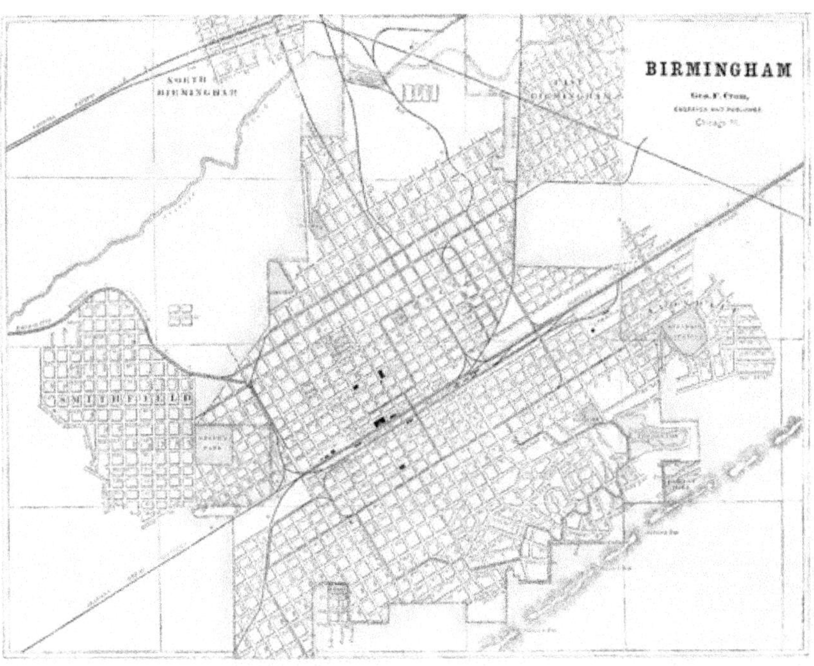
BIRMINGHAM
Geo. F. Cram,
NORTH BIRMINGHAM
SMITHFIELD

CHARLESTON
SOUTH CAROLINA
Geo. F. Cram,
ENGRAVER AND PUBLISHER
Chicago Ill.
ASHLEY RIVER
COOPER RIVER
TOWN CREEK
DRUM ISLAND
PUBLIC CEMETERY
CEMETERY

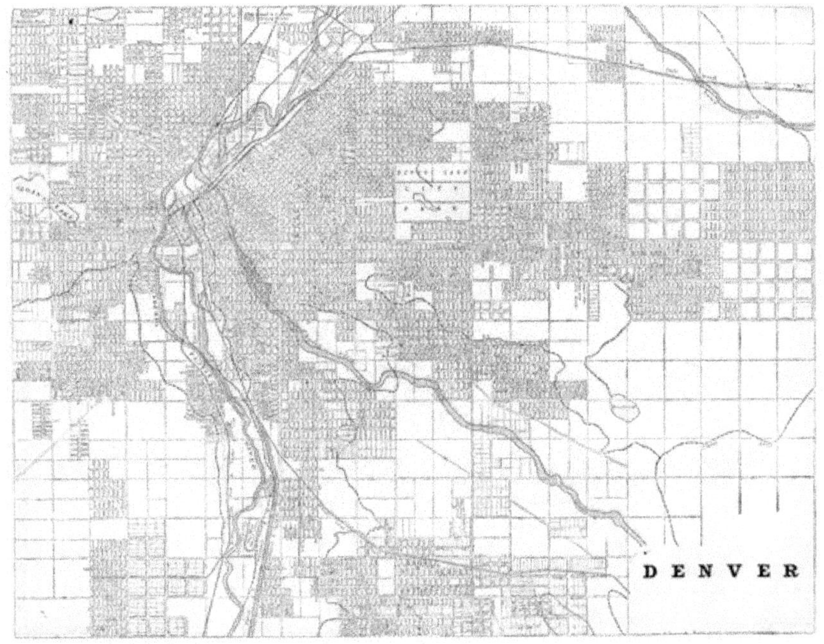
DENVER

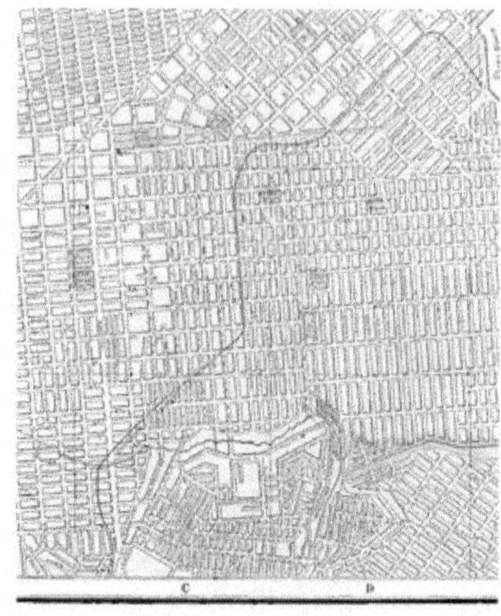
C
D

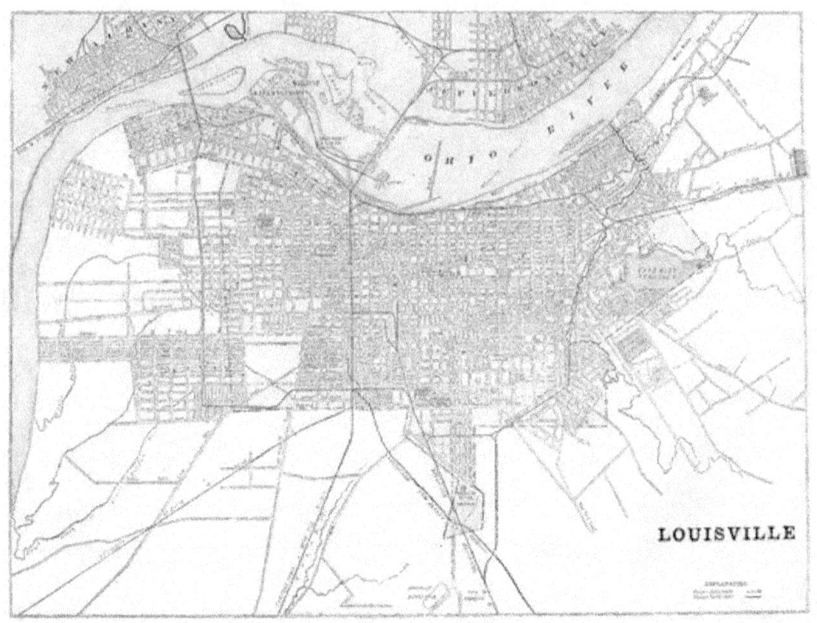
OHIO
LOUISVILLE

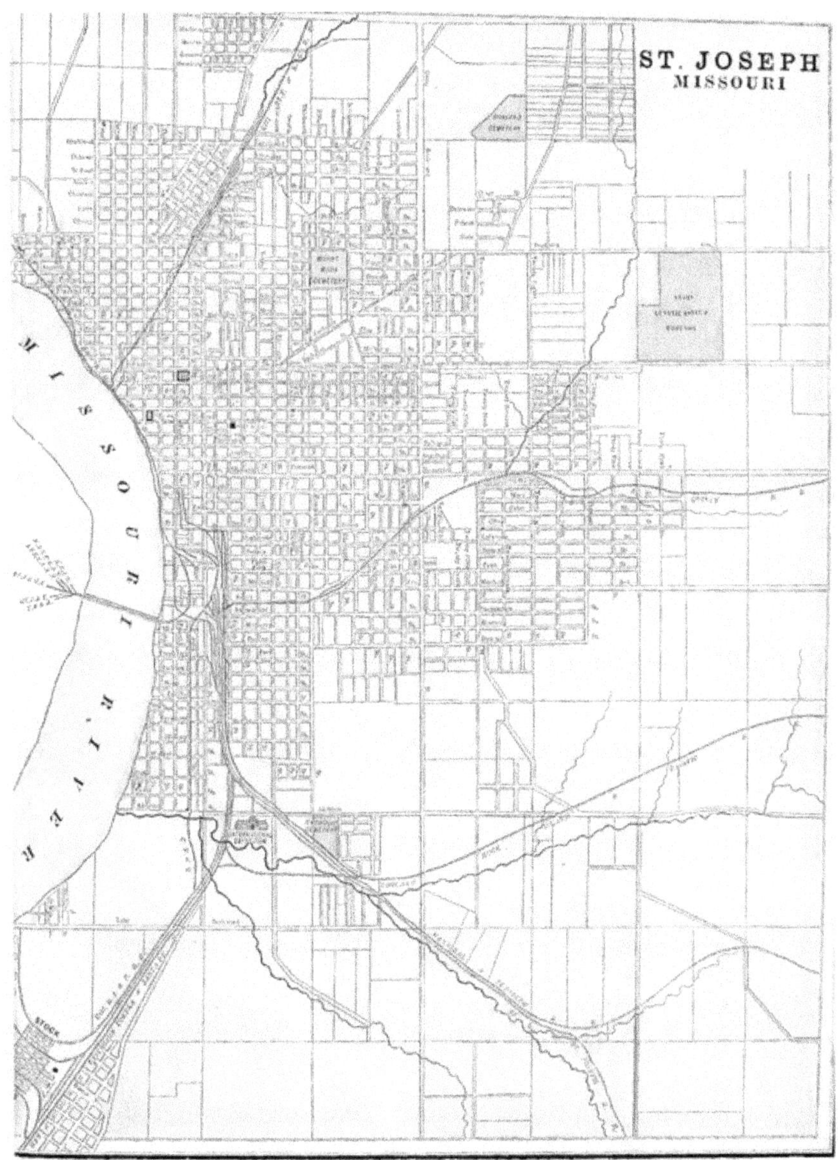
ST. JOSEPH
MISSOURI
MISSOURI RIVER

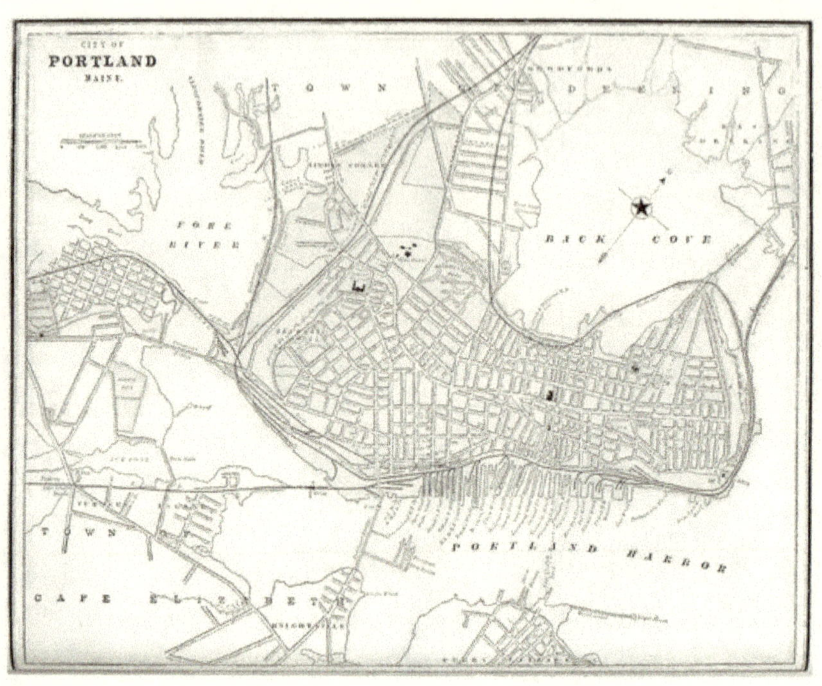
CITY OF
PORTLAND
MAINE.
FORE RIVER
BACK COVE
PORTLAND HARBOR
CAPE ELIZABETH

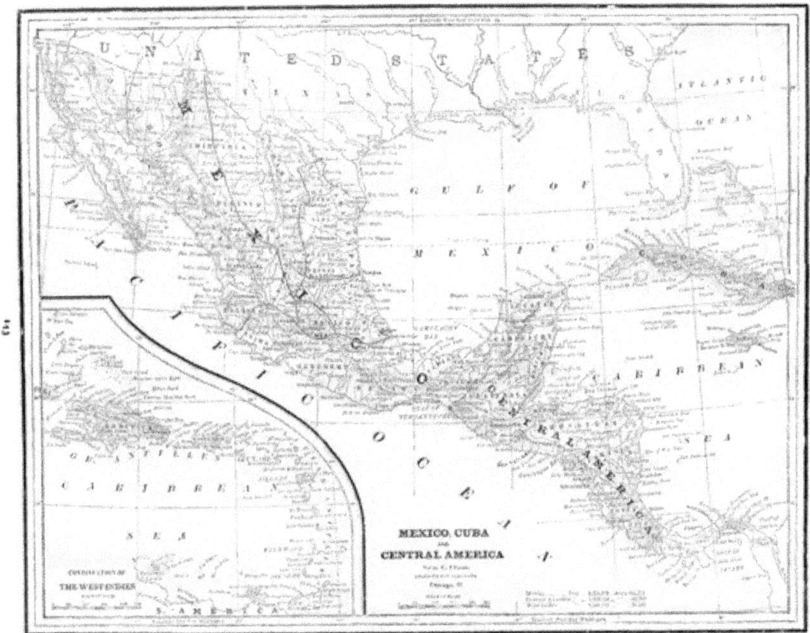
UNITED STATES
ATLANTIC OCEAN
GULF OF MEXICO
MEXICO
CUBA
CARIBBEAN SEA
CENTRAL AMERICA
PACIFIC OCEAN
ANTILLES
CARIBBEAN SEA
THE WEST INDIES
S. AMERICA
MEXICO, CUBA
and
CENTRAL AMERICA

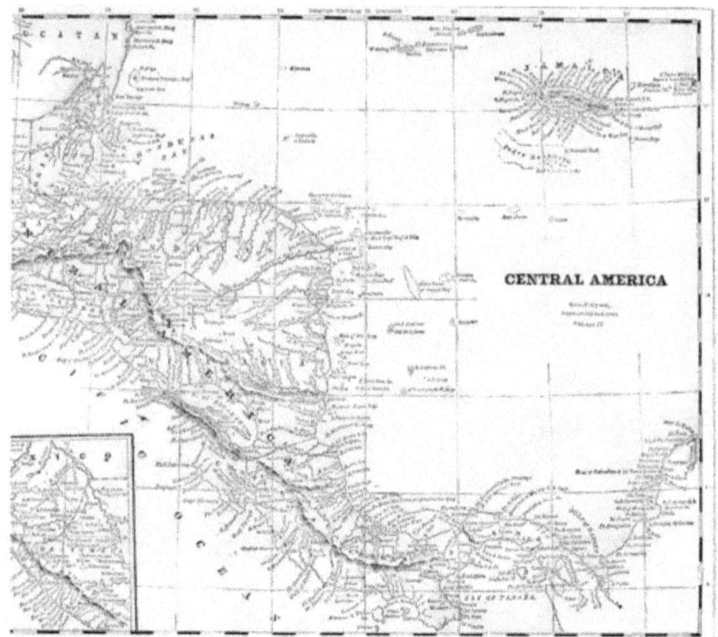
CENTRAL AMERICA
BAY OF PANAMA

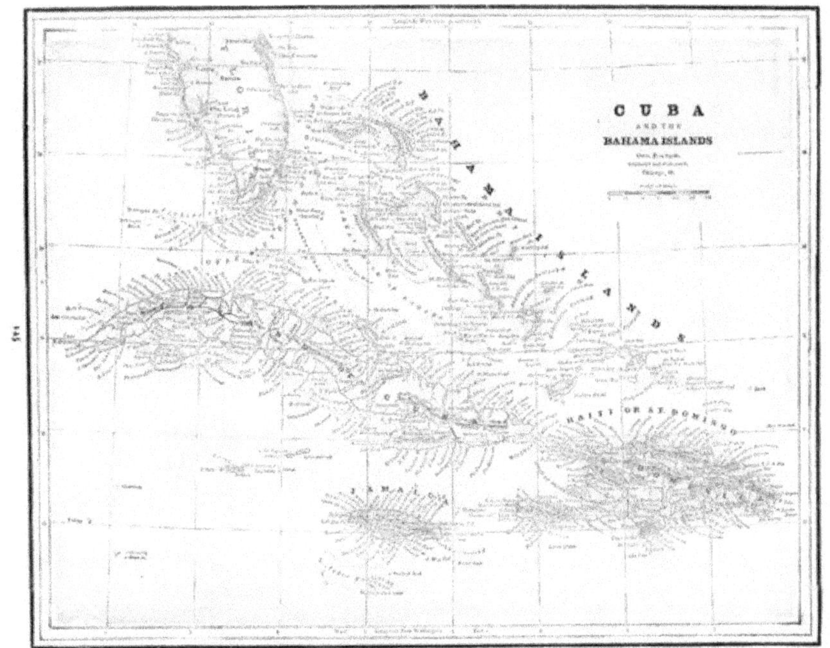
CUBA
AND THE
BAHAMA ISLANDS
HAITI OR ST. DOMINGO

UNITED STATES OF COLOMBIA
ECUADOR
BOLIVIA
SOUTH PACIFIC OCEAN
ATLANTIC OCEAN
SOUTH AMERICA

ENGLAND
& WALES
N O R T H
S E A
I R I S H S E A
BRISTOL CHANNEL
NORTHUMBERLAND
K E N T

SCOTLAND.
N O R T H
S E A
SUTHERLAND
KINCARDIN
FORFAR
HADDINGTON
SELKIRK
KIRKCUDBRIGHT
HEBRIDES
WESTERN
ISLES
SEA OF THE
HEBRIDES
ATLANTIC
OCEAN
E N G L A N D

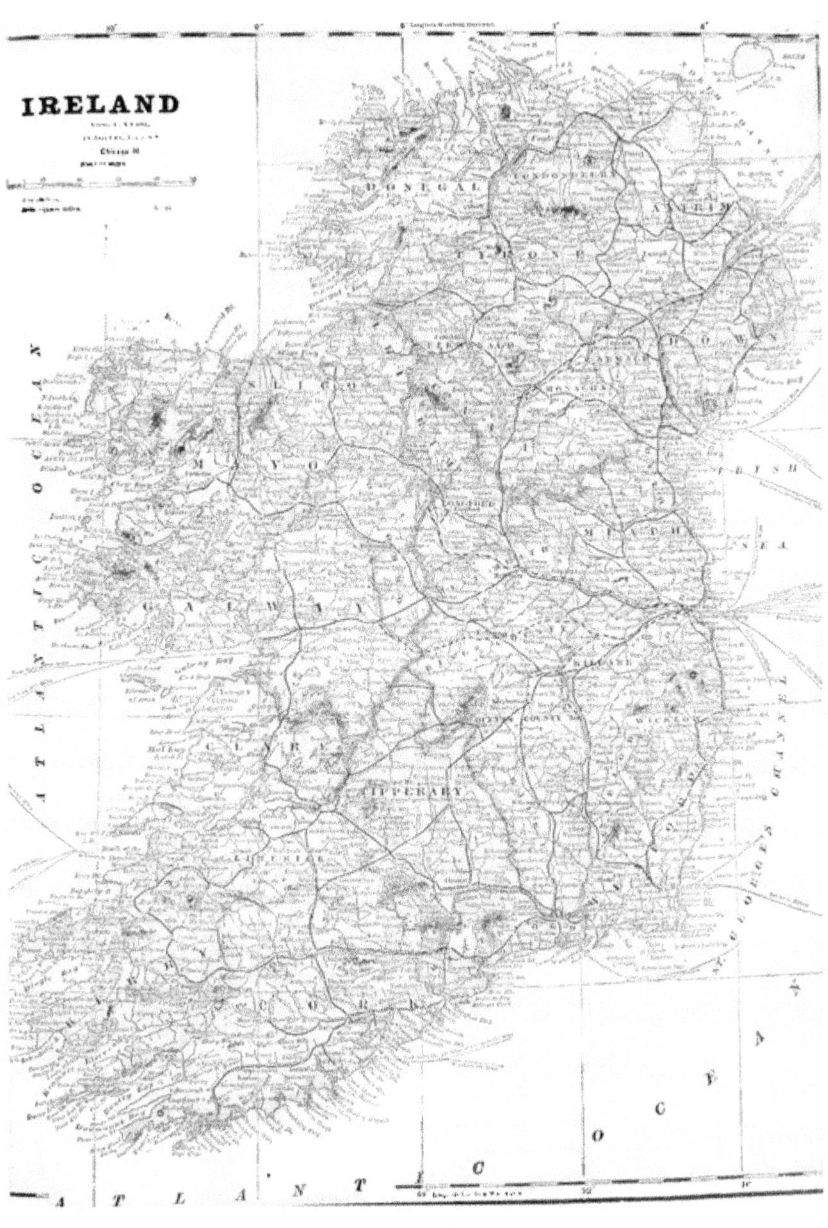
IRELAND
DONEGAL
ANTRIM
TYRONE
DOWN
MONAGHAN
SLIGO
MAYO
GALWAY
MEATH
CLARE
TIPPERARY
IRISH
SEA
ATLANTIC OCEAN

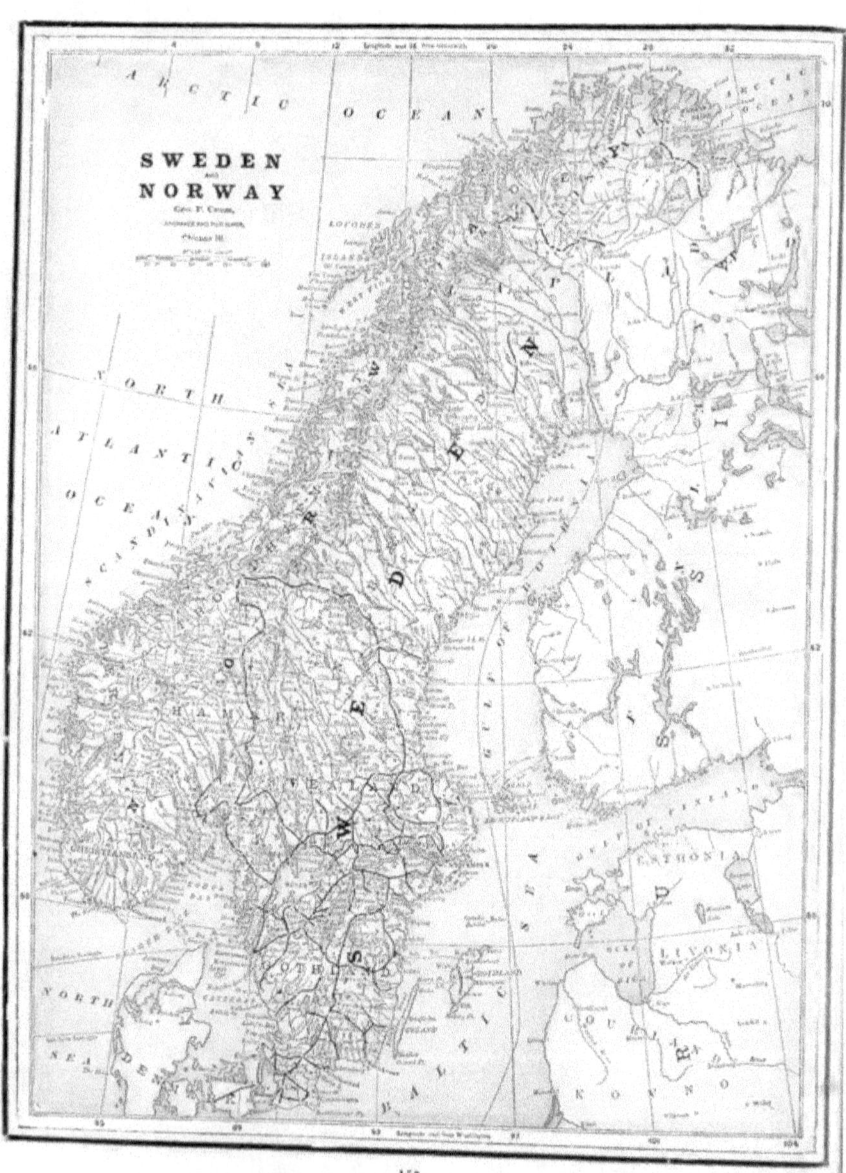
ARCTIC OCEAN
SWEDEN
NORWAY
NORTH ATLANTIC OCEAN
GULF OF BOTHNIA
GULF OF FINLAND
ESTHONIA
LIVONIA
COURLAND
KOVNO
BALTIC SEA
NORTH SEA
GOTHLAND
SVEALAND
LOFODEN ISLANDS

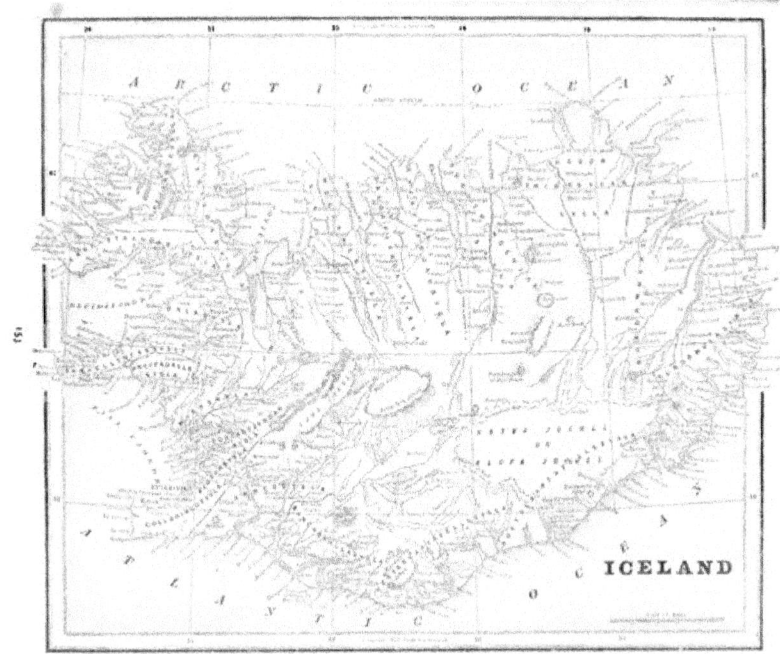
ARCTIC OCEAN
ATLANTIC OCEAN
ICELAND

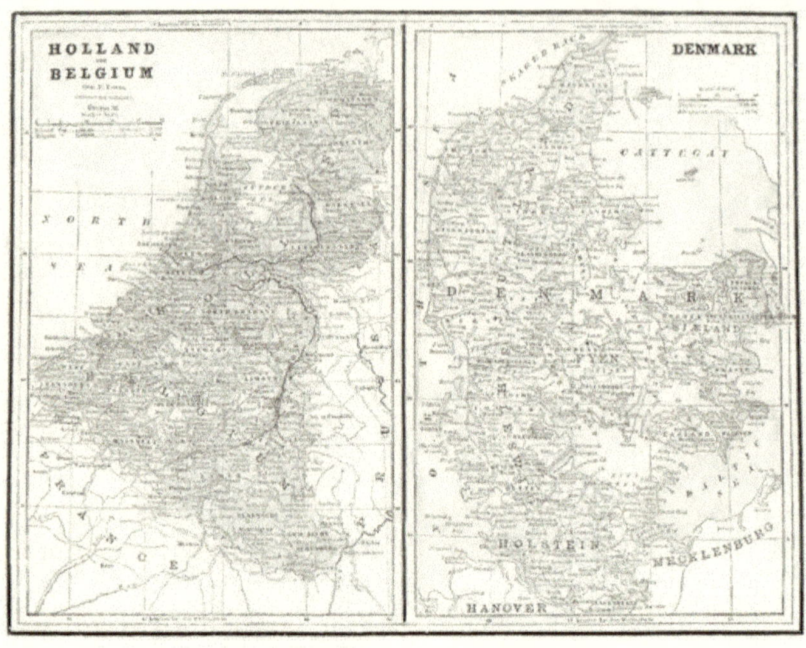
HOLLAND
BELGIUM
DENMARK
NORTH
SEA
CATTEGAT
DENMARK
SJÆLAND
FYEN
HOLSTEIN
MECKLENBURG
HANOVER
FRANCE

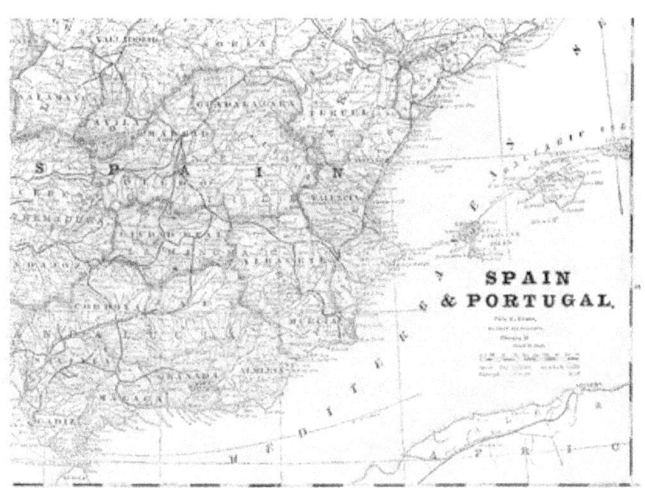
SPAIN
& PORTUGAL.
S P A I N
GUADALAJARA
TERUEL
MADRID
AVILA
VALENCIA
CIUDAD REAL
MURCIA
GRANADA
ALMERIA
MALAGA
CADIZ

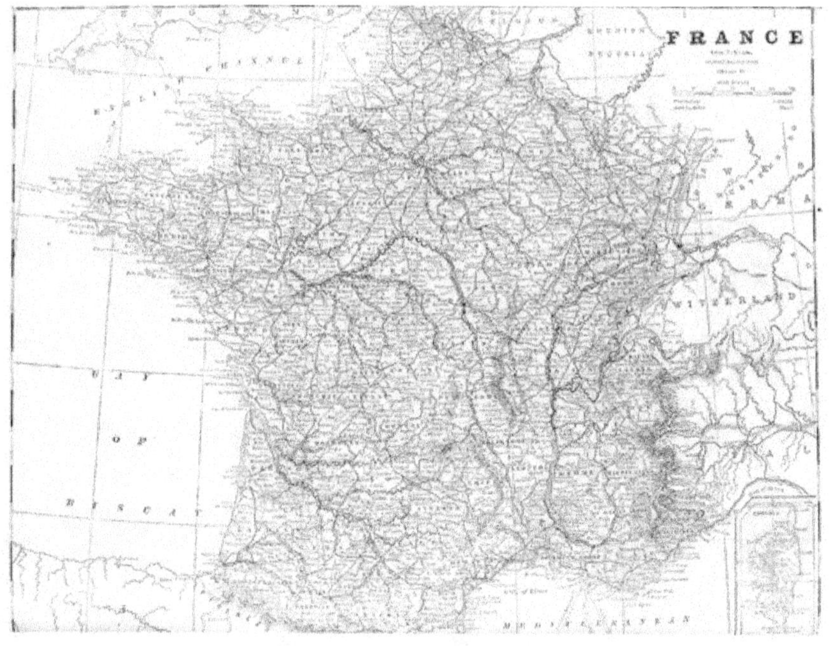
FRANCE

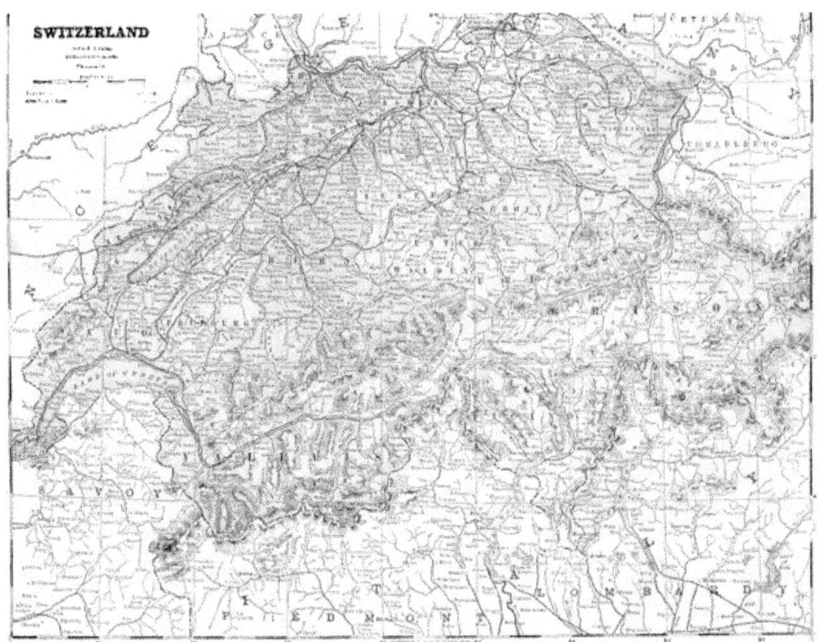
SWITZERLAND
SAVOY
PIEDMONT
LOMBARDY

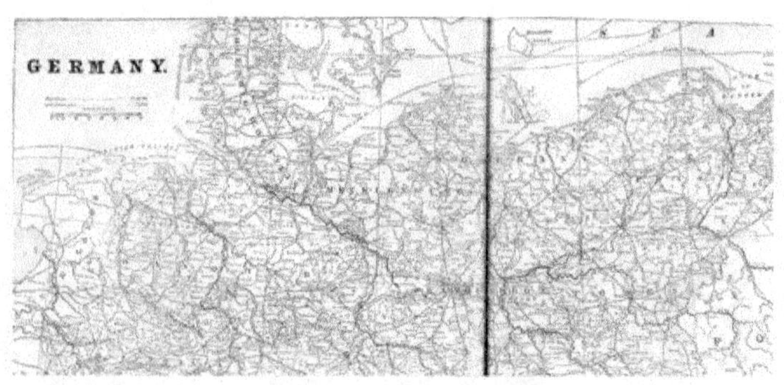
GERMANY.
S E A

R U S S I A
HUNGARY
TRANSYLVANIA
ROUMANIA
SERVIA
TURKEY
AUSTRIA

ITALY
CORSICA
SARDINIA
SICILY
TUSCANY
UMBRIA
ABRUZZO
MOLISE
BASILICATA
LIGURIAN SEA
TYRRHENIAN
SEA
MEDITERRANEAN
SEA
IONIAN
SEA
GULF OF TARANTO
Lipari Islands
Gulf of Hammamet

GREECE.
ACARNANIA AND ETOLIA
PHOCIS
EUBOEA
MOREA
ARGOLIS
ARCADIA
PELOPONNESUS
MESSENIA
LACONIA
KOLOKYTHIA
IONIAN SEA
Longitude East from Washington

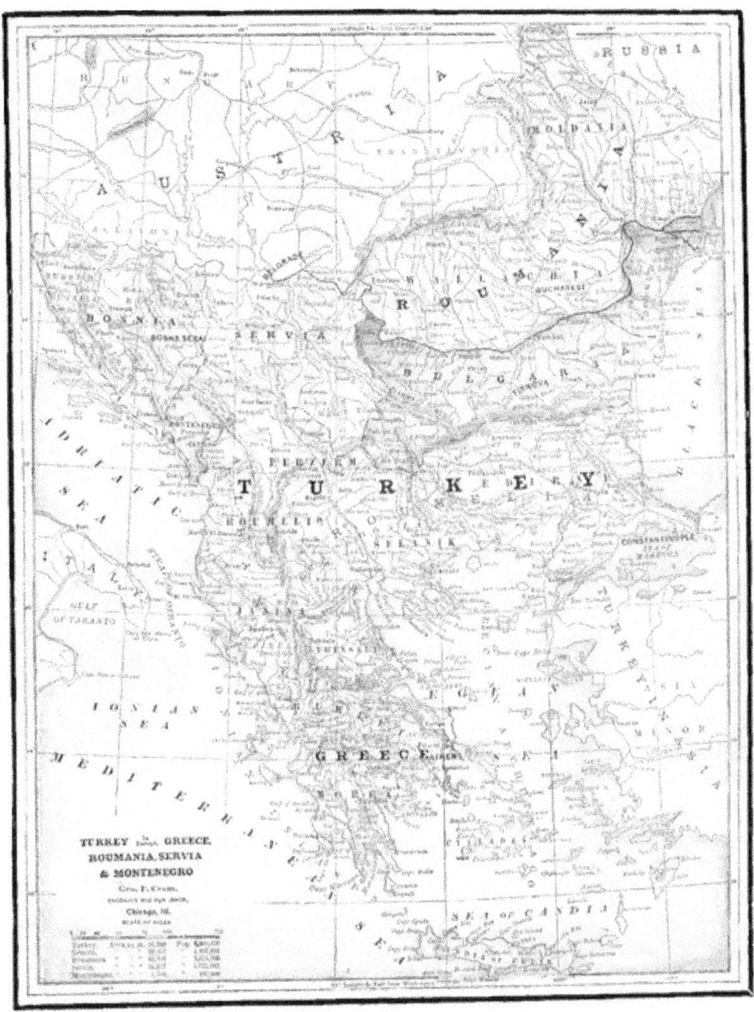
TURKEY in Europe, GREECE, ROUMANIA, SERVIA & MONTENEGRO
Chicago, Ill.
RUSSIA
AUSTRIA
HUNGARY
TRANSYLVANIA
MOLDAVIA
WALLACHIA
ROUMANIA
BUCHAREST
BELGRADE
BOSNIA
SERVIA
BULGARIA
MONTENEGRO
TURKEY
ROUMELIA
SELANIK
CONSTANTINOPLE
THESSALY
GREECE
ATHENS
MOREA
CYCLADES
ADRIATIC SEA
IONIAN SEA
MEDITERRANEAN SEA
GULF OF TARANTO
ITALY
SEA OF CANDIA
ASIA MINOR
BLACK SEA
AEGEAN SEA

TURKISH EMPIRE
IN
EUROPE AND ASIA.
BLACK SEA
MEDITERRANEAN SEA
AFRICA
ARABIA

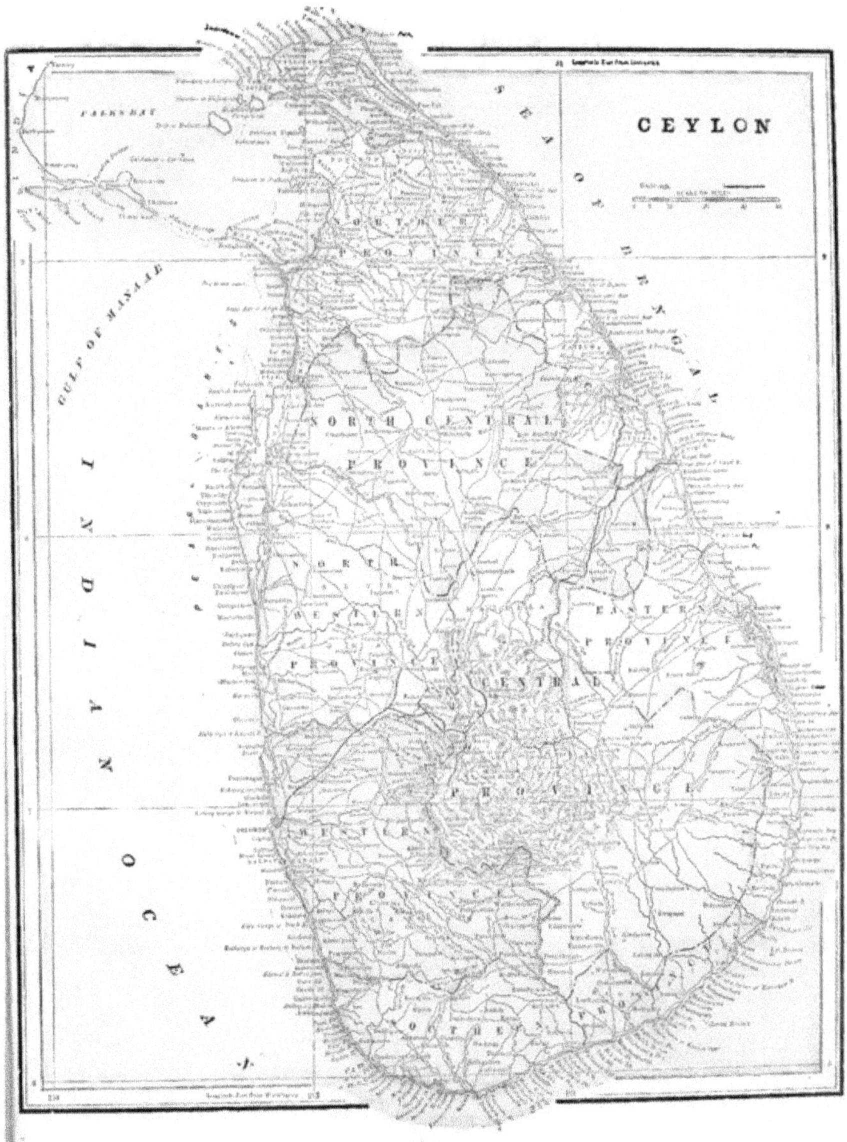
CEYLON
PALKS BAY
GULF OF MANAAR
BAY OF BENGAL
INDIAN OCEAN
NORTHERN PROVINCE
NORTH CENTRAL PROVINCE
NORTH WESTERN PROVINCE
EASTERN PROVINCE
CENTRAL PROVINCE
WESTERN PROVINCE
SOUTHERN PROVINCE

ARCTIC OCEAN
NORWAY
SWEDEN
RUSSIA
AUSTRIA
BLACK SEA
TURKEY
TURKEY IN ASIA
ASIA
RUSSIA.

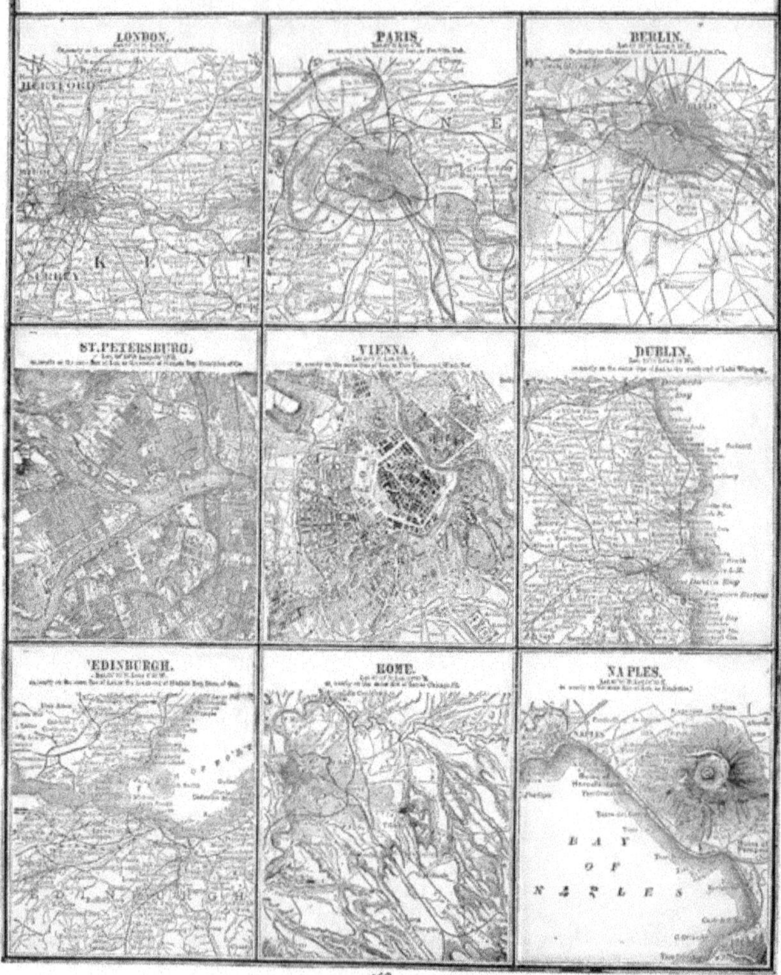
PRINCIPAL CITIES OF THE OLD WORLD,
COMPARING THEIR LATITUDE WITH POINTS ON THE AMERICAN CONTINENT.
LONDON.
PARIS.
BERLIN.
ST. PETERSBURG.
VIENNA.
DUBLIN.
EDINBURGH.
ROME.
NAPLES.
BAY OF NAPLES

PRINCIPAL CITIES OF THE OLD WORLD,

COMPARING THEIR LATITUDE WITH POINTS ON THE AMERICAN CONTINENT.

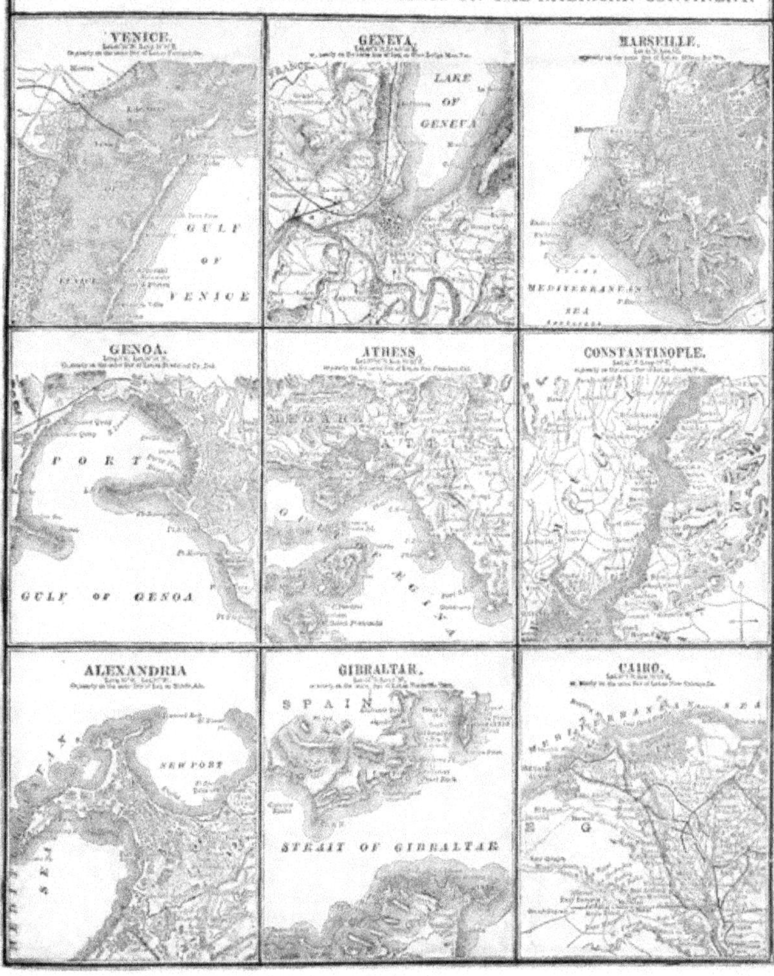

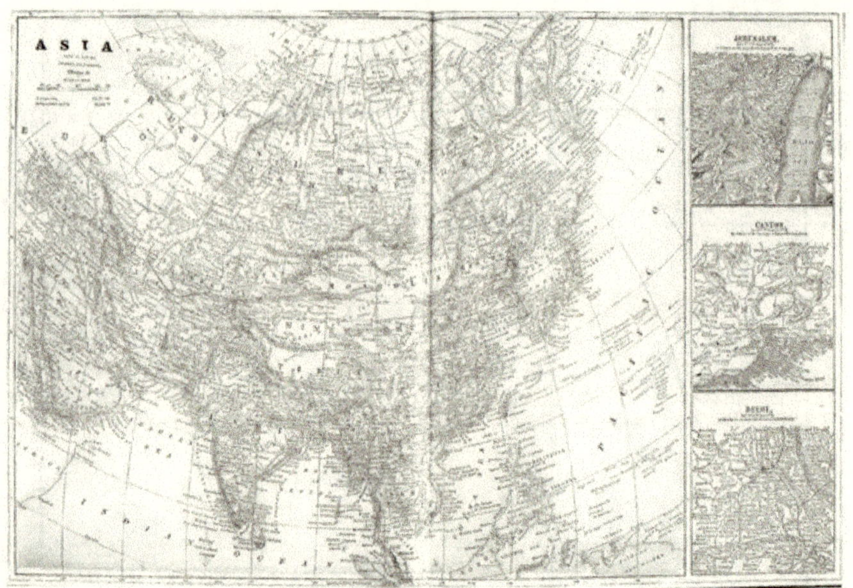
ASIA
CANTON

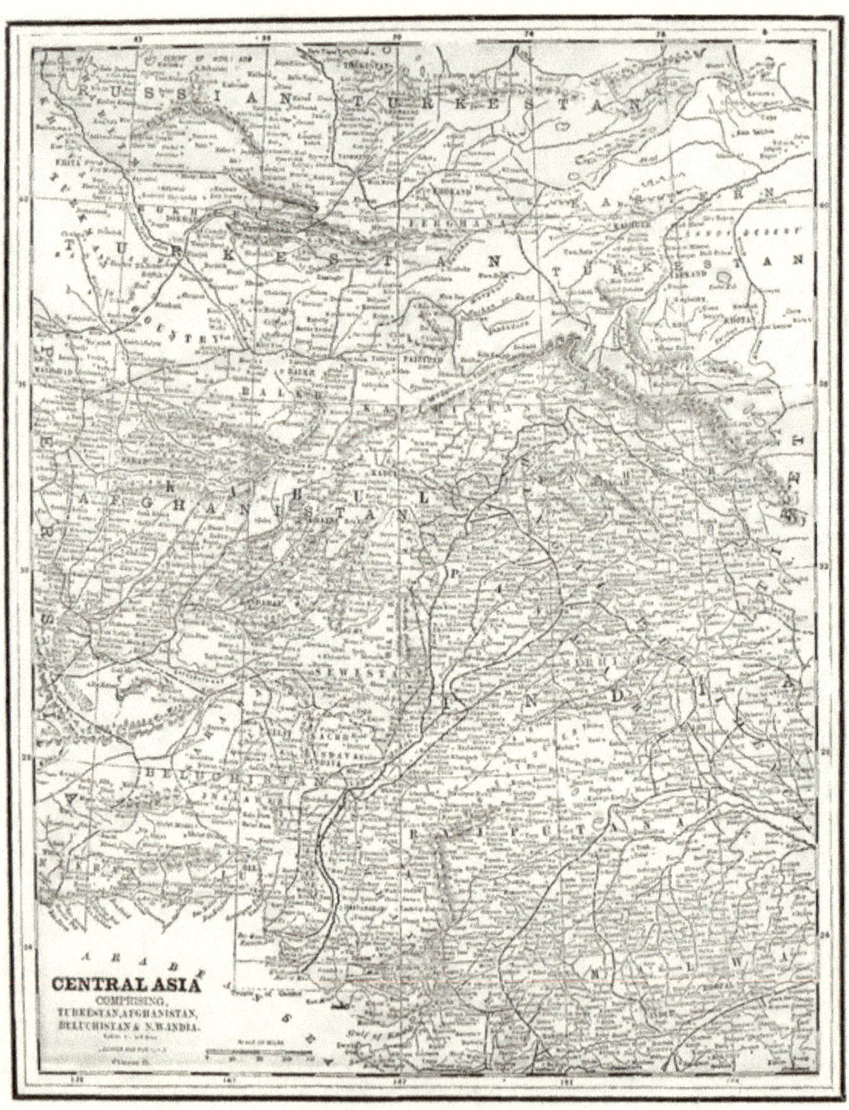
CENTRAL ASIA
COMPRISING,
TURKESTAN, AFGHANISTAN,
BELUCHISTAN & N.W. INDIA.
R U S S I A N
T U R K E S T A N
E A S T E R N
T U R K E S T A N
A F G H A N I S T A N
K A B U L
B E L U C H I S T A N
R A J P U T A N A
M A L W A
I N D I A
F E R G H A N A
A R A B I A N

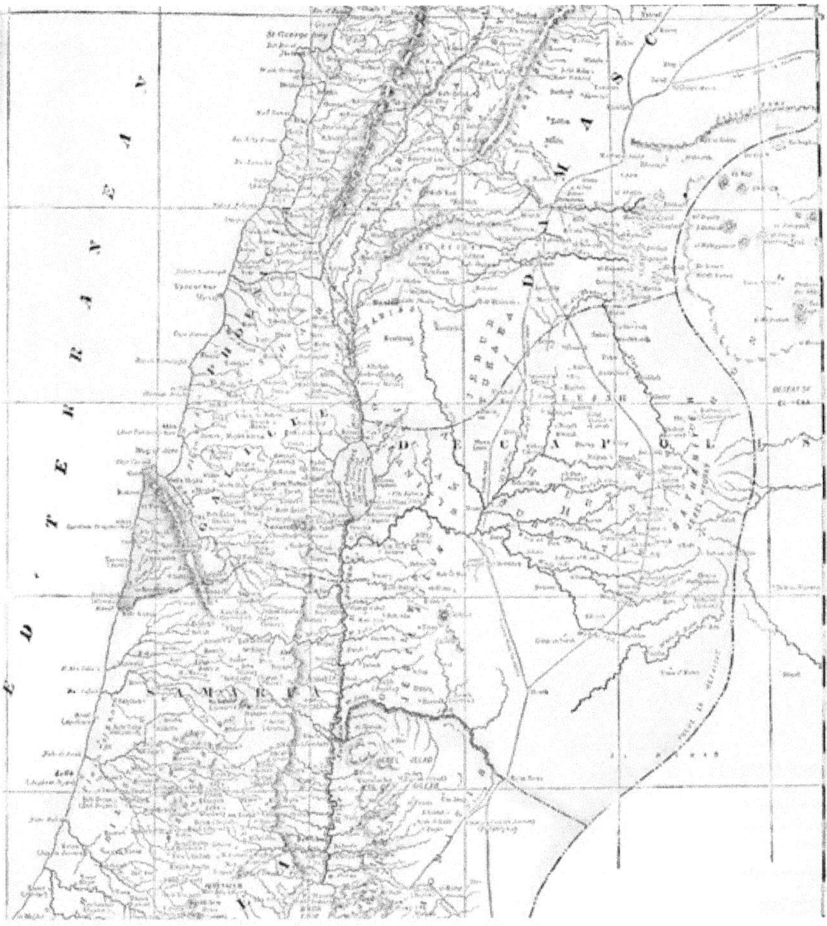

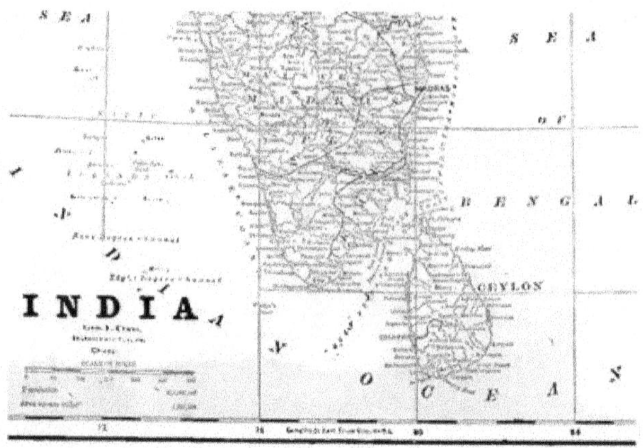
S E A
S E A
O F
B E N G A L
CEYLON
MADRAS
INDIA
O C E A N

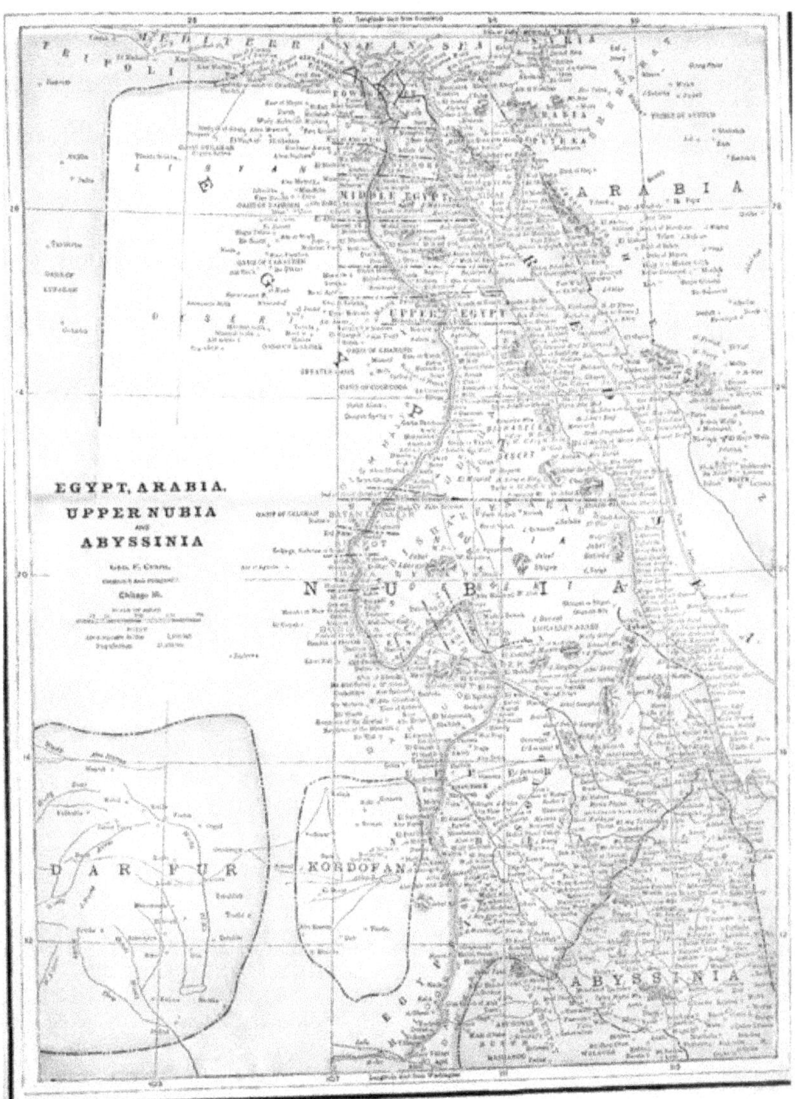
EGYPT, ARABIA,
UPPER NUBIA
AND
ABYSSINIA
MIDDLE EGYPT
UPPER EGYPT
ARABIA
NUBIA
ABYSSINIA
DAR FUR
KORDOFAN

KEY TO VIEW OF HOLY LAND.

No. 1--BAALBEC.

Heliopolis, or "City of the Sun," as it is sometimes called, is situated in the valley between the Lebanon and Anti-Lebanon ranges of mountains, 160 miles north of Jerusalem. The Temple was of great extent, being 500 by 500 feet on either side. A part of the main building is still standing, supported by columns of immense size and length,—some of them being 60 feet high and from four to six feet in diameter. On the top of these columns are beautiful Corinthian capitals, finely carved, equal or superior to anything found in this country. At one place amid the ruins are found six of these immense columns standing upright, not having been shaken down by the earthquake. They can be seen at a long distance.

No. 8--DAMASCUS,

Is situated 147 miles east of the Anti-Lebanon range of mountains, on the plain, surrounded by large olive groves and mulberry trees, poplars, terebinths, etc., and looks beautiful from a distance. It is called "The Gem of the East"; the "Pearl of the Orient." It is a place of 120,000 inhabitants; is surrounded by walls, and has many beautiful mosques and minarets which look picturesque and graceful, seen from a distance. The river Abana runs through the city, supplying the inhabitants with water. The river Pharpar also runs across the plain south of the city and the whole plain is thus watered, and produces abundant crops. Damascus has a history of 4,000 years. Abraham obtained his here, on his way to the Holy Land. Naaman, the leper, lived here; Benhadad, also. I. Kings, 15-18.

No. 21, BEIRUT,

Is on the coast, 147 miles from Jerusalem, and is the seaport of Damascus, the capital of Lebanon, and has 80,000 inhabitants, 12 newspapers, many common schools, 3 Female Seminaries, 1 Medical College, a Normal School, and 8 High Schools.

No. 24, SIDON,

One of the oldest cities mentioned in the Bible, is situated also on the sea, and was founded by Sidon, the son of Canaan. It is a place of 10,000 inhabitants. Around and in the suburbs of the city are immense orange groves, and tropical fruits of all kinds grow there, also.

No. 34,--DAN,

A city in the north of Palestine, 25 miles north of the Sea of Galilee, situated on a hill at the base of Mt. Hermon. There are some old ruins to be found, placed in an oval form, covering about three-quarters of an acre. From the west side of the hill flows one of the tributaries of the Jordan River. Here the golden calf was set up to worship, by Jeroboam; here the tribe of Dan lived, 140 miles north of Beersheba.

No. 55, TYRE,

Is also on the coast, and about 25 miles south of Sidon. It is built out on a peninsula or neck of land extending into the sea. It was formerly on an island, and was strongly fortified—so much so that Nebuchadnezzar laid siege to the city for a space of twelve years without success, and abandoned it; but Alexander captured it after a siege of six months, building a bridge or causeway out to the island with the ruins of the old city. It is a city of 5,000 inhabitants to-day, and a "place to spread nets upon."

No. 57,--ACCHO,

Or Ptolemais, is 8 miles north of Mt. Carmel, on the Bay of Accho, a picturesque looking city of about 8,000 inhabitants. It was so strong a city that the Israelites never completely subdued it. Viewed from the north, at a little distance off, the city appears planted with trees, and presents an attractive appearance; but within the streets are narrow and dirty. It was here that the most fearful and bloody contest of the Crusades took place, and it was the last place of any importance in which the Crusaders held out against the Saracens. Its common European name is St. Jean de Acre.

No. 102,--NAZARETH,

Is found in the picture of the Holy Land 65 miles north of Jerusalem, in a valley, amid the hills of Galilee. It is picturesquely situated, as it is surrounded on all sides by hills, with a beautiful valley opening out in front of it. It is a place of 8,000 inhabitants. It was the home of our Saviour during his childhood. The fountain from whence the inhabitants draw water is a little way out of the city. The hill of precipitation, over which the enraged Jews would have thrown the Saviour, is a little to the north-west.

No. 119, SAMARIA,

Is 30 miles, a little west of north from Jerusalem, situated on a hill that rises up out of a beautiful valley. It was once the capital of Israel, and was built by Omri, and surrounded with a wall, B. C. 925. It was rebuilt by Herod in the time of our Saviour, and many beautiful palaces erected, the columns of which stand to-day in many places, some of them 20 feet in height, with Corinthian capitals on the top. Here is found the reported tomb of John the Baptist, covered by the ruins of the church called by his name—found on the top of the hill.

150, JERUSALEM,

The "Holy City," is situated among the mountains, 2,540 feet above the level of the Mediterranean Sea; is a city of 30,000 inhabitants of various sects and denominations—Mohammedans, Jews, Turks, Christians, &c. The city stands on the site of the old city, 60 feet above the original foundation, on Mt. Zion and Mt. Moriah. The walls of the city are from 38 to 75 feet in height and 12 feet in thickness. There are 10 gates, 5 open and 5 closed. The streets are very narrow. The prominent buildings in the city are the Church of the Holy Sepulchre, Mosque of Omar, Jewish and Armenian Synagogues, Mosque of Elaksa, Church of St. Ann, Castle of Goliath, etc. Seen from the Mt. of Olives, the city looks picturesque, but it is now only a shadow of its former greatness and beauty—when it was the wonder of the world and "the joy of the whole earth."

193, BETHANY,

Is found just over the Mount of Olives, 2 miles from Jerusalem, on the road to Jericho. It is a small village, where some ancient ruins are to be found.

190, BETHLEHEM,

Is 5 miles south of Jerusalem, on a hill, and a city of 8,000 inhabitants. A large church stands over the place where tradition says that the Saviour was born. In one of the large rooms lamps are kept continually burning, and in the floor is a silver star which indicates the place, over the cave, where the shepherds are said to have found the Saviour in the manger.

208, HEBRON,

Is situated in a valley, 18 miles south of Jerusalem, and contains about 10,000 inhabitants. It was the home of Abraham, and no doubt his remains could be found to-day in the cave of Machpelah, where he was buried, and where he buried his wife Sarah.

233.--DEAD SEA,

The Dead Sea is a singular body of water, being 46 miles long and 10 miles wide, surrounded by high and rugged mountains, 2,000 and 3,000 feet in height. The water is one-quarter salt, and contains bitumen, potassium and many kinds of acid, making it unpleasant to the taste. No fish can live in it.

234.--SEA OF CALILEE,

This beautiful sea is in the northern part of the Holy Land, and is 13 miles long, 6 miles wide, and 600 feet below the Mediterranean. Ruins of the cities of Capernaum and Chorazin are found on its shores. Here the Saviour made his home, and 22 out of the 33 miracles which he wrought were performed upon or near this sea.

THE RIVER JORDAN,--g.

The River Jordan runs almost the entire length of the Holy Land, and is called the Descender. It is 1,700 feet above the Mediterranean Sea at its source, and at its mouth, where it empties into the Dead Sea, it is 1,300 feet below the Mediterranean—falling 3,000 feet in its course of 200 miles.

The exact extent of the Holy Land as given to Abraham in the original promise, and as more minutely defined in a subsequent renewal of the original charter (Num. xxxiv: 1-12) is not easily determined at this distance of time, when localities of many places are lost. It is evident the Israelites did not actually possess the full extent of territory embraced in the original grant, and it is further evident that two different boundaries of the land are given in two different places. According to the above passage from Numbers, the length of the Promised Land, north and south, is about 180 miles, and its breadth, east and west, about 90 miles at the south end and about 40 miles at the northern limit. This variation is occasioned by the slope of the Mediterranean coast in a south-westerly direction.

In Genesis God said to Abraham, "Unto thy seed have I given this land, from the river of Egypt unto the great river, the river Euphrates."

The smallness of Palestine often elicits surprise, when the number of people that inhabited it are considered and the magnitude of the events that have there transpired. It is about as large as the States of Connecticut and Rhode Island combined, and has an area of some 12,000 square miles.

The general surface of the country is mountainous, but these mountains often stand in majestic contrast with broad, flowing, fertile valleys, beautiful plains, verdant hills, or, perhaps, are spread out upon their sides and summits into rich table lands. There are many barren mountains and plains, and frightful deserts.

Moses said to the Israelites: "The land whither thou goest in to possess it, is a land of hills and valleys, and drinketh water of the rain of heaven; a land which the Lord thy God careth for."

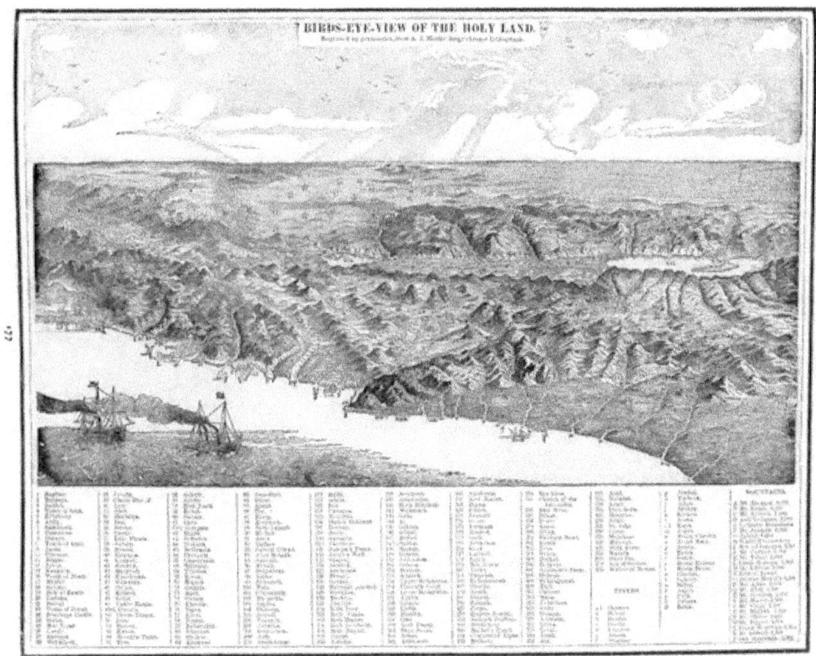
BIRDS-EYE-VIEW OF THE HOLY LAND.

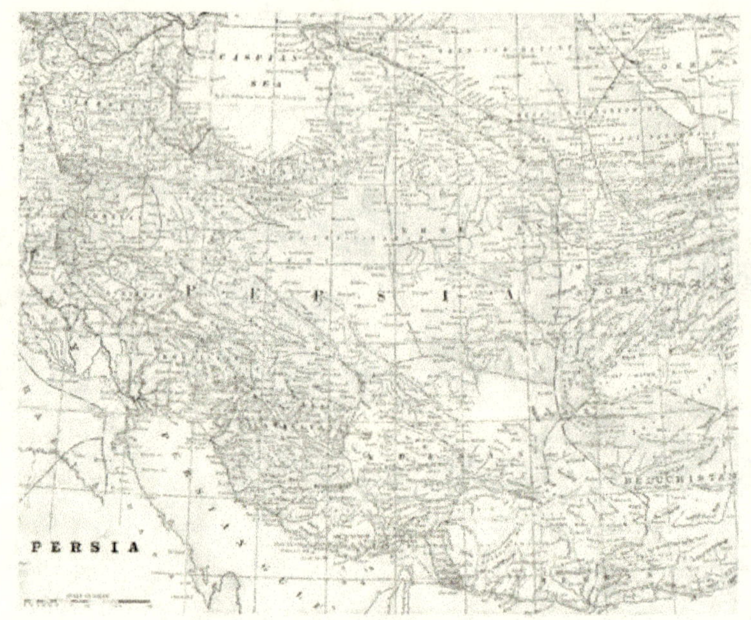
CASPIAN
SEA
P E R S I A
PERSIA

WHANG HAI
OR
YELLOW
SEA
TUNG HAI
OR
EASTERN SEA

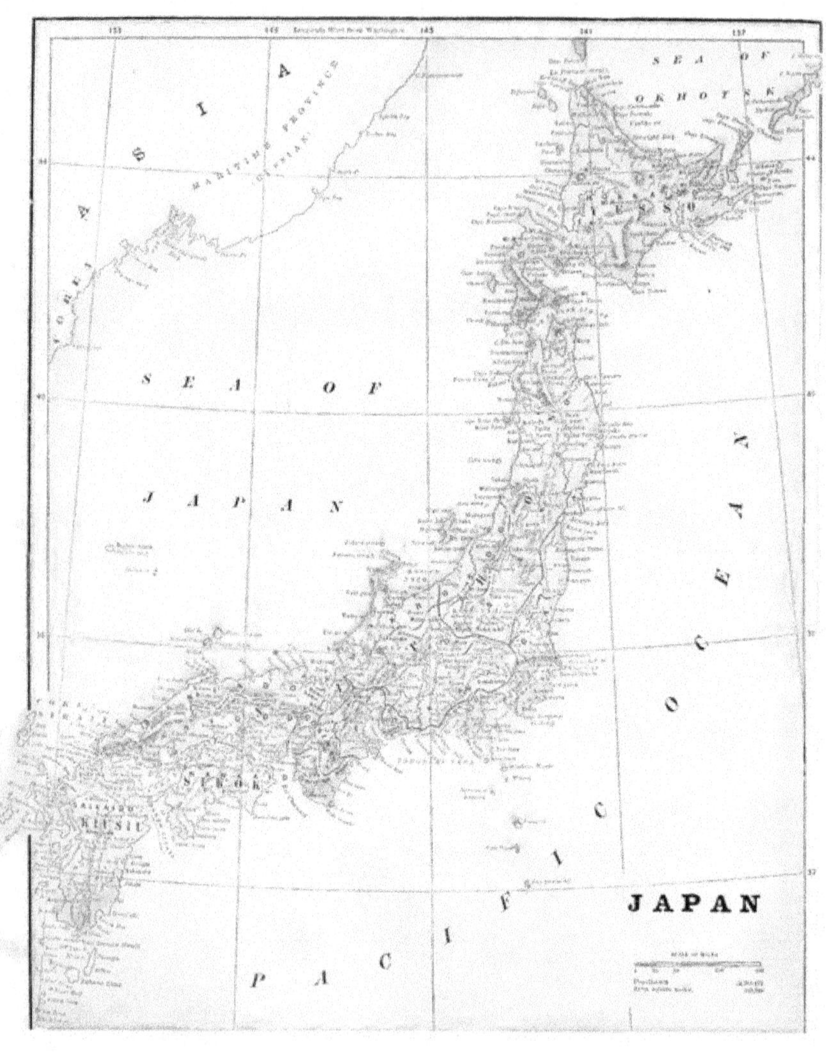
A S I A
MARITIME PROVINCE
(RUSSIAN)
SEA OF
OKHOTSK
YESSO
S E A O F
J A P A N
P A C I F I C O C E A N
SIKOK
KIUSIU
JAPAN

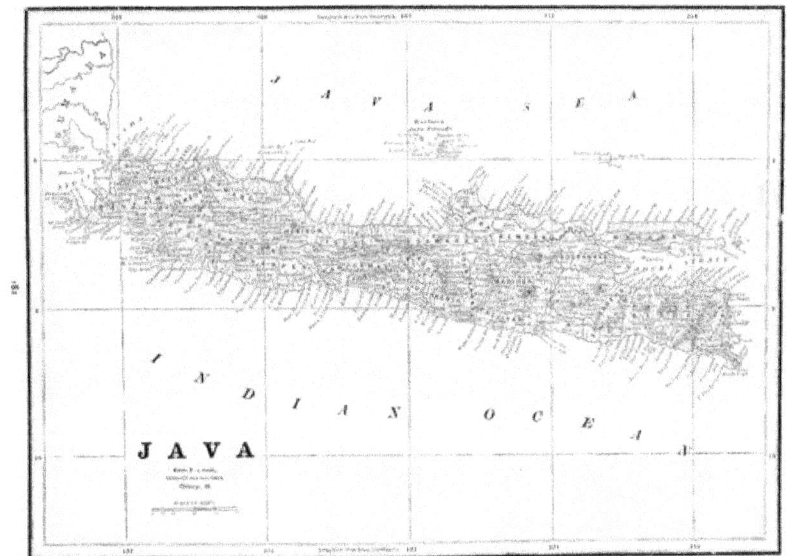

J A V A S E A
I N D I A N O C E A N
J A V A

SUMATRA
ACHEEN
COUNTRY OF THE BATTAKS
PENINSULA
LAMPONG
JAVA
BANCA
INDIAN OCEAN

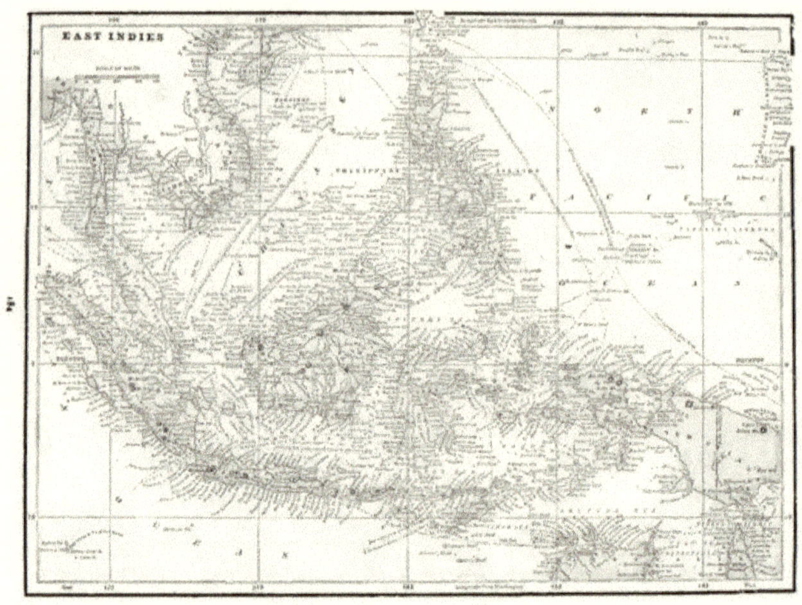
EAST INDIES

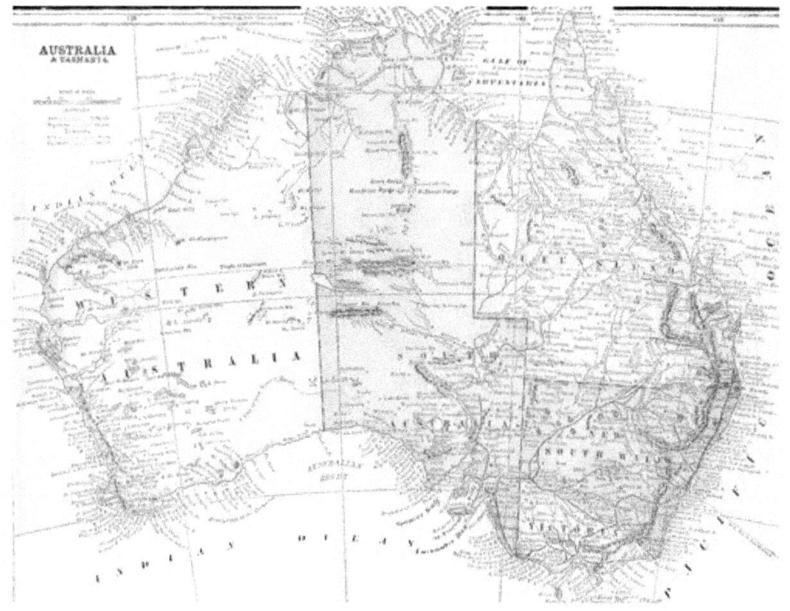
AUSTRALIA
& TASMANIA
GULF OF
CARPENTARIA
WESTERN
AUSTRALIA
SOUTH
NEW
SOUTH WALES
VICTORIA
AUSTRALIAN
BIGHT
INDIAN OCEAN

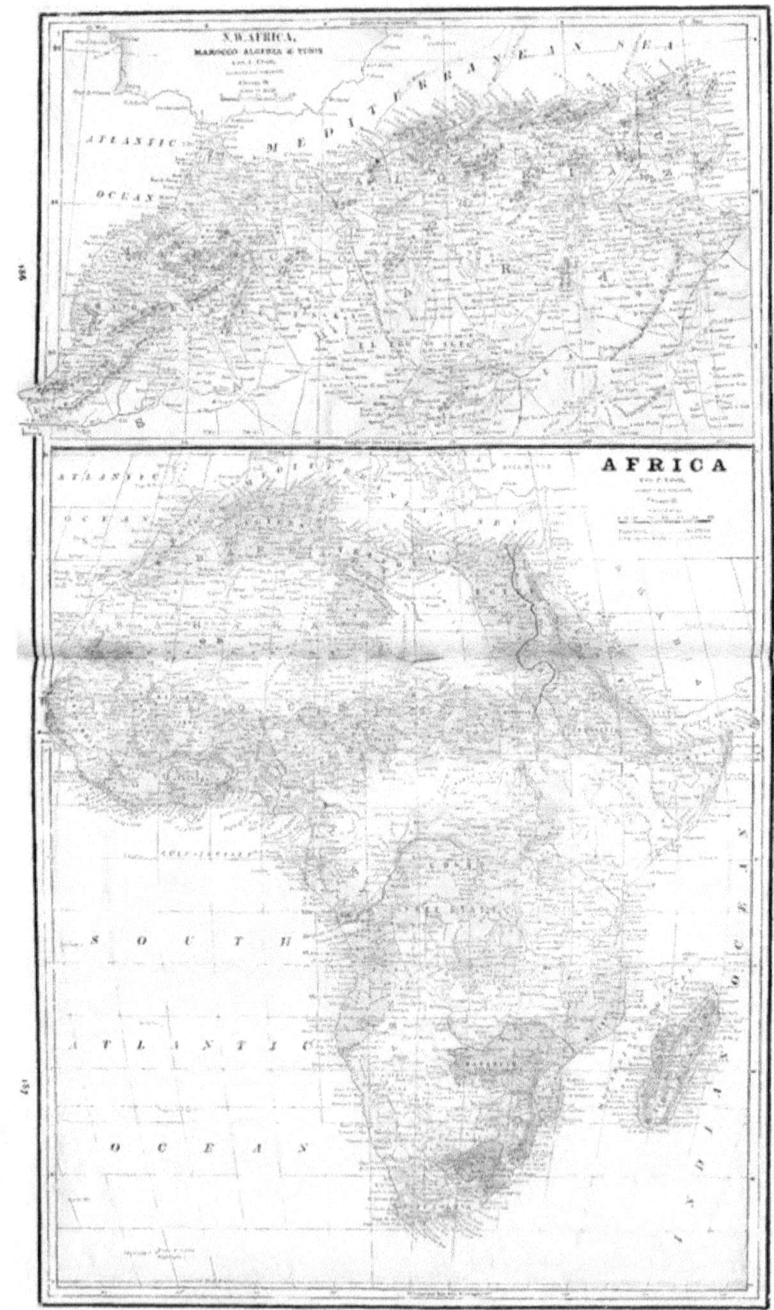
N.W. AFRICA,
MAROCCO ALGERIA & TUNIS
MEDITERRANEAN SEA
ATLANTIC
OCEAN
AFRICA
ATLANTIC
OCEAN
SOUTH
ATLANTIC
OCEAN

SOUTH AFRICA
CAPE COLONY
INDIAN OCEAN

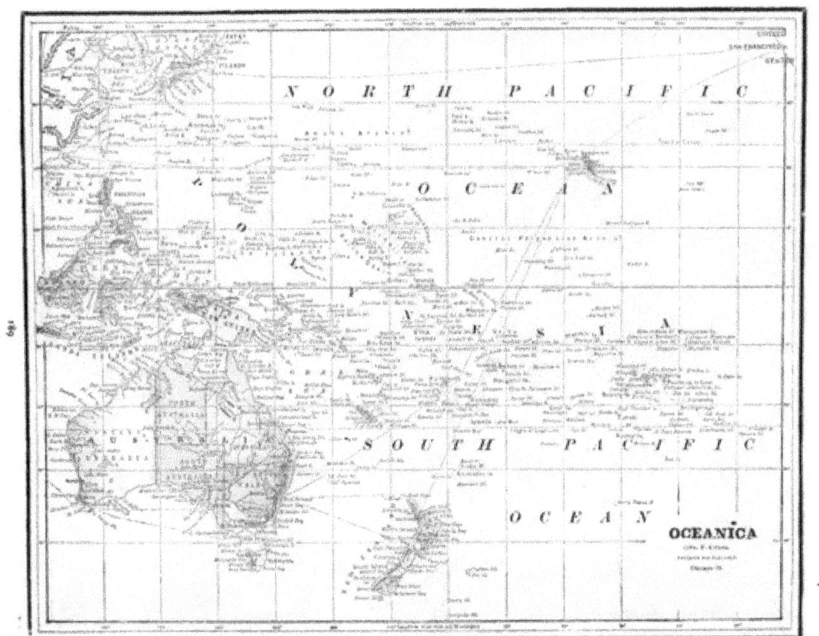
NORTH PACIFIC
OCEAN
POLYNESIA
SOUTH PACIFIC
OCEAN
OCEANICA

HISTORICAL

AND

CHRONOLOGICAL

UNITED STATES

FROM 986 

TO 1891

DESIGNED TO SIMPLIFY THE STUDY OF HISTORY,

AND AS A

VALUABLE AID IN GIVING A CLEAR, RAPID, CONDENSED COURSE OF PRACTICAL INSTRUCTION IN THE HISTORY OF OUR OWN COUNTRY, ENABLING ONE THROUGH THE MEDIUM OF THE EYE, TO READILY

LOCATE FACTS OF HISTORY

AND FIX THEM CLEARLY IN THE MEMORY.

PERIOD I. 1491 TO 1606. 116 YEARS.

DISCOVERY.

Discoveries before 1492.

9th century. Northmen at Iceland.

986. Eric the Red, at Greenland.

Later. Biörn and Lief at Newfoundland.

1000. Vinland.—Supposed to be southeast coast of New England.

Note.—Historians differ regarding the authenticity of the above events.

English Sovereigns. Tudors.—1485.—Henry VII, 24 years.

PERIOD I.

1491 *Report of committee unfavorable to Columbus' scheme.

1492 *Columbus received a patent from Ferdinand and Isabella, of Spain.—April 17.

COLUMBUS discovered America, at San Salvador, one of the Bahamas.—October 12.

1493 Columbus discovered Jamaica and other islands.—Second voyage.

1497 CABOTS discovered the continent at Labrador.—June 24.

1498 Columbus discovered South America at the mouth of the Orinoco.—Third voyage.—August 1.

*Vasco da Gama first doubled the Cape of Good Hope.—India.

1499 Americus Vespucci, after whom America was named, visited South America.

1500 Cortereal, of Portugal, seeking India, explored coast of Labrador. 1500

1502 Columbus explored coast in Gulf of Mexico.—Fourth voyage.

1506 *Death of Columbus.—May 20.

1509 *Accession of Henry VIII to the throne of England.—April 22.

1509. Henry VIII, 38 years.

1511 Havana, Cuba, settled by Velasquez.

1512 PONCE DE LEON discovered and named Florida.—March 27.

(Ponce de Leon in search of Fountain of Immortal Youth.)

1513 Balboa discovered the Pacific Ocean.—Called it the South Sea.

1517 Cordova discovered Mexico.

1519 *Expedition of Cortez against Mexico.

1520 MAGELLAN, a Portuguese, in the service of Spain, explored the Straits of Magellan.—Named the Pacific Ocean.

De Ayllon's expedition to Carolina.—Called it Chicora.

1521 CORTEZ conquered Montezuma in Mexico.—New Spain.

1522 *First circumnavigation of the globe by Magellan's ship.

1524 VERRAZZANO explored the coast from Carolina to Newfoundland.—New France. 1525

1528 Expedition of Narvaez to Florida.—4 survivors reached Mexico.

1532 Pizarro in Peru put to death the Inca.—Lima founded.

1534 Cartier, under Roberval, explored Gulf and River St. Lawrence.

1539 DE SOTO'S expedition to Florida.—10 vessels, 600 men.

1541 De Soto discovered the Mississippi River.—Died in 1542.

Coronado explored the country about the Upper Rio Grande.

1542 Cabrillo, a Portuguese in the service of Spain, explored coast of California.

Edward VI, 6 years—1547.

1547 *Accession of Edward VI to the throne of England.—January 28. 1550

1553 *Accession of Mary I to throne of England. July 6.

1553.—Mary I, 5 years.

1558 *Accession of Elizabeth to the throne of England.—November 17.

1558. Elizabeth, 45 years.

1562 Huguenots.—Coligny sent Ribault to South Carolina.—Port Royal entrance.

1564 Huguenots.—Laudonniere settled on St. John's River, Florida.

1565 Menendez destroyed Huguenots on St. John's River, Florida.

ST. AUGUSTINE, Florida, founded by Menendez. Oldest European town in the United States.—August 29.

1568 *Spanish prisoners hung by De Gourges on the site of the Menendez massacre.

1576 Frobisher, seeking route to India, cruised about Newfoundland. 1575

1579 Sir Francis Drake explored the Pacific Coast.—New Albion.

(Sir Francis Drake the first Englishman to circumnavigate the globe.)

1582 *Calendar of Pope Gregory XIII.—October 5 made October 15.

Santa Fe, N. M., founded by Espejo.—Second oldest European town in the United States.

1583 Sir Humphrey Gilbert attempted the settlement of Newfoundland.

1584 SIR WALTER RALEIGH sent Amidas and Barlow to explore the coast of Carolina.

(Virginia named in honor of Elizabeth, the virgin queen.)

1585 Raleigh's second expedition.—Grenville attempted to settle Roanoke Island.

1587 Raleigh's third expedition.—John White attempted to settle Roanoke Island.

(Virginia Dare, the first white child born in America.)

1602 Gosnold explored the Southeast coast of New England.—Named Cape Cod. 1600

1603 *Accession of James I to the throne of Great Britain.—March 24.

Stuarts. 1603.—James I, 22 years.

Champlain explored the coast of Newfoundland.

1605 Port Royal, N. S. (now Annapolis), settled under DeMonts.—Acadia.

(Port Royal, the first permanent French settlement in America.)

1606 JAMES I chartered the London Company.—South Virginia, 34° to 38° lat., and from ocean to ocean.—Also Plymouth Company.—North Virginia, 41° to 45° lat.—April 10.

(Both companies had jurisdiction from 38° to 41° lat.)

*Not on the map.

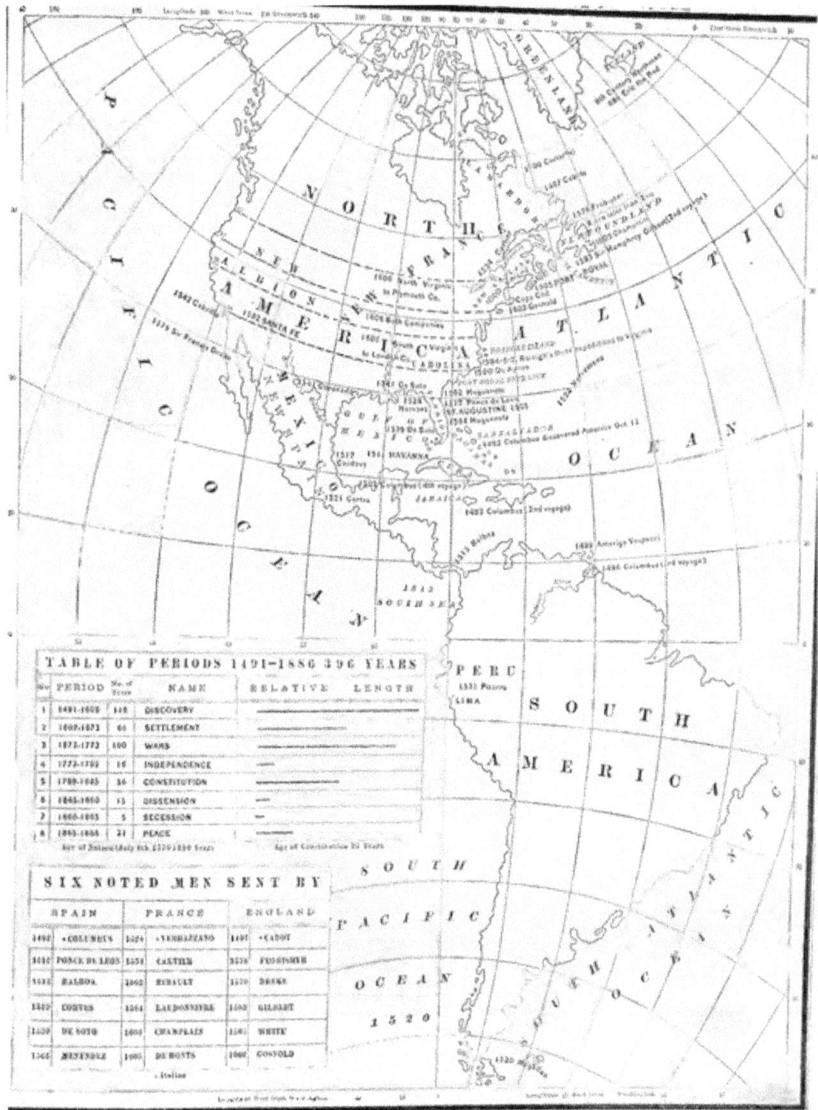

TABLE OF PERIODS 1491–1886 396 YEARS

No.	PERIOD	No. of Years	NAME	RELATIVE LENGTH
1	1491-1607	116	DISCOVERY	
2	1607-1673	66	SETTLEMENT	
3	1673-1773	100	WARS	
4	1773-1789	16	INDEPENDENCE	
5	1789-1845	56	CONSTITUTION	
6	1845-1860	15	DISSENSION	
7	1860-1865	5	SECESSION	
8	1865-1886	21	PEACE	

Age of Independence July 4th 1776 [illegible] Years — Age of Constitution [illegible] Years

SIX NOTED MEN SENT BY

SPAIN		FRANCE		ENGLAND	
1492	*COLUMBUS	1524	*VERRAZZANO	1497	*CABOT
1512	PONCE DE LEON	1534	CARTIER	1576	FROBISHER
1513	BALBOA	1562	RIBAULT	1579	DRAKE
1519	CORTES	1564	LAUDONNIERE	1583	GILBERT
1539	DE SOTO	1603	CHAMPLAIN	1587	WHITE
1565	MENENDEZ	1605	DE MONTS	1602	GOSNOLD

* Italian

PERIOD II. 1607 TO 1673. 66 YEARS.

SETTLEMENT.

James I.—Continued.

1607 JAMESTOWN, Va., settled by the London Company.—May 13.

Settlement by the Plymouth Company, at the mouth of the Kennebec, unsuccessful.

1608 Quebec settled by the French, under Champlain.—July 3.

1609 CHAMPLAIN discovered Lake Champlain.—July.

HENRY HUDSON, in the service of the Dutch, discovered the Hudson River.—September 6.

1610 "Starving Time" in Virginia.—Absence of Captain John Smith.

1613 Pocahontas married Rolfe at Yorktown, Va.—April.

1614 CAPTAIN JOHN SMITH explored coast of and named New England.

NEW NETHERLANDS granted to the Amsterdam Company.—40° to 45° lat. and sea to sea.—October 11.

NEW AMSTERDAM (now New York City) settled by the Dutch.

1615 Fort Orange (now Albany, N. Y.,) settled.

1616 The culture of tobacco began in Virginia.

1619 FIRST REPRESENTATIVE ASSEMBLY in America met at Jamestown, Va.—July 30.

NEGRO SLAVERY introduced at Jamestown by the Dutch.—August.

1620 GREAT PATENT granted to Plymouth Company.—40° to 48° lat. and ocean to ocean.—November 3.

PLYMOUTH, Mass., settled by the Puritans.—December 11.

(Compact signed on the Mayflower before landing.—November 11.)

1621 Treaty with Massasoit, chief of the Wampanoags.—Fifty years' peace.—March 22.

1622 Gorges and Mason's grant between the Merrimac and Kennebec Rivers.

OPECHANCANOUGH'S WAR.—First Indian massacre in Virginia.—347 whites killed.—March 22.

1623 PORTSMOUTH and Dover, N. H., settled by Gorges and Mason.

1625 *Accession of Charles I to the throne of Great Britain.—March 27.

1625 1625.—Charles I, 24 years.

1628 ENDICOTT'S GRANT from the Plymouth Company, from three miles south of the Charles River to three miles north of the Merrimac River, and from ocean to ocean.—March 19.

Salem, Mass., settled by the Massachusetts Bay Company.—Gov. John Endicott.—September 6.

1629 Order of Patroons founded by the Dutch in New Netherlands.

1630 Warwick's Grant, "westward from Narragansett River, 120 miles along the coast, west to the Pacific Ocean."

BOSTON founded by Winthrop.

1631 *Warwick's Grant transferred to Lords Say, Brooke and others.—March 19.

*Mason named his grant New Hampshire.

*Gorges named his grant Maine.

1632 MARYLAND granted to Lord Baltimore.

1633 WINDSOR, Conn., settled by William Holmes, from Plymouth, Mass.

1634 MARYLAND settled at St. Mary's by Calvert.—March 27.

1636 PROVIDENCE, R. I., founded by Roger Williams.

1637 PEQUOT WAR in Connecticut.—First Indian war in New England.

1638 DELAWARE settled near Wilmington by Swedes and Finns.—New Sweden.

New Haven, Conn., settled by Eaton and Davenport.—April 18.

HARVARD COLLEGE founded by bequest of John Harvard, at Cambridge, Mass.—September 14.

1639 *First printing press in America, at Cambridge, Mass.—January.

1641 *New Hampshire settlements united to Massachusetts.

1643 UNITED COLONIES of New England formed.—May 19.

1644 SECOND INDIAN MASSACRE in Virginia.—300 whites killed.—April 18.

1645 CLAIBORNE'S REBELLION in Maryland.—Gov. Calvert fled to Virginia.

1649 *Charles I, King of Great Britain, beheaded.—January 30.

1649 1650 Commonwealth: —Cromwells, 11 years.

1650 FIRST SETTLEMENT IN NORTH CAROLINA, on the Chowan River, near Edenton.

1653 *Oliver Cromwell appointed Lord Protector of Great Britain.—December 16.

1655 RELIGIOUS WAR in Maryland between Protestants and Catholics.

New Sweden conquered by the Dutch.

1656 Quakers came to Massachusetts.—Cruel treatment by Puritans.

1660 *Monarchy restored in Great Britain.—Charles II as King.—May 29.

Stuarts Restored: 1660.—Charles II, 25 years.

*Navigation acts passed restricting colonial trade.

1663 CLARENDON GRANT to Lord Clarendon and others.—March 24.

(This grant extended from 30° to 36° lat. and ocean to ocean.)

Charter of Rhode Island, giving religious liberties, granted.—July 8.

1664 NEW NETHERLANDS granted to the Duke of York and Albany.—March 12.

NEW JERSEY granted to Berkeley and Carteret.—June 24.

Stuyvesant surrendered New Amsterdam (New York City).

Fort Orange, N. Y., named Albany.—September 24.

ELIZABETH, N. J., settled by emigrants from Long Island.

1665 Connecticut and New Haven united under the name of Connecticut.—May.

Second charter of Carolina.—Boundary extended to 29° lat.—June 30.

Clarendon Colony, near Wilmington, N. C., permanently settled.

1670 DETROIT, Mich., settled by the French.

Carteret Colony settled on Ashley River near Charleston, S. C.

1671 Marquette established the mission of St. Ignatius, at Michilimackinac.

1673 Virginia granted to Culpepper and Arlington.

THE EIGHT INDIAN FAMILIES.

Algonquins, Iroquois, Dakotas or Sioux, Catawbas, Cherokees, Uchees, Choctaws or Mobilians, and Natchez.

*Not on the map.

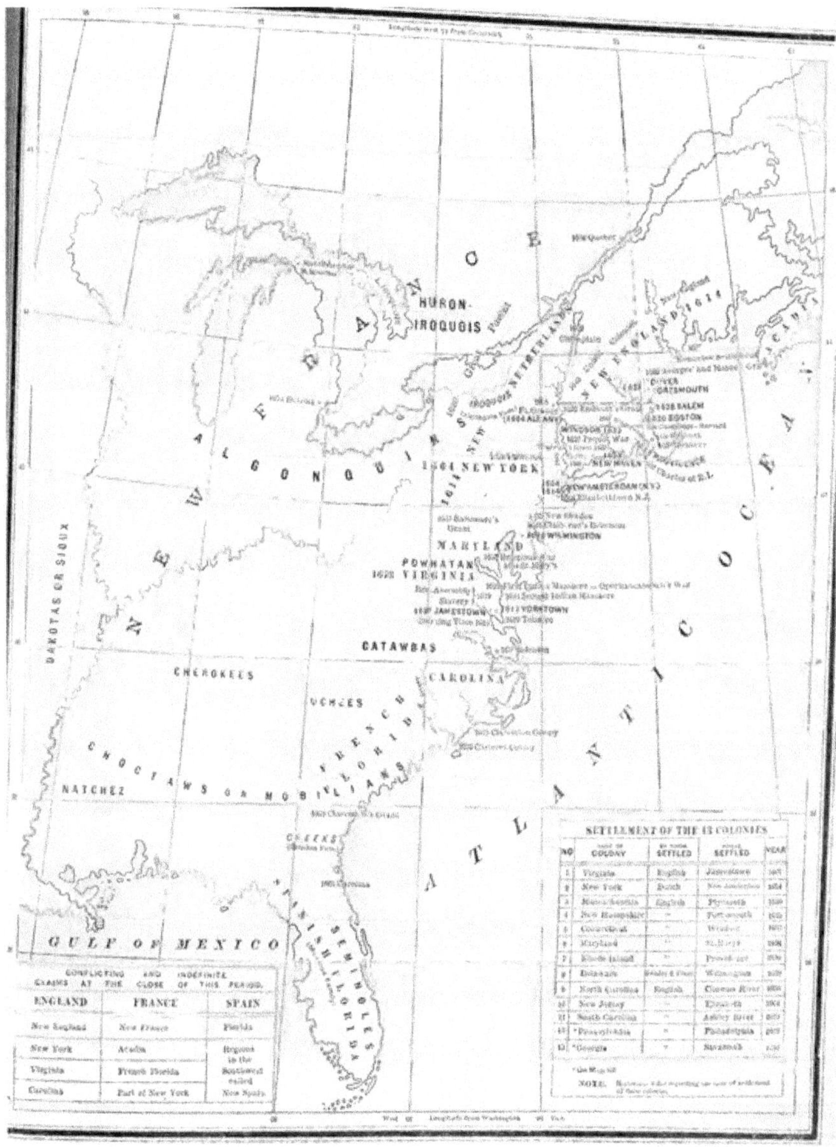
NEW FRANCE
HURON-IROQUOIS
ALGONQUINS
1664 NEW YORK
NEW NETHERLAND
NEW ENGLAND
ACADIA
MARYLAND
POWHATAN
VIRGINIA
1607 JAMESTOWN
CATAWBAS
CHEROKEES
CAROLINA
UCHEES
CHOCTAWS OR MOBILIANS
FRENCH FLORIDA
NATCHEZ
CREEKS
DAKOTAS OR SIOUX
SEMINOLES
SPANISH FLORIDA
GULF OF MEXICO
ATLANTIC OCEAN
1626 SALEM
1630 BOSTON
NEW AMSTERDAM
WILMINGTON
YORKTOWN
SETTLEMENT OF THE 13 COLONIES
NO
COLONY
SETTLED
YEAR
Virginia
English
Jamestown
New York
Dutch
New Hampshire
Maryland
North Carolina
New Jersey
South Carolina
Ashley River
Pennsylvania
Philadelphia
Georgia
Savannah
NOTE.
CONFLICTING AND INDEFINITE CLAIMS AT THE CLOSE OF THIS PERIOD.
ENGLAND
FRANCE
SPAIN
New England
New France
Florida
New York
Acadia
Regions in the Southwest called New Spain
Virginia
French Florida
Carolina
Part of New York

PERIOD III. 1673 TO 1773. 100 YEARS.

WARS.

1673 Marquette and Joliet explore the Mississippi River to the Arkansas.
1674 MARQUETTE FOUNDED MISSIONARY STATION at Chicago, Ill.
1675 Marquette founded a mission at Kaskaskia, Ill.
King Philip's War in New England began.
1676 BACON'S REBELLION against Berkeley, in Virginia.—100 years before independence.
QUINTIPARTITE DEED formed East and West Jersey.—West to the Quakers and east to Carteret.—Dividing line from Little Egg Harbor to lat. 41° 40′ on the northernmost branch of the Delaware River.
1680 Charleston, S. C., founded by the removal of the Carteret Colony.
1681 PENNSYLVANIA granted to William Penn, by Charles II.—March 4.
1682 LA SALLE explored the Mississippi to its mouth.—Named Louisiana.
DELAWARE ("the three lower counties") granted to William Penn.—August 24.
PHILADELPHIA founded by William Penn.
1684 *Massachusetts' charter declared null and void by English court.—June 18.
1685 *Accession of James II to the throne of Great Britain.—February 6.
1686 Arrival of Sir Edmund Andros, Governor of all New England.—December 20.
1687 CHARTER OF CONNECTICUT concealed in the Charter Oak at Hartford.—October 31.
1689 *Accession of William III and Mary II to the throne of Great Britain.—February 13.
*KING WILLIAM'S WAR between Great Britain and France.—Lasted 8 years.
1690 Burning of Schenectady, N. Y., by French and Indians.—Feb. 8.
PORT ROYAL taken by the British under Phipps.—May.
1691 *Massachusetts, Plymouth, Maine and Nova Scotia united.—Gov. Phipps.—October 7.
1692 Phipps' witchcraft court at Salem, Mass.
(Twenty persons convicted of witchcraft and put to death.)
1694 *Death of Mary II, Queen of Great Britain.—December 28.
1697 *Treaty of Ryswick closed King William's War.—No change in territory.—October 30.
1699 Captain William Kidd, the pirate, at Gardener's Bay, Long Island.
1702 *Accession of Anne to the throne of Great Britain.—March 8.
*QUEEN ANNE'S WAR began.—Great Britain against France and Spain.—Lasted 11 years.
1704 First permanent newspaper in America, the "Boston News Letter."—April 24.
1710 Port Royal, N. S., captured by the British and named Annapolis.—October 2.
1711 Indian war with the Corees in North Carolina.
1713 Tuscaroras join the Iroquois in New York, making the Six Nations.
*TREATY OF UTRECHT closed Queen Anne's War.—April 11.
(This treaty gave Great Britain the Hudson Bay region, Newfoundland and Acadia.)
1714 *Accession of George I to the throne of Great Britain.—August 1.
1715 Yamassee War in Carolina.
1718 NEW ORLEANS founded by the French under Bienville.
1727 *Accession of George II to the throne of Great Britain.—June 11.
1729 CAROLINA divided.—Clarendon, or middle colony, moved to Charleston.
(Albemarle Colony became North Carolina.
(Carteret Colony became South Carolina.)
1732 WASHINGTON born in Westmoreland County, Va.—February 22.
GEORGIA granted to Oglethorpe.—Included part of Carolina.—June 9.
1733 SAVANNAH, Ga., founded by Oglethorpe.—February 12.
1739 *SPANISH WAR between Great Britain and Spain declared.—October 23.
(This with King George's war lasted 9 years.)
1740 Invasion of Florida by Oglethorpe.
1742 Invasion of Georgia by the Spanish.
1744 *SPANISH WAR merged into KING GEORGE'S WAR.—France allied with Spain.

1745 LOUISBURG, the Gibraltar of America, captured by Pepperell.—June 17.
1748 *TREATY OF AIX LA CHAPELLE closed King George's War.—October 18. 1750
(Both parties to restore their respective conquests.)
1749 Ohio Company, of London, received a grant of 6,000,000 acres on Ohio River.
1751 *NEW STYLE Gregorian Calendar adopted by Great Britain.—11 days cut, September 3 to 14.
1753 WASHINGTON sent to Ft. Le Bœuf by Gov. Dinwiddie of Virginia.
1754 Washington returned to Williamsburg.—January 6.
*FRENCH AND INDIAN WAR.—Most important of the colonial wars.
WASHINGTON defeated Jumonville at Mountain Meadows.—May 28.
ALBANY CONVENTION adopted plan of union prepared by Franklin.—June 19.
(Plan rejected by the crown and people.)
Washington defeated at Ft. Necessity by De Villiers.—June 3.
1755 ALEXANDRIA CONVENTION, Va.—Colonial governors met Braddock.—April 14.
Ft. Beau Sejour, N. S., surrendered to the British.—June 16.
Ft. Gaspereau surrendered to the British.—June 17.
BRADDOCK'S DEFEAT on the Monongahela River, Pa.—Braddock mortally wounded.—July 9.
Battle of Lake George.—Lyman under Johnson defeated Dieskau.—September 8.
Johnson established Ft. William Henry.—Received a baronetcy and £5,000.
1756 *WAR DECLARED by Great Britain after two years' fighting.—May 18.
MONTCALM captured Oswego, 1,400 men, stores and money.—Aug. 14.
1757 Ft. William Henry surrendered to Montcalm.—August 9.
(Massacre by Indians after Monroe capitulated.)
1758 Lord Howe killed in a fight near Ticonderoga.—July 6.
Abercrombie repulsed by Montcalm at Ticonderoga.—July 8.
LOUISBURG, N. S., taken by Amherst and Boscawen.—July 26.
Ft. Frontenac (now Kingston, Ca.), surrendered to Bradstreet.—August 27.
Grant defeated by Aubrey at Ft. Duquesne.—September 21.
FT. DUQUESNE, Pa., captured by Forbes.—Named Ft. Pitt.—Nov. 25.
1759 FT. NIAGARA surrendered to Johnson.—Death of Prideaux.—July 25.
Battle of Montmorenci, near Quebec.—Montcalm repulsed Wolfe.—July 31.
Crown Point, N. Y., taken by Amherst.—August 4.
PLAINS OF ABRAHAM, QUEBEC.—Wolfe and Montcalm mortally wounded.—September 13.
Quebec surrendered to the British.—September 18.
1760 Cherokee War in Georgia.
Battle of Sillery, Ca.—De Levi attempts to recover Quebec.—Apr. 28.
*Accession of George III to the throne of Great Britain.—Oct. 25. 1760—George III.—60 years.
1762 LOUISIANA ceded to Spain by France.
*Pontiac's conspiracy to unite the Indian nations.
1763 *TREATY OF PARIS closed the French and Indian War.—Feb. 10.
(Practically all territory east of the Mississippi River ceded by France to Great Britain.—Two Islands near Newfoundland and island and town of New Orleans retained by France.)
Florida ceded to Great Britain by Spain, treaty of Paris.—Feb. 10.
East and West Florida established by George III.—October 7.
Pontiac's War broke out.—Ottawas.
Siege of Detroit by the Indians unsuccessful.—May.
1764 St. Louis, Mo., settled by the French.
West Florida extended to the mouth of the Yazoo.—June 6.
*ENGLISH DEBT greatly increased by French and Indian War.
1765 *Stamp Act passed by Parliament.—March 22.
1766 *Stamp Act repealed.—March 19.
1767 *Bill imposing a tax on glass, paper, etc., passed.—June 29.
1770 The Boston Massacre.—March 5.
*All duties except on tea repealed by Parliament.—April 12.

*Not on the map.

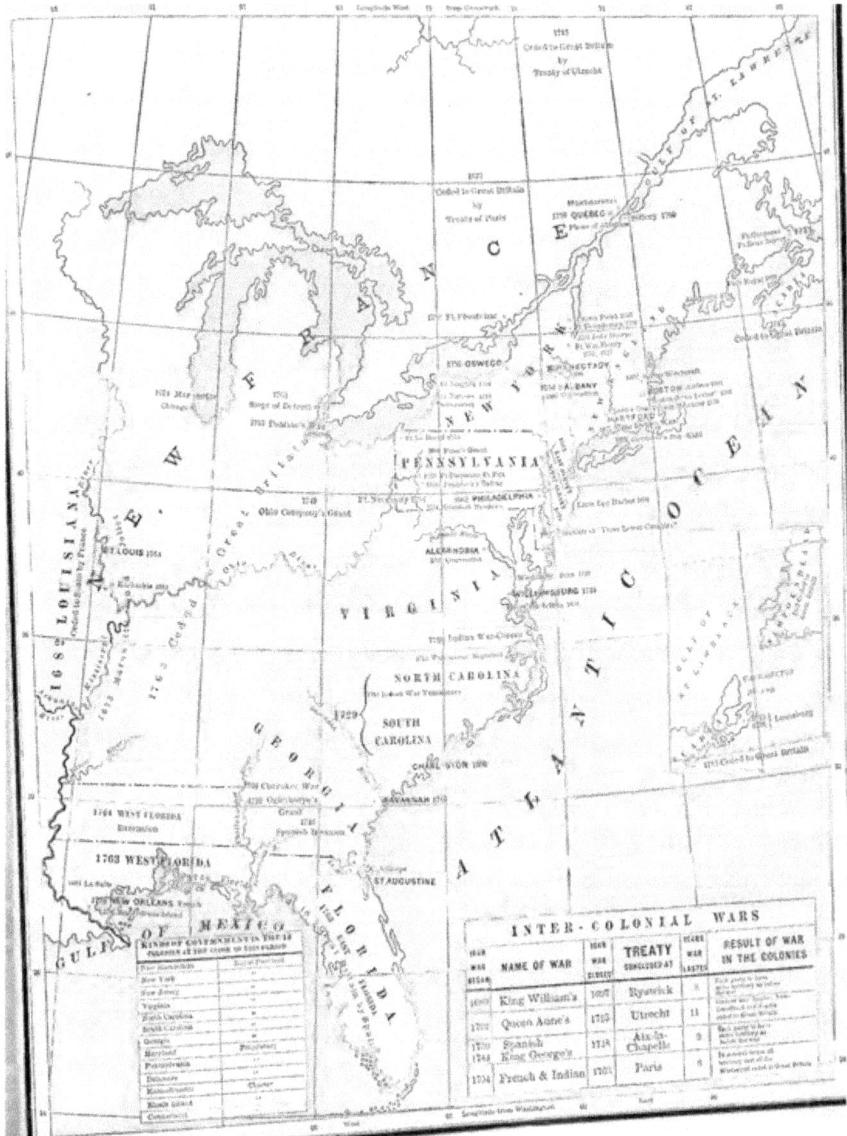

NEW FRANCE
NEW YORK
PENNSYLVANIA
VIRGINIA
NORTH CAROLINA
SOUTH CAROLINA
GEORGIA
FLORIDA
LOUISIANA
1763 WEST FLORIDA
ATLANTIC OCEAN
GULF OF MEXICO
QUEBEC
OSWEGO
ALBANY
BOSTON
HARTFORD
PHILADELPHIA
ALEXANDRIA
CHARLESTON
SAVANNAH
ST. AUGUSTINE
ST. LOUIS
NEW ORLEANS
Ohio Company's Grant
INTER-COLONIAL WARS
NAME OF WAR
TREATY
RESULT OF WAR IN THE COLONIES
King William's
Queen Anne's
Spanish
King George's
French & Indian
Utrecht
Aix-la-Chapelle
Paris

PERIOD IV. 1773 TO 1789. 16 YEARS.

INDEPENDENCE.

1773 "Boston Tea Party."—Three cargoes of tea destroyed.—December 16.

1774 *Boston Port Bill enacted.—March 25.
Green Mountain Boys' Rebellion, led by Ethan Allen.
*First Continental Congress met at Philadelphia.—September 5.
*Declaration of rights passed by Congress.—October 14.

1775 BATTLE OF LEXINGTON, Mass.—First blood of the Revolutionary War.—April 19.
Allen and Arnold capture Ticonderoga, N. Y.—May 10.
*Continental Congress met at Philadelphia.—May 10.
Americans capture Crown Point, N. Y.—May 12.
A declaration of independence at Charlotte, Mecklenburgh County, N. C.—May 20.
*Howe, Clinton and Burgoyne arrived at Boston.—May 25.
*Washington elected Commander-in-Chief.—June 15.

BATTLE OF BUNKER HILL.—Death of Gen. Joseph Warren.—June 17.
Montreal surrendered to Montgomery.—November 12.
Battle of Quebec.—Death of Montgomery.—December 31.

1776 Norfolk destroyed by Lord Dunmore.—January 1.
*Boston evacuated by British troops.—March 17.
*Resolution for independence offered by Richard Henry Lee.—June 7.
Clinton attacked Col. Moultrie at Sullivan's Island, S. C.—June 28.

DECLARATION OF INDEPENDENCE at Philadelphia.—July 4.—(Thomas Jefferson supposed to be the author.)
Battle of Long Island, N. Y.—Putnam against Howe.—August 27.
*New York City abandoned by the Americans.—September 15.
Battle of White Plains, N. Y.—Howe defeated Washington.—October 28.
Fort Washington captured by Gen. Howe.—November 16.
Fort Lee captured by Cornwallis.—November 20.
*Washington's Retreat through New Jersey.—December.
*General Lee captured in New York by British scouts.—December 13.

BATTLE OF TRENTON, N. J.—Washington captured 1,000 Hessians.—December 26.

1777 Battle of Princeton, N. J.—Cornwallis lost 1,000 men.—January 3.
Tryon's first expedition against Connecticut.—Danbury burned.—April.
Battle of Ridgefield, Conn.—Arnold's bravery.—Wooster's death.—April 27.
Meigs' expedition against the British at Sag Harbor, Long Island.—May 23.
*National flag with 13 stars and stripes, adopted by Congress.—June 14.
Lafayette, DeKalb and party arrive at Georgetown, S. C.—June 25.
Ticonderoga abandoned by the Americans.—July 6.
Battle of Hubbardton, Vt.—Americans defeated.—July 7.
Fort Schuyler besieged by St. Leger.—August.
Battle of Oriskany, N. Y.—Death of Gen. Herkimer.—August 6.
Battle of Bennington, Vt.—Americans successful.—August 16.
Battle of Brandywine or Chad's Ford, Pa.—Washington and Howe.—September 11.
First Battle of Stillwater, or Bemis' Heights.—September 19.
Battle of Paoli, Pa.—Midnight defeat of Wayne.—September 21.
Philadelphia entered by the British under Howe.—September 26.
Battle of Germantown, Pa.—Washington lost 1,200 men.—October 4.
Fts. Clinton and Montgomery, posts in the Highlands, N. Y., captured.—October 6.
Second Battle of Stillwater, or Saratoga.—American victory.—Oct. 7.

SURRENDER OF BURGOYNE to Gates, near Saratoga, N. Y.—October 17.
(This seems the pivotal event of the war.)
Hessians repulsed at Ft. Mercer, N. J.—October 22.
*Articles of Confederation adopted by Congress.—November 15.
Ft. Mifflin abandoned by Americans.—November 16.

VALLEY FORGE, Pa.—American army encamped.—December 19.

1778 *Independence of the United States acknowledged by France.—Jan. 14.
*Treaty of Alliance with France signed at Paris.—February 6.
Ohio settled at Marietta by a Colony under Rufus Putnam.—April 7.
*British Peace Commission arrived at Philadelphia.—May 31.
*Philadelphia evacuated by Clinton, successor of Howe.—June 18.
Battle of Monmouth Court-house, N. J.—Clinton retreated to New York.—June 28.
Wyoming Massacre, Pa., by Tories and Indians.—July 3.
*Articles of Confederation adopted by Congress.—July 9.
Battle of Rhode Island, near Quaker Hill.—August 29.
Cherry Valley Massacre, N. Y., by Butler and Brandt.—November 11.
Battle of Savannah.—City captured by the British.—December 29.

1779 Sunbury captured by the British, last American post in Georgia.—January 9.
Battle of Kettle Creek, Ga.—Defeat and death of Col. Boyd (British).—February 14.
Battle of Brier Creek, Ga.—Prevost defeated Ashe.—March 3.
Stony Point and Verplanck's Point, N. Y., captured by the British.—June 1.

George III. 1779 Continued.

*Spain declared war against Great Britain.—June 16.
Stono Ferry, S. C., Americans repulsed.—June 20.
Tryon's expedition against Connecticut.—New Haven plundered.—July.
STONY POINT, N. Y., captured by Wayne.—July 15.
Battle of Penobscot, Me.—Americans defeated by British fleet.—July 25.
British surprised at Paulus Hook (now Jersey City), N. J., by Lee.—August 19.
Sullivan's Expedition against the Indians in New York.—August.
Battle of Chemung Creek, near Elmira, N. Y.—August 29.
Savannah besieged by French and Indians.—September-October.
*John Paul Jones captured two frigates off the northeastern coast of England.—September 23.
D'Estaing and Lincoln repulsed at Savannah, Ga.—October 9.

1780 Clinton and Arbuthnot besieged Charleston, S. C.—March 29.
Battle of Monk's Corner, S. C.—Tarleton defeated Americans.—April 14.
Surrender of Charleston, S. C., to the British by Lincoln.—May 12.
Tarleton massacred 300 Americans at the Waxhaws, S. C.—May 29.
Battle of Springfield, N. J.—Knyphausen and Greene.—June 23.

ADMIRAL DE TERNAY AND ROCHAMBEAU arrived at Newport, R. I., with 6,000 men.—July 10.
Battle of Rocky Mount, S. C.—Americans repulsed.—July 30.
Battle of Hanging Rock, S. C.—Sumter defeated by the British.—August 6.
Battle of Camden, or Sanders Creek.—Gates lost 1,000 men.—August 16.
Battle of Fishing Creek, S. C.—Sumter defeated by Tarleton.—August 18.

ARNOLD attempted to betray West Point, N. Y., to Sir Henry Clinton.—September 23.
*Andre executed as a spy at Tappan, N. Y.—October 2.
Battle of King's Mountain, N. C.—Ferguson defeated and killed.—October 7.
Battle of Fishdam Ford, S. C.—Sumter defeated Wemyss.—November 12.
Battle of Blackstocks, S. C.—Sumter defeated Tarleton.—November 20.

1781 Revolt of American troops at Morristown, N. J.—January 1.
Battle of the Cowpens.—Tarleton defeated by Morgan.—January 17.
Arnold's depredations at Richmond and other points in Virginia.—January.
Retreat of Morgan and Greene through North Carolina to Virginia, pursued by Cornwallis.—February 3-14.
*Ratification of the Articles of Confederation by the States announced.—March 1.

*NEW YORK CESSION to the General Government of territory between Lake Erie and the Cumberland Mountains.—March 1.
(New York the first to cede territory to the United States. She claimed a vast domain covering the Northwest. Not shown on the map.)
Battle of Guilford Court-house, N. C.—Greene repulsed by Cornwallis.—March 15.
Battle of Hobkirk's Hill, or second Camden, S. C.—Greene defeated by Rawdon.—April 25.
Battle of Ft. Ninety-six.—Greene repulsed.—June 19.
*Isaac Hayne executed as a traitor by the British at Charleston, S. C.—August 4.
*Arnold's expedition to Connecticut.—Attempt to divert the attention of Washington.
Battle of Ft. Griswold.—New London, Conn., burned by Arnold.—September 6.
Battle of Eutaw Springs, S. C.—Greene closed the campaign in the Carolinas.—September 8.
Siege of Yorktown by Washington and Count de Grasse.—October.
SURRENDER OF CORNWALLIS at Yorktown, Va., with 7,000 men.—Oct. 19.

1782 *Preliminary Articles of Peace signed at Paris.—November 30.

1783 Florida re-ceded to Spain by Great Britain.—January 20.
*Cessation of hostilities proclaimed in the American army.—April 11.

DEFINITIVE TREATY OF PEACE signed at Paris (original territory).—September 3.
Washington resigned his commission at Annapolis, Md.—December 23.
Fitch unsuccessfully applied steam to navigation on the Hudson. (Fitch predicted the present use of steam.)

1784 Virginia Cession of territory to the General Government.—March 1.
Virginia Reserve, between the Little Miami and Scioto Rivers.

1785 Massachusetts Cession of territory to the General Government (between parallels 42° 2' and 43° 30').—April 19.

1786 Connecticut Cession to the General Government (between parallels 41° and 42° 2').—September 14.
(Western or Connecticut Reserve, from Pennsylvania to a line 120 miles west.)
Shay's Rebellion in Massachusetts.—War debt troubles.—Paper money demanded.

1787 Territory Northwest of the River Ohio formed by Congress.—July 13.
(The first territorial division formed by the United States.)
South Carolina Cession.—A strip "12 or 14 miles wide" west to the Mississippi River.—August 9.
*Constitution agreed upon by convention at Philadelphia.—September 17.

1788 *Constitution ratified by the requisite number of States.

*Not on the map.

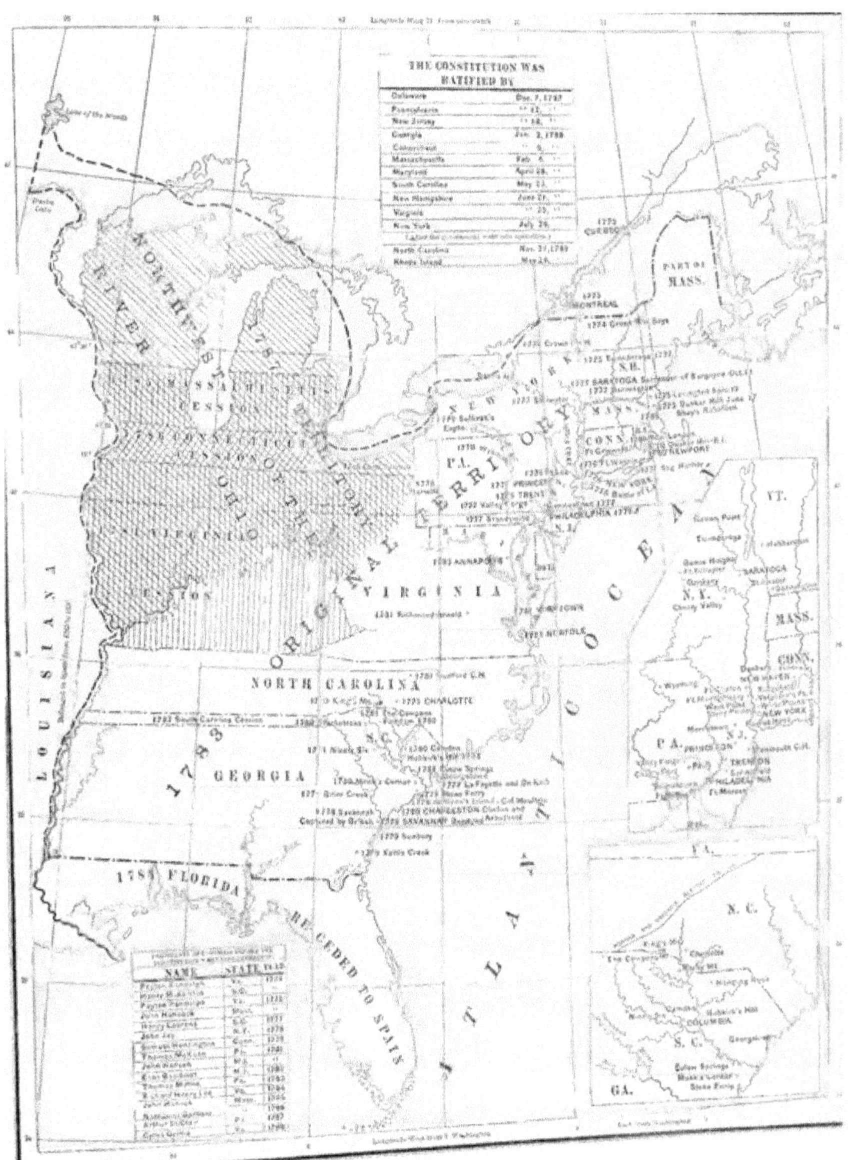

PERIOD V. 1789 TO 1845. 56 YEARS.

CONSTITUTION.

1789 FIRST CONGRESS under the Constitution met at New York.—March 4.
*WASHINGTON inaugurated President.—April 30.
1790 NORTH CAROLINA CESSION of territory to the General Government.—February 25.
Territory south of the River Ohio formed.—May 26.
District of Columbia located and bounded.—July 16.
Harmar defeated by Little Turtle at Maumee Ford, now Ft. Wayne, Ind.—October 22.
*FIRST TEN AMENDMENTS to the Constitution proclaimed in force.—December 15.
1791 Vermont admitted into the Union.—Generally laid down as part of New York.—March 4.
United States Bank established at Philadelphia.—February 25.
St. Clair defeated by the Indians in Ohio.—November 4.
1792 Kentucky admitted into the Union.—June 1.
1793 *Washington began second presidential term.—March 4.
1794 Wayne's campaign against the Indians in Ohio.
Whisky insurrection in Pennsylvania.—Opposition to duties on liquors.
*JAY'S TREATY with Great Britain at London.—November 19.
1795 *WAYNE'S TREATY with the Indians at Greenville, Ohio.—August 3.
*Treaty of Peace with Algiers.—November 28.
1796 Tennessee admitted into the Union.—June 1.
1797 *JOHN ADAMS inaugurated President.—March 4.
1798 *ELEVENTH AMENDMENT to the Constitution declared in force.—January 8.
Mississippi Territory formed.—April 7.
*Washington accepted an appointment as general-in-chief.—July 13.
1799 WASHINGTON died at Mt. Vernon, Va., aged 67 years.—December 14.
1800 Indiana Territory formed.—July 4.
Louisiana ceded to France by Spain by secret treaty.—October 1.
SEAT OF GOVERNMENT removed to Washington, D. C.—Congress met November 17.
1801 *THOMAS JEFFERSON inaugurated President.—March 4.
*Tripoli declared war against the United States.—June 10.
MILITARY ACADEMY established at West Point, N. Y.—March 16.
1802 GEORGIA CESSION of territory to the General Government.—April 24.
Ohio admitted into the Union.—November 29.
1803 LOUISIANA ceded to the United States (see also Map VI.) by France for \$5,000,000 francs.—April 30.
(By this cession the United States claimed to the present western boundary of Florida.)
1804 *The Philadelphia destroyed by Decatur at Tripoli.—February 16.
Duel between Hamilton and Burr at Hoboken, N. J.—July 11.
*TWELFTH AMENDMENT to the Constitution declared in force.—September 25.
Orleans Territory formed. (See also Map VI.)—October 1.
District of Louisiana formed. (Same as Louisiana cession less Orleans Territory. See Map VI.)—October 1.
1805 Louisiana Territory formed. (Same as District of Louisiana. See Map VI.)—March 3.
*Jefferson began second presidential term.—March 4.
*Treaty of peace concluded with Tripoli.—June 4.
Michigan Territory formed.—June 30.
1806 *BONAPARTE'S BERLIN DECREE.—November 21.
1807 *BRITISH "ORDERS IN COUNCIL" requiring goods to land in Great Britain.—January 7.
Aaron Burr tried for treason at Richmond, Va.—Acquitted September 1.
FULTON successfully applied steam to navigation on the Hudson.—September 14.
The Chesapeake attacked by the Leopard off the coast of Virginia.—June 22.
*BRITISH "ORDERS IN COUNCIL" prohibited trade with France and allies.—November 11.
*BONAPARTE'S MILAN DECREE prohibited trade with English colonies.—December 17.
1808 *BONAPARTE'S BAYONNE DECREE ordered seizure of United States vessels.—April 17.
1809 *Non-Intercourse Act prohibiting trade with Great Britain and France passed.—February 27.
Illinois Territory formed.—March 1.
*JAMES MADISON inaugurated President.—March 4.
1810 *BONAPARTE'S RAMBOUILLET DECREE.—132 American vessels seized and sold.—March 23.
1811 *George, Prince of Wales, appointed regent of Great Britain.—February 5.
BATTLE between the President and Little Belt off Virginia.—May 16.
BATTLE OF TIPPECANOE, Ind.—Harrison defeated the Indians.—November 7.
1812 Louisiana admitted into the Union. (See also Map VI.)—April 30.
*WAR WITH GREAT BRITAIN proclaimed by the United States.—June 19.
HULL'S EXPEDITION against Ft. Malden, Ca.—July.
Ft. Mackinaw captured by British and Indians.—July 17.
First battle of Brownstown, Mich.—British defeated Van Horn.—August 5.
Second battle of Brownstown, or Maguaga.—Americans victorious.—August 9.
*British sloop Alert taken by the Essex off Newfoundland.—August 13.
HULL'S SURRENDER of the fort and city of Detroit.—August 16.
THE GUERRIERE, a British frigate, captured by the Constitution off Massachusetts.—August 19.
BATTLE OF QUEENSTON, Ca.—Van Rensselaer wounded.—Brock killed.—October 13.
BATTLE OF LEWISTON, N. Y.—Cowardly conduct of American militia.—October 13.
British ship Frolic captured the Frolic and Wasp off North Carolina.—October 18.
*British ship Macedonia captured by the United States off Canary Islands.—October 25.
Missouri Territory formed. (Same as Louisiana Territory. See Map VI.) December 7.
*British frigate Java captured by the Constitution off Bahia, Brazil.—December 29.
1813 BATTLE OF FRENCHTOWN, Mich.—Winchester defeated by Proctor.—January 22.
British brig Peacock captured by the Hornet off Demarara, South America.—February 24.
*Madison began second presidential term.—March 4.
BATTLE OF YORK, Ca. (now Toronto).—Explosion of British magazine.—April 27.
FT. MEIGS besieged by 2,000 British and Indians under Proctor.—May 1.
(Gen. Clay with 1,200 Kentuckians dispersed besiegers.—May 5.)
Prevost makes an unsuccessful attack on Sackett's Harbor.—May 29.
THE CHESAPEAKE, Captain Lawrence, captured by the Shannon in Massachusetts Bay.—June 1.
DEFENSE OF FT. STEPHENSON, Ohio (now Lower Sandusky), by Maj. Croghan.—August 2.
*American brig Argus captured by the Pelican in the English Channel.—August 14.
1813 THE CREEK WAR.—Massacre of Ft. Mimms, Ala.—August 30.
British brig Boxer captured by the Enterprise off Maine.—September 5.
PERRY'S VICTORY at the west end of Lake Erie.—September 10.
(Perry, 9 vessels, 54 guns. Barclay, 6 vessels, 63 guns.)
BATTLE OF THE THAMES, or MORAVIAN TOWNS, Ca.—October 5.
(Tecumseh killed and the Indian confederacy broken.)
Battle of Talladega, Ala.—Jackson defeated the Creeks.—November 9.
BATTLE OF CHRYSLER'S FIELD, Ca.—British repulsed.—November 11.
*Porter made a successful cruise on the Pacific with the Essex.
1814 BATTLE OF TOHOPEKA, OR HORSE SHOE BEND, Ala.—Close of the Creek War.—March 27.
*American frigate Essex captured by the Phœbe and Cherub off Chili.—March 28.
Wilkinson repulsed at La Colle Mill, Ca., on the Richelieu river.—March 30.
British brig Epervier captured by the Peacock off Florida.—April 29.
*British sloop Reindeer captured by the Wasp near the British Channel.—June 28.
GENERALS SCOTT AND RIPLEY captured Ft. Erie, Ca.—July 3.
BATTLE OF CHIPPEWA, Ca.—Scott defeated Riall.—July 5.
BATTLE OF LUNDY'S LANE, Ca.—The most obstinate of the war.—July 25.
(Drummond, British, and Brown, Scott and Jesup, Americans, wounded.)
FIRST BATTLE OF FT. ERIE.—Drummond with 5,000 men repulsed.—August 15.
Ross dispersed Americans at Bladensburg, Md.—August 24.
WASHINGTON, D.C., captured by Ross.—Public buildings burned.—August 24.
BATTLE OF LAKE CHAMPLAIN.—Downie, British, surrendered his fleet to McDonough.—September 11.
BATTLE OF PLATTSBURG, N. Y.—Prevost, British, defeated by McComb.—September 11.
Ross defeated Americans at North Point, Md.—Death of Ross.—September 12.
Brooke bombarded Ft. McHenry, Md., without success.—September 13.
British bombarded Ft. Boyer, Mobile Bay, without success.—September 15.
SECOND BATTLE OF FT. ERIE.—Brown dispersed besiegers.—September 17.
Jackson drove the British from Pensacola, Fla.—November 7.
AMERICAN FLOTILLA surrendered to the British at Lake Borgne, La.—December 14.
Convention at Hartford, Conn., opposed to the war.—December 15.
*Battle nine miles from New Orleans, La.—Jackson retired to intrenchments.—December 23.
*TREATY OF GHENT, Belgium (peace), signed.—December 24.
1815 BATTLE OF NEW ORLEANS.—14 days after treaty of peace.—January 8.
(Packenham lost 2,600 men and was killed.—The Americans lost 7 men.)
British squadron captured the frigate President off New Jersey.—Jan. 15.
*British Cyane and Levant captured by Constitution off Madeira Islands.—February 20.
*War against Algiers declared by Congress.—March 2.
*British brig Penguin captured by the Hornet off Brazil.—March 23.
1816 *Bank of the United States rechartered for 20 years.—Capital \$35,000,000.—April 10.
Indiana admitted into the Union.—December 11.
1817 Alabama Territory formed. (Same as present State of Alabama.)—March 3.
*JAMES MONROE inaugurated President.—"Era of good feeling."—March 4.
Seminoles and Creeks began depredations in Georgia and Alabama.
Mississippi admitted into the Union.—December 10.
1818 Jackson seized Spanish forts in Florida.
Joint occupation of Oregon by Great Britain and the United States agreed upon.—42° to 54° 40′ latitude. (See Map VI.)
Pensacola, Fla., seized by Jackson.—Spanish officials sent to Cuba.—May 27.
Illinois admitted into the Union.—December 3.
1819 FLORIDA ceded to the United States by Spain.—February 22.
Arkansas Territory formed. (See Map VI.)—July 4.
Alabama admitted into the Union.—December 14.
1820 *Accession of George IV to the throne of Great Britain.—January 29.
*MISSOURI COMPROMISE passed.—Slavery prohibited north of parallel from south boundary of Missouri to Pacific Ocean, but established in Missouri.—March 3.
Maine admitted into the Union.—March 15.
1821 Mexico became independent of Spain.—(See Map VI.)—February 24.
*Monroe began second presidential term.—March 5.
Missouri admitted into the Union. (See Map VI.)—August 10.
1822 Florida Territory formed.—March 3.
*"MONROE DOCTRINE" enunciated in the annual message.—December 2.
1824 *LAFAYETTE visited the United States.—August 24.
1825 *JOHN QUINCY ADAMS inaugurated President.—"Era of prosperity."—March 4.
1826 *Death of two ex-Presidents.—Adams and Jefferson.—July 4.
1829 *ANDREW JACKSON inaugurated President.—March 4.
PARTISAN APPOINTMENTS in the civil service began.
1830 *Accession of William IV to the throne of Great Britain.—June 26.
PETER COOPER'S ENGINE.—B. & O. R. R., the first to transport passengers.—August 28.
1831 *Death of ex-President Monroe.—July 4.
1832 BLACK HAWK WAR in Wisconsin and Illinois.
"Nullification" in South Carolina.—Convention met at Columbia.—Oct. 25.
1833 *Jackson began second presidential term.—March 4.
1834 Indian country formed. (See Note Period VI.)—June 30.
1835 *SEMINOLE WAR began in Florida.
Gen. Thompson and others killed at Ft. King, Fla.—December 28.
Major Dade and 100 men massacred in Florida.—December 28.
1836 Texas became independent of Mexico. (See Map VI.)—April 21.
Arkansas admitted into the Union. (See Map VI.)—June 15.
Wisconsin Territory formed. (See Map VI.)—July 4.
CREEK WAR began in Georgia.
1837 Michigan admitted into the Union.—Doubled the original 13.—January 26.
*MARTIN VAN BUREN inaugurated President.—March 4.
*Accession of Victoria to the throne of Great Britain.—June 20.
Battle of Okeechobee, Fla.—Taylor defeated the Indians.—December 25.
1838 Canadian rebellion.—Attempt to gain independence.
Iowa Territory formed. (See Map VI.)—July 4.
1841 *WILLIAM HENRY HARRISON inaugurated President.—March 4.
*DEATH OF PRESIDENT HARRISON.—April 4.
*JOHN TYLER inaugurated President.—April 6.
1842 *Close of the Seminole War.—Peace proclaimed.—August 14.
DORR'S REBELLION in Rhode Island.—Attempt to obtain a constitution.
1844 MORSE'S TELEGRAPH established between Baltimore and Washington.
1845 Florida admitted into the Union.—March 3.
Iowa admitted into the Union. (See Map VI.)—March 3.

George III.—Continued. | 1789.—Washington, 2 terms. | 1797.—John Adams, 1 term. | 1801.—Jefferson, 2 terms. | 1809.—Madison, 2 terms. | 1811.—Prince of Wales Regent. | 1817.—Monroe, 2 terms. | 1820.—George IV.—10 years. | 1825.—John Q. Adams, 1 term. | 1829.—Jackson, 2 terms. | 1830.—William IV.—7 years. | 1837.—Van Buren. | 1837.—Victoria. | 1841.—Harrison.—Tyler.

* Not on the map.

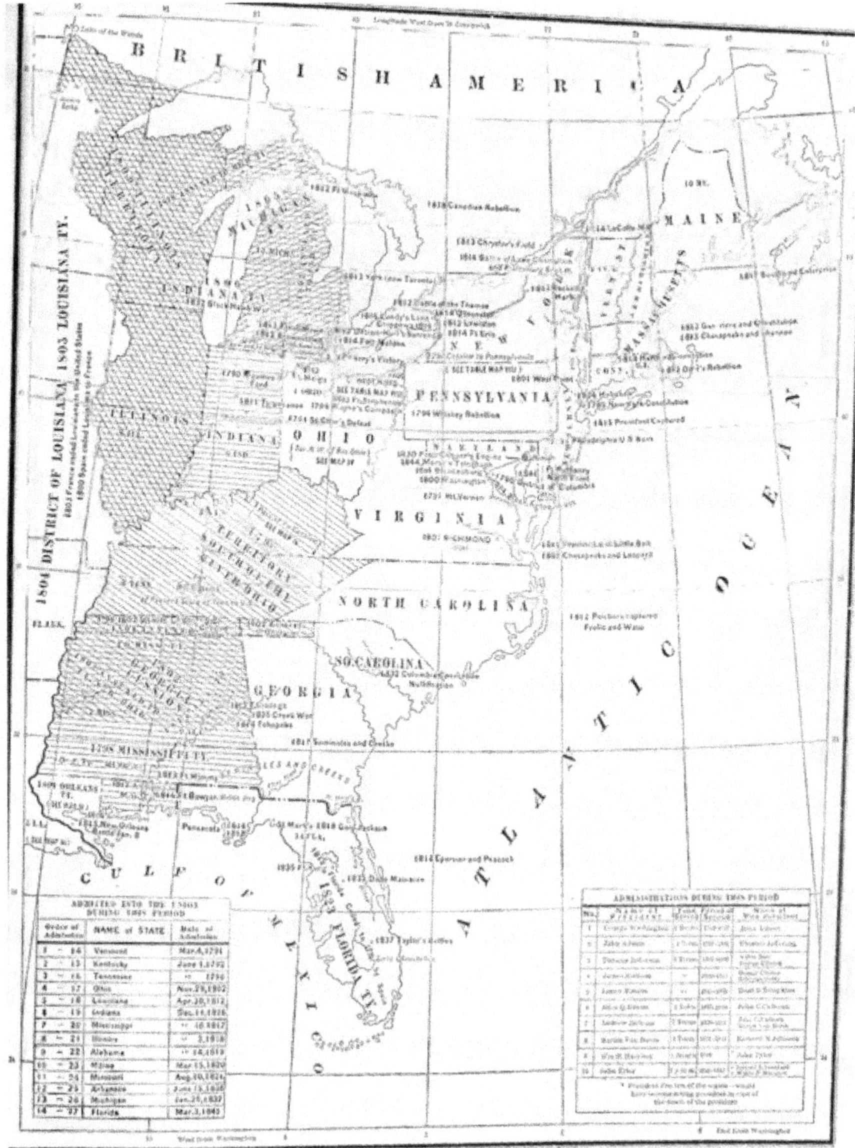
BRITISH AMERICA
MAINE
MASSACHUSETTS
NEW YORK
PENNSYLVANIA
1794 Whiskey Rebellion
OHIO
INDIANA
ILLINOIS
VIRGINIA
NORTH CAROLINA
SO. CAROLINA
GEORGIA
1798 MISSISSIPPI TY.
1804 DISTRICT OF LOUISIANA 1803 LOUISIANA TY.
1822 FLORIDA TY.
ATLANTIC OCEAN
GULF OF MEXICO
1815 New Orleans
Pensacola
1837 Taylor's Battles
1814 Epervier and Peacock
1835 Dade Massacre
1838 Canadian Rebellion
1807 Chesapeake and Leopard
1812 Potomac captured Frolic and Wasp
1815 President captured
Philadelphia U.S. Bank
1817 Seminoles and Creeks
ADMITTED INTO THE UNION DURING THIS PERIOD
ADMINISTRATIONS DURING THIS PERIOD

PERIOD VI. 1845 TO 1860. 15 YEARS.

DISSENSION.

1845 *JAMES K. POLK inaugurated President.—March 4.

*Naval Academy opened at Annapolis, Md.—October 10.

*Gun Cotton invented.

Texas admitted into the Union.—December 29.

1846 MEXICAN WAR.—Thornton's party captured east of the Rio Grande.—April 26.

Fort Brown bombarded from Matamoras.—May 3-9.

Taylor marched from Point Isabel to relieve Ft. Brown.—May 7.

BATTLE OF PALO ALTO.—Taylor defeated 6,000 Mexicans under Arista.—May 8.

Battle of Resaca de la Palma.—Taylor captured La Vega.—May 9.

Congress declared war to exist by act of Mexico.—May 13.

Matamoras captured by Taylor.—May 18.

Oregon boundary established by treaty with Great Britain.—June 15.

FREMONT defeated Californians at Sonoma, Cal.—June 25.

KEARNEY'S MARCH from Ft. Leavenworth, Kan., began.—June 30.

California declared independent by American settlers at Sonoma.—July 4.

Monterey, Cal., captured by Com. Sloat.—July 7.

California declared a part of the United States at Monterey.—July 7.

Yerba Buena, Cal. (now San Francisco), captured by Com. Montgomery.—July 9.

Com. Stockton arrived at Monterey, Cal.—July 23.

*WILMOT PROVISO offered, prohibiting slavery in acquired territory.—August 8.

Santa Fe, N. M., occupied by Kearney.—August 18.

Monterey, Mex., under Ampudia, captured by Taylor.—September 24.

DONIPHAN'S MARCH from Santa Fe to Saltillo.

Tampico, Mex., possessed by Com. Connor.—November 14.

Battle of Bracito, N. M.—Doniphan victorious.—December 25.

El Paso, Mex., occupied by Doniphan.—December 27.

Iowa re-admitted into the Union with present boundaries.—December 28.

1847 Battle of San Gabriel River, Cal.—Kearney defeated Californians.—January 8.

Yerba Buena named San Francisco.—January.

BATTLE OF BUENA VISTA.—Taylor's last battle.—Santa Anna defeated.—February 23.

Battle of Sacramento, Mex.—Doniphan victorious.—February 28.

VERA CRUZ and Ft. San Juan d'Ulloa surrendered to Scott.—March 27.

Battle of Cerro Gordo Pass.—Scott defeated Santa Anna.—April 18.

PUEBLA taken without a battle.—Scott remained three months.—May 15.

Mormons under Brigham Young arrived at Salt Lake Valley.—July 24.

BATTLE OF CONTRERAS.—Mexicans defeated in twenty minutes.—August 20.

Battle of Cherubusco.—Mexicans retreated.—August 20.

Worth captured Molino del Rey, outer defense of Chapultepec.—September 8.

FORTRESS OF CHAPULTEPEC captured.—September 13.

1847 CITY OF MEXICO entered by Americans under Scott.—September 14.

Lane defeated Santa Anna at Huamantla.—October 9.

1848 Gold discovered on a branch of the Sacramento, Cal.—January 19.

TREATY OF PEACE signed at Guadaloupe Hidalgo.—Feb. 2.

("First Mexican Cession" ceded to the United States.)

*John Quincy Adams died.—February 23.

Wisconsin admitted into the Union.—May 29.

Oregon Territory formed.—August 14.

*Ex-President Van Buren first candidate of the Free Soil Party.

1849 Minnesota Territory formed.—March 3.

*ZACHARY TAYLOR inaugurated president.—March 5.

1850 *DEATH OF PRESIDENT TAYLOR.—July 9.

*MILLARD FILLMORE inaugurated President.—July 10.

*COMPROMISE OF 1850, or "Omnibus Bill" passed.—September 9.

(Repealed Missouri Compromise of 1820.)

California admitted into the Union.—September 9.

Utah Territory formed.—September 9.

*Fugitive slave law passed.—September 18.

*Slave Trade prohibited in the District of Columbia.—September 17.

TEXAS CESSION of Territory to the General Government.—November 25.

Present Unorganized Territory a part of the Texas Cession.—November 25.

New Mexico Territory formed.—December 13.

1853 Washington Territory formed.—March 2.

*FRANKLIN PIERCE inaugurated President.—March 4.

*Death of Vice President William R. King at Cahawba, Ala.—April 18.

GADSDEN PURCHASE from Mexico.—December 30.

1854 KANSAS-NEBRASKA BILL, repealing Compromise of 1850, passed.—March 3.

Kansas Territory formed.—May 30.

Nebraska Territory formed.—May 30.

*Ostend Manifesto issued by American ministers.—October 21.

1855 *Kansas troubles.—Emigration from slave and free States.

*Niagara Suspension Bridge completed.

1857 *JAMES BUCHANAN inaugurated President.—March 4.

*DRED SCOTT DECISION.—Opinion delivered by Chief Justice Taney.—March 6.

Trouble with Mormons in Utah.—Military sent by the United States.

1858 Minnesota admitted into the Union.—May 11.

*FIRST MESSAGE by the Atlantic Cable.—August 16.

1859 Oregon admitted into the Union.—February 14.

JOHN BROWN seized United States Arsenal at Harper's Ferry. (See Map VII.)—October 16.

*Victoria Bridge, Montreal, opened.

NOTE.—In 1834 Missouri Territory became the Indian Country. That part of the Territory east of the Missouri and White Earth Rivers, except a parcel in the Northwestern part of the present State of Missouri, as shown on the map, was annexed to Michigan Territory. These changes could not be shown by the parallel lines without confusion. (See Map VI and Table following Map VIII.)

*Not on the Map.

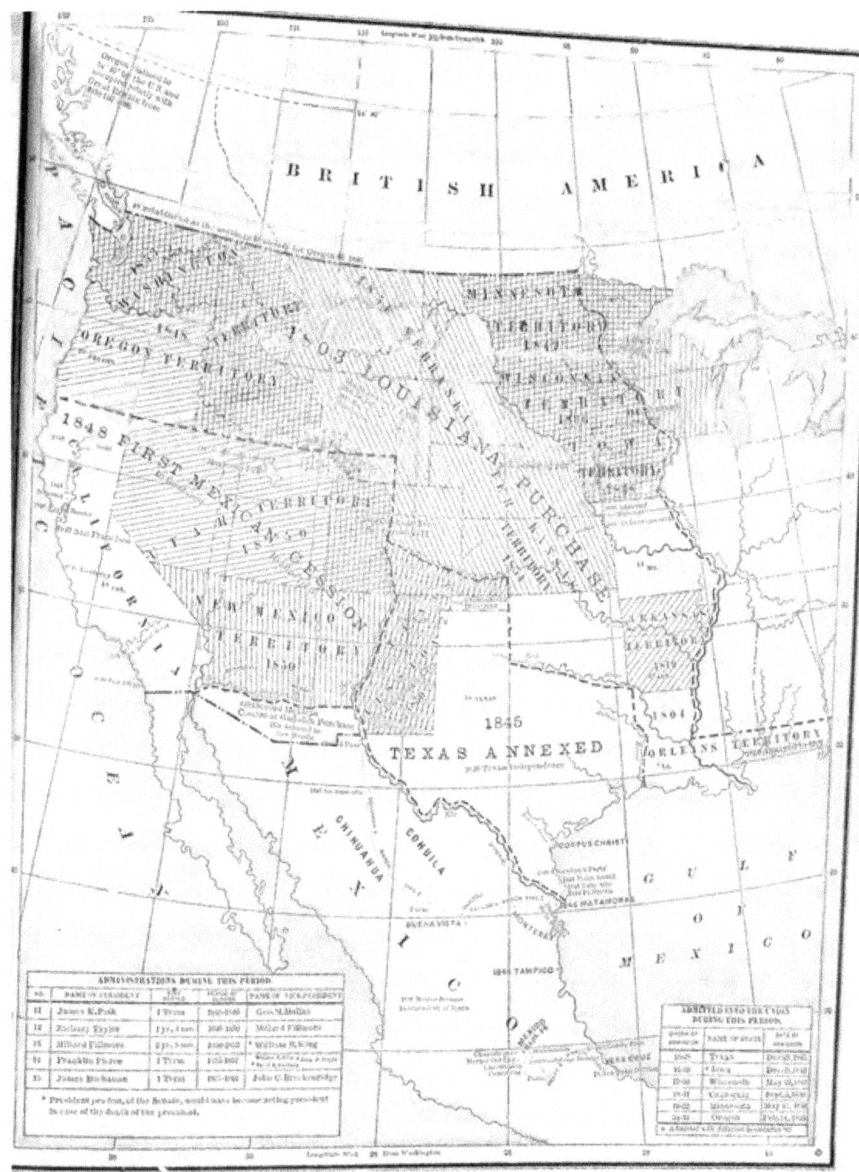
BRITISH AMERICA
PACIFIC OCEAN
WASHINGTON TERRITORY
1848 OREGON TERRITORY
1803 LOUISIANA PURCHASE
NEBRASKA TERRITORY
1854
KANSAS TERRITORY
1854
MINNESOTA TERRITORY
1849
WISCONSIN TERRITORY
1836
IOWA TERRITORY
1838
1848 FIRST MEXICAN CESSION
CALIFORNIA
UTAH TERRITORY
1850
NEW MEXICO TERRITORY
1850
ARKANSAS TERRITORY
1819
1845
TEXAS ANNEXED
1804
ORLEANS TERRITORY
MEXICO
CHIHUAHUA
COAHUILA
CORPUS CHRISTI
1846 MATAMORAS
MONTEREY
BUENA VISTA
1846 TAMPICO
VERA CRUZ
GULF OF MEXICO
ADMINISTRATIONS DURING THIS PERIOD

PERIOD VII. 1860 TO 1865. 5 YEARS.

SECESSION.

1860 SOUTH CAROLINA seceded.—(For seceding States see table on map)—December 20.

1861 Star of the West fired upon off Charleston Harbor.—January 9.
Kansas admitted into the Union.—January 29.
CONFEDERATE GOVERNMENT organized at Montgomery, Ala.—February 8.
*JEFFERSON DAVIS, president; ALEXANDER H. STEPHENS, vice-president.—February 9.
Colorado Territory formed.—(See Map VIII.)—February 28.
Dakota Territory formed.—(See Map VIII.)—March 2.
Nevada Territory formed.—(See Map VIII.)—March 2.
*ABRAHAM LINCOLN inaugurated president.—March 4.
FT. SUMTER, S. C., bombarded by Beauregard.—April 12.
United States arsenal at Harper's Ferry destroyed by Federals.—April 18.
Gosport navy-yard destroyed by Federals (Norfolk, Va.).—April 20.
Battle of Philippi, W. Va.—Confederate defeat.—June 3.
BATTLE OF BIG BETHEL, Va.—Pierce defeated.—June 10.
Battle of Romney, Va.—Federal victory.—June 11.
Battle of Boonville, Mo.—Lyon victorious.—June 17.
Battle of Carthage, Mo.—Gov. Jackson and Sigel.—Indecisive.—July 5.
Battle of Rich Mountain, W. Va.—Rosecrans victorious.—July 11.
Battle near Centreville, Va.—July 18.
CONFEDERATE CAPITAL changed to Richmond, Va.—July 20.
BATTLE OF BULL RUN, Va.—McDowell defeated.—July 21.
Battle of Dug Spring, Mo.—Lyon victorious.—August 2.
Battle of Wilson's Creek, Mo.—Lyon killed.—August 10.
BATTLE OF HATTERAS INLET, N. C.—Federal victory.—August 28-29.
Columbus, Ky., seized and fortified by Confederates.—September 4.
Grant occupied Paducah, Ky.—September 6.
BATTLE OF LEXINGTON, Mo.—Price defeated Mulligan.—September 12-20.
BATTLE OF BALL'S BLUFF or EDWARDS' FERRY.—Baker killed.—October 21.
*Scott retired and McClellan appointed general-in-chief.—November 1.
Battle of Port Royal Entrance, S. C.—Federals victorious.—November 7.
Battle of Belmont, Mo.—Grant and Polk.—Indecisive.—November 7.
*MASON AND SLIDELL taken from the Trent.—November 8.

1862 Battle of Mill Springs, Ky.—Thomas victorious.—January 19-20.
Ft. Henry, Tenn., captured by Foote.—February 6.
Battle of Roanoke Island, N. C.—Burnside victorious.—February 8.
Ft. Donelson, Tenn., surrendered to Grant.—February 16.
Battle of Pea Ridge, Ark.—Curtis victorious.—March 6-8.
THE VIRGINIA (Merrimac) destroyed the Cumberland and Congress at Hampton Roads, Va.—March 8.
BATTLE BETWEEN THE VIRGINIA AND MONITOR at Hampton Roads, Va.—March 9.
Battle of New Madrid, Mo.—Pope victorious.—March 14.
Battle of New Bern, N. C.—Burnside victorious.—March 14.
Battle near Winchester, Va.—Shields victorious.—March 23.
BATTLE OF PITTSBURG LANDING or SHILOH, Tenn.—Grant defeated Beauregard.—A. S. Johnson killed.—20,000 men lost.—April 6-7.
ISLAND No. 10, with 6,000 men, captured by Foote and Pope.—April 7.
Battle of Ft. Pulaski, Ga.—Gillmore victorious.—April 10-11.
FARRAGUT'S FLEET passed Fts. Jackson and St. Philip, La.—April 24.
NEW ORLEANS, La., captured by Farragut's fleet.—April 25.
New Orleans, La., occupied by Federals under Butler.—May 1.
Battle of Williamsburg, Va.—McClellan victorious.—May 5.
Norfolk, Va., captured by Wool.—May 10.
Hanover Courthouse, Va., captured by Fitz John Porter.—May 27.
Beauregard evacuated Corinth, Miss.—May 27.
BATTLE OF SEVEN PINES AND FAIR OAKS, Va.—McClellan victorious.—May 31 and June 1.
*LEE appointed to chief command of the Confederate army.—June 3.
Gunboat fight near Ft. Pillow, Tenn.—June 4.
Davis, successor of Foote, captured Memphis, Tenn.—June 6.
SEVEN DAYS' BATTLES in Virginia.—McClellan and Lee.—June 26 to July 1.
(Mechanicsville, June 26; Gaines' Mill, 27; Chickahominy, 28; Savage's Station, 29; White Oak Swamp, 29-30; Glendale, 30; Malvern Hill, July 1.)
Battle of Cedar Mountain, Va.—Jackson victorious.—Winder killed.—August 9.
*Sioux war in Minnesota began.—August.
POPE'S BATTLES between Manassas and Washington, D. C.—August 26 to September 1.
(The more important were Groveton, August 29; second Bull Run, 30; Chantilly, September 1.—Victorious campaign for Lee.—Kearney and Stevens killed.)
Battle of Richmond, Ky.—Kirby Smith victorious.—August 30.
INVASION OF MARYLAND by Lee.—Crossed the Potomac near Point of Rocks.—September 4-7.
BATTLE OF SOUTH MOUNTAIN, Md.—McClellan victorious.—September 14.
HARPER'S FERRY, with 12,000 men, surrendered to Jackson by Miles.—September 15.
BATTLE OF ANTIETAM, Md.—McClellan and Lee.—September 17.
Munfordville, Ky., captured by Confederates.—September 17.
Battle of Iuka, Miss.—Rosecrans victorious.—September 19-20.
BATTLE OF CORINTH, Miss.—Rosecrans victorious.—October 3-4.
Battle of Perryville, Ky.—Unsuccessful attack by Bragg.—October 8.
Battle of Prairie Grove, Ark.—Blunt victorious.—December 7.
BATTLE OF FREDERICKSBURG, Va.—Lee victorious.—Federals lost 12,000 men.—December 13.
Battle of Kinston, N. C.—Foster victorious.—December 14.
BATTLE OF STONE RIVER or MURFREESBORO', Tenn.—December 31 to January 3.
(One of the fiercest of the war.—Rosecrans victorious.)

1863 *EMANCIPATION PROCLAMATION issued by Lincoln.—January 1.
Battle of Ft. Hindman or Arkansas Post.—McClernand victorious.—Jan. 11.
SECOND EXPEDITION TO THE YAZOO.—Grant arrived at Young's Point, La.—February 2.
Arizona Territory formed.—(See Map VIII.)—February 24.
*NATIONAL BANK ACT Approved.—February 25.
Idaho Territory formed.—(See Map VIII.)—March 3.
THIRD EXPEDITION TO THE YAZOO, under Porter.—March 15.

1863 Ft. Sumter, S. C. bombarded by the Federals.—Repulsed unsuccessful.—April 7.
Grierson's cavalry raid through Mississippi.—Left La Grange, Tenn., April 17.
Battle of Port Gibson, Miss.—McClernand victorious.—May 1.
BATTLE OF CHANCELLORSVILLE, Va.—Lee victorious.—Federals lost 17,000 men.—May 2-3.
BATTLE OF FREDERICKSBURG, Va.—Early victorious.—May 3-4.
Battle of Raymond, Miss.—McPherson victorious.—May 12.
Battle of Big Black River, Miss.—McClernand victorious.—May 17.
Battle of Vicksburg, Miss.—Federals repulsed.—May 22.
Battle of Port Hudson, La.—Federals repulsed.—May 27.
Battle of Brandy Station, Va., by cavalry.—Gregg victorious.—June 9.
*MARYLAND AND PENNSYLVANIA invaded by Lee.—June.
West Virginia admitted into the Union.—June 20.
Morgan's raid.—Crossed the Cumberland River near Burkesville, Ky.—June 22.
BATTLE OF GETTYSBURG, Pa.—Meade and Lee.—50,000 men lost.—July 1-3.
Battle of Helena, Ark.—Attack by Holmes repulsed.—July 4.
SURRENDER OF VICKSBURG to Grant by Pemberton.—July 4.
PORT HUDSON, La., surrendered to Banks.—July 8.
*Riots in New York City.—opposition to the draft.—July 13-16.
Jackson, Miss., destroyed by Sherman.—July 16.
Ft. Wagner, S. C., captured by Federals.—September 6.
Chattanooga, Tenn., occupied by Crittenden.—September 9.
Little Rock, Ark., occupied by Steele.—September 10.
BATTLE OF CHICKAMAUGA, Ga.—Bragg victorious.—Rosecrans lost 16,000 men.—September 19-20.
BATTLES OF CHATTANOOGA AND LOOKOUT MOUNTAIN.—Federals defeat Bragg.—November 23-25.
Battle of Knoxville, Tenn.—Longstreet raised the siege.—December 4.

1864 Sherman's raid from Vicksburg,—reached Meridian, Miss.—February 14.
Battle of Olustee or Ocean Pond, Fla.—Finnegan defeated Seymour.—February 20.
BANKS' RED RIVER EXPEDITION moved up the river.—March 12.
Battle of Mansfield or Sabine Cross-roads.—Banks defeated.—April 8.
Battle of Pleasant Hill, La.—Banks victorious.—April 9.
Battle of Ft. Pillow, Tenn.—Captured by Forrest.—April 12.
Plymouth, N. C., surrendered to Confederates under Hoke.—April 20.
Bermuda Hundred seized and intrenched by Butler.—May 5.
BATTLES OF THE WILDERNESS.—Between Grant and Lee.—40,000 men lost.—May 5-6.
SHERMAN'S GEORGIA CAMPAIGN, with 100,000 men began from Chattanooga, Tenn.—May 7.
BATTLE OF SPOTTSYLVANIA COURT-HOUSE, Va.—30,000 men lost.—May 10.
BATTLE OF RESACA, Ga.—Sherman defeated Johnston.—May 13-15.
Battle of Newmarket, Va.—Sigel defeated.—May 15.
BATTLES OF NORTH ANNA, Va.—Federals victorious.—May 23-27.
Montana Territory formed.—(See Map VIII.)—May 26.
Battle of Dallas, Ga.—Sherman victorious.—May 25-28.
Battle of Totopotomoy Creek, Va.—May 30.
BATTLE OF COLD HARBOR, Va.—Grant repulsed by Lee.—June 1-3.
BATTLE OF PETERSBURG, Va.—Grant repulsed.—10,000 men lost.—June 15-18.
Siege of Petersburg, Va., by Grant began.—June 18.
*THE ALABAMA sunk by the Kearsarge off Cherbourg, France.—June 19.
Battle of Kenesaw Mountain, Ga.—Sherman repulsed.—June 27.
INVASION OF MARYLAND by Early.—Washington, D. C., threatened.—July 5-21.
Battle of Monocacy, Md.—Early defeated by Wallace.—July 9.
BATTLES AT ATLANTA, Ga.—Sherman victorious.—McPherson and Walker killed.—July 20-28.
Chambersburg, Pa., attacked and burned by McCausland.—July 30.
BATTLE OF PETERSBURG.—Explosion of mine.—Federal repulse.—July 30.
BATTLE OF MOBILE BAY, Ala.—Farragut victorious.—August 5.
Weldon Railroad, running south from Richmond, seized by Federals.—August 18.
Battle of Ream's Station, Va.—Weldon Railroad.—Hancock repulsed.—August 25.
Battle of Jonesboro', Ga.—Sherman victorious.—August 31 and September 1.
ATLANTA, Ga., occupied by Sherman.—September 2.
Battle of Winchester, Va.—Sheridan victorious.—September 19.
Battle of Fisher's Hill, Va.—Sheridan victorious.—September 22.
Nevada admitted into the Union.—(See Map VIII.)—October 31.
BATTLE OF FRANKLIN, Tenn.—Schofield victorious.—November 30.
Ft. McAllister, Ga., captured by Hazen.—December 13.
Battle of Nashville, Tenn.—Thomas victorious.—December 15-16.
SAVANNAH, Ga., occupied by Sherman's army.—December 22.

1865 FT. FISHER, N. C., captured by Porter and Terry.—January 15.
SHERMAN'S MARCH northward from Savannah, Ga.—February 1.
COLUMBIA, S. C., surrendered to Federals.—Sherman's march.—February 17.
Charleston, S. C., occupied by Federals.—Sherman's march.—February 18.
Wilmington, N. C., captured by Schofield.—February 22.
*Lincoln began second presidential term.—March 4.
Battle of Averysboro', N. C.—Sherman victorious.—March 16.
Battle of Bentonville, N. C.—Sherman victorious.—March 19.
Armies of Sherman, Terry and Schofield united at Goldsboro', N. C.—March 23.
BATTLE OF FT. STEDMAN, at Petersburg, Va.—Indecisive.—March 25.
Battle of Dinwiddie Court-house, Va.—Sheridan victorious.—March 31.
BATTLE OF FIVE FORKS, Va.—Sheridan victorious.—April 1.
BATTLE OF PETERSBURG, Va.—Grant carried outer lines.—April 1-2.
Battle of Selma, Ala.—Wilson captured the city.—April 2.
PETERSBURG AND RICHMOND occupied by Grant.—April 3.
LEE SURRENDERED TO GRANT at Appomattox Court-house, Va.—April 9.
Mobile, Ala., occupied by Canby.—April 12.
PRESIDENT LINCOLN assassinated at Washington, D. C.—April 14.
*ANDREW JOHNSON inaugurated President.—April 15.

*Not on the map.

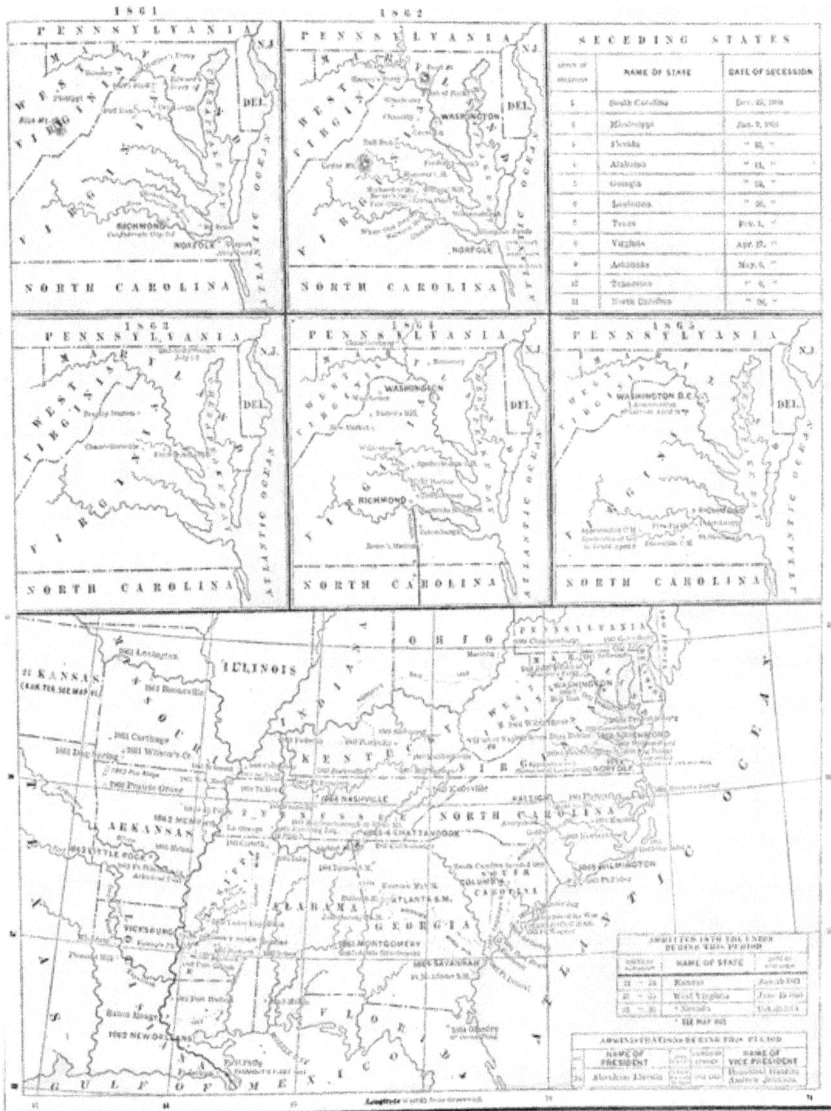
1861
1862
1863
1864
1865
PENNSYLVANIA
N.J.
DEL.
WEST VIRGINIA
VIRGINIA
MARYLAND
WASHINGTON
RICHMOND
NORFOLK
NORTH CAROLINA
ATLANTIC OCEAN
SECEDING STATES
NAME OF STATE
DATE OF SECESSION
South Carolina
Mississippi
Florida
Alabama
Georgia
Louisiana
Texas
Virginia
Arkansas
Tennessee
North Carolina
WASHINGTON D.C.
KANSAS
ILLINOIS
OHIO
KENTUCKY
ARKANSAS
ALABAMA
GEORGIA
FLORIDA
1864 NASHVILLE
1862 NEW ORLEANS
VICKSBURG
1861 MONTGOMERY
1865 SAVANNAH
1865 WILMINGTON
GULF OF MEXICO
SEE MAP 103

PERIOD VIII. 1865 TO 1891. 26 YEARS.

PEACE.

Johnson—Continued. Victoria—Continued.

1865 *Thirteenth Amendment to the Constitution declared in force.—December 18.
1866 *Fenian raids into Canada.
Tennessee reconstructed by act of July 24.
Civil War proclaimed at an end.—August 20.
1867 Nebraska admitted into the Union.—March 1.
*Reconstruction Act passed over President's veto.—March 2.
*Tenure of Office Act passed over President's veto.—March 2.
Downfall of Maximilian in Mexico. (Shot at Queretaro.)—June 19.
Alaska purchased of Russia.—June 20.
Dominion of Canada established.—July 1.
1868 *Secretary Stanton declared removed from office by President Johnson.—February 21.
*Johnson's impeachment trial began.—March 30.
*Johnson acquitted by a vote of 35 to 19, not two-thirds.—May 26.
Arkansas reconstructed.—June 22.
Alabama, Florida, Georgia, Louisiana and North Carolina reconstructed.—June 25.
Wyoming Territory formed.—July 25.
*Fourteenth Amendment to the Constitution declared in force.—July 28.
*General amnesty proclaimed by President Johnson.—December 25.

1869—Grant, two terms.

1869 *Ulysses S. Grant inaugurated President.—March 4.
PACIFIC RAILROAD (Union and Central) completed.—May 10. (Length, 1,930 miles; cost, $252,000,000.)
WOMAN SUFFRAGE in Wyoming.—December 6.
1870 Virginia reconstructed.—January 27.
Mississippi reconstructed.—February 3.
*Fenian raids into Canada resumed.
Texas reconstructed.—March 30.
*Fifteenth Amendment to the Constitution declared in force.—March 30.
*War between France and Germany began July 19; ended May 10, 1871.
(Sales of arms difficulties in the United States resulted from this war.)
1871 National Park established in Yellowstone Valley.—February 28.
*LEGAL-TENDER LAWS declared constitutional by the Supreme Court.—May 1.
Fire at Chicago, Ill.—Estimated loss, $300,000,000.—October 10-12.
*TREATY OF WASHINGTON, providing for arbitration on the Alabama claims, etc., agreed upon by Joint High Commission.—December 15.
*CIVIL SERVICE REFORM.—Commission established by act of March 3, promulgated report December 19.
1872 *National Bureau of Education established.—February 8.
*GENEVA AWARD.—$15,500,000 awarded to the United States by the arbitrators on the Alabama claims, etc.—September 14.
SAN JUAN boundary dispute decided in favor of the United States.—San Juan Island to the United States.—October 21.
Fire at Boston, Mass.—Estimated loss, $100,000,000.—Nov. 9-10.
Modoc war in California began.—November 29.
1873 *Credit Mobilier.—Committee appointed December 2, 1872, to investigate frauds in the construction of the Pacific Railroad reported.—February 24.
*"Salary Grab" act passed.—March 3.
*Grant began second presidential term.—March 4.
1875 *Act providing for specie payments on January 1, 1879, approved.—January 14.
*Death of Vice-President Wilson, at Washington, D. C.—November 22.
Thomas W. Ferry, President *pro tempore* of the Senate.
1876 Centennial Exhibition opened at Philadelphia, May 10; closed November 10.
Colorado admitted into the Union.—August 1.
*Presidential election.—November 7.
(Contest between the Republican and Democratic parties as to its validity.)

1877—Hayes.

1877 *ELECTORAL COMMISSION provided for by act of January 29.
*Hayes and Wheeler declared elected by Congress.—March 2.
*Rutherford B. Hayes inaugurated President.—March 5.
*President Hayes' civil service order issued.—June 22.
*War between Russia and Turkey began.—Ended 1878.
Railroad riots at Pittsburgh, Albany, Chicago, St. Louis, etc.—July 22-24.
1878 Yellow fever in Louisiana, Mississippi, Tennessee, Kentucky, etc.
*Silver dollar made legal tender over President's veto.—Feb. 28.
*Gold sells at par in Wall street.—December 17.
1879 *RESUMPTION OF SPECIE PAYMENTS.—Act of January 14, 1875.—January 1.
*Jeannette sails from San Francisco to North Pole.—July 9.
1880 *Increasing Emigration.—456,000 immigrants arrived during year ending December 31.
*Population of United States over 50,000,000.—Tenth census.

1881—Garfield—Arthur.

1881 *James A. Garfield inaugurated President.—March 4.
President Garfield shot at Washington, D. C.—July 2.
*Death of President Garfield at Long Branch, N. J.—Sept. 19.
*Chester A. Arthur inaugurated President, at New York City.—September 19.
*500,000 immigrants arrived in the United States during the nine months ending September 30.
Centennial Celebration at Yorktown.—October 19.
*Survivors of Jeannette heard from.—December 20.
1882 *Terrible accident at Spuyten Duyvil, N. Y.—January 13.
*Guiteau, the assassin, found guilty, January 25.—Hung June 30.
*Transit of Venus.—December 6.
1883 *New York and Brooklyn Bridge opened.—May 24.
*Great Strike of Telegraphers' Brotherhood in the U. S.—July 19—August 18.
*Northern Pacific Railroad open for traffic.—September 8.
*Two Cent Letter Postage goes into effect throughout the U. S.—October 1.
*Lord Lansdowne inaugurated Governor-General of Canada vice the Marquis of Lorne.—October 23.
1884 *Bodies of Jeannette explorers arrive in New York.—February 20.
Washington Monument completed.—December 6.
Opening of "World's Fair and Cotton Centennial Exposition" in New Orleans.—December 16.

1885—Cleveland.

1885 Dedication of Washington Monument.—February 21.
*GROVER CLEVELAND inaugurated President.—March 4.
Rebellion in Saskatchewan, British America, began March 25; Riel captured May 15, and executed at Regina.—November 16.
*Revised Old Testament published.—May 21.
*Bartholdi Statue of Liberty arrived in New York.—June 19.
Niagara Park thrown open to the public.—July 15.
GENERAL U. S. GRANT died at Mount McGregor, N. Y., July 23, and buried at Riverside Park, N. Y.—August 8.
Flood Rock, East River, blown up.—October 10.
*Gen. Geo. B. McClellan died.—October 29.
*Vice-President Thos. A. Hendricks died.—November 25.
*Wm. H. Vanderbilt, the noted millionaire, died.—December 8.
*U. S. Senate passed the Presidential Succession bill.—Dec. 17.
1886 *Gen. Winfield S. Hancock died.—February 9.
*Horatio Seymour died.—February 12.
*John B. Gough, noted temperance lecturer, died.—February 18.
*Great labor agitations throughout the U. S.—May 1.
*Railroad strike in the Southwest ended.—May 4.
Anarchists explode a dynamite bomb, killing and wounding many policemen and citizens, at Haymarket Square, Chicago.—May 4.
*Odell, Ill., wrecked by the wind.—May 22.
Grover Cleveland, President of U. S., married to Miss Frances Folsom.—June 2.
Judge David Davis died at Bloomington, Ill.—June 26.
Samuel J. Tilden died.—August 4.
The Great Anarchist Trial commenced at Chicago, Ill., at 10 a. m., June 21, and ended at 10 a. m. August 20. The jury brought in a verdict of murder in the first degree in the case of seven of defendants, and one to serve fifteen years in prison.—June 21, August 20.
Dedication of the famous Bartholdi statue of "Liberty Enlightening the World."—October 28.
Death of Ex-President Chester A. Arthur.—November 18.
Death of General John A. Logan.—December 26.
1887 The Inter-state Commerce bill passes the Senate.—January 14.
The President signs the Inter-state Commerce bill.—February 4.
Rev. Henry Ward Beecher died.—March 8.
Wm. A. Wheeler, ex-Vice-President of U. S., died.—June 4.
Terrible railroad accident near Chatsworth, Ill.; nearly 100 killed.—Aug. 10.
Gov. Oglesby commutes the sentence of Samuel Fielden and Michael Schwab, the Chicago Anarchists, to imprisonment for life.—November 10. Louis Lingg commits suicide.—Nov. 10. August Spies, A. R. Parsons, Adolph Fischer and Geo. Engel executed.—Nov. 11.
1888 Terrible blizzard in New York and vicinity.—March 12-13.
Ex-Senator Roscoe Conkling died.—April 18.
Democratic National Convention at St. Louis nominated Grover Cleveland, of New York, for President, and Allen G. Thurman, of Ohio, for Vice-President.—June 6.
Republican National Convention at Chicago nominated Benjamin Harrison, of Indiana, for President, and Levi P. Morton, of New York, for Vice-President.—June 25.
Philip H. Sheridan, General of U. S. Army, died.—Aug. 5.
The President signed the Chinese Exclusion Bill.—Oct. 1.
The Presidential and Congressional Elections were held. Benjamin Harrison was elected President of U. S., and Levi P. Morton, Vice-President.—Nov. 6.

1889—Harrison.

1889 The President signs bill making the following new States: North Dakota, South Dakota, Montana and Washington.—Feb. 22.
President Benjamin Harrison and Vice-President Levi P. Morton inaugurated.—March 4.
The proclamation opening the Territory of Oklahoma, was issued by the President, March 23, the proclamation to take effect April 22, at high noon.
Centennial celebration throughout the United States.—April 30.
Terrible flood at Johnstown, Pa., caused by bursting of a reservoir. The entire valley of the Conemaugh flooded. Loss of life estimated about 5,000. Loss of property almost incalculable.—May 31, June 1.
The business portion of Seattle, Washington, destroyed by fire.—June 6.
Disastrous fire at Spokane Falls, Washington.—August 4.
The Cronin trial began August 26, ended December 16. John F. Beggs was acquitted; John Kunze, guilty of manslaughter, three years, and Daniel Coughlin, Patrick O'Sullivan and Martin Burke receive life sentences.
1890 Terrible storm passes over the Mississippi Valley.—March 27.
Samuel J. Randall died.—April 13.
Great floods in Mississippi Valley during April.
The World's Fair bill passed the Senate.—April 21.
President Harrison signs the World's Fair Bill.—April 25.
Monument to Robert E. Lee was unveiled at Richmond, Va.—May 29.
Idaho became a State.—July 3.
Wyoming became a State.—July 10.
Death of Gen. Clinton B. Fisk.—July 9.
Death of Major-General John C. Fremont.—July 13.
The McKinley Tariff bill signed by President Harrison.—Oct. 1.
New Tariff bill went into effect.—Oct. 6.
Outbreak of the Indians.—Dec.
Death of Sitting Bull.—Dec. 15.
The President issued a proclamation announcing the fact that the World's Fair will be held in Chicago in 1893.—Dec. 24th.
Death of Gen. F. E. Spinner, Ex-Treasurer of U. S.—Dec. 31.
1891 Death of Wm. Windom, Secretary of the Treasury.—Jan. 29.
Death of Admiral David D. Porter.—Feb. 13.
Death of Gen. W. T. Sherman.—Feb. 14.
A mob in New Orleans attack the jail and kill eleven Italians who were indicted for the murder of David Hennessey. Intense excitement all over the country.—March 14.
Death of P. T. Barnum, the great showman.—April 7.

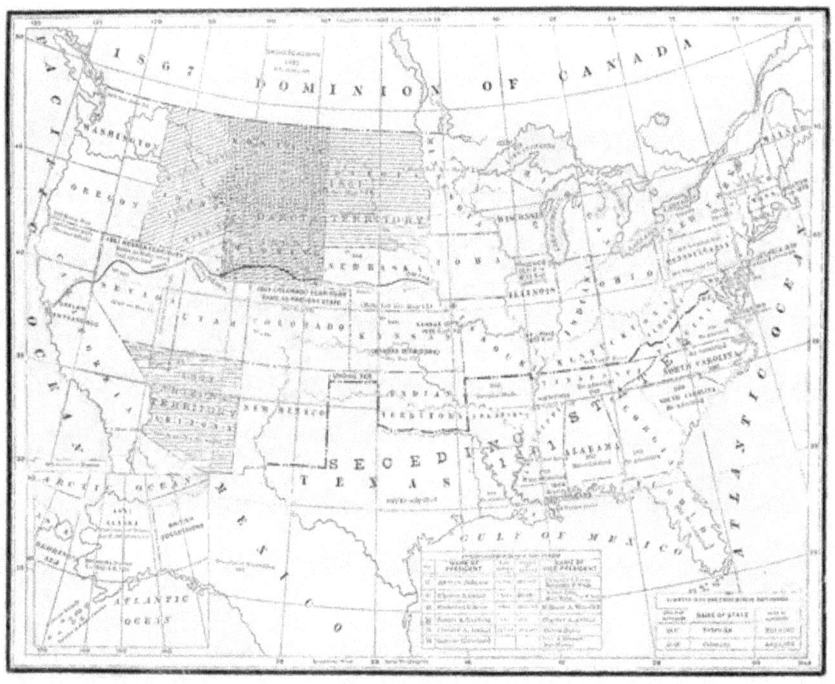

1867 DOMINION OF CANADA
WASHINGTON
OREGON
DAKOTA TERRITORY
NEBRASKA
IOWA
NEVADA
UTAH
COLORADO
ILLINOIS
OHIO
NEW MEXICO
INDIAN TERRITORY
NORTH CAROLINA
ALABAMA
SECEDING
TEXAS
MEXICO
GULF OF MEXICO
ATLANTIC OCEAN
ARCTIC OCEAN
ATLANTIC OCEAN

EXISTENT AND OBSOLETE DIVISIONS OF THE UNITED STATES.[*]

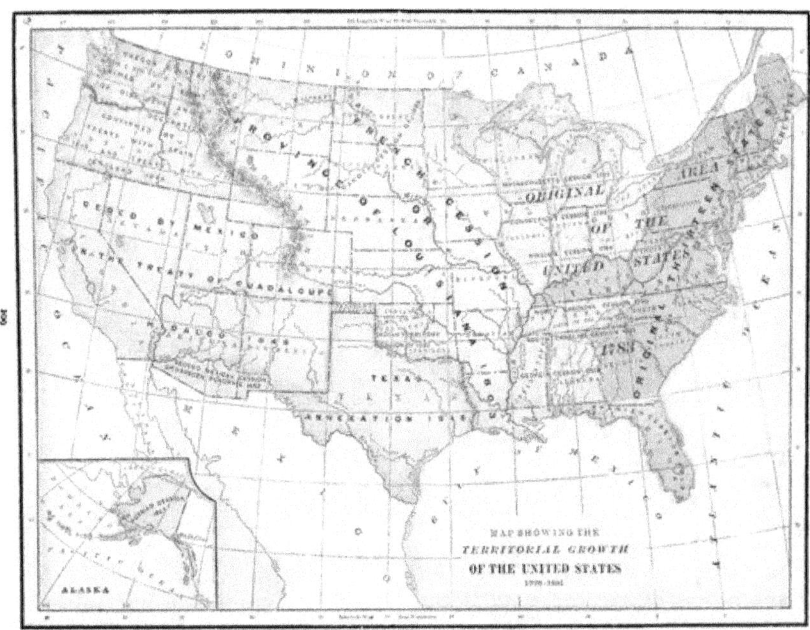
DOMINION OF CANADA
PROVINCE
FRENCH CESSION
OF LOUISIANA
ORIGINAL
AREA
OF THE
UNITED STATES
1783
ORIGINAL THIRTEEN STATES
CEDED BY MEXICO
BY THE TREATY OF GUADALUPE
HIDALGO 1848
TEXAS
ANNEXATION 1845
ALASKA
MAP SHOWING THE
TERRITORIAL GROWTH
OF THE UNITED STATES

POLITICAL PARTIES OF THE UNITED STATES.

INTRODUCTION — PROGRESS OF THE COLONIES TO NATIONAL UNION, 1607-1789.

First Steps Toward Colonial Liberty and Union, 1607-43.

1607 First permanent English settlement in America, at Jamestown, Virginia—105 persons, with few laborers or artisans and no families. The planting of English colonies in America had been provided for, the year before, by two royal letters-patent, to the London and Plymouth companies.

∴ The government of England at that time was a monarchy limited by Magna Charta, [illegible]

1614. New Amsterdam, now New York, and Fort Orange, now Albany, occupied by Dutch **traders**, in virtue of the discovery of that region, five years **before**, by Henry Hudson, in the service of the Netherlands.

1619. First representative government in America, the general assembly of Virginia, composed of a governor, council and two representatives from each **town** or "hundred." Slavery introduced into Virginia by **the** purchase of twenty African slaves from Dutch traders.

∴ The political troubles in England and the persecution of Puritans and Independents [illegible] many of them to emigrate. Their principles of brotherhood, freedom and equality, [illegible] by the qualification of church fellowship, [illegible] took deep root in America.

1620. Arrival of the Pilgrim Fathers (refugees in Holland since 1608) at Cape Cod, in New England, (so named in 1614). First political union of free and equal men **formed** by them in "The Compact of Liberty," **as** follows: "**In** the name of God, Amen. We, whose names **are** hereunder written, (41 male adults,) the loyal subjects of **our dread** sovereign lord, King James . . . having undertaken **for the** glory of God and advancement of the Christian **Faith** and honor of our king and country, a voyage to **plant the** first colony in the northern part of Virginia, do **by these** presents, solemnly and mutually, in the presence **of God and one** another, covenant and combine ourselves **together into a** civil body politic for our better ordering and **preservation** and furtherance of the ends aforesaid, and by **virtue** hereof, to enact, constitute and frame such just and **equal laws**, ordinances, acts, constitutions and offices, from **time to time**, as shall be thought most meet and convenient **for** the general good of the colony, unto which **we** promise all due submission and obedience. In witness whereof we have hereunto subscribed our names at Cape Cod, this eleventh day of November. . . . Anno Domini, 1620. Plymouth Colony founded by the Pilgrim Fathers.

∴ In England, growing hatred of despotism and love of freedom. Puritans, Independents, [illegible] royalists [illegible] supporters of the divine right of kings. Parliament [illegible] the king. The rise of political parties in the modern sense: the Court and Country parties.

1621. First written constitution, given to Virginia, granted an elective legislature and **trial by** jury. First Navigation Act, prescribing export **of Virginia** tobacco direct to England. First Charter or patent to John Pierce and associates from the Council of Plymouth, for the benefit of the Plymouth colony.

1623. Settlements at Dover and Portsmouth in Laconia, now New Hampshire, under patents to Mason and Gorges. First permanent settlement in New Netherlands of thirty Walloon families, **at** and **near** New Amsterdam.

1624. Virginia made a royal province, its measure **of** independence and freedom giving offense **to** the king, **who** now entrusted its government to **a governor and** twelve councillors, chosen by himself.

∴ First debate on colonial affairs in parliament: "America," said Calvert, "is not annexed to the realm nor within the jurisdiction of parliament; you have therefore no right to interfere." "We make laws for Virginia," said a member, "a bill passed by the Commons and the Lords, if it receives the king's assent, will control the patent." [illegible]

1627. Purchase by the Plymouth colonists from the non-emigrating members, of the **remaining** interest in the colony.

1628. First Union of **New England settlements** for the suppression of Morton **of Merry Mount, now** Braintree, Mass.

∴ In England, "The Petition of Rights," embodying the most pressing grievances, agreed to by both houses and reluctantly accepted by the king.

1629. First Charter to the Governor and Colony of Massachusetts Bay. Arrival of Puritans at Salem and Charlestown. The government transferred to the colonists, with the right to elect governor, deputy-governor and eighteen assistants, constituting the "General Court" or legislature. In New Netherlands, the establishment of "Patroons," or founders of colonies of not less than fifty persons, with the right of lordship or government under a "Charter of Liberties," granted by the Dutch West India Company.

∴ Parliament dissolved and not again convened for eleven years, because of its opposition to arbitrary taxation by the king.

1630. Charter of Plymouth colony granted to William Bradford and others, with a right to the soil, previously withheld. The arrival of 1,500 Puritans gave rise to several new settlements in Massachusetts Bay Colony. Local Self-Government in those settlements. First "General Court" of Massachusetts Bay, held in Boston. Carolana, now North and South Carolina, granted by the king to Robert Heath.

1631. Franchise Limited to church members by the second "General Court" of Massachusetts Bay. "Laconia" divided by Mason and Gorges, the proprietors, the former taking what he named New Hampshire, and the latter taking all to the east thereof. Warwick's patent to Connecticut, granted in 1630, transferred to Lord Say and Seal, Lord Brooke and others.

1632. Maryland granted to Lord Baltimore. Sixteen delegates sent to general court of Massachusetts Bay, by eight towns of the colony. Plymouth Colony passed an act imposing a penalty for declining office: $100 for refusing to be governor, and $50 for refusing to be a councillor or magistrate.

1633. First election of selectmen in the Massachusetts towns.

1634. Maryland settled by a Catholic colony, with representative government and religious toleration. English Commission appointed to supervise colonial affairs, with the right to revoke charters. Preparation for resistance in Boston, and refusal to surrender charter. 24 delegates from towns obtained seats in the general court. Allegiance sworn to colonial authorities instead of the crown, in Massachusetts, by the "Freeman's Oath."

∴ In England various forms of illegal taxation. These and other acts are upheld by the court of star-chamber and other venal tribunals.

1635. First representative assembly in Maryland; its laws declared void by Lord Baltimore, who claimed the right to initiate legislation. Renewed attempts to withdraw its charter from Massachusetts Bay in the interest of the English patentees. First voting by ballot, for delegates to the general court of Massachusetts Bay. First grand jury at Boston. Political disturbances in Maryland and Virginia. First Puritan settlement in Connecticut, from Plymouth Colony.

1636. Town government in Massachusetts recognized by law of general court. Puritan colony at Hartford. The governor of Virginia sent back by Charles I. to rule the province, "if but for a day," in denial of the pretensions of the colonists. Providence, R. I., founded by Roger Williams and associates, under a compact: "To submit themselves in active and passive obedience to all such orders and agreements as should be made for the public good of the body in an orderly way, by major consent of the present inhabitants, masters of families, incorporated together into a township, and such others as they shall admit into the same, only in civil things." No taxation in Plymouth Colony except by consent of the freemen in public assembly. First code of laws of Plymouth Colony compiled. Military union of New England Colonies in the Pequod War.

∴ In England, trial of John Hampden for resistance to illegal taxation.

1637. First project of political union of colonies, proposed by Plymouth to Massachusetts Bay, in May, and by Connecticut in August, failed because "the apprehensions of Connecticut dictated such extreme reserve in relation to grants of power to the proposed Confederacy, that Massachusetts did not deem it advisable to promote the scheme."

∴ Renewal of Navigation Act of 1621, requiring the shipment of Virginia tobacco direct to England.

1638. Disinclination to union, "Because some pre-eminence was yielded to Massachusetts." Connecticut favored the right of veto in each colony on the acts of the confederacy, by which arrangement Massachusetts claimed "all would have come to nothing." Second colony in Rhode Island by Coddington and other friends of Anne Hutchinson, under the compact: "We, whose names are underwritten, do hereby solemnly, in the presence of Jehovah, incorporate ourselves into a body politic, and as He shall help, will submit our persons, lives and estates unto our Lord Jesus Christ, the King of kings and Lord of lords, and to all those perfect and absolute laws of His Holy Word of Truth, to be judged and guided thereby." They chose a governor, deputy-governor and five assistants.

Exeter colony established in what is now New Hampshire by dissenters from Massachusetts. New Haven colony established by fresh arrivals of Puritans from England, who formed the "Plantation Covenant:"

"That, as in matters that concern the gathering and ordering of a church, so likewise in all public offices which concern civil order, as choice of magistrates and officers, making and repealing of laws, dividing allotments of inheritance, and all things of like nature, they would "be ordered by the rules which the Scripture held forth."

Surrender **of Charter of Massachusetts again refused** to demand **of royal commissioners. Swedish Colony settled** on the Delaware.

1639. Project of Colonial Union renewed by Connecticut, was rejected by Massachusetts, "not being satisfied with having an equal vote in the Confederacy with the smaller colonies." A constitution framed by Connecticut colonists, the assembly comprising an elected representative from each town, besides the governor and six magistrates elected by the whole colony. A house of burgesses provided for in Maryland, to consist of representatives elected by the people. First printing press, at Cambridge, Mass. First assembly of New Haven Colony. Settlement of Brunswick, in "the province of Maine," put itself under the government of Massachusetts Bay. The Government of Plymouth Colony changed from universal to representative democracy. Newport, R. I., colony established by dissenters **from** Anne Hutchinson's colony.

1640. Number of colonists of all ages in **New** England since the landing of the Pilgrims, about twenty-one thousand.

∴ Meeting of the Long Parliament, which, despite some drawbacks, did more for the progress of civil liberty than any parliament before or since.

1641. The Charter of Plymouth Colony surrendered by Wm. Bradford to the whole body of freemen. "The body of Liberties" of Massachusetts Bay, a constitution or code of 100 enactments, providing among other matters, that "there shall never be any bond slavery, villeinage or captivity among us, unless it be lawful captives taken in war, or such as willingly sell themselves or are sold **to** us;" and that "there should be no monopolies, **but of** such new inventions as were profitable to the country, and that for a short time only."

∴ Taxation without consent of parliament abolished in England, also the court of star-chamber, the high commission court and all arbitrary tribunals. 1642. Beginning of the Civil War. The designations Court and Country parties give place, for a time, to Royalist and Republican, nicknamed Cavaliers and Roundheads respectively, by their opponents.

1642. Committee on colonial union appointed by Massachusetts Bay to confer with similar representatives of other colonies. House of burgesses in Virginia authorized by the king, the upper house to comprise the governor and council. Religious-political feuds in Maryland retard the progress of the colony.

1643. Toleration of all Forms of Religion in Rhode Island. Religious Intolerance in Virginia; all nonconformists to the Church of England ordered "to depart the colony with all conveniency." Servitude in punishment of crimes abolished in Virginia. All exports and imports of New England exempted from duty by Parliament.

United Colonies of New England established by delegates from the colonies of Plymouth, Connecticut, New Haven and the General Court of Massachusetts Bay, mainly for mutual protection against their enemies, the union which was only an advisory body, to consist of two commissioners from each colony. Such as it was it lasted until 1686. Rhode Island was not invited because its people were regarded as schismatics, and when it sought admission was refused unless it would submit to Plymouth Colony.

Enlarged Area and Scope of Colonial Liberty and Union. First Steps toward Freedom of Religion and Free Schools, 1644-90.

1644. Union of Colonies in Rhode Island under a charter with a more democratic government. Division of the general court of Massachusetts into two chambers, insuring greater freedom to the direct representatives of the people.

1645. Progress in New Netherlands promoted by treaty with Indians. Slavery discountenanced in Massachusetts by return of two kidnapped slaves. Civil war in Maryland, eventuating some years later in extension of popular privileges.

1646. Colonial freedom vindicated by Governor Winslow, of Plymouth Colony, from disloyalty to England.

1647. Complete freedom of religion established by assembly of Rhode Island: "All men may walk as their consciences persuade them, without molestation—every one in the name of his God."

∴ In England the republican army under Cromwell emerged

[illegible] parliament and [illegible] the king, who [illegible] the proposal of [illegible] parliaments, [illegible] and [illegible] representation, and liberty of conscience [illegible] [illegible] England [illegible]. Execution of the king, abolition of monarchy and of the House of Lords, establishment of the Commonwealth.

1649. Free schools established by law in Massachusetts; intolerance in Virginia; political discrimination against Puritans; population of Virginia, 15,000 whites, 300 negroes. Act of toleration in Maryland, granting freedom of worship to all Christian sects. The Commonwealth willingly accepted by New England; Virginia, loyal to royalty, proclaimed Charles II. king, whence its name of "Old Dominion."

1650. Colonial Peace and Progress promoted by settlement of boundary dispute between New Haven and New Netherlands by a Joint Commission. General Assembly of Maryland divided into two chambers; no taxation without consent of lower house established. Colony established on Chowan River, in what is now North Carolina.

*** In England Military government under [illegible] of the "Rump" Parliament (comprising about [illegible] members of the Long Parliament) who [illegible] most of the [illegible] [illegible] themselves and [illegible] a Council of State to administer the government.

1651. Attempted Subversion of the charter of Rhode Island, with a view to its absorption by the larger colonies. Colonial commerce forbidden to foreign vessels by English Navigation Act—first appearance of the prohibitive system in commerce.

1652. Submission of Virginia to the Commonwealth, taxation only with consent of the assembly and other principles of political liberty being guaranteed. Proprietary government in Maryland temporarily abolished by the Commonwealth. Slave trade and slavery of more than ten years abolished in Rhode Island, they had never existed in Providence Plantations[illegible] authorized in New Netherlands. Popular freedom in New Netherlands in conflict with Governor Stuyvesant. Demand for elective municipal government for New Amsterdam granted by the States General after having been refused by the governor, who strongly disapproved of such "imprudent entrusting of power with the people."

1653. First municipal election in New Amsterdam. First popular representation in New Netherlands; a republican delegate convention of nineteen members, representing eight districts, submitted a statement of grievances to Governor Stuyvesant, who ordered them to disperse "under pain of his high displeasure," saying, "We derive our authority from God and the Company, not from a few ignorant subjects; and we alone can call the inhabitants together." The appeal of the convention taken to Holland by their advocate. Proprietary authority re-established in Maryland. The governor's assumption of the illegality of previous administration followed by his deposition, and the re-establishment of the government by commissioners.

*** The Long Parliament, as represented by the "Rump," dismissed by Cromwell, who became by the grace of [illegible] "Barebones' Parliament," Lord Protector of the Three Kingdoms. The vigorous but arbitrary and personal government of the protector is more severe but a less deeply rooted despotism than that of the late king. 1654. The new parliament—[illegible] members for England and [illegible] for Scotland and Ireland, with electoral qualification of £200, freehold or movable—[illegible] dissolved without passing a single bill.

1654. Disfranchisement of Roman Catholics in Maryland by the Protestant majority in the assembly; violent antagonism of Catholic and Protestant parties resulted in temporary anarchy; the commissioners ordered by Cromwell, "not to busy themselves about religion, but to settle the civil government."

1655. European sovereignties in America diminished by the conquest of New Sweden by New Netherlands. Civil War in Maryland; defeat of the Catholic party.

*** In England a conspiracy to restore the monarchy crushed; the country divided into twelve military governments.

1656. First arrival of Quakers in New England; their arrest and imprisonment in Boston under the general law against heresies, and re-shipment to England.

1657. Violent intolerance in Massachusetts against Quakers. Concessions to popular liberty by proprietor in Maryland secured re-establishment of his authority.

*** 1658. Death of Cromwell; accession of his son. 1659. Assembling of parliament, and its dissolution by the army; establishment of Committee of Safety; the nation [illegible] [illegible] of Richard Cromwell as protector; [illegible] of anarchy. 1660. The Convention Parliament called, by Gen. Monk, [illegible] by acclamation, accession of Charles II., general amnesty except to regicides; the army disbanded, except 1,000 cavalry and [illegible]—the first royal standing army; the parliament dissolved.

1660. Colonial commerce hampered by renewal of navigation acts. General acceptance of the Restoration in the colonies. The royal governor Berkeley restored in Virginia, and proprietary government fully re-established in Maryland.

1661. No Taxation in Massachusetts without consent of general court. Religious intolerance in Virginia resulting from re-establishment of Church of England. Royal order for arrest of fugitive regicides in New England failed of execution, through lack of zeal of the colonial authorities. Last Quaker execution in New England, at Boston.

1662. Extension of Franchise to members of the Church of England in Massachusetts demanded by the king. First charter of Connecticut, including New Haven colony, granted an enlarged degree of popular liberty.

1663. Colonial trade restricted to England by an amendment to the navigation acts. Royal patent for Carolana (Carolina) issued to Lord Clarendon and others, with freedom of conscience to colonists, and the right to elect governor and legislature. Franchise limited in Connecticut by property qualification of £20, besides personal property.

1664. Clarendon County Colony established in Carolina. New Netherlands granted by Charles II. to his brother, the Duke of York, and name changed to New York. The portion of New York now known as New Jersey, granted by the Duke of York to Lord Berkeley and Sir Geo. Carteret. Submission of New Netherlands to the duke's fleet, appointment of an English governor by him. Failure of royal commissioners to enforce a larger measure of royal authority in Massachusetts. No taxation without consent of legislature affirmed by Rhode Island.

1665. Free schools provided for New England towns. New Jersey formed into a separate government, with an elective assembly, liberty of conscience, and no taxation without consent of the assembly.

1666. First colonial naturalization act, in Maryland.

1667. Conquest of New Netherlands sanctioned by Treaty of Breda. Tyrannical exactions in New York, by the Duke of York's governors: "If there is any more murmuring against the taxes," said the governor, "make them so heavy that the people can do nothing but think how to pay them." The promise of a representative assembly evaded, and the settlers required to purchase new deeds to their lands.

1668. First general assembly of New Jersey.

1670. Carteret colony founded at "Old Charlestown," in Carolina. The "Grand Model" or "Fundamental Constitutions," framed by John Locke, introduced into Carolina, but found not practical enough to form a basis for colonial legislation. Absence of free schools and printing a subject of thanksgiving to Governor Berkeley of Virginia.

1670-2. Discontent of New Jersey colonists, and resistance to quit-rent claim of proprietary governor.

1672. Governor deposed by assembly of New Jersey, and replaced by another son of the proprietor.

*** First import on [illegible] commerce, "based upon the principle that the colonies were established at the cost, and for the benefit of the mother country."

1673. Proprietary government in Virginia, by royal grant to Earl of Arlington and Lord Culpepper for 31 years. New York taken by the Dutch, July 30.

1674. New York restored to England by Treaty of Westminster, February 19, and surrendered to English governor, October 31.

1675. Resistance of Connecticut to the assumption of dominion by the governor appointed by the Duke of York, whose new patent covered from the Connecticut to the Delaware. Prosperity of New England checked by the Indian War of King Philip.

1676. Bacon's "Rebellion" in Virginia and success of the popular party under his leadership. First election by universal suffrage, of assembly of Virginia, and no taxation without consent of assembly affirmed. Arbitrary government in Virginia in conflict with the "rebels," who burned Jamestown. Death of Bacon, subjugation of his followers and hanging of the leaders. The royal expectation of subjection of Massachusetts again disappointed. The spirit of popular liberty in Carolina strengthened by arrival of refugees from Virginia—Bacon's patriots.

1677. Maine transferred to Massachusetts by purchase from heirs of original proprietor. Oppression in Virginia not relieved by recall of Berkeley.

*** In England the names Court and Country parties, which had [illegible] after the Restoration, replaced respectively by those of Tory and Whig.

1678. Universal suffrage in Maryland, in electing assembly. Conflict in Virginia between the popular assembly and royal governor.

1679. First royal province in New England; Maine and New Hampshire separated, and the rights of the deceased proprietor of the latter awarded to his son, Robert Mason, whose nominee for governor was commissioned by the king, but denied recognition by "the [illegible] people of New Hampshire." First collector of customs and surveyor-general of New England at Boston, thwarted by the people and refused redress by the colonial courts.

*** Habeas corpus act in England, after repeated passage of the [illegible] by the Commons since 1668. The avowed aim of the king was to establish an absolute monarchy with the aid of Tories and Catholics, whose church was to be established by law. Impeachment of Catholic peers by Parliament.

1680. Arbitrary government in Virginia continued by the proprietor-governor Culpepper. Indian captives sold into slavery from Carolina. Duties on imports without its consent declared "illegal and unconstitutional" by assembly of New Jersey.

1681. Pennsylvania granted to William Penn, whose aim was "to establish a free commonwealth without respect to the color, race or religion of its inhabitants," and especially as a refuge for the members of his own faith, the Quakers.

*** After repeated angry dissolutions parliament was again dissolved, and the power of the crown became nearly absolute; no parliament for four years.

1682. Arrival of Penn in his colony; formation of Treaty of Shakamaxon with the Indians; calling of a general assembly, and passage of a code of laws.

1683. First School in Pennsylvania. First assembly or convention of Freeholders in New York; supreme legislative power declared to be in the governor, the council and the people; no taxation without consent of assembly; trial by jury; soldiers should not be quartered on the people; martial law should not be proclaimed; no person who accepted the general doctrines of religion should be persecuted.

1684. Treaty of Albany, between governors of New York and Virginia and the chiefs of the Iroquois, promoted peace and prosperity in the colonies. Virginia again a royal province, by revocation of grant to Arlington and Culpepper; the liberty of the colonists not enhanced by the change. Charter of Massachusetts declared forfeit by the English courts.

1685. Charter of Massachusetts declared void by King James, who appointed Joseph Dudley president of all New England.

*** Accession of James II. and confirmance of the royal [illegible] for absolute power. Liberty of conscience declared, [illegible] to relieve the Catholics. Rebellions in England and Scotland [illegible]. The King's Bench affirmed the right of the crown to set aside acts of parliament. 1686. Increasing alarm and discontent in England and Scotland.

1686. First printing press in Pennsylvania. Huguenot exiles arrive in the colonies. Liberty-loving victims of Jeffreys' bloody assizes transported to Virginia. Despotism in New England under Governor-General Andros, December 19, 1686, to April 18, 1689.

1687. Charter of Connecticut hidden from Andros.

1688. First protest against negro slavery, by Quakers in Pennsylvania. Area of despotism enlarged by addition of New York and New Jersey to the jurisdiction of Andros.

Despotism in Carolina overthrown; trial and punishment of Governor Sothel by the assembly; peace, progress and freedom under his successors. Despotism in Virginia resisted by an assembly "more turbulent than any which had preceded," armed insurrection prevented by the Revolution in England.

*** The Revolution. Flight of King James to France, the throne declared vacant; accession of William and Mary; declaration of rights; principles established, that a sovereign would forfeit his right to the nation's allegiance, and that the chief end of government is the public good; overthrow of absolutism, triumph of parliament, and the way opened for the gradual extension of civil and religious liberty to the great body of the people.

1689. Government of Maryland wrested from the Catholic party. Despotism overthrown from Maine to Pennsylvania by the imprisonment of Andros in Boston; Committee of Safety appointed, and Assembly convened, former charter declared in force; William and Mary proclaimed sovereigns, and provisional government of Massachusetts sanctioned by them. Despotism overthrown in New York; Leisler's insurrection in favor of William and Mary. Progress of Maine retarded by Indian disturbances. First public school in Pennsylvania founded by Quakers of Philadelphia. King William's War begun, between England and France and their American colonies; development of these retarded by war, which however promoted future liberty and union by the severe discipline of a common danger and the necessity of concerting broader measures of attack and defense, as well as statesmanship.

1690. Progress of Virginia promoted by the appointment of a more liberal governor.

A broader colonial union instituted by the assembling at New York of a congress of delegates from Massachusetts, Plymouth, Connecticut and New York colonies, to take counsel together and project plans for the general safety of all the colonies and for the invasion of Canada.

Liberty and Union Promoted by Growth of Colonies, by Wars and Treaties, Founding of Newspapers, and a Wider Intercolonial Public Opinion. 1691-1754.

1691. Progress retarded in New York by the conflicts of local factions. Catholics disfranchised in Maryland, at its change from a proprietary to a royal province. Separation of Delaware from Pennsylvania.

1692. Pennsylvania taken from Penn, and its government annexed to that of New York. New Charter uniting Massachusetts, Plymouth and the Eastern colonies, slightly reactionary in asserting petty royal prerogatives, gave rise to party distinctions of "Liberty Men" and "Prerogative Men." Religious freedom denied and progress retarded in Massachusetts by executions for witchcraft; the delusion at its height.

1693. Government of Delaware annexed to New York.

1694. Proprietary government restored to Penn in Pennsylvania and Delaware. County schools established in Maryland.

1695. A Puritan colony from Massachusetts

established in Carolina. Civil and religious liberty in Carolina promoted by the appointment of a Quaker governor.

1696. Project of colonial union by Penn:

"That the several colonies do meet once a year, and oftener if need be during war, and once in two years in peace, by stated deputies to debate and resolve of such measures as are most advisable for their better understanding and the public tranquillity and safety."

Slavery discouraged by resolution of the yearly meeting of Quakers. Colony of New York invaded by the French from Canada. Colonial affairs entrusted to English Boards of Trade and Plantations, more especially as to enforcement of navigation acts, which proved an instrument of oppression and a seed of discontent and revolution.

1697. King William's War ended by the Peace of Ryswick. Prosperity of New York promoted by appointment of a liberal governor.

1700. Military union of colonies promoted by apportionment of contingents to each in the event of war with Indians or French.

1701. Slavery discountenanced in Boston by instructions to representatives in the general court to labor "to put a period to negroes being slaves." Property qualification for suffrage, 50 acres of real or £50 of personal property, required by new charter of liberties of Pennsylvania. Religious freedom denied in New York and New England to "Jesuit and popish priests," as alleged "incendiaries."

1702. Colonial prosperity retarded by Queen Anne's War. Delaware permanently separated from Pennsylvania. Progress of New York hindered by a selfish and profligate governor. Free grammar school established in New York.

1703. Growth of liberty in American colonies as reported to English government: "Commonwealth notions improve daily, and if not checked in time, the rights and privileges of British subjects will be thought too narrow."

1704. First permanent newspaper, the Boston News Letter.

1705. Growth of liberty in Virginia through an interregnum of five years in the office of governor.

1706. The franchise restored to dissenters in Carolina.

1707. New Jersey's remonstrance against arbitrary acts of the governor, asserted the principle that "liberty is too valuable a thing to be easily parted with."

⁂ First united parliament of Great Britain. Growing importance to the kingdom of her American colonial trade.

1710. First notable German immigration, several thousand settling in New York, Pennsylvania, Virginia and Carolina.

⁂ 1711. Property qualifications of country members of parliament fixed by a Tory ministry at £600, and of borough members at £300 a year. Divine right of kings, passive obedience of subjects and [illegible] of Whigs [illegible] by the dominant party in church and state.

1712. Military union of Virginia and Carolina against Tuscarora Indians. Abolition of slavery in Pennsylvania declared by its assembly to be "neither just nor convenient."

1713. Queen Anne's War closed by treaty of Utrecht. The prosperity of the colonies further promoted by treaty of Portsmouth, between New England and the lately hostile Indians. Continued dissatisfaction of the colonies with the governors and other royal officials. All of Maine annexed to government of Massachusetts.

⁂ 1714. Accession of George I. The government almost entirely in the hands of parliament, which was itself an aristocracy divided into two great parties fighting for place and power.

1715. Progress of Carolina retarded by Indians and pirates.

1716. Two thousand slaves in Massachusetts.

1717. Increase of New England commerce shown by the clearing from the port of Boston alone, of 1,247 vessels in three years.

1718. Freedom of the press curtailed by official censorship in New England.

1719. Boston Gazette and American Weekly Mercury of Philadelphia established. Colonial manufactures discouraged by parliament, as tending to lessen dependence on Great Britain.

1721. New England Courant established; its free criticism punished by imprisonment of publisher.

1722. Discontent of New England at the continued enforcement of the royal prerogative of selecting the best forest trees.

⁂ Parliament authorized the acceptance from Quakers of an affirmation instead of an oath, and some other attempts were made by the Whigs to promote religious liberty, through which the principle of toleration became gradually established.

1725. New York Gazette established.

1727. Excessive importation of slaves vigorously condemned by leaders of opinion in Carolina.

⁂ Accession of George II. The first fourteen years of his reign were marked by the political conflict between Walpole and the opposition.

1728. The Maryland Gazette established at Annapolis.

1729. Proprietary government of Carolina sold to the crown, and two royal governments, North and South Carolina, established. First large Irish immigration, settling chiefly in Maryland and Virginia.

1731. Colonial manufactures create alarm in England, as they "would interfere with the profit made by the British merchants."

1732. South Carolina Gazette and Rhode Island Gazette established. Royal charter for colonizing Georgia with released poor debtors. Export of colonial manufactures forbidden by the "hat act." "I will leave the taxation of America," said Walpole, "to some of my successors who have more courage than I have."

1733. All sugar imported into the colonies taxed under the "importation act." First Georgia colony, 35 families, settled at Savannah; slavery and rum excluded; Jewish colonists received despite the remonstrance of the Georgia trustees in England. Massachusetts' remonstrance against official encroachments rebuked by the home government, "as a high insult tending to shake off the dependence of the colony upon the kingdom." Indian treaties at Philadelphia and in Georgia.

1734. Freedom of colonial press vindicated by the acquittal of the publisher of the New York Weekly Journal, which had opposed the claim of the governor for unearned "back pay."

1736. The Virginia Gazette established. Increase of the Georgia colony by the arrival of Wesleyans and Moravians.

1738. Slave insurrection in South Carolina quelled.

1739. Stamp act proposed by Governor Keith of Pennsylvania.

1740. First law defining slavery in South Carolina.

⁂ A motion of censure in parliament of Walpole's unscrupulous system of political corruption, defeating opposition by purchasing the necessary majority. His secret service outlay from 1731 to 1741 was £1,453,400, relatively a much larger sum then than now.

1741. The General Magazine and Historical Chronicle issued by Franklin. Panic in New York, from apprehension of a negro insurrection, subsided only after burning and hanging some of the alleged conspirators.

1742. Patent declined by Franklin, on his stove, on the ground that, "as we are benefited by the inventions of others, we should be willing to devote our own to the general welfare."

1743. Georgia colony deprived of the fostering care of its founder, Oglethorpe, by his return to England.

1744. King George's War begun, the American section of the war of the Austrian succession. Treaty of Lancaster, Pa., to forestall French intrigues with Indians of the English colonies.

1745. The fall of Louisburg, "the Gibraltar of America," "filled Europe with amazement and America with joy" at the prowess of the colonial troops, and exerted no little influence on the progress of the colonies toward independence.

1747. Surrender of impressed seamen at Boston to the demand of the citizens.

1748. Opposition of New York assembly to the demands of royal officials. Arbitrary colonial government promoted, and the English constitution menaced by the doctrine of the divine right of kings and the duty of non-resistance. King George's War closed by Treaty of Aix-la-Chapelle. First export of cotton, a small lot from Charleston. Manufacture of fire-arms in Massachusetts.

1749. Stamp act suggested by a royal official of Boston. First female academy, by Moravians, at Bethlehem, Pa. Peace of Georgia menaced by the intrigues with the half-breed "queen of the Creeks."

1750. Divine right of kings and non-resistance vigorously denounced from a Boston pulpit—an "impious bargain," said Mayhew, "between the sceptre and the surplice;" a "fabulous and chimerical" doctrine; if rulers oppress, resistance is "lawful and glorious." Colonial manufactures of iron declared "a common nuisance" by parliament, and prohibited under a penalty of £200.

1751. Colonial union urged from a royal official standpoint. The receiver-general of New York recommended that there should be held by authority of parliament, "an annual meeting of commissioners from all the colonies at New York or Albany. From upwards of 40 years' observation upon the conduct of provincial assemblies, and the little regard paid by them to instructions," he was satisfied that "a British parliament must oblige them to contribute, or the whole would end in altercation and words."

1752. Colonial union projected by Franklin, who declared that, "a voluntary union entered into by the colonies themselves would be preferable to one imposed by parliament; for it would be perhaps not much more difficult to procure, and more easy to alter and improve, as circumstances should require and experience direct." Colonial affairs more fully entrusted to the Board of Trade and Plantations in England.

1753. Colonial taxation urgently pressed by the Board of Trade to obtain "a revenue with which to fix settled salaries on the northern governors and defray the cost of Indian alliances."

1754. The French and Indian War, begun by a conflict between the colonial pioneers of England and France in America, and destined to settle the conflicting colonial claims of the two nations, was not formally declared until May 17, 1756, in Europe, where it became known as the Seven Years' War, 1756-63.

Franklin's plan of colonial union, or general constitution of the colonies, adopted at Albany by a convention of twenty-five delegates from seven colonies—New York 5, Massachusetts 5, New Hampshire 4, Pennsylvania 4, Connecticut 3, Rhode Island and Maryland 2—Connecticut's members alone dissenting.

It provided for a president-general, to be appointed and paid by the crown, and a grand council, to be elected by the colonial assemblies, "in proportion to the money arising out of each colony to the general treasury," "yet so as that the number to be chosen by any one province be not more than seven nor less than two," with stated annual meetings, "power to choose their speaker," power to make general laws, affecting Indian relations, new settlements, army and navy—"but they shall not impress men in any colony without the consent of the legislature;" to levy taxes—"rather discouraging luxury than loading industry with unnecessary burthens;" all laws made by them "shall not be repugnant, but as near as may be agreeable to the laws of England, and shall be transmitted to the king in council for approbation," having previously received the assent of the president-general in America.

As the compromises of statesmen are always objectionable to extremists, the "Plan of Union" was rejected. "The Assemblies all thought there was too much prerogative in it, and in England it was thought to have too much of the democratic," wrote Franklin.

Colonial Liberty and Union Stimulated by the Exactions of the British Government, 1755-65.

1755. Future independence foreshadowed; "In another century," wrote John Adams in his diary, "all Europe will not be able to subdue us. The only way to keep us from setting up for ourselves is to disunite us." Permanent settlement on the Penobscot by immigrants from Massachusetts.

1756. War declared between England and France, by the former on May 17, and by the latter on June 9. The campaign in America not important, but rather to the advantage of the French.

⁂ William Pitt, prime minister of England.

1757. Restoration of Liberty in Pennsylvania attempted by commissioning Franklin as agent to England, "to represent the unhappy state of the province, that all occasion of dispute hereafter might be removed by an act of the British legislature." Anti-colonial resolution in parliament, "that the claim of right in a colonial assembly to raise and apply public money by its own act alone, is derogatory to the crown and to the rights of the people of Great Britain," promoted discontent in the colonies. Disasters of the campaign felt by the colonists to be largely due to the inefficiency or cowardice of the English commanders, and accompanied by a deepening sense of the injustice of being required to supply men and money for operations in the management of which they had no voice. Somewhat more than half the army were colonial troops, and taxation became so heavy that it sometimes took two-thirds the income of colonial landowners.

1758. Massachusetts insisted on controlling its own war-fund. Campaign favorable to English and colonial arms—the capture of Louisburg, Fort Frontenac and Fort Du Quesne. Treaty of Easton, Pa., with Indian tribes, north and west of the Ohio.

1759. Project of stamp act rejected by Pitt; "I will never burn my fingers," said he, "with an American stamp act." Progress of South Carolina retarded by ill treatment of Cherokees and the resulting war with that tribe. British and colonial arms successful—capture of forts Niagara, Ticonderoga, Crown Point and Quebec.

1760. War with the French ended by conquest of Canada, and the promised surrender of western out-posts, and war with their Indian allies temporarily suspended. Colonial discontent increased by fresh orders for enforcement of navigation acts. Colonial self-government advocated by Franklin before the Board of Trade and Plantations in England, and generally accepted by American leaders as a right inherent in the people. Population of the colonies estimated at 310,000 blacks, and 1,385,000 whites, marked by great diversity of social, religious and race views and customs, and yet becoming gradually impressed with the sense of an underlying identity of interests as against England, and the necessity of less intolerant and antagonistic relations among themselves, but with little opportunity for wide interchange of views between the inhabitants of the different, and especially the more distant colonies.

⁂ Accession of George III., who with the aid of the Tory party ruled as well as reigned, especially after Lord North became premier in 1770. Hence all the attacks on American liberty have been justly regarded as royal acts.

1761. Writs of assistance from the superior court of Massachusetts in support of the alleged right, under the importation act of 1733, of universal search for smuggled goods, argued before the court by James Otis, who inveighed against them "as instruments of slavery on the one hand, and villainy on the other." "Then and there," said John Adams in later years, "was the first scene of the first act of opposition to the arbitrary claims of Great Britain. Then and there the child Independence was born." Slave-trade discountenanced by heavy duties in Virginia and South Carolina. Subservience of colonial paternity promoted by grant of commissions to remain in force during the pleasure of the king.

1763. Canada and Florida ceded to England by Treaty of Paris, closing the Seven Years' War. Future independence of colonies promoted by cession of Canada. "There now," said a French statesman, "we have arranged matters for an American rebellion in which England will lose her empire in the West." This view was shared by some Tory statesmen in England, who thought that the continuance of French dominion in Canada would tend to insure the permanent dependence and loyalty of the British colonies to the mother country. English domination in the West vainly resisted by the late Indian allies of the French, under Pontiac. Confiscation of vessels engaged in the contraband sugar trade with the colonies ordered by parliament, almost destroying colonial commerce with the West Indies. Colonial taxation and representation declared inseparable. The imposition of taxes only by the representatives of the people claimed **by the** colonists **to** be their constitutional right as Englishmen; **and** as they were represented only in their colonial assemblies, to those alone belonged the right to levy taxes and **duties**; great speech of Samuel Adams, in Boston, in vindication of the principle. "If we are not represented in **the** body that taxes us, and we submit," said he, "we are slaves."

1764. The right of taxing the colonies insisted on, by resolution of the British House of Commons. Great agitation throughout the colonies; contrary resolutions passed everywhere; formal remonstrances addressed to the king and the two houses of parliament; and colonial agents sent to England to prevent if possible the passage of the act. Boundary controversy between New Hampshire and New York, involving the settlements in what became Vermont, decided in England in the interest of the royal officials of New York, subjecting settlers to re-purchase of lands.

1765. Colonial taxation by parliament established by passage of American stamp act. Patrick Henry's resolutions in the House of Burgesses of Virginia proclaimed the principle of **no** taxation without consent of the body which represents those who pay the taxes, and were adopted by a majority of one. American congress proposed by James Otis in the general court of Massachusetts.

Colonial congress or convention at New York, sometimes called the stamp act congress, composed of twenty-seven delegates from nine colonies: New York 4; Massachusetts, Connecticut, New Jersey, Pennsylvania, Maryland and South Carolina, 3 each; Rhode Island and Delaware, 2 each—"without the least claim of pre-eminence, one over the other." Letters of concurrence were received from the assemblies of Virginia, New Hampshire, North Carolina and Georgia. "We should stand," said **a** South Carolina delegate, "upon the **common** ground of those natural rights that we feel and **know** as men. . . . There ought to be no New-England man, **no** New-Yorker, known on the continent, but all of us Americans." They adopted a declaration of rights, a petition to the king, and a memorial to both houses of parliament. In England its suggestions **were** ignored and it was sneered at in parliament as "a federal union assembled without **any** regulation on **the** part of **the** supreme power."

Colonial Liberty and Union Promoted by the Attempts of Great Britain to Enforce Taxation, by Defensive Organizations, and by Correspondence between Colonial Assemblies—the Unarmed Struggle.

1765-75.

1765. Union Promoted by General Resistance to Stamp Act, which was characterized as "the folly of England and the ruin of America." Stamps destroyed or reshipped; stamp officers burned in effigy and forced to fly or resign; Sons of Liberty organized under a pledge to defend liberty and resist oppression with their lives, if necessary; colonial importers agreed not to trade with England until the act should be repealed; Daughters of Liberty and other societies, pledged to the making and wearing of home-spun, organized. "Nothing will now save us," wrote Gadsden, "but acting together. The province that endeavors to act separately must fall with the rest, and be branded besides with everlasting infamy." Whig and Tory, as party names, came into more general use, respectively, the friends and foes of the people.

1766. Delusive hope of freedom on repeal of stamp act. The right of colonial taxation re-asserted by parliament, with the right "to bind the colonies in all cases whatsoever." In the repeal discussion Pitt declared: "You have no right to tax America. I rejoice that America has resisted. Three millions of our fellow-subjects so lost to every sense of virtue as tamely to give up their liberties would be fit instruments to make slaves of the rest." Colonial rejoicing over repeal; the leaders not deceived by its superficial character; the qualifying resolution led Samuel Adams to declare that "the conduct of England is permitted and ordained by the unsearchable wisdom of the Almighty for hastening the independence of these colonies."

1767. Colonial taxation renewed by duties on glass, white-lead, painters' colors, paper and tea, imported into the colonies. Renewal of discontent and agitation in America. Arbitrary government attempted in Massachusetts by the governor's dismissal of the assembly and his refusal to call another. Regulation of local affairs claimed in North Carolina, in a general convention—thence called Regulators.

1768. Liberty menaced in New York by the presence of British troops and the suspension of the assembly for refusing to vote military supplies. Colonial liberty promoted by John Dickinson's "Letters of a Farmer," which were republished in England by Franklin, and translated into French and published in Paris. Non-importation societies reorganized. The people ripe for riot and insurrection, but kept in check by the prudence of their leaders. "To insult and tear each other to pieces," said Otis, "was to act like madmen." "Our cause," said Dickinson, "is a cause of the highest dignity. . . . I hope it will not be disgraced in any colony by a single rash step." "The day dawns," wrote William Livingston, "in which the foundation of this mighty empire is to be laid by the establishment of a regular American constitution. . . Before seven years roll over our own heads the first stone must be laid. . . . No circumstance, whether prosperous or adverse, can happen to our parent; nay, no conduct of hers, whether wise or imprudent, no possible temper on her part, will put a stop to this building." "No assembly on the continent will ever concede that parliament has a right to tax the colonies," wrote Roger Sherman. "The right of unfettered discussion," said the same, "is inalienable, and we must maintain it." "We cannot believe," wrote William Williams, "that they will draw the sword on their own colonies; but if they do our blood is more at their service than our liberties." "You [the Massachusetts assembly] are right, and that is sufficient for me," wrote John Morin Scott, a Son of Liberty of New York. "We will fight the tory faction here, and the British regulars too, if necessary." "We must maintain," wrote Richard Stockton, "the natural and chartered rights of the colonists, but by peaceful and lawful means." "Let these truths be indelibly impressed on our minds," wrote the covert author of a hand-bill circulated in New York, "that we cannot be free without being secure in our property; that we cannot be secure in our property if, without our consent, others may as by right take it away; that taxes imposed by parliament do thus take it away; that duties laid for the sole purpose of raising money are taxes; that attempts to lay such should be instantly and firmly opposed." Commotion in Boston because of seizure without a warrant of the sloop Liberty for alleged violation of the revenue law, pronounced by royal governor to be "an insurrection rather than a riot." A general spirit of insurrection declared by royal officials to be prevailing throughout the province.

Colonial union promoted by circular of Massachusetts to the other colonial assemblies, by whom it was cordially adopted despite the vigorous opposition and threats of the royal governors. By parliament it was declared to be "a seditious paper," and the assembly was ordered to apologize for their "rash and hasty proceeding," which declining to do, they were dismissed. "Let Britons rescind their measures," said Otis, "or they are lost forever." By the royal minister, in his correspondence with the colonial governors, it was characterized as a document "of most dangerous and factious tendency." Liberty menaced in Massachusetts by encampment of royal troops on Boston Common; refusal of colonial authorities to furnish military supplies. Popular liberty asserted in Massachusetts in a six days' convention, at Boston, of delegates from ninety-six towns, the governor having refused to summon the regular assembly. Circle of liberty completed by letter of North Carolina (Nov. 30), which was the last of the colonies to reply to the circular of Massachusetts.

1769. A purpose of independence and subversion of the constitution charged on Massachusetts by the king at the opening of parliament. The transportation of the Massachusetts leaders to England for trial suggested in parliament. Colonial union promoted by resolutions of Virginia's house of burgesses, claiming for that body "the sole right of imposing taxes," and "the lawfulness and expediency of procuring a concert of the colonies in case of the violated rights by America," of which a copy was sent "to every legislature in America," with request to concur.

Union of colonies in a general Congress, "which should exercise legislative power for them all," suggested by New York assembly, "without waiting for further aggressions." Colonial independence foreseen in England: "I now warn ministers," said Col. Barre in the House of Commons, "that, if they persist in their wretched course of oppression, the whole continent of North America will rise in arms, and these colonies perhaps be lost to England forever." Freedom of legislation menaced in the opinion of the Massachusetts assembly by the presence of armed troops in Boston, and they declined to discuss any subject but the redress of grievances. Toryism and loyalism of New York assembly censured by the people in mass meeting. The resolution declared by the assembly to be "an infamous and scandalous libel."

1770. Aversion to English rule deepened in New York by the cutting down by the soldiers of the people's emblem of freedom, the liberty pole. Hostility to royal government intensified in Massachusetts by the bloody altercation between soldiers and citizens, known as "the Boston massacre." Removal of royal troops from the city on demand of the people. Whig and Tory still more widely used to designate, respectively, those who favored the popular cause, or the pretensions of the crown. The right to tax the colonies re-asserted by parliament, by retaining the duty on tea, upon the repeal of the act of 1767. To this the colonies responded by continuing their non-importation societies as to tea. "The little conveniences and comforts of life," wrote the merchant, George Mason, "when set in competition with our liberty, ought to be rejected, not with reluctance but with pleasure." The spirit of liberty fostered in New York by the trial and imprisonment of Alex. McDougall, a Son of Liberty, charged with the authorship of obnoxious hand-bill, "To the Betrayed Inhabitants of the City and Colony of New York," which led to the mass meeting of citizens and their censure of the assembly. On being sentenced to imprisonment for contempt, he said, "I rejoice that I am the first to suffer for liberty since the commencement of our glorious struggle."

1771. Freedom of discussion honored by the attentions paid to McDougall in prison, and by his release. Arbitrary government strengthened in North Carolina by defeat of the Regulators and the execution of six of their leaders.

1772. The struggle for liberty renewed in Massachusetts by an act of parliament requiring the payment of salaries of governor and judges from colonial funds without the consent of assembly, which declared the act to be subversive of their chartered rights and therefore void. Summary vindication of liberty by the people of Providence by capturing and burning the royal revenue schooner Gaspee. Co-operation of patriots promoted by formation of committees of correspondence throughout Massachusetts.

1773. Inter-colonial co-operation of patriots begun by Virginia assembly in appointing a committee of correspondence to represent the colony in communicating with the other colonies. Union against British aggression promoted by Sons of Liberty and Committees of Correspondence. Taxation without representation resisted in the anti-tea agitation: the sending of tea by Great Britain into the colonies declared, at a meeting of citizens of Philadelphia, to be "an attack on the liberties of America." Anti-tea hand-bill in Boston declared that "the hour of destruction, or manly opposition to the machinations of tyranny" had arrived, and it summoned the people, at the ringing of the bells, "to make united and successful resistance to this last, worst and most destructive measure of administration." Tea thrown overboard by the "Boston Tea Party" some days later. Tea sent back from Philadelphia and New York, on demand of the people.

1774. The act of defiance of the Boston Tea Party applauded throughout the colonies, but declared by the English government to be "open rebellion," which "must be punished." Local delegate convention of Boston and vicinity deliberated on methods of defense against oppression, urged stricter observance of non-importation compact, and sent a circular letter to other colonies. Repression of liberty in Massachusetts by acts of parliament: the Boston Port bill, forbidding commerce with that city; the bill for regulating the government of Massachusetts Bay, making the governor's council and the supreme court independent of the people, and forbidding town meetings without the consent of the governor; and the Murder bill, providing that officials charged with murder should be removed from the province for trial.

In relation to these bills, Burke exclaimed in parliament: "What can Americans believe but that England wishes to despoil Americans of all liberty, of all franchise, and by the destruction of the charters to reduce them to a state of the most abject slavery," and Pownall prophesied that these arbitrary measures would drive the Americans [illegible] a general congress and perhaps resorting to arms. If the Americans do not reject these bills, said another member, "they are the most abject slaves upon earth, and nothing the ministers can do is base enough for them," while still another added: "I am sorry to say that not only the House has fallen into this error, but the people approve of the measure. The people, I am sorry to say, have been misled. But a short time will prove the evil tendency of this bill. If there ever was a nation rushing headlong to ruin, it is this."

1774. New York assembly tainted with Toryism and not in sympathy with the tendency of the times toward revolution. Liberty maintained in Virginia. The House of Burgesses, being dissolved for non-compliance with the governor's wishes, constituted itself the Provincial Assembly of Virginia, and declared for a general congress as suggested by New York five years before. Free deliberation maintained in Massachusetts, whose assembly, dissolved by the governor, refused to separate before it had declared for a general congress.

Impending revolution: "They were rushing towards revolution," says Bancroft, "and they knew it not."

The Continental Congress met in Philadelphia, September 5, and organized by electing Peyton Randolph, of Virginia, as president. It comprised fifty-five delegates from twelve colonies, Georgia only not represented. This was virtually the birth of the republic, as the people thenceforth looked to that body as the guiding spirit of the colonies in their struggle with the British government. Congress indorsed non-importation, requesting colonial merchants "not to send any order to Great Britain, and to delay the execution of any order already sent;" they approved "the opposition of the inhabitants of Massachusetts Bay to the execution of the late acts of parliament; and if the same shall be attempted to be carried into execution by force, in such case all America ought to support them in their opposition;" they formulated a Declaration of Colonial Rights; and agreed upon fourteen articles of American Association, the second of which was: "We will neither import nor purchase any slave imported after the first day of December next." Jefferson had previously declared in the Virginia legislature, that the "abolition of domestic slavery is the greatest object of desire in these colonies where it was unhappily fixed in their infant state." They wrote an "Address to the People of Great Britain," a "Memorial to the Inhabitants of the several British-American Colonies," a "Petition to the King," and an "Address to the Inhabitants of the Province of Canada."

The ruling idea of congress and the people was to obtain for the several colonies the rights guaranteed by the British constitution as modified and enlarged by their charters and established political privileges without hostility to a constitutional monarchy or any deliberate purpose of separation from the mother country. "No such thing as independence," said Washington, in October, 1774, "is desired by any thinking man in America." By giving to each delegation only a single vote, this congress laid the foundation for future union on the basis of equality of colonies. Of their labor, Lord Chatham spoke thus in the House of Lords: "When your lordships look at the papers transmitted to us from America; when you consider their decency, firmness and wisdom, you cannot but respect their cause, and wish to make it your own. For myself, I must declare and avow, that in all my reading and observation—I have read Thucydides (and it has been my favorite study) and have studied and admired the master states of the world—that for solidity of reasoning, force of sagacity, and wisdom of conclusion, under such a complication of difficult circumstances, no nation or body of men can stand in preference to the general congress at Philadelphia." Henry Middleton, of South Carolina, chosen president. Adjournment of Congress, October 26, to meet May 10, 1775, unless redress should be granted.

Virtual revolution and abolition of royal authority in Massachusetts. The general court having been called by the governor, and the call rescinded because of anticipated insubordination, they constituted themselves a Provincial Congress of 260 members, which assumed executive and legislative powers, and actually represented the sovereignty of the people of Massachusetts, appointing a Committee of Safety to protect the interests of the people during adjournments. Preparations for war in Massachusetts by enrollment of 12,000 minute men—to take the field at a minute's notice—under authority of the Provincial Congress. Their acts denounced by the governor. Anticipation of war by the British government, which forbade importation of military stores into the colonies; seizure by the colonists of arms and ammunition.

1775. A provincial convention, followed by a provincial congress, in North Carolina, to replace the assembly dissolved by the governor for daring to approve the acts of the Continental Congress. Provincial conventions in Maryland and New Jersey, replacing assemblies. Obstruction of elections for delegates to Congress by royal governors under direction of British government. New York assembly declining to appoint delegates to Congress, they were appointed by a convention, and the assembly was replaced by a provincial congress, May 22, which was succeeded by the state legislature, three years later. First society for the abolition of slavery, in Philadelphia.

Liberty, Union and Independence Won by War. Period of Armed Struggle. Whigs and Tories. The Revolutionary Government. 1775-81.

1775. The Whig or Patriot Party, during the period between the battle of Lexington and the Declaration of Independence (April 19, 1775, to July 4, 1776), were willing to continue in the relation of colonists provided their rights as such were properly guaranteed by Great Britain.

The War of Independence precipitated by the Battle of Lexington, and the contingency of eventual separation from the mother country more widely entertained. "That there be any who pant after independence," wrote John Adams, earlier in the year, "is the greatest slander," and Jefferson afterwards wrote, "Before the 19th of April, 1775, I had never heard a whisper of a disposition to separate from Great Britain." It had been hoped that a "durable union between Britain and the Colonies" could be amicably established, but actual hostilities dispelled the illusion. A despotic king, who was incapable of entertaining even the conception of popular freedom, and a pliant ministry, whose subserviency to his arbitrary will was the surest guarantee of its continuance in power, were engaged in a continued and unscrupulous attempt to revolutionize the government of Great Britain, and were utterly impervious to all apprehension of danger from the conflict they were determined to force upon the colonies in vindication of the alleged rights of the crown.

The Second Continental Congress met at Philadelphia, May 10, comprising delegates from twelve colonies, Georgia remaining unrepresented until July, Peyton Randolph, of Virginia, elected president. Without a formal renunciation of allegiance they proceeded to assume several of the functions of a general government, sent a second petition to the king which may be regarded as the last official expression of loyalty to the crown. John Hancock, of Massachusetts, elected president, May, 24, to succeed Peyton Randolph who had resigned to take his seat in the Virginia House of Burgesses. Declaration of independence by settlers of Mecklenburg county, North Carolina. Election of George Washington as commander-in-chief of the continental army by Congress. A Tory newspaper office—New York Gazetteer—destroyed by patriots of New Haven. Assumption of national powers by Congress, in voting bills of credit.

A form of Confederation sketched by Franklin on the basis of his "Plan of Union," of 1754, but with less recognition of the royal claims, and designed to be perpetual in case reconciliation with the crown should prove a vain hope, failed to receive the attention of Congress, which was still unwilling to take so decisive a step, hoping to receive a favorable reply to their humble petition; and was repudiated by others because it gave too great powers to Congress. "The idea of destroying all provincial distinctions," said Rutledge, of South Carolina, "and making everything of the most minute kind bend to what they call the good of the whole, is, in other terms, to say that these colonies must be subject to the government of the eastern provinces. . . . I am resolved to vest the Congress with no more power than what is absolutely necessary, and to keep the staff in our own hands; for I am confident, if surrendered into the hands of others, a most pernicious use will be made of it." Virtual sovereignty asserted by the expulsion of Dr. Benjamin Church from Congress, for disloyalty. Prospect of independence not less favorable because of the military operations of the year.

1776. Union Typified in the hoisting of the first American flag over the camp at Boston. Liberty, union and independence promoted by Paine's "Common Sense." Separation from Massachusetts, and establishment of a temporary state government by New Hampshire. Patriots encouraged by the triumph of their arms in compelling the evacuation of Boston. A state constitution adopted by South Carolina. Independence proclaimed by Rhode Island. To work for colonial independence urged on the delegates of Virginia in Congress, by the House of Burgesses. Negotiations for aid from France begun. Recommendation of Congress to the colonial assemblies that they severally "adopt such governments as shall best conduce to the happiness and safety of their constituents in particular, and America in general." Connecticut and Rhode Island content with the governments they had formed under their charters, did not frame new constitutions until 1818 and 1842, respectively. British authority in the colonies abrogated by Congress, and British property declared a lawful prize. Independence formally enunciated in Congress by Lee's Resolutions, June 7; and committee to draft a declaration of independence appointed, June 8, also a committee on foreign relations and a board of war. Declaration of rights adopted by Virginia convention. Lee's Resolutions passed by twelve colonies, July 2, New York's delegates not voting in the absence of instructions.

Declaration of Independence adopted by Congress, July 4. Birth of the Nation. A committee appointed to devise a seal for the United States of America, though no design was actually adopted until June 20, 1782. The royal statue in New York transformed into bullets. Declaration of Independence signed August 2, by fifty-four delegates of thirteen colonies, two being absent. "We must be unanimous," said President Hancock, "there must be no pulling different ways; we must all hang together." "Yes," said Franklin, "we must all hang together, or we shall all hang separately."

Sovereignty exercised by Congress in passing a pension act, and a homestead act in favor of those who should serve in the army to the close of the war. Sovereignty asserted by refusing to confer with British commissioners except on the basis of recognition of Independence. Adoption of state constitutions by New Jersey (July 2), Virginia (July 5), Pennsylvania (July 15), Maryland (Aug. 14), Delaware (Sept. 20), North Carolina (Dec. 18); and New York declared her independence of Great Britain. Proclamation of pardon by British commander to all who would lay down their arms. Rhode Island occupied by British troops. Congress removed to Baltimore, Dec. 20, to escape capture by the British. Patriots encouraged by an important victory at Trenton. Negotiations for aid from France resumed under leadership of Franklin. Slaveholding declared incompatible with membership by the Society of Friends. Military operations of the year not encouraging.

1777. Patriots encouraged by Washington's success in New Jersey. Independence of Vermont, with abolition of slavery, declared. State constitutions adopted by Georgia and New York. Financial aid from France, without recognition of independence. Return of Congress to Philadelphia, March 4. Exchange of prisoners refused by Washington because of the inhuman treatment of Americans in British prison-ships. United States flag adopted by Congress. First anniversary of Independence celebrated. Congress removed to Lancaster Sept. 27, and thence to York, Pa., Sept. 30. Philadelphia taken by British. The patriot cause strengthened by surrender of Gen. Burgoyne. Board of war created to replace committee of Congress.

Union and Independence promoted by the adoption by Congress of the "Articles of Confederation and Perpetual Union." Henry Laurens, of South Carolina, elected president, succeeding Hancock, who left that body to fight for his country as first major-general of Massachusetts militia. Military operations of the year indecisive.

1778. Independence of the United States recognized by France in a treaty of alliance and commerce. Plan of reconciliation by Lord North, based upon the old relations between the crown and the colonies, though adopted by parliament, failed to affect the United States, which had meanwhile passed far beyond that phase of political evolution. The patriot cause advanced by the evacuation of Philadelphia; and by the arrival of a French fleet and a French minister to the United States, as well as by the reception at the French court of the embassy from the United States. Increase of the United States territory by the conquest of the Northwest by Virginia troops under Col. George Rogers Clark. Congress returned to Philadelphia, July 2.

Permanent union certain through the adoption of the Articles of Confederation by eight states before July 9, and three others before the close of the year. In framing that instrument an overwrought idea of liberty and local independence operated on the minds of many of the patriotic delegates against granting to the central government the necessary powers, entailing dangerous weakness and even the risk of ultimate failure. Even the name of United States was tainted in the minds of some by a suspicion of centralization, and Confederated States was preferred as savoring less of consolidated power, so jealous were they of authority and so impressed with the difficulty of exercising great powers without abuse.

The Whig, Patriot or Revolutionary party, divided in Congress, in the State legislatures and among the people at large into two sections, which might be designated as State-rights Whigs and Strong-government Whigs, both being in accord as to the prosecution of the war and separation from Great Britain, but differing as to the powers to be entrusted to the central or union government. The form adopted was a genuine political victory to the former, who were in a majority and in the main had control of the government, although several of the most active civil and military leaders in the Revolution were of the opposite section. "The States separately," said Washington, "are too much engaged in their local concerns. If the great whole is mismanaged, the States individually must sink into the general wreck." John Jay, of New York, elected president of Congress. Military operations of the year indecisive.

1779. The patriot cause strengthened by the naval victory of Paul Jones. Financial credit of the United States very low, its bills being worth in gold only about three per cent. of their face value. An American minister to Spain commissioned. Samuel Huntington, of Connecticut, chosen president. A Board of Admiralty replaced naval committee of Congress. Military operations restricted by the diminished numbers of the American troops.

1780. Demand by Congress on the States to enlarge the army to 35,000 men. Gradual abolition of slavery enacted by Pennsylvania. French aid of 6,000 troops received by the United States. A state constitution adopted by Massachusetts. Negotiations with Holland begun by United States. Depreciation of the currency to about two and one-half per cent.

1781. Suffering, destitution and discontent of the army, with mutiny of some troops, because of arrears of pay and lack of proper supplies.

National union made permanent by the adoption by Maryland (last of the thirteen to accept,) of the Articles of Confederation, March 1. Congress adjourned.

Congress reassembled under the Articles of Confederation March 2. Thomas McKean, of Delaware, chosen president, July 10. John Hanson, of Maryland, chosen president, November 5.

The Tory, Royalist or Loyalist party were willing that the colonies should remain subject to Great Britain, without any guarantee of chartered or otherwise established rights and usages. They constituted the opposition to the Whigs, Patriots or Revolutionists during the unarmed struggle of 1765 to 1775, in the controversy with the mother country. After the war began they gave aid and comfort to the enemy by enlistments (to the number of perhaps 25,000, from first to last,) and otherwise. There were many more, who for various causes were non-combatants, but no less virulent in their denunciations of the "rebels," on that account. After the Declaration of Independence, their positions became more critical, as by that instrument they were made disloyalists to the new government and to their respective States, all of which assumed sovereignty and could not be indifferent to these internal enemies. With the sanction of Congress, penalties of confiscation, imprisonment, banishment and minor restrictions were imposed by the several legislatures. But, as a rule, after the voluntary expatriation of the more violent and obnoxious of them, the patriots were content with keeping a close watch on their movements, to prevent as far as possible their being of service to the public enemy, to the undisguised chagrin of the more ardent Whigs, whose feelings were voiced by the vigorous outburst of Joseph Hawley: "Can we subsist—did any state ever subsist—without exterminating traitors? It is amazingly wonderful that, having no capital punishment for our intestine enemies, we have not been utterly ruined before now."

1775. Tories under Gov. Dunmore defeated in Virginia.

1776. Tories disarmed by order of Congress, "as now are Americans who take the part of the oppressors." Tories defeated and routed [illegible] in North Carolina. [illegible] Tories to Halifax, on the evacuation of Boston. [illegible] of a noted Tory parson from York, Pa., for continuing to publicly **pray** for the king.

1778. Toryism made more odious by its **massacres in** Wyoming and Cherry valleys.

1779. Toryism and cupidity made yet more odious, by **the** [illegible] inflicted on Americans [illegible] by the British fleet.

1780. Tories and their British allies defeated, and [illegible] of the most violent and cruel of **the** Tory leaders [illegible], in South Carolina, by [illegible].

1781. Tory hopes blasted by the surrender **of Cornwallis,** and [illegible] left to the mercy of their [illegible], **except that** a few of the most [illegible] were [illegible] to escape the **vengeance** of the patriots in a [illegible] vessel.

When the British troops finally quit the shores of the United States, many Tories removed across the border into Canada and New Brunswick. After some years the British parliament voted them an indemnity of [illegible], and several received "annuities, half-pay **as** military officers, large grants of lands, and shared with other subjects in the patronage of the crown." Some **of the** less prominent remained in the United States and were **soon** lost sight of among the loyal masses.

Liberty, Union and Independence assured in Peace. Divergence of Political Views among the Patriots. The Confederation Government, 1781-89.

1781. A French Fleet in aid of the United States drove the British from Chesapeake Bay. Virtual close of the war by the surrender of Cornwallis, Oct. 19.

1782. Independence of the United States recognized by Holland. Suggestion of kingship spurned by Washington. "My eyes have grown dim," said he, "in the service of my country; but I have never doubted her justice." An emblem of National sovereignty adopted by Congress in the great seal of the United States and its motto *E pluribus Unum*. The king authorized by parliament, in May, to make peace. Elias Boudinot, of New Jersey, made president of Congress, Nov. 4. Preliminary treaty of peace with Great Britain, Nov. 30.

1783. Independence of the United States recognized by Sweden, Denmark, Spain and Russia, successively. Cessation of hostilities proclaimed by Washington. Independence of the United States established by a definite treaty of peace with Great Britain, Sept. 3. Evacuation of New York, their last foothold, by the British. Final emigration of Tories. Surrender of his commission by Washington. A State constitution, with abolition of slavery, adopted by New Hampshire, to take effect in June, 1784.

The later presidents of Congress, and temporary capitals. Thomas Mifflin, chosen president of Congress, Nov. 3, [illegible] was succeeded by Richard Henry Lee, Nov. 30, 1784; Nathaniel Gorham, June 6, 1786; Arthur St. Clair, Feb. 2, 1787; and Cyrus Griffin, Jan. 22, 1788. Congress removed to Princeton, June 30, and to Annapolis, Nov. 26, 1783; to Trenton, Nov. 1, 1784; to New York, Jan. 11, 1785, which was the capital of the United States until 1790, whence it removed until the establishment of the permanent capital at Washington in 1800.

State-rights Whigs, as they were named a few years later,—State-sovereignty or State-supremacy Whigs, they might perhaps more appropriately have been called—may be said to have had control of the government under the Articles of Confederation, though, party lines not being strictly drawn, men of contrary opinion were not excluded from place or power. The central government, as previously stated, was regarded by them as a delegated authority, with the chief elements of sovereignty reserved to each State, on which account the members of the party were sometimes called particularists. Favorable to the individual States as was this form of government, they had hesitated "to conclude the compact, which was to unite the strength, wealth and councils of the whole." That their views were purely patriotic there is no reason to doubt, and that they sprang from a jealous vigilance to preserve their dearly bought liberties and not from any wish to needlessly enfeeble the central authority, is evidenced by the fact that they restricted with a like rigidity the powers of the State executives. As was observed by a French contemporary, "the mere name of authority inspired terror." They held that the largest measure of local self-government was the best safeguard against oppression. The several States had established their governments, exercising all the essential rights of real sovereignty, and it was no easy task to induce them to surrender any large measure of those powers to constitute a strong central authority which all the bitter experiences of the past had taught them to regard as possessed of abhorrent tendencies dangerous to liberty. The Continental Congress itself was nothing else than an assemblage of delegates commissioned by the several colonial assemblies and afterwards by the State legislatures, without even a semblance of direct popular or national representation. Their conception of the government was of a loose confederation of the States with a carefully restricted central delegated authority for the more convenient discharge of foreign relations and some general purposes affecting the internal relations of the States, but without possessing any of the essential attributes of sovereignty, properly so called. When, in 1783, Gen. Greene was soliciting relief for his half-fed soldiers from the legislature of South Carolina, a member exclaimed: "A Cromwell was dictating to free men, threatening them with a mutinied army; trying to build up Congress on the ruins of state rights."

The divergence of political views between the two sections of American patriots, the State-rights and the strong-government Whigs (see below) became more decided on the establishment of peace with England, and the recognition of the independence of the United States by the leading nations of the world. The period from 1783 to 1787 was much occupied in the discussion of their opposing theories, with an increasing preponderance of opinion in favor of a stronger government than was supplied by the Articles of Confederation. There was thus gradually developed a desire for a constitutional convention to reconsider and amend the existing form of government.

The first definite conception and proposal of a constitutional convention dates back a few years. July 21, 1782, on motion of General Schuyler (at the suggestion of his son-in-law, Alexander Hamilton) in the New York legislature, it was resolved: "That the foregoing important end [the collection of the taxes due the general government, by its own officers] can never be attained by partial deliberations of the States separately; but that it is essential to the common welfare that there should be, as soon as possible, a conference of the whole on the subject; and that it would be advisable, for this purpose, to propose to Congress to recommend, and to each State to adopt, the manner of assembling a general convention of the States, specially authorized to revise and amend the Confederation, reserving a right to the respective legislatures to ratify their determinations." But the project lay in abeyance several years.

"A new system of government which should act, not on the States, but directly on individuals, and vest in Congress full powers to carry its laws into effect," was suggested by Noah Webster in a pamphlet issued 1784.

In 1785, commissioners appointed by Maryland and Virginia to form some equitable agreement for the peaceable navigation of the waters common to both States, found themselves unable to establish a satisfactory settlement, whereupon the legislature of Virginia invited the other States to send delegates to Annapolis, Md., the ensuing year, to determine how existing defects in the government in regard to inter-state commercial relations could best be remedied. In 1785 Washington deplored that through the "illiberality, jealousy and local policy of the States," the Confederation was sinking, "in the eyes of Europe, into contempt."

In September, 1786, the delegates of Virginia, Pennsylvania, Delaware, New Jersey and New York assembled at Annapolis to deliberate on the subject indicated. The result of their deliberations was that they advised Congress to call a convention to revise the Articles of Confederation.

The permanency of the Confederation was meanwhile seriously menaced. A project of separation into three confederacies was entertained by some. Insurgents in western North Carolina formed the short-lived State of Frankland. There was an insurrection against Pennsylvania in the Wyoming valley. The territory of Maine projected a revolt from Massachusetts and the formation of a State. At Exeter, New Hampshire, a mob demanded of the legislature the issue of paper money and a remission of taxes. In December, what has become known as Shays' Rebellion broke out in Massachusetts. It was due to the general poverty and distress arising from the heavy taxes occasioned by the late war, and was precipitated by the attempt to legally collect these debts by forced sales, in consequence of which many worthy people were threatened with the loss of their homesteads. Taxation was growled at, or resisted in other parts of the country. Debt weighed heavily on all classes. Among other results of this widespread distress and discontent was the direction of the thoughts of many to the lack of adequate powers in the Confederation to provide for the payment of the war debt or secure the public peace.

In February, 1787, Congress passed a resolution calling on the States to send delegates to a general convention for "the sole and express purpose of revising the Articles of Confederation, and reporting to Congress and the several legislatures such alterations and provisions therein as should, when agreed to in Congress and confirmed by the States, render the Federal Constitution adequate to the exigencies of the government and the preservation of the Union."

Strong Government or Federal Sovereignty Whigs is an appropriate designation of the opponents of the State-rights Whigs. In the first year of the Confederation government they were in a decided minority, but as the weakness of that form became more manifest, the party grew in numbers, or, rather (as there was no party organization on either side), the number of those who entertained the views indicated by that name, was largely increased. They were dissatisfied with the limited powers entrusted to Congress, and the consequent inefficiency of its executive measures, justly complaining of a constitution of government that made the central authority weak at home and despised abroad. "There ought to be a principle," said Hamilton, "capable of resisting the popular current." ... It "is idle, that there must be a permanent will." They wish to endow the central government, through the voluntary concessions of the States, with the attributes of sovereignty in the exercise of the functions with which it was charged for the welfare of the whole people. "A thirst for power," wrote Washington, "and the bantling (I liked to have said the monster) sovereignty, which has taken such fast hold of the States individually, will, when joined by the many whose personal consequence in the line of State politics will in a measure be annihilated, form a strong phalanx against it."

These were perhaps extreme views, but all Strong-government Whigs desired a complete revision of the Articles of Confederation, regarding them as utterly inadequate to the purposes for which they were adopted. They claimed that the permanence of free institutions was dependent on an extension of the powers of the central government, and that without such enlargement it would be impossible to preserve the union of the States, command the respect of foreign nations or form with these equal commercial treaties. "We are one nation today," said Washington, "and thirteen tomorrow. Who will treat with us on these terms?" "If the American States," suggested an English writer, "choose to send consuls, receive them, and send a consul to each State. Each State will soon enter into all necessary regulations with the consul, and this is the whole that is necessary."

"The United States in Congress," said a native critic of the Articles of Confederation, "have exclusive power for the following purposes without being able to execute one of them:

"1. They make and conclude treaties, but can only recommend the observance of them.

"2. They may appoint ambassadors, but cannot defray even the expenses of their tables.

"3. They may borrow in their own name on the faith of the Union, but cannot pay a dollar.

"4. They may coin money, but they cannot purchase an ounce of bullion.

"5. They may make war and determine what number of troops are necessary, but cannot raise a single soldier.

"6. In short, they may declare everything, but can do nothing."

The Formation and Adoption of the Constitution, 1787-89. Federalists and Anti-Federalists.

The Federal Convention, now more generally known, from the result of its labors, as the Constitutional Convention, met in Philadelphia, in May, 1787, in response to the call of Congress three months before, every State except Rhode Island being represented. It was organized by the election of Washington as presiding officer, and its deliberations extended from May 25 to September 17.

In the first formal speech, by Edmund Randolph, it was suggested that "a national government ought to be established, consisting of a supreme legislature, executive and judiciary." Originally convened to revise the Articles of Confederation, they found so much to change that they concluded to form a new Constitution. As the result of their labors, by a provision of the original call, was to be submitted to conventions of the several States for adoption, they felt at liberty to make that departure from the first design, and signalized it by the well-known preamble to the Constitution: "We, the people of the United States, in order to form a more perfect union, establish justice, insure domestic tranquility, provide for the common defence, promote the general welfare, and secure the blessings of liberty to ourselves and our posterity, do ordain and establish this Constitution for the United States of North America." The instrument thus announced, and by one of its provisions requiring for its ratification only the adoption by nine States, founded a free representative democracy, based on universal suffrage, "a government of the people, by the people, and for the people," with the powers of government divided into three independent divisions: the legislative or Congress, the executive or President, and the judiciary or Supreme Court, with freedom of religion, of speech and of the press, trial by jury, the right of every citizen to petition, and to bear arms, and many other important provisions "to secure the blessings of liberty."

The Constitution was signed by thirty-nine of the fifty-five delegates composing the Convention, but of the other sixteen some were absent and only three of those present refused to sign. The State-rights Whigs, or Confederationists, and Strong-government Whigs, or Nationalists, (these in greater number as being the promoters of the desired change) went into Convention with little prospect of agreement. But as all were anxious to better the existing form, moderate men of both parties, with the aid of a middle class who were not specially committed to either, were enabled by compromises and concessions to harmonize the jarring elements and effect the desired end—a union or federation of the States, possessed in its own right of independent and dominant sovereign powers, but without prejudice to the local domination or sovereignty of the States within their respective borders.

The Northwest Territory. During the session of the Convention an act, only less momentous than the Constitution in its influence on liberty, was passed by Congress under this title: "An ordinance for the government of the territory of the United States northwest of the Ohio," in which, among other valuable provisions, it was ordained that "There shall be neither slavery nor involuntary servitude in the said territory, otherwise than in the punishment of crimes, whereof the party shall have been duly convicted."

The Draft of the Constitution was sent forward to Congress, which on September 28, 1787, "Resolved, That the said report [the Constitution] with the resolution and letter accompanying the same, be transmitted to the several legislatures, in order to be submitted to a convention of delegates chosen in each State by the people thereof, in conformity to the resolves of the Convention made and provided in that case."

The division of parties now became more decided and new names began to prevail, based on their relations to the new Constitution. During the debates in the Federal Convention and in the several State conventions which were called for its adoption, those who favored it were called Federalists, while those who opposed were from that circumstance known as Anti-federalists, successors, respectively, of the Strong-government and State-rights Whigs already described.

The new government assured. The Constitution (Art. VII.) provided that, "The ratification by nine States shall be sufficient for the establishment of this Constitution between the States so ratifying the same." It was ratified by the States, as follows: Delaware, December 7, Pennsylvania, December 12, New Jersey, December 18, of that year; Georgia, January 2, Connecticut, January 9, Massachusetts, February 6, Maryland, April 28, South Carolina, May 23, New Hampshire (the ninth State), June 21, Virginia, June 26, New York, July 26, 1788, North Carolina, November 21, 1789, and Rhode Island, May 29, 1790.

September 13, 1788, Congress appointed the first Wednesday in January, 1789, for the choosing of presidential electors, the first Wednesday in February for casting the ballots for president and vice-president, and the first Wednesday in March "for commencing proceedings under the Constitution," but owing to delays in coming together, the first Congress did not have a quorum until April 6, and the president was not inaugurated until April 30, 1789.

POLITICAL PARTIES FROM 1789 TO THE PRESENT TIME.

1789 to 1793—George Washington, President.

States voting, 10; their electoral vote, 73; not cast, 4.

FEDERALIST; *Electoral vote, 56.* — The sixty-nine electoral votes of both parties were cast for Washington as the first choice of all for President. "In you," said the Senate in reply to his inaugural, "all parties confide." He was politically in accord with the Federalists, but his personal fitness and his great services made him the universal choice. He reciprocated the confidence of his political opponents by selecting his cabinet partly from among them and by a studied and sincere impartiality. Party lines are, however, clearly recognizable in the choice of vice-president. John Adams, fully identified with the Federalist party, not only received thirty-four votes, the greatest number cast for any one candidate for that office, but of the remaining thirty-five, twenty-two were cast for other Federalists, leaving only thirteen electoral votes to represent the strength of the Anti-federalist party.

This Federalist victory was in fact but the continuance of that already won in the Constitutional Convention and the ten State conventions which had adopted the new form of government. They alone could be entrusted with carrying it into effect, while their opponents might be trusted to keep a watchful eye on their avowed purpose to enlarge its scope. In their leading measures the Federalists evinced a decided tendency to increase the functions and powers of the general government, as well by new statutes to that end, as by such interpretation of the Constitution—its implied and constructive grants of central authority—as favored their views. Hence they and their successors in that line of thought are known as Loose, or Broad Constructionists.

The Federalists denied the adaptability of "the masses" for self-government, and regarded them as inclined to oppose the rights of property as well as the pretensions of a superior or ruling class, to which the Federalists considered themselves as belonging. The party comprised prosperous merchants, capitalists, large land-owners, theorists and thinkers who imagined the British government to be so nearly perfect that they were more desirous of imitating than improving it, and those distinguished for inherited prestige and social standing. They lacked faith in the people.

ANTI-FEDERALIST; *Electoral vote, 13.* — *No opposing candidate for the presidency.*

The Anti-federalist was a short-lived party. They were known as Particularists and State-rights Whigs until the meeting of the Constitutional Convention, May 14, 1787, but upon the acceptance of the Constitution by Rhode Island, May 29, 1790, that designation was no longer applicable. Indeed it was never appropriate, and had always been protested against. They did not oppose a league or union, nor the Constitution, but only the Federalist views of them. There were no truer patriots than their leaders. But the objectionable epithet continued to be applied until they adopted the more significant name of Republicans.

1793 to 1797—GEORGE WASHINGTON, President—Second Term.

States voting, 15; total electoral vote, 135; not cast, 3.

FEDERALIST; *Electoral vote, 77.* — Several of the more prominent leaders of the Federalist party regarded the Constitution merely as the best that could then be "extorted from the grinding necessity of a reluctant nation." "The Federal government," said Hamilton, "may then triumph over the State governments, and reduce them to entire subordination, dividing the larger States into smaller districts," and be "able to protect the men of property from the depredations which the democratic spirit is apt to make on property." In 1792 he characterized the Constitution as "a shilly-shally thing of mere milk and water, and only good as a step to something better;" and in 1802 he was "still laboring to prop the frail and worthless fabric." "State attachments and State importance," said Gouverneur Morris, "have been the bane of this country. We cannot annihilate them, but we may perhaps take out the teeth of the serpents."

Party lines were distinctly drawn between them and their opponents, the Republicans, whom they called Democratic Republicans, and the French party, because of the odium then attaching to the word democrat by reason of the excesses of the Jacobins, or radical democrats of the French Revolution. The Federalists, on the other hand, were characterized by their opponents, with equal freedom, as Aristocratic and Monarchical Republicans, and the British party.

REPUBLICAN; *Electoral vote, 55.* — *No opposing candidate for the presidency.*

The Republican party of 1792 may be said to consist of such persons as, though adhering to the strict construction views of the late Anti-federalists and the State-rights views of these and their predecessors, the Particularists, had determined to give the Constitution a fair trial and due obedience, while resisting the "implied and constructive" theory of the Federalists. "I own," said Jefferson, the leader and founder of the party, "that I am not a friend to a very energetic government: it is always oppressive."

Among the leading principles of the party were the sovereignty, if not the supremacy of the States, without prejudice however to the limited sovereignty of the Federal government in its own sphere; the value of local self-government as a safeguard of free institutions as well as an economy in internal administration. Their aim was to foster simple and inexpensive, rather than showy and complicated forms of administration. They claimed that thus had independence been won, and that thus it could be best maintained, and prosperity and happiness be more widely distributed among a self-governing people.

1797 to 1801—JOHN ADAMS, President.

States voting, 16; total electoral vote, 138.

FEDERALIST; *Electoral vote, 71.* — The leaning of the party to strong government views and its partiality to the British in the European conflicts of the period culminated in the introduction and enactment through its influence, of the Alien and Sedition laws of 1798. One required fourteen years' residence before naturalization; a second authorized the president to "order any alien whom he should judge to be dangerous to the peace and liberties of America to depart from the United States;" a third provided that, upon declaration of war against, or invasion of the United States, all former subjects of the hostile power might be arrested, secured or removed at the discretion of the president, requiring only the formality of a proclamation. Though worded with careful comprehensiveness, these Alien laws were chiefly directed against the French, because of their ultra-democracy, and British refugees in America. The Sedition Act made it a misdemeanor, punishable by a fine not to exceed $5,000, and imprisonment not to exceed five years, to combine against government measures or officials; and subjecting to fine and imprisonment any one who should print or publish "any false, scandalous and malicious writings against the government of the United States, or either House of Congress, or the President, with intent to defame them, or to bring them into contempt or disrepute." These measures justified the charges of their opponents and lost the party the confidence of the people.

REPUBLICAN; *Electoral vote, 68.* — *Thomas Jefferson, candidate for the presidency.*

The current views of the party are fairly indicated by the following extracts, of two years' later date:

From the Kentucky Resolutions of 1799: "That the principle and construction contended for by sundry of the State legislatures, that the General government is the exclusive judge of the extent of the powers delegated to it, stop not short of despotism—since the discretion of those who administer government, and not the Constitution, would be the measure of their powers. That the several States who formed that instrument, being sovereign and independent, have the unquestionable right to judge of the infraction; and that a nullification by those sovereignties of all unauthorized acts done under color of that instrument, is the rightful remedy; that this Commonwealth does under the most deliberate reconsideration declare that the said Alien and Sedition Laws are, in their opinion, palpable violations of the said Constitution."

From Virginia Resolutions of 1798: "This Assembly doth explicitly and peremptorily declare that it views the powers of the Federal government, as limited by the plain sense and intention of the instrument constituting that compact, as no further valid than they are authorized by the grants enumerated in that compact; and that in case of a deliberate, palpable and dangerous exercise of other powers, not granted by said compact, the States who are parties thereto have the right and are in duty bound to interpose for arresting the progress of the evil and for maintaining, within their respective limits, the authorities, rights and liberties appertaining to them.

"The General Assembly doth also express its deep regret, that a spirit has, in sundry instances, been manifested by the Federal government to enlarge its powers by forced constructions of the constitutional charter which defines them; ... so as to consolidate the States by degrees into one sovereignty, the obvious tendency and inevitable result of which would be to transform the present republican system of the United States into an absolute, or at best a mixed monarchy.

"The General Assembly doth particularly protest against the palpable and alarming infractions of the Constitution in the two late cases of the Alien and Sedition Acts."

1801 to 1805—Thomas Jefferson, President.

States voting, 16; total electoral vote, 138.

REPUBLICAN; *Electoral vote, 73.* — *Platform of 1800 abridged;* 1. "Inviolable preservation of the Federal constitution, according to the true sense in which it was adopted by the States. 2. Opposition to monarchizing its features. 3. Preservation to the States of the powers not yielded by them to the Union. 4. A rigorously frugal administration of the government, ... and resistance to all measures looking to a multiplication of offices and salaries. 5. Reliance for internal defense solely upon the militia, till actual invasion, ... and opposition to the policy of a standing army in time of peace. 6. Free commerce with all nations, political connection with none, and little or no diplomatic establishment. 7. Opposition to linking ourselves by new treaties with the quarrels of Europe. 8. Freedom of religion. 9. Freedom of speech and of the press. 10. Liberal naturalization laws. 11. Encouragement of science and the arts to the end that the American people may perfect their independence of all foreign monopolies, institutions and influences."

From Jefferson's inaugural, 1801; "I will compress them ['The essential principles of our government,'] within the narrowest compass they will bear:"

"Equal and exact justice to all men, of whatever State or persuasion, religious or political; peace, commerce and honest friendship with all nations, entangling alliances with none; the support of the State governments in all their rights as the most competent administrations for our domestic concerns and the surest bulwark against anti-republican tendencies; the preservation of the general government, in its whole constitutional vigor, as the sheet-anchor of our peace at home and safety abroad; a jealous care of the right of election by the people." (*Continued under Jefferson's second term.*)

FEDERALIST; *Electoral vote, 65.* — *John Adams, candidate.* President Adams was held responsible by many prominent Federalists for the injury done to the party by the Alien and Sedition laws, and his known desire for re-election offended others who felt that past success was jeopardized by his candidacy. Against the Sedition Act especially, Hamilton, the most popular of the party's leaders, had vainly remonstrated. "Let us," said he, "not establish a tyranny. Energy is a very different thing from violence. If we take no false step, we shall be essentially united; but if we push things to the extreme, we shall then give to parties body and solidity." Hamilton had long been estranged from Adams; and the latter was regarded by many as an unwise party leader, because of personal peculiarities as well as public measures.

The party was defeated by 68 to 71 electoral votes, and never recovered political ascendency; but it had done good work and deserved well of the country. It had established the Union by the Federal Constitution, a work which otherwise might not have been achieved but by a slow political evolution. It had funded the public debt and established the finances of the new nation on a creditable basis; had put into practical operation the complex machinery of the new government, and had added the first ten Amendments to the Constitution, having shown an unusual degree of political courage in accepting them from the opposition.

1805 to 1809—THOMAS JEFFERSON, President—Second Term.

States voting, 17; total electoral vote, 176.

REPUBLICAN; *Electoral vote, 162.* (*Continued from Jefferson's first term*). "a mild and safe corrective of abuses which are lopped by the sword of revolution where peaceable remedies are unprovided; absolute acquiescence in the decisions of the majority—the vital principle of republics, from which there is no appeal but to force, the vital principle and immediate parent of despotism; a well-disciplined militia—our best reliance in peace, and for the first moments of war, till regulars may relieve them; the supremacy of the civil over the military authority; economy in the public expense, that labor may be lightly burdened; the honest payment of our debts and sacred preservation of the public faith; encouragement of agriculture, and of commerce as its handmaid; the diffusion of information and the arraignment of all abuses at the bar of public reason; freedom of religion; freedom of the press; freedom of person under the protection of the habeas corpus; and trial by juries impartially selected—these principles form the bright constellation which has gone before us and guided our steps through an age of revolution and reformation. The wisdom of our sages and the blood of our heroes have been devoted to their attainment. They should be the creed of our political faith—the text of civil instruction—the touchstone by which to try the services of those we trust; and should we wander from them in moments of error or alarm, let us hasten to retrace our steps, and to regain the road which alone leads to peace, liberty and safety."

From Jefferson's Letters, in 1801, in relation to removals from office: . . . "I lament sincerely that unessential differences of opinion should ever have been deemed sufficient to interdict half the society from the rights and the blessings of self-government, to proscribe them as unworthy of every trust. It would have been to me a circumstance of great relief, had I found a moderate participation of office in the hands of the majority. I would gladly have left to time and accident to raise them to their just share. But their total exclusion calls for prompter corrections. I shall correct the procedure, but, that done, return with joy to that state of things when the only question concerning a candidate shall be: Is he honest? Is he capable? Is he faithful to the Constitution?"

"Some removals I know must be made. They must be as few as possible, done gradually, and bottomed on some malversation or inherent disqualification." . . . . "officers who have been guilty of gross abuses of office, such as marshals packing juries, &c., I shall now remove, as my predecessor ought in justice to have done. The instances will be few, and governed by strict rule, not party passion. The right of opinion shall suffer no invasion from me." . . . . "The measures we shall pursue and propose for the amelioration of the public affairs will be so confessedly salutary as to unite all men not monarchists in principle."

FEDERALIST; *Electoral vote, 14.* *Charles C. Pinckney, candidate.* Through dissensions among the leaders, as well as by reason of the great political sagacity of Jefferson, who has perhaps never been surpassed as a party leader, the Federalists had sunk into a hopeless minority.

1809 to 1813—JAMES MADISON, President.

States voting, 17; total electoral vote, 176; not cast, 1.

REPUBLICAN; *Electoral vote, 122.* The party continued in the line marked out by the genius of Jefferson, and no one was more willing to accept his guidance than the new president. The government had been administered for eight years under Republican principles to the general satisfaction of the people, and there were no grounds for a marked change of policy. The disturbed relations with England remained unimproved, but Jefferson and Madison were equally loath to proceed to extremities by declaring war. The Embargo Act of the former administration had some influence in decreasing the Republican majority in the electoral college, but a schism in the party and the less popularity of the candidate had probably more influence in producing that result. The ascendency of the party throughout the nation was not, however, seriously impaired, nor were any new principles of party politics broached. Even its bitterest opponents had been compelled to recognize its patriotism and fidelity to the Constitution.

Madison, personally, had been a wise and zealous promoter and defender of that instrument, and his influence in molding it to its existing form was second to none. He has, indeed, been styled "the father of the Constitution." "I hold for a fundamental point," said he, in April, 1787, "that an individual independence of the States is utterly irreconcilable with the idea of aggregate sovereignty. I think, at the same time, that a consolidation of the States into a simple republic is not less unattainable than it would be inexpedient. Let it be tried whether any middle ground can be taken."

"Let the national government be armed with a positive and complete authority in all cases where uniform measures are necessary, as in trade. . . . Let it also retain the powers which it now possesses. . . . Let this national supremacy be extended also to the judiciary. . . . The legislative department may be divided into two branches . . . . A national executive will also be necessary. . . . An article . . . guaranteeing the States against internal as well as external dangers."

George Clinton, candidate of a section of the Republican party, received six of the nineteen electoral votes of his own State, New York.

FEDERALIST; *Electoral vote, 47.* *Charles C. Pinckney, candidate.* The Federalists being in opposition since 1801, their views had become somewhat modified. They were no longer strenuous advocates of the "implied and constructive" powers of the Federal government. They had opposed the purchase of Louisiana on the ground, among others, that the Constitution did not entrust Congress with such powers; and they railed at the Embargo Act, as not included in the power to regulate commerce. "This measure rekindled the old fires of party. He that was for the Embargo was a 'Democrat;' he that was against it, a 'Federalist.' It was a wall between the parties . . . in every State, city, county, town, village and hamlet . . . and in every class and condition of the people."

1813 to 1817—JAMES MADISON, President—Second Term.

States voting, 18; total electoral vote, 218; not cast, 1.

REPUBLICAN; *Electoral vote, 128.* The Republicans had entered on the campaign of 1808 with the avowal that "its only choice lay between the embargo and war, and war should be avoided as long as possible;" and Madison had endeavored by diplomacy and remonstrance to avert a rupture with England. This course having proved ineffective, and the insults to the nation having grown more intolerable because of his forbearance, the leaders of the party demanded that he should yield to the wishes of the people, and the declaration of war against Great Britain was approved by him June 18th, 1812. The presidential campaign of the year hinged on that measure and some minor domestic conditions: Sectional jealousy of Virginia, as "the mother of presidents;" the antagonism of a peace faction which on religious grounds deprecated war with Great Britain, "the bulwark of Protestantism" and "the world's last hope;" and the partisanship of the Federalists who opposed it as an administration measure. The president having committed himself to war, was a strenuous advocate and promoter by word and work of all that it implied, and was supported by the great body of the people, though some of the New England States refused to supply their quotas of troops, and a few misguided Federalists gave aid and comfort to the enemy.

Otherwise the political views of the party underwent no serious change, and the following brief analysis of the Constitution by Madison shows his appreciation of the unique and nicely-balanced American system of government which secures sovereignty to the Federal as well as the State authorities within their respective spheres. "The Constitution," said he, "is in strictness neither a national nor a federal constitution, but a composition of both. In its foundation it is federal, not national; in the sources from which the ordinary powers of the government are drawn it is partly federal and partly national; in the operation of these powers it is national, not federal; in the extent of them, again, it is federal, not national; and, finally, in the authoritative mode of introducing amendments it is neither wholly federal nor wholly national."

FEDERALIST; *Electoral vote, 89.* *De Witt Clinton, candidate.* The supporters of Clinton were partly Federalists and partly disaffected Republicans, the coalition being designated Clintonians.

Clintonian Platform Abridged: 1. Opposition to the congressional caucus system of nominating presidential candidates; 2, to an official regency self-constituted to prescribe tests of political faith and tests of political orthodoxy; 3, to a monopoly of the highest offices by particular States, and especially to the continuance of a Virginian in the presidency; 4, to the continuance of Mr. Madison in an office which, in view of our pending difficulties with Great Britain, requires an incumbent of greater decision, energy and efficiency; 5, to the lingering inadequacy of preparation for the war; 6, Avowal of the existing necessity of placing the country in a condition for aggressive action for the conquest of Canada; 7, Advocacy of the election of De Witt Clinton.

Hartford Convention of Federalists recommended the adoption, by the five New England States represented, of measures: 1, To protect their citizens from the Federal military draft; 2, their own coasts with their own militia; 3, to organize their militia with full control by the respective States; 4, to labor for amendments to the Constitution—1, to ignore slaves as a basis of representation; 2, to require two-thirds vote of both Houses for admission of new States; 3, to restrict Congress in laying embargoes to sixty days; 4, to require two-thirds vote of both Houses to decree commercial non-intercourse with foreign nations; 5, the same to declare aggressive war; 6, to exclude naturalized citizens from Federal offices; 7, to limit the president to one term, and to exclude from the immediate succession a citizen of the same State.

1817 to 1821—JAMES MONROE, President.

States voting, 19; total electoral vote, 221; not cast, 4.

REPUBLICAN; *Electoral vote, 183.* No marked change of party views characterized the election of Monroe. He was recognized as the natural successor of Madison, as the latter was of Jefferson. The happy termination of the war had given the party such a hold on popular confidence that they could afford to be more tolerant of their opponents' views and even to engraft some of them on their own principles. An effort was made to wipe out party lines, and the president's wishes in that direction were reinforced by the advice of Gen. Jackson, "to exterminate that monster called party spirit." "The chief magistrate of a great and powerful nation," he added, "should never indulge in party feelings. His conduct should be liberal and disinterested; always bearing in mind, that he acts for the whole and not a part of the community." On his tour of inspection of national defenses, the president in reply to an address at Kennebunk, Maine, spoke as follows: "You are pleased to express a confident hope that a spirit of mutual conciliation may be one of the blessings which may result from my administration. This indeed would be an eminent blessing, and I pray it may be realized. Nothing but union is wanting to make us a great people. The present time affords the happiest presage that this union is fast consummating. It cannot be otherwise; I daily see greater proofs of it. The further I advance in my progress in the country, the more I perceive that we are all Americans—that we compose but one family—that our republican institutions will be supported and perpetuated by the united zeal and patriotism of all. Nothing could give me greater satisfaction than to behold a perfect union among ourselves—a union which is necessary to restore to social intercourse its former charms, and to render our happiness, as a nation, unmixed and complete. To promote this desirable result requires no compromise of principle, and I promise to give it my continued attention, and my best endeavors."

As early as 1785 Monroe had favored an enlargement of the powers of Congress under the Articles of Confederation, and although distrustful of what he deemed the too liberal grant of power to the Federal government by the Constitution, and its too limited recognition of the rights of the citizen, upon the adoption of the first ten amendments to that instrument guaranteeing those rights, he became its consistent supporter, and during his term, like his predecessor, adopted some of the measures that were originally characteristic of Federalist views. He was, however, always mindful of the principle of popular sovereignty. "It is only," said he in his inaugural, "when the people become ignorant and corrupt—when they degenerate into a populace—that they are incapable of exercising sovereignty." From these causes his administration became known as "the era of good feeling."

FEDERALIST; *Electoral vote, 34.* *Rufus King, candidate.* The party organization was continued until this election, but its standard-bearer was only the leader of a forlorn hope. It had forfeited whatever hold it had retained through the two administrations of Jefferson and the first of Madison on the confidence of the people, by its factious antagonism to the War of 1812-15, and by the proceedings of the Hartford Convention of 1814. The strong government principles for which it stood had been proved unnecessary by the happy issue of a war conducted by their political opponents.

1821 to 1825—JAMES MONROE, President—Second Term.

States voting, 24; total electoral vote, 235; votes not cast, 3.

REPUBLICAN; *Electoral vote, 231.* The president's policy had been so wise and liberal that the "era of good feeling" had been fully established at the period of his second election. By a process of natural selection in politics some of the more valuable principles of the Federalists had been adopted, and the Republican party of the period embraced "hope," as well as "strict constructionists," while awaiting a new differentiation of political issues of sufficient importance to form the bases of new parties. The president had increased the army and navy in numbers and efficiency, strengthened the national defences, encouraged commerce, favored the United States bank, and promoted the general welfare by many prudent measures regardless of their origin, whether Federalist or Republican. Somewhat similarly the Federalist party before its final dissolution had changed places with its old antagonists, having become "strict constructionists" of the powers of the general government in the late war.

It was a period when, says Benton, "the word economy had an existence **in** fact as well **as** in name. It was my first year **in** Congress; and while economy **was** claimed as a distinctive Republican virtue (for the name of Democrat had not been taken), I owe it to candor and to justice to say that I **saw** the same regard for economy in the Federal members (for neither had they at that time changed their name) that **I** did in the Republican. Less **than** $13,000,000 a year for working the government at that **time**."

The Monroe Doctrine, from the President's message of Dec. 2d, 1823.

. . . "The citizens of the United States cherish sentiments the most friendly in favor of the liberty and happiness of their fellow-men on the other side of the Atlantic. In wars of the European powers, in matters relating to themselves, we have never taken any part, nor does it comport with our policy to do so. It is only when our rights are invaded, or seriously menaced, that we resent injuries, or make preparation for our defense. The political system of the allied powers is essentially different in this respect from that of America. This difference proceeds from that which exists in our respective governments; and **to** the defense of our own, which has been achieved by **the loss** of so much blood and treasure, and matured by **the wisdom** of our most enlightened citizens and under which **we** have enjoyed unexampled felicity, this whole nation is devoted. We owe it, therefore, to candor and the amicable relations existing between the United States and those powers to declare that we should consider any attempt on their part to extend their system to any portion of this hemisphere as dangerous to our peace and safety. With the existing colonies or dependencies of **any** European power we have not interfered; but with the governments which have declared their independence, and maintained it, and whose independence we have, on great consideration and on just principles, acknowledged, we could **not** view any interposition for the purpose of oppressing them, or controlling in any other manner their destiny, by any European power, in any other light than as the manifestation of an unfriendly disposition toward the United States.

. . . Our policy in regard to Europe, which **was** adopted at an early stage of the wars which have so long agitated that quarter of the globe, nevertheless remains the **same**, which is, not to interfere in the internal concerns of **any of** its powers; to consider the government *de facto* **as** the legitimate government for us; to cultivate friendly relations with it, and to preserve those relations by a frank, firm and manly policy; meeting, in all instances, the just claims of every power, submitting to injuries from none. But **in** regard to these continents (North and South America) circumstances are eminently and conspicuously different. It is impossible that the allied powers should extend their political system to any portion of either continent without endangering **our** peace and happiness."

John Quincy Adams, candidate of a small faction of Republicans and former Federalists, prevented the re-election of Monroe from being unanimous.

1825 to 1829—John Quincy Adams, President.

States voting, 24; total electoral vote, 261; **not cast, 1.**

REPUBLICAN: *Electoral vote, 261. Popular vote, 352,062.* } Republican principles, somewhat modified by the responsibilities of actual administration of **the government** for a quarter of a century as well as by **the influences** of the opposition, had now gained **complete** ascendancy. Soon after the establishment of **the government** under the Constitution, and indeed **while its** adoption was under consideration, "we broke," said **Jefferson**, "into two parties, each wishing to give the government a different direction; the one—the Republican—to strengthen the most popular branch; the other—the Federal—the more permanent branches and to extend their permanence." The contests of a generation had ended, leaving the former party without organized opposition. There were four candidates for the presidency in 1824, all Republicans, and no political issues, whence the campaign was nicknamed, rather disrespectfully, as "the scrub race for the presidency." No candidate having received a majority, the contest was carried into the House of Representatives, which elected Mr. Adams, who had received only 84 electoral votes and a popular vote of 105,321. He might be characterized as the Eastern or New England candidate, and was backed by the prestige of his father, the influence of the unorganized Federalists, and the more effective aid of the "loose-constructionist Republicans" under the leadership of Henry Clay.

Andrew *Jackson—Electoral vote,* **99; Popular** *vote, 155,872.*

Andrew Jackson might be characterized as the military-prestige candidate, and he received the largest number of electoral votes, but was defeated in the House of Representatives by an alleged coalition of the friends of Henry Clay with his own partisans. The representatives of districts which had given a majority for Jackson were considered to have betrayed their trust in voting for Adams in the House, and though their action was legal they lost caste with their constituents and were relegated to private life at the ensuing Congressional election, when friends of Jackson were very generally chosen. Thus were public men taught to recognize that the preferences of the people could not be disregarded with impunity, even where Constitutional rights only were exercised. It also led to the abolition of the caucus system of nominating presidential candidates. The first choice of the people was not the nominee of the caucus, and this earlier attempt of the same Congress to dictate the choice of the people was so effectively rebuked that congressional caucus nominations were replaced by the Convention system. The caucus was characterized by Rufus King as "a new, extraordinary, self-created central power, stronger than the power of the Constitution, which has risen up at the seat of government."

Wm. H. Crawford—Electoral **vote, 41, Popular** *vote, 44,282.*

William Harris Crawford was the candidate **of** the Congressional caucus. He was Secretary of the Treasury at the time of his nomination, had previously been Secretary of War, Minister to France, and a Senator from Georgia. Bred a lawyer he entered public life at the age of thirty-one as a member of the State legislature and while in the United States senate was regarded as **its** ablest member. His chance of winning the presidency was marred by being the nominee of the caucus at a time when it had begun to be unpopular, and when its claims to the confidence of the people were antagonized by three rival candidates of great local and personal popularity.

Henry Clay—Electoral vote, 37; Popular vote, 46,587.

Henry Clay, the fourth presidential candidate, represented the "loose-constructionist" wing of the great party to which all the candidates belonged, and was personally and locally popular in his section. When defeated in the electoral college and barred from election by the House as the candidate receiving the least number of votes, he threw his influence in favor of Adams and secured his election. In regard to his action in the matter there is no reason to doubt the truth of his own statement made to a friend, Jan. 28, 1825: "My position in regard to the presidential contest is highly critical, and such as to leave me no path on which I can move without censure. I have pursued in regard to it the rule which I always observe in the discharge of my public duty. I have interrogated my conscience as to what I ought to do, and it tells me **I** ought to vote for Mr. Adams."

1829 to 1833—Andrew Jackson, President.

States voting, 24; total electoral vote, 261.

DEMOCRATIC: *Electoral vote, 178; Popular vote, 647,231.* } During the previous administration the Republican party became divided, on the lines which has constituted the underlying basis of separation in all our political history, into "strict," and "loose-constructionists" of the powers of Federal government. The former finally adopted the party name Democratic, which at first had been directed at them as a reproach and which for many years had been used to qualification of and interchangeably with their chosen name Republican. There was, however, but little change of principles, except, as before stated, by gradual political evolution as affected by the antagonism of the Federalists, their own ripened experience in administration and the beneficial influence of increased confidence in the good working qualities of the Constitution as established and amended. The election of Jackson was regarded as a triumph of the people over the political leaders, who were held to have proved recreant to their trust in the previous election. His military successes, years before, had made him the idol of the people who looked upon him as one of themselves, and had a well-founded confidence in his sincerity as well as his instinctive sympathy with their wants and wishes. His views, as indicated by his inaugural, did not differ essentially from those of his more immediate predecessors. He promised "to take care not to confound the reserved powers of the separate States with those which they had granted to the Confederacy;" to recognize the constitutional limits as well as extent of his official powers—affirming in that connection that "the recent demonstration of public sentiment in the late election inscribes on the list of executive duties, in characters too legible to be overlooked, the task of Reform"—to improve the finances; to correct abuses; to strengthen the militia; and to cultivate friendly relations with foreign **nations**. In his first message he indicated a preference for electing the president and vice-president by direct vote of the people. "It was never designed," he said, "that **their** choice should in any case be defeated, either by the intervention of electoral colleges, or by the agency confided under certain contingencies to the House of Representatives. Experience proves that in proportion as agents to secure the will of the people are multiplied, there is danger of their wishes being frustrated. Some may be unfaithful. All are liable to err. So far, therefore, as the people can with convenience speak, it is safer for them to express their own will." With characteristic directness he removed officials for differing with him in political opinion, and he is held responsible for the introduction into American politics of the spoils system. "During the first year of his administration there were nearly seven hundred removals from office, not including subordinate clerks. During the forty years preceding there had been but sixty-four." He had forcibly deprecated such removals a few years before, and it is only fair to assume that his change of views was due to what he deemed a political necessity. He was, he said, "too old a soldier to leave his garrison in the hands of his enemies."

NATIONAL REPUBLICAN; *Electoral vote, 83; Popular vote, 508,064.* } *John Q. Adams, candidate.*

The "loose-constructionist" wing of the late Republican party assumed the name of the National Republican, the qualifying adjective helping to appropriately designate the inheritance from the disbanded Federalists of the principle which might be described as the Nation above the States. They also favored a protective tariff while their opponents represented substantially a tariff for revenue only. In the matter of internal improvements at national expense they also favored a broader sweep of the principle involved than did the Democrats who had adopted it as it were under protest, and to be exercised only with great discretion as an implied consequence of the military, commercial or other powers of the Federal government.

The Nullification Faction in South Carolina assumed form by an act of the State legislature, in November, 1832, nullifying the Tariff Act of Congress, as unconstitutional, to which President Jackson promptly replied by sending troops and issuing a proclamation, saying, among other things, "If South Carolina considers the revenue laws unconstitutional, and has a right to prevent their execution in the port of Charleston, there would be a clear constitutional objection to their collection in every other port, and no revenue could be collected anywhere; for all imports must be equal."

1833 to 1837—ANDREW JACKSON, President—Second Term.

States voting, 24; total **electoral vote, 288; not cast, 2.**

DEMOCRATIC; *Electoral vote, 219; Popular vote, 687,502.* } **"The people of the** United **States," said Jackson, in his Nullification** Proclamation **of** 1832, "formed **the** Constitution, acting **through the** State Legislatures in making the compact, **to meet and** discuss its **provisions, and** acting in separate **conventions** when they **ratified those** provisions; but the terms **used in** the Constitution show it **to** be a government **in which the** people of **all the** States collectively are represented. We are one **people** in the choice of President and Vice-president. **Here the** States have no other agency than to direct the mode **in** which the votes shall be given. The people then, and not the States, are represented in the executive branch. . . . In the House of Representatives, the members are all representatives of the United States, not representatives of the particular States from which they come. They are paid by the United States, not by **the State**, nor **are** they accountable to it for any act done in the performance of their legislative functions.

"The Constitution of the United States, then, forms a government, not a league; and whether it be formed by compact between the States, or in any other manner, its character is the same. It is a government in which all the people are represented, which operates directly on the people individually, not upon the States. They retained all the power they did not grant; but each State having expressly parted with so many powers as to constitute, jointly with the other States, a single nation, cannot from that period possess any right to secede, because such secession does not break a league, but destroys the unity of the nation, and any injury to that unity is not only a breach which could result from the contravention **of** a compact, **but** is an offense against the whole Union. To say that any State may at pleasure secede **from** the Union, is to say that the United States are not **a nation**, because it would be a solecism to contend that **any part** of a nation might dissolve its connection with the **other** parts, to their injury or ruin, without committing an offense. Secession, like any other revolutionary act, may **be morally** justified by the extremity of oppression; but to **call it a** constitutional right is confounding the meaning **of terms.**"

John Floyd, candidate of the Nullification Faction, received the eleven electoral votes of South Carolina.

NATIONAL REPUBLICAN; *Electoral vote, 49; Popular vote, 530,189.* } *Henry Clay, candidate.*

"*Resolved*,—That an adequate protection to American industry is indispensable to the prosperity of the country

[illegible]

ANTI-MASONIC; [illegible]

1837 to 1841—Martin Van Buren, President.

States voting, 26; total electoral vote, 294.

DEMOCRATIC; [illegible]

WHIG; [illegible]

1841 to 1845—WILLIAM HENRY HARRISON, President.

WHIG; [illegible]

DEMOCRATIC; [illegible]

LIBERTY ("ABOLITION"); [illegible]

1845 to 1849—JAMES KNOX POLK, President.

DEMOCRATIC; [illegible]

WHIG; [illegible]

LIBERTY; [illegible]

1849 to 1853—ZACHARY TAYLOR, President.

WHIG; [illegible]

tion, or manifest haste and want of consideration by Congress.... 3. Upon the subjects of the tariff, the currency, the improvement of our great highways, rivers, lakes and harbors, the will of the people, as expressed through their representatives in Congress, ought to be respected and carried out by the executive. 4. I sincerely rejoice at the prospect of peace.... The principles of our government, as well as its true policy, are opposed to the subjugation of other nations and the dismemberment of other countries by conquest."

DEMOCRATIC; *Electoral vote, 127; Popular vote, 1,220,544.* } *Lewis Cass, candidate. Platform condensed:* "1. Resolved, That the American Democracy place their trust in the intelligence, the patriotism, and the discriminating justice of the American people. 2. We regard this [trust] as a distinctive feature of our political creed.... and contrast it with the creed and practice of federalism, under whatever name or form.... 3. The Democratic party.... renew and re-assert before the American people the declaration of principles avowed by them on a former occasion." [Here follow resolutions 1, 2, 3 and 4, of 1844. 8.... "No more revenue ought to be raised than is required to defray the necessary expenses of the government, and for the gradual but certain extinction of the debt.... [Here follows resolution 5, of 1840, with the addition]: "And that the results of Democratic legislation, in this and all other financial measures, ... have demonstrated.... their soundness, safety and utility in all business pursuits." [Here follow resolutions 7, 8 and 9, of 1840, and 10 and 11 of 1844.] 15, 16 and 17. Justify the war with Mexico, and compliment the army for its services therein. 18. Tenders fraternal congratulations to National Convention of the Republic of France. 19. Declares the duty of the Democratic party "to sustain and advance among us constitutional liberty, equality and fraternity, by continuing to resist all monopolies".... 20. Orders a copy of these resolutions to be forwarded to the French Republic. 21. Recapitulates the chief measures of Polk's administration and declares that "it would be a fatal error to weaken the hands of a political organization by which these great reforms have been achieved, and risk them in the hands of their known adversaries".... 22. Compliments and congratulates President Polk. 23. Presents Lewis Cass as candidate.

FREE SOIL; *Electoral vote, 0; Popular vote, 291,263.* } *Martin Van Buren, candidate. Platform of 1848.*—An eloquent and impassioned appeal, in a three-fold preamble and sixteen resolutions, against the extension of slavery, from which the following are brief extracts: "A common resolve to maintain the rights of free labor against the aggressions of the slave power, and to secure free soil to a free people." "We propose no interference by Congress with slavery within the limits of any State." "It was the settled policy of the nation [from 1784 to 1800] not to extend, nationalize or encourage .... slavery, and to this policy .... the government ought to return." "Congress has no more power to make a slave than to make a king." "The only safe means of preventing the extension of slavery into territory now free, is to prevent its extension into such territory by an act of Congress." "We accept the issue which the slave power has forced upon us; and to their demand for more slave States and more slave territory, our calm but final answer is, no more slave States and no more slave territory." "There must be no more compromises with slavery; if made, they must be repealed." "We demand cheap postage for the people." "River and harbor improvements.... are objects of national concern." "The free grant to actual settlers.... of reasonable portions of the public lands, under suitable limitations, is a wise and just measure of public policy." "Honor and patriotism require the earliest practical payment of the public debt." "We inscribe on our banner, 'Free Soil, Free Speech, Free Labor and Free Men,' and under it we will fight on, and fight ever, until a triumphant victory shall reward our exertions."

LIBERTY LEAGUE; } *Gerrit Smith, candidate.* The Liberty League, the radical wing of the Free-Soil, or Liberty Party. *Platform*—The duty and the right of the Federal government to abolish slavery even in the slave States. *Motto*—Duty is ours, results are God's.

1853 to 1857—FRANKLIN PIERCE, President.

States voting, 31; total electoral vote, 296.

DEMOCRATIC; *Electoral vote, 254; Popular vote, 1,601,474.* } *Platform of 1852* was mainly composed of planks borrowed from the platforms of 1840, 1844 and 1848, with these additions: "The Democratic party of the Union, standing on this national platform, will abide by, and adhere to a faithful execution of the acts known as the Compromise measures settled by last Congress, 'the act for reclaiming fugitives from service labor,' included." "The Democratic party will resist all attempts at renewing in Congress, or out of it, the agitation of the slavery question, under whatever shape or color the attempt may be made." "The Democratic party will faithfully abide by and uphold the principles laid down in the Kentucky and Virginia resolutions of 1792 and 1798, and in the report of Mr. Madison to the Virginia legislature in 1799." "The war with Mexico, upon all the principles of patriotism and the law of nations, was a just and necessary war on our part, in which no American citizen should have shown himself opposed to his country." "We rejoice at the restoration of friendly relations with our sister republic of Mexico, and earnestly desire for her all the blessings and prosperity which we enjoy under republican institutions, and we congratulate the American people on the results of that war, which have so manifestly justified the policy and conduct of the Democratic party, and insured to the United States indemnity for the past and security for the future."

"In view of the condition of popular institutions in the old world, a high and sacred duty is devolved with increased responsibility upon the Democracy of this country, as the party of the people, to uphold and maintain the rights of every State, and thereby the union of States, and to sustain and advance among them constitutional liberty, by continuing to resist all monopolies and exclusive legislation for the benefit of the few at the expense of the many, and by a vigilant and constant adherence to those principles and compromises of the Constitution, which are broad enough and strong enough to embrace and uphold the Union as it is, and the Union as it should be, in the full expansion of the energies and capacity of this great and progressive people."

WHIG; *Electoral vote, 42; Popular vote, 1,386,578.* } *Winfield Scott, candidate. Platform.*—Substantially a repetition of former announcements of the same character, with the additions: "The Union should be revered and watched over as the palladium of our liberties." "As the people make and control the government, they should obey its constitution, laws and treaties as they would retain their self-respect and the respect which they claim and will enforce from foreign powers." "The Federal and State governments are parts of one system, alike necessary for the common prosperity, peace and security, and ought to be regarded alike with a cordial, habitual and immovable attachment." "The series of acts of the 32nd Congress, the act known as the Fugitive Slave Law included, are received and acquiesced in by the Whig party."

FREE DEMOCRACY; *Electoral vote, 0. Popular vote, 156,149.* } *John P. Hale, candidate. Platform.*—Substantially a reiteration of former principles, with additions suited to the times: "Slavery is a sin against God, and a crime against man, which no human enactment nor usage can make right." "The Fugitive Slave Law of 1850 is repugnant to the Constitution.... we therefore deny its binding force on the American people, and demand its immediate and total repeal." "Slavery is sectional and freedom national." "We recommend.... the amicable settlement of [international] difficulties by a resort to decisive arbitrations." "The Free Democratic party is not organized to aid either the Whig or Democratic wing of the great slave compromise party of the nation, but to defeat them both." "We inscribe Free Soil, &c., [as in 1848]."

1857 to 1861—JAMES BUCHANAN, President.

States voting, 31; total electoral vote, 296.

DEMOCRATIC; *Electoral vote, 174; Popular vote, 1,838,169.* } *Platform.*—Substantially reiterates former documents of the same kind, with additions: "It is proper that the American democracy should clearly define its relations thereto [a party claiming to be exclusively American, the "Know Nothing" party], and declare its determined opposition to all secret political societies, by whatever name they may be called." "No party can justly be deemed national, constitutional, or in accordance with American principles, which bases its exclusive organization upon religious opinions and accidental birthplace." "We reiterate with renewed energy of purpose the well-considered declarations of former conventions upon the sectional issue of domestic slavery, and concerning the reserved rights of the States." "Claiming fellowship with, and desiring the co-operation of all who regard the preservation of the Union under the Constitution as a paramount issue, and repudiating all sectional parties and platforms concerning domestic slavery which seek to embroil the States and incite to treason and armed resistance to law in the territories, and whose avowed purpose, if consummated, must end in civil war and disunion, the American democracy recognize and adopt the principles contained in the organic laws establishing the territories of Nebraska and Kansas, as embodying the only sound and safe solution of the slavery question." "There are questions connected with the foreign policy of this country which are inferior to no domestic questions whatever." "The time has come for the people of the United States to declare themselves in favor of free seas and progressive free trade throughout the world." "We should hold sacred the principles of the Monroe doctrine." "The Democratic party will expect of the next administration that every proper effort be made to insure our ascendency in the Gulf of Mexico." "The administration of Franklin Pierce has been true to the Democratic principles, and therefore true to the great interests of the country."

REPUBLICAN; *Electoral vote, 114; Popular vote, 1,341,264.* } *John C. Fremont, candidate. Platform condensed:* ".... Opposed to the repeal of the Missouri Compromise.... *Resolved,* That the maintenance of the principles promulgated in the Declaration of Independence, and embodied in the Federal Constitution, is essential to the preservation of our republican institutions, and that the Federal Constitution, the rights of the States, and the union of the States shall be preserved.... That we deny the authority of Congress, of a Territorial legislature, of any individual or association of individuals, to give legal existence to slavery in any Territory of the United States, while the present Constitution shall be maintained. That the Constitution confers upon Congress sovereign power over the Territories of the United States for their government, and that in the exercise of this power it is both the right and the imperative duty of Congress to prohibit in the Territories those twin relics of barbarism—polygamy and slavery. That .... the dearest constitutional rights of the people of Kansas have been fraudulently and violently taken from them.... that for this high crime against the Constitution, the Union and humanity, we arraign the administration, the President, his advisers.... before the country and before the world .... That Kansas should be immediately admitted as a State of the Union with her present free constitution.... That .... the Ostend circular was in every respect unworthy of American diplomacy.... That a railroad to the Pacific .... is imperatively demanded .... and that the Federal government ought to render immediate and efficient aid.... That .... the improvement of rivers and harbors of a national character.... is authorized by the Constitution .... That we invite the affiliation and co-operation of the men of all parties.... as the spirit of our institutions, as well as the constitution of our country, guarantees liberty of conscience and equality of rights among citizens, we oppose all proscriptive legislation affecting their security."

The more radical wing of the Whig party in the North, and the Free-Soil party, with fresh accessions from anti-slavery Democrats, may be regarded as the chief components of the Republican party, organized under that name in February, 1854.

AMERICAN ("Know-Nothing"); *Electoral vote, 8; Popular vote, 874,534.* } *Millard Fillmore, candidate.*

Platform.—"Humble acknowledgment to the Supreme Being..... The perpetuation of the Federal Union..... the bulwark of American independence.... Americans must rule America.... No person shall be selected for political station.... who recognizes any allegiance.... to any foreign power..... Unqualified recognition and maintenance of the reserved rights of the several States.... and non-interference of Congress..... Citizens of the United States, permanently residing in any Territory thereof, to frame their constitution and laws.... No State or Territory ought to admit others than citizens of the United States to the right of suffrage, or of holding political office..... A continued residence of twenty-one years.... an indispensable requisite for citizenship hereafter.... Opposition to any Union between Church and State; no interference with religious faith or worship; no test oaths for office.... a strict economy in public expenditures..... Enforcement of all laws constitutionally enacted until said laws shall be repealed, or shall be declared null and void."

WHIG, *Remnant of.* } The remnant of the Whig party declared: "They have no new principle to announce; no new platform to establish; but are content to broadly rest, where their fathers rested, upon the Constitution of the United States, wishing no safer guide, no higher law," but proceeded to make some additions to their former announcements of principles.

1861 to 1865—ABRAHAM LINCOLN, President.

States voting, 33; total electoral vote, 303.

REPUBLICAN; *Electoral vote, 180; Popular vote, 1,866,352.* } *Platform.*—"*Resolved,* That the history of the nation during the last four years has fully established the propriety and necessity of the organization and perpetuation of the Republican party.... and demand its peaceful and constitutional triumph.... That the Federal Constitution, the rights of the States, and the union of the States must and shall be preserved. That to the Union of the States this nation owes its unprecedented increase in population, its surprising development of material resources, its rapid augmentation of wealth, its happiness at home and its honor abroad; and we hold in abhorrence all schemes for disunion.... and we denounce those threats of disunion.... That the maintenance inviolate of the rights of the States.... is essential to that balance of powers on which the perfection and endurance of our political fabric depends.... That the present Democratic administration has far exceeded our worst apprehensions, in its measureless subserviency to the exactions of a sectional interest.... That a return to rigid economy and accountability is indispensable to arrest the systematic plunder of the public treasury by favored partisans.... That the pere dogma, that the Constitution, of its own force, carries slavery into any or all of the Territories of the United States, is a dangerous political heresy, at variance with the explicit provisions of that instrument.... is revolutionary in its tendency, and subversive of the peace and harmony of the country. That the normal condition of all the territory of the United States is that of freedom.... and we deny the authority of Congress, [etc. as in 1856]. That we brand the recent re-opening of the African slave trade, under the cover of our national flag.... as a crime against humanity and a burning shame to our country and age.... In the recent vetoes, by their Federal governors, of the acts of the legislatures of Kansas and Nebraska prohibiting slavery in those Territories, we find a practical illustration of the boasted Democratic principle of non-intervention and popular sovereignty, embodied in the Kansas-Nebraska bill, and a demonstration of the deception and frauds involved therein. That Kansas should, of right, be immediately admitted as a State under the constitution recently formed.... sound policy requires such an adjustment of imposts as to encourage the development of the industrial interest of the whole country..... We protest.... against any view of the homestead policy which regards the settlers as paupers or suppliants for public bounty.... The Republican party is opposed to any change in our naturalization laws..... River and harbor improvements.... are authorized by the Constitution..... A railroad to the Pacific ocean is imperatively demanded..... We invite the co-operation of all citizens.... who substantially agree with us...."

DEMOCRATIC; *Electoral vote, [illegible]; Popular vote, [illegible].* *J. C. Breckenridge, candidate.* *Platform.*—"That of 1856 reaffirmed with these additions: All citizens have an equal right to settle with their property [slaves included] in any Territory. It is the duty of the Federal government.... to protect, when necessary, the rights of persons and property in the Territories..... When the settlers in a Territory having an adequate population form a state constitution in pursuance of law, the right of sovereignty commences.... and the State thus organized ought to be admitted into the Federal Union, whether its constitution prohibits or recognizes the institution of slavery.... in favor of the acquisition of Cuba on such terms as shall be honorable.... Enactments .... to defeat.... Fugitive Slave Law.... are.... revolutionary in their effect.... Imperative duty of this government to protect the naturalized citizen in all his rights, whether at home or in foreign lands, to the same extent as its native-born citizens..... One of the greatest necessities of the age is.... the construction of a Pacific railroad.... at the earliest practicable moment."

Independent Democratic; *Electoral vote, 12; Popular vote, [illegible].* *Stephen A. Douglas, candidate.*

Platform.—Substantially as the other division of the party, with an express pledge to abide by the decisions of the Supreme Court in relation to slavery in the Territories.

CONSTITUTIONAL UNION; *Electoral vote, 39; Popular vote, [illegible].* *John Bell, candidate.* *Platform.*—"Experience has demonstrated that platforms adopted by the partisan conventions of the country have had the effect to mislead and deceive the people, and at the same time to widen the political divisions of the country, by the creation and encouragement of geographical and sectional parties; therefore, *Resolved*, That it is both the part of patriotism and duty to recognize no political principles other than the Constitution of the country, the Union of the States, and the enforcement of the laws."

1865 to 1869—Abraham Lincoln, President—Second Term.

States *voting, 25; their electoral vote, 233; States in secession, 11; their electoral vote, 81; total States, 36; total vote, 314.*

REPUBLICAN; *Electoral vote, 212; Popular vote, [illegible].* *Andrew Johnson, elected Vice-President, succeeded to the Presidency upon the death of Lincoln, April 15, 1865.*

Platform.—"*Resolved*, that it is the highest duty of every American citizen to maintain, against all their enemies, the integrity of the Union and the paramount authority of the Constitution.... and.... we pledge ourselves.... to do everything in our power to aid the government in quelling, by force of arms, the Rebellion now raging against its authority, and in bringing to the punishment due to their crimes the rebels and traitors arrayed against it..... We approve the determination of the government ....not to compromise with rebels, nor to offer them any terms of peace, except such as may be based upon an 'unconditional surrender of their hostility'.... and to prosecute the war with the utmost possible vigor to the complete suppression of the Rebellion..... As slavery was the cause, and now constitutes the strength of this Rebellion, ...we uphold and maintain the acts and proclamations by which the government, in its own defence, has aimed a death-blow at the gigantic evil..... That the thanks of the American people are due to the soldiers and sailors.... that the nation owes to them some permanent recognition. .... That we approve and applaud the practical wisdom.... with which Abraham Lincoln has discharged, under circumstances of unparalleled difficulty, the great duties and responsibilities of the presidential office..... We deem it essential to the general welfare that harmony should prevail in the national councils, and we regard as worthy of public confidence and official trust those only who cordially indorse the principles proclaimed in these resolutions..... The government owes to all men employed in its armies, without regard to distinction of color, the full protection of the laws of war..... That foreign immigration.... should be fostered and encouraged by a liberal and just policy. That we are in favor of the speedy construction of the railroad to the Pacific coast. That the national faith, pledged for the redemption of the public debt, must be kept inviolate..... That we approve the position taken by the government, that the people of the United States can never regard with indifference the attempt of any European power to overthrow by force, or to supplant by fraud, the institutions of any republican government on the western continent...."

RADICAL; *John C. Fremont, candidate, Who withdrew and recommended the support of the regular Republican ticket, which recommendation was followed.*

Platform.—"The Federal Union shall be preserved.... The Constitution and laws.... must be observed.... The Rebellion must be suppressed.... and without compromise.... The rights of free speech, free press, and the *habeas corpus* be held inviolate, save in districts where martial law has been proclaimed.... The Rebellion has destroyed slavery; and the Federal Constitution should be amended [accordingly].... Integrity and economy.... in the administration.... in time of war, the want of them is criminal..... The right of asylum.... is a recognized principle of American liberty.... The 'Monroe Doctrine' [also].... The gratitude and support of the nation are due to the faithful soldiers. The one-term policy for the presidency.... should be maintained by Constitutional amendment.... The President and Vice-President shall be elected by a direct vote of the people..... Reconstruction of the rebellious States belongs to the people, through their representatives in Congress, and not to the Executive. That the confiscation of the lands of the rebels, and their distribution among the soldiers and actual settlers, is a measure of justice."

DEMOCRATIC; *Electoral vote, 21; Popular vote, [illegible].* *George B. McClellan, candidate.*

Platform.—"*Resolved*, That in the future, as in the past, we will adhere with unswerving fidelity to the Union under the Constitution.... That after four years of failure to restore the Union by the experiment of war, during which, under the pretense of a military necessity of a war power higher than the Constitution, the Constitution itself has been disregarded in every part.... justice, humanity, liberty, and the public welfare demand that immediate efforts be made for a cessation of hostilities, with a view to an ultimate convention of all the States.... that.... peace may be restored on the basis of the Federal Union of all the States. That the direct interference of the military authority.... in the recent elections.... was a shameful violation of the Constitution; and the repetition of such acts.... will be held as revolutionary, and resisted.... That the aim and object of the Democratic party is to preserve the Federal Union and the rights of the States unimpaired;.... and they hereby declare that they consider the administrative usurpations of extraordinary and dangerous powers not granted by the Constitution.... as calculated to prevent a restoration of the Union.... That the shameful disregard of the administration to its duty.... to our fellow-citizens.... prisoners of war.... deserves the severest reprobation.... That the sympathy of the Democratic party is heartily and earnestly extended to the soldiery .... and the sailors."

SECESSIONIST; *Electoral vote, 81.* *Jefferson Davis, president of the confederacy of 11 seceded States. The Right of Secession* formally assumed, December 20, 1860: "We, the people of South Carolina, in convention assembled, do declare and ordain.... that South Carolina, in the exercise of her sovereign will as an independent State, acceded to the Federal Union [May 23, 1788].... and that, in the exercise of the same sovereign will, it is her right.... to secede from the said Federal Union."

The other seceding States took the same ground.

"Our new government," said Alex. H. Stevens, March 21, 1861, "is founded upon exactly the opposite idea [to the equality of races]; its foundations are laid, its cornerstone rests upon the great truth that the negro is not equal to the white man; that slavery—subordination to the superior race—is his natural and normal condition..... The negro, by nature, or by the curse against Canaan, is fitted for that condition which he occupies in our system..... and by experience we know that it is best, not only for the superior but for the inferior race, that it should be so. It is, indeed, in conformity with the ordinance of the Creator."

1869 to 1873—ULYSSES S. GRANT, President.

States voting, 34; their electoral vote, 294; States not reconstructed, 3; their electoral vote, 23; total States, 37; total vote, 317.

REPUBLICAN; *Electoral vote, [illegible]; Popular vote, [illegible].* *Platform.*—"We congratulate the country on the assured success of the Reconstruction policy of Congress, as evidenced by the adoption, in the majority of the States lately in rebellion, of constitutions securing equal civil and political rights to all..... The guarantee by Congress of equal suffrage to all loyal men at the South was demanded by every consideration of public safety, of gratitude, and of justice, and must be maintained .... We denounce all forms of repudiation as a national crime. It is due to the labor of the nation that taxation should be equalized and reduced as rapidly as the national faith will permit. The national debt, contracted as it has been for the preservation of the Union for all time to come, should be extended over a fair period for redemption..... The best policy to diminish our burden of debt is to so improve our credit that capitalists will seek to loan us money at lower rates of interest than we now pay and must continue to pay, so long as repudiation, partial or total, open or covert, is threatened or suspected. The government .... should be administered with the strictest economy. We profoundly deplore the tragic death of Abraham Lincoln, and regret the accession to the presidency of Andrew Johnson..... No citizen.... must be liable to arrest and imprisonment by any foreign power for acts done or words spoken in this country.... The bounties and pensions provided by the laws for the brave defenders of the nation are obligations never to be forgotten..... Foreign immigration .... should be fostered and encouraged by a liberal and just policy. This convention declares itself in sympathy with all oppressed people who are struggling for their rights.... We favor the removal of the disqualifications and restrictions imposed upon the late rebels, in the same measure as the spirit of disloyalty shall die out, and as may be consistent with the safety of the loyal people. That we recognize the great principles laid down in the immortal Declaration of Independence as the true foundation of democratic government; and we hail with gladness every effort toward making these principles a living reality on every inch of American soil."

DEMOCRATIC; *Electoral vote, [illegible]; Popular vote, [illegible].* *Horatio Seymour, candidate.* *Platform.*—"The Democratic party.... demand.... Immediate restoration of all the States to their rights in the Union under the Constitution, and of civil government to the American people. Amnesty for all past political offences, and the regulation of the elective franchise in the States by their citizens. Payment of all the public debt as rapidly as practicable, and where.... the law.... does not provide that they shall be paid in coin, they ought in right and justice to be paid in the lawful money of the United States. Equal taxation.... including government bonds. .... One currency for the government and the people, ... the producer and the bondholder. Economy in the administration.... reduction of the standing army and navy; the abolition of the Freedmen's Bureau..... A tariff for revenue.... Such equal taxation as will afford incidental protection to domestic manufactures.... Reform of abuses.... to the end that the usurpation of Congress and the despotism of the sword may cease. Equal rights and protection for naturalized and native-born citizens at home and abroad..... We arraign the radical party for its disregard of right and the unparalleled oppression and tyranny which have marked its career..... We regard the reconstruction acts (so called) of Congress as usurpations, and unconstitutional, revolutionary, and void.... Our soldiers and sailors.... must ever be gratefully remembered..... The public lands should be distributed as widely as possible among the people.... and to none but actual occupants.... Andrew Johnson.... is entitled to the gratitude of the whole American people..... This convention sympathizes cordially with the workingmen. Thanks.... tendered.... Salmon P. Chase for.... impartiality.... on the trial of President Andrew Johnson."

NOT RECONSTRUCTED; *Electoral vote, 23.* Three States, Virginia, Mississippi, and Texas, had not complied with the requirements of Congress.

1873 to 1877—ULYSSES S. GRANT, President—Second Term.

States voting, 37; total electoral vote, 366; rejected, 17.

REPUBLICAN; *Electoral vote, [illegible]; Popular vote, [illegible].* *Platform.*—"During eleven years of supremacy it has accepted with grand courage the solemn duties of the time. It suppressed a gigantic rebellion, emancipated four millions of slaves, decreed the equal citizenship of all, and established universal suffrage. Exhibiting unparalleled magnanimity, it criminally punished no man for political offenses.... The recent amendments to the Constitution should be cordially sustained because they are right, not merely tolerated because they are law.... Complete liberty and exact equality in the enjoyment of all civil, political and public rights should be established and effectually maintained throughout the Union, by efficient and appropriate State and Federal legislation.... The national government should seek to maintain honorable peace with all nations, protecting its citizens everywhere.... Any system of civil service under which the subordinate positions of the government are considered rewards for mere party zeal is fatally demoralizing; and we therefore favor a reform of the system.... We are opposed to further grants of public lands to corporations and monopolies, and demand that the national domain be set apart for free homes for the people. The annual revenue.... should furnish a moderate balance for the reduction of the principal [of the public debt]; and.... except.... what tax upon tobacco and liquors, should be raised by duties upon importations ....so adjusted as to.... promote the industries .... of the whole country. We hold in undying honor the soldiers and sailors whose valor saved the Union.... It is the duty of our government to guard with jealous care the rights of adopted citizens against the assumption of unauthorized claims by their former governments..... The franking privilege ought to be abolished, and a way prepared for speedy reduction in the rates of postage.... Recognizes the duty of so shaping legislation as to secure full protection and the amplest field for capital; and for labor, the creator of capital, the largest opportunities and a just share of the mutual profits. Congress and the President have only fulfilled an imperative duty in .... the protection of the ballot-box; and ....are entitled to the thanks of the nation. We denounce repudiation of the public debt, in any form or disguise, as a national crime .... Mindful of its obligations to the loyal women of America .... their admission to wider fields of usefulness is viewed with satisfaction .... Approves the action of Congress in extending amnesty to those lately in rebellion .... Proposes to respect the rights reserved by the people to themselves as carefully as the powers delegated by them to the States and to the Federal government .... It is the duty of the general government to adopt such measures as may tend to encourage and restore American commerce and ship-building. We believe that the modest patriotism.... and the illustrious services of Ulysses S. Grant have commended him to the heart of the American people.... Henry Wilson .... is worthy to associate with our great leader...."

DEMOCRATIC and LIBERAL REPUBLICAN; *Electoral vote, 63; Popular vote, 2,834,079.* *Horace Greeley, candidate.* *Platform*—"We, the Democratic electors of the United States, in convention assembled, do present the following principles, already adopted at Cincinnati [by the Liberal Republicans], as essential to just government.

Liberal Republican Platform.—"We, the Liberal Republicans.... proclaim the following principles as essential to just government: .... The equality of all men before the law .... The union of the States, emancipation and enfranchisement, and to oppose any re-opening of the questions settled by the 13th, 14th and 15th Amendments.... The immediate and absolute removal of all disabilities imposed on account of the Rebellion.... Local self-government, with impartial suffrage, will guard the rights of all citizens more securely than any centralized power.... The supremacy of the civil power.... The civil service.... a mere instrument of partisan tyranny.... is a scandal and reproach upon free institutions. .... No president shall be a candidate for re-election.... A system of Federal taxation which shall not unnecessarily interfere with the industry of the people.... We denounce Repudiation in every form and guise.... Speedy return to specie payment is demanded.... We remember with gratitude the heroism and sacrifices of the soldiers and sailors.... We are opposed to all further grants of lands to railroads or other corporations.... It is the duty of the government, in its intercourse with foreign nations, to cultivate the friendships of peace...."

DEMOCRATIC, "STRAIGHT OUT;" *Electoral vote, 0; Popular vote, 29,489.* *Charles O'Conor, candidate.*—*Platform.*—"Fidelity to our constitutional system is the only protection for either [liberty or progress].... The people of each State voluntarily created their State, and the States voluntarily formed the Union .... for foreign and inter-state relations .... All governmental powers whether State or Federal, are trust powers .... limited to the written letter of the constitution and the laws.... The interests of labor and capital should not be permitted to conflict. Labor is entitled to permanent consideration. Principle is to be preferred to power. Betrayed at Baltimore [by Democratic indorsement of Liberal Republicanism] into a false creed, and a false leadership by the convention, we repudiate both...."

LABOR REFORM; *Electoral vote, 0; Popular vote, included in O'Conor's pop. vote above.* *David Davis, candidate, declined; Charles O'Conor, candidate.*

Platform.—"Duty of the government to establish a just standard of distribution of capital and labor, by providing a purely national circulating medium.... The national debt should be paid in good faith.... The burdens of government should be so adjusted as to bear equally on all classes.... exemption of bonds.... a violation of all just principles.... To admit free all such articles of common use as we can neither produce nor grow, and lay duties for revenue mainly upon articles of luxury.... Chinese labor .... should be prohibited.... All mechanics and day-laborers employed by the government, directly or indirectly, [should work only] eight hours a day.... Abolition of contract labor in prisons.... Money needed for prosecuting wars .... to be collected from the wealthy.... Duty of the government to exercise its power over railroad and telegraph corporations.... Reform in the civil service .... Limiting the occupancy of the presidential chair to one term.... Granting general amnesty.... Subjection of military to civil authorities.... To supervise the patent laws.... Fitness.... should be the only recommendation to public office, either appointive or elective...."

PROHIBITION; *Electoral vote, 0; Popular vote, 5,608.* *James B. Black, candidate.* *Platform.*—"Traffic in intoxicating beverages is a dishonor to Christian civilization, a political wrong of unequalled enormity .... not capable of being regulated or restrained by any system of license whatever, and imperatively demands, for its suppression, effective legal prohibition, both by State and National legislation.... There can be no greater peril to a nation than existing party competition for the liquor vote.... We will individually use all efforts to persuade men from the use of intoxicating liquors .... Competency, honesty and sobriety are indispensable qualifications for holding office.... Removals.... for mere political differences of opinion are wrong.... Salaries of public officers should take the place of fees.... President.... should be elected directly by the people .... In favor of a sound national currency.... Rates of ocean and inland postage.... should be made as low as possible by law.... Opposed to all discrimination in favor of capital against labor, as well as all monopoly and class legislation.... The removal of the burdens imposed by the traffic in intoxicating drinks will emancipate labor, and will practically promote labor reform.... Suffrage .... without regard to sex.... Extension of common schools is a primary duty of the government.... A liberal policy.... to promote foreign immigration."

REVENUE REFORM, or FREE TRADE; *Wm. S. Groesbeck, candidate.*

ANTI-SECRET SOCIETY; *Charles Francis Adams, candidate.*

1877 to 1881—Rutherford B. Hayes, President.

States voting, 38; total electoral vote, 369.

REPUBLICAN; *Electoral vote, 185; Popular vote, 4,033,950.* *Platform.*—"When in the economy of Providence, this land was to be purged of human slavery, and when the strength of the government of the people, by the people, and for the people, was to be demonstrated, the Republican party came into power. Its deeds have passed into history, and we look back to them with pride. Incited by their memories to high aims for the good of our country and mankind, and looking to the future with unfaltering courage, hope and purpose, we, the representatives of the party .... make the following declaration of principles: The United States is a nation, not a league.... The Republican party has preserved these governments [National and State] to the 100th anniversary of the nation's birth.... The permanent pacification of the southern section of the Union, and the complete protection of all its citizens in the free enjoyment of all their rights, is a duty to which the Republican party stands sacredly pledged.... National credit demands that this promise [redemption of the United States notes in coin] be fulfilled by a continuous and steady progress to specie payment.... The invariable rule in appointments should have reference to the honesty, fidelity and capacity of the appointees.... All others [subordinate places] to be filled by persons selected with sole reference to the efficiency of the public service.... Will hold all public officers to a rigid responsibility.... The public school system.... is the bulwark of the American Republic.... The revenue.... must be largely derived from duties.... which.... should be adjusted to promote interests of American labor and advance the prosperity of the whole country. We reaffirm our opposition to further grants of the public lands to corporations and monopolies.... The same protection shall be afforded to the adopted American citizen that is given to the native-born.... Duty of Congress to fully investigate the effect of the immigration and importation of Mongolians upon the moral and material interests of the country.... The honest demands of women for additional rights, privileges, and immunities, should be treated with respectful consideration.... It is the right and duty of Congress to prohibit and extirpate in the Territories that relic of barbarism, polygamy.... The pledges which the nation has given to her soldiers and sailors must be fulfilled.... We sincerely deprecate all sectional feeling and tendencies. We therefore note with deep solicitude that the Democratic party counts.... upon the electoral vote of a united South.... We charge it with being the same in character and spirit as when it sympathized with treason.... The national administration merits commendation.... We present as our candidates.... Rutherford B. Hayes and Wm. A. Wheeler."

DEMOCRATIC; *Electoral vote, 184; Popular vote, 4,284,885.* *Samuel J. Tilden, candidate.* *Platform.*—"We.... do hereby declare the administration of the Federal government to be in urgent need of immediate reform.... We do here re-affirm our faith in the permanence of the Federal Union, our devotion to the Constitution.... with its amendments universally accepted as a final settlement of the controversies engendered by the Civil War.... In absolute acquiescence in the will of the majority—the vital principle of republics; in the supremacy of the civil over the military authority; in the total separation of Church and State, for the sake alike of civil and religious freedom; in the equality of all citizens before just laws of their own enactment; in the liberty of individual conduct, unvexed by sumptuary laws; in the faithful education of the rising generation, that they may preserve, enjoy, and transmit these best conditions of human happiness and hope—we behold the noblest products of a hundred years of changeful history; but while upholding the bond of our Union and great charter of these our rights, it behooves a free people to practice also that eternal vigilance which is the price of liberty.... Reform is necessary to.... establish, in the hearts of the whole people, the Union.... now to be saved from a corrupt centralism.... To establish a sound currency, restore the public credit, and maintain the national honor. We denounce the failure, for all these eleven years of peace, to make good the promise of the legal-tender notes.... and the improvidence which.... has taken.... in Federal taxes thirteen times the whole amount of the legal-tender notes, and squandered four times their sum.... The financial imbecility.... which.... has made no advance toward Resumption.... We demand a judicious system of preparation [for resumption].... Reform is necessary in the sum and modes of Federal taxation.... We denounce the present tariff, levied upon nearly 4,000 articles, as a masterpiece of injustice, inequality and false pretence.... Reform is necessary in the scale of public expense.... To put a stop to the profligate waste of public lands.... To correct the omissions of a Republican Congress, and the errors of our treaties.... which have stripped our fellow citizens of foreign birth.... of the shield of American citizenship .... and demand such modifications of the treaty with the Chinese Empire .... as shall prevent further importation.... of the Mongolian race.... [As to] the false issue with which they [the Republicans] would enkindle sectarian strife in respect to the public schools.... [And] fight anew the dying embers of sectional hate.... In the civil service.... From none, in the higher grades of the public service, President, [&c.].... those and all others in authority are the people's servants .... All these abuses, wrongs and crimes, the product of sixteen years' ascendency of the Republican party, create a necessity for reform, confessed by the Republicans themselves.... Reform can only be had by a peaceful civic revolution.... Do cordially indorse the action of the present House.... in reducing.... the expenses of the Federal government.... The soldiers and sailors.... have a just claim upon the care.... of their fellow-citizens."

INDEPENDENT or GREENBACK; *Electoral vote, 0; Popular vote, 81,740.* *Peter Cooper, candidate.* *Platform.*—"Called into existence by the necessities of the people.... for financial reform and industrial emancipation .... Demand.... repeal of the specie-resumption act.... United States note.... 3.65 interest.... the best circulating medium ever devised.... Paramount duty of the government.... the full development of all legitimate business.... Protest against any further issue of gold bonds for sale in foreign markets.... Against sale of bonds for .... purchasing silver to be used as a substitute for.... fractional currency...."

AMERICAN NATIONAL, or ANTI-SECRET SOCIETY; *Electoral vote, 0; Popular vote, — —.* *James B. Walker, candidate.* *Platform of 1872:* "Ours is a Christian and not a heathen nation.... God requires and man needs a Sabbath.... Prohibition.... the true policy on the temperance question.... Charters of all secret lodges.... should be withdrawn.... Our amended Constitution should be preserved inviolate.... Arbitration.... [between] nations is the most direct and sure method of securing.... a permanent peace.... The Bible should be associated with books of science and literature in all our educational institutions.... Land and other monopolies shall be discountenanced.... The government should furnish.... an ample and sound currency and a return to specie payment.... Maintenance of the public credit, protection to all loyal citizens and justice to Indians are essential to the honor and safety of the nation.... We demand the abolition of the electoral college...."

PROHIBITION; *Electoral vote, 0; Popular vote, 9,522.* *Green C. Smith, candidate.* *Platform.*—Substantially the same as in 1872, with some of the religious planks from the American National of 1875

1881 to 1885—**JAMES A. GARFIELD**, President.

States voting, 38; total electoral vote, 369.

REPUBLICAN; *Electoral vote, 214; Popular vote, 4,449,053.* } *Chester A. Arthur President, on the death of Garfield, Sep. 19, 1881. Platform.*—"The Republican party.... at the end of twenty years since the Federal government was first committed to its charge, submits.... **its brief** report.... It suppressed **a** rebellion which **had** armed nearly **a** million of men.... **It** reconstructed **a union** of the States with freedom, **instead of** slavery, **as** its corner-stone. It transformed four **million of** human beings from the likeness of things **to the rank of** citizens. It relieved Congress from **the** infamous **work of** hunting fugitive slaves, and charged **it to see that slavery does** not exist. It has raised the value of **our paper currency from** thirty-eight per cent. **to the par of gold. It has restored**.... payment in **coin**.... **and has given us a** currency absolutely good.... **Railways have increased from** 31,000 **miles** in 1860 to more **than 82,000 miles in 1879. Our foreign trade** has increased **from $700,000,000 to $1,150,000,000**.... and our exports, **which were $20,000,000 less than our** imports in 1860, **were $264,000,000 more than our imports in 1879.** Without **resorting to loans, it has, since the war** closed, defrayed **the ordinary expenses of** government.... the interest **on** the public **debt**.... annually **over** $30,000,000 for soldiers' **pensions**.... $888,000,000 **of the** public debt, and by refunding **the balance at** lower rates has reduced the annual interest **charge from** nearly $151,000,000 to less than $89,000,000. **All the in**dustries.... revived, labor in demand, wages.... **increased**.... evidences of **a** coming prosperity **greater**.... **than ever**.... Upon this record.... asks **for continued support and** confidence. We affirm that **the work of the last twenty years** has been such **as to commend itself to the favor of the nation,** and that **the fruits** of the costly victories.... **should be** preserved. **The** Constitution.... **a supreme law, not a** mere contract.... the boundary **between the** powers delegated and those reserved is **to be determined** by **the** National, and not **by the** State **tribunals**.... **It is** the duty of the National government **to aid that work [education]** by the State] to the extent of **its constitutional ability**.... That the Constitution be **so amended as.... to forbid** the appropriation of public **funds to the support of** sectarian schools [by any State].... **The duties.... for revenue** should be so discriminated **as to favor American labor.... no** further [land] grant **to** any **railway or other** corporation.... the twin barbarity, **polygamy must die**.... everywhere protection.... to citizens.... **The** duty.... to.... improve water **courses and** harbors.... To **do** them, who **preserved the republic** in the day **of** battle, perpetual honor, **is**.... the.... sacred duty of **the** American people.... The unrestricted immigration **of** the Chinese.... an evil of great magnitude.... The **purity and** patriotism of.... [President] Hayes.... [his] **efficient, just and** courteous discharge of the public business.... **We charge** upon the Democratic party the habitual **sacrifice of** patriotism and justice **to a** supreme and insatiable **lust for** office **and** patronage. [here follows a lengthy **arraignment** of that party.] The reform **of** the civil service should be thorough, radical and complete."

DEMOCRATIC; *Electoral vote, 155; Popular vote, 4,442,035.* } *Winfield S. Hancock, candidate.—Platform.*—"We pledge ourselves anew to the Constitutional doctrines and traditions of the Democratic party.... embodied in the platform of the last national convention.... Opposition to centralization.... **no sumptuary laws**.... separation **of** Church and State.... **common schools** fostered and protected. Home rule.... **honest money**.... convertible into coin.... strict maintenance of **public** faith.... tariff for revenue only.... subordination **of the** military **to** the civil power, and a general and **thorough** reform of **the** civil service. The right to a free **ballot is a** right preservative **of all** rights; and must **and shall be** maintained in every part of the United States. **The existing** administration is the representative of **conspiracy** only.... **and** demands a reform, by statute, **which shall** make it **forever** impossible **for a** defeated candidate **to** bribe his **way to** the seat of **a** usurper by billeting villains upon the people. The great fraud **of** 1876-7.... struck a great blow at **our** system **of representative government.** The Democratic party, **to** preserve **the country from the** horrors **of** a civil war, submitted.... **The resolution of** Samuel **J.** Tilden, **not** again **to be a candidate**.... **is re**ceived.... **with** deep sensibility.... **by purifying the pub**lic service [he] merits **the** lasting **gratitude of his country** and party. **Free** ships, and a living chance **for American** commerce **upon** the **seas; and** upon the **land no discrimi**nation in **favor** of transportation lines, corporations or monopolies.... No more Chinese immigration.... Public money and public credit for public purposes solely, and public land for actual settlers. The Democratic party **is** the friend of labor and the laboring man, and pledges itself to protect him alike from the cormorants and the commune. We congratulate the country upon the honesty and thrift of the Democratic Congress...."

NATIONAL ("GREENBACK"); *Electoral vote, 0; Popular vote, 308,578.* } *James B. Weaver, candidate.*

Platform.—"The civil government should guarantee the divine right of every laborer to the result of his toil.... and we condemn, as unworthy of our civilization, the barbarism which imposes upon wealth-producers a state of drudgery as the price of a bare animal existence.... The associated monopolies, the international syndicates and other income classes demand dear money, cheap labor and a strong government, and, hence, a weak people.... The right to make and issue money is a sovereign power.... The delegation of this right to corporations is a surrender of the central attribute of sovereignty.... All money.... should be issued.... by the government.... The bonds.... should be paid as rapidly as practicable.... Legal-tender currency should be substituted for the notes of the national banks, the national banking system abolished, and the unlimited coinage of silver, as well as of gold, established by law. Labor should be so protected by National and State authority as to equalize its burdens and insure a just distribution of its results. The eight-hour law should be enforced.... contract convict labor abolished.... Slavery being simply cheap labor, and cheap labor simply slavery, the importation of Chinese serfs tends to.... degrade American labor.... Railroad land grants forfeited.... should be immediately reclaimed.... and the public domain reserved.... for actual settlers.... Moderate, fair and uniform rates for passenger and freight traffic. We denounce.... as dangerous to liberty the action of the old parties in fostering.... gigantic.... corporations and monopolies.... We condemn the cruel class legislation of the Republican party, which, while professing great gratitude to the soldier, has most unjustly discriminated against him, and in favor of the bondholder.... We demand a graduated income tax. We denounce.... the efforts.... to restrict the right of suffrage. We are opposed to an increase of the standing army.... and the insidious scheme to establish an enormous military power under the guise of militia laws. We demand absolute democratic rules.... of Congress.... and taking from committees a veto power greater than that of the President. We demand a government of the people, by the people, and for the people, instead of a government of the bondholder, by the bondholder, and for the bondholder; and we denounce every attempt to stir up sectional strife as an effort to conceal monstrous crimes against the people.... We have no quarrels with individuals, wage no war on classes, but only against vicious institutions...."

PROHIBITION; *Electoral vote, 0; Popular vote, 10,305.* } *Neal Dow, candidate. Platform.*—"Substantially as in previous years, with a more general exposition of the evils of intemperance, to the individual, the family, the state and society in general, morally, religiously, intellectually, socially, financially and politically; and an arraignment of the Republican, Democratic, and National parties for passive or negative devotion on that subject."

1885 to 1889—Grover Cleveland, President.

States voting, 38; total electoral vote, 401.

DEMOCRATIC; *Electoral vote, 219; Popular vote, 4,911,017.* } *Platform.*—"The Democratic party recognizes that new issues are born.... and old issues perish. But the fundamental principles of the Democracy.... will ever remain the.... only security for the continuance of free government. The preservation of personal rights, the equality of all citizens before the law, the reserved rights of the States and the supremacy of the Federal Government within the limits of the Constitution will ever form the true basis of our liberties.... But it is indispensable.... that the government should not always be controlled by one political party. Frequent change of administration is as necessary as a constant recurrence to the popular will.... The Republican party, so far as principle.... is a reminiscence, in practice it is an organization for enriching those who control its machinery.... Frauds and jobbery.... in every department.... have called for reform.... A change is demanded.... Also necessary in 1876, but the will of the people was then defeated by a fraud.... against 1880.... by the lavish use of money.... The Republican party, during its legal, its stolen, and its bought tenures of power, has steadily decayed.... Its platform promises are now a list of its past failures. [Here follows a categorical arraignment of the government.] Unnecessary taxation is unjust taxation. We denounce it for having failed to relieve the people from crushing war taxes.... The Democratic party pledges itself to purify the administration from corruption, to restore economy, to revive the respect of the law, and to reduce the taxation to the lowest limit consistent with due regard to the preservation of the faith of the nation to its creditors and pensioners.... It is pledged to revise the tariff in a spirit of fairness to all. But in making a reduction in taxes it is not proposed to injure any domestic industries, but rather to promote their healthy growth.... All taxation shall be limited to the requirements of economical government.... Reduction.... can and must be effected without depriving American labor of the ability to compete successfully with foreign labor.... Internal revenue is a war tax.... and should be sacredly devoted to the relief of the people from the remaining burdens of the war.... We favor an American continental policy, based upon more intimate commercial and political relations with the fifteen republics.... but entangling alliances with none.... We believe in honest money, the gold and silver coinage of the Constitution, and a circulating medium convertible into such money without loss.... Equal and exact justice to all citizens, of whatever nativity, race, color, or persuasion.... A free ballot and a fair count.... We oppose sumptuary laws.... We favor honest civil-service reform.... and fixed salaries [of officials].... separation of Church and State.... and free education by common schools.... While we favor all legislation which will tend to the equitable distribution of property, to the prevention of monopoly.... and against corporate abuses.... we hold that the welfare of society demands a scrupulous regard for the rights of property.... Labor should be fostered.... We favor the repeal of all laws restricting the free action of labor, and the enactment of laws by which labor organizations may be incorporated.... The public lands.... to be kept as homesteads for actual settlers.... all unearned lands.... granted to railroad corporations.... should be restored to the public domain, and that no more grants of land shall be made to corporations, or allowed to fall into their ownership of alien absentees.... Opposed to converting the General Government into a machine for collecting taxes to be distributed among the States.... Our country ought never to be a lazaretto for the deportation of the pauper labor of other countries.... or its importation as an instrument with which capital can defeat American workingmen.... Labor has a right to demand a just share of the profits of its own production.... Monopoly engenders two classes, the very rich and the very poor, both of which are equally harmful to a republic, which should give to its people equal rights and equal privileges under the law.... All corporate bodies.... performing public duties, are public servants.... Frequent change of officers is necessary to counteract.... tendencies to a caste of life officers.... and punishment of frauds.... and embezzlements.... American civilization demands that against the immigration or importation of Mongolians to these shores our gates be closed.... It is an imperative duty of this government to efficiently protect all rights of persons and property of every American citizen in foreign lands, and demand and enforce full reparation for any violation thereof.... We recall the acquisition of Louisiana, Florida, California and the adjacent Mexican territory by purchase alone, and contrast.... with the purchase of Alaska, the sole fruit of a Republican administration of nearly a quarter of a century. The Federal government should care for and improve the Mississippi river and other great waterways of the Republic.... Under a long period of Democratic rule and policy our merchant marine was.... outstripping that of Great Britain. Under twenty-four years of Republican.... our commerce has been left to British bottoms.... [and they] have managed to surrender to Great Britain.... the control of the markets of the world.... Instead of.... its false pretense of friendship for American labor, expressed by imposing taxes, we demand.... freedom for American labor by reducing taxes.... We offer to Samuel J. Tilden in his withdrawal from public career not only our respectful sympathy and esteem, but also.... the pledge of our devotion to the principles and cause now inseparable.... from his name.... The great issue of reform and change in administration is submitted to the people...."

REPUBLICAN; *Electoral vote, 182; Popular vote, 4,848,334.* } *James G. Blaine, candidate. Platform.*—"The Republicans.... renew their allegiance to the principles upon which they have triumphed in six successive presidential elections, and congratulate the American people on the attainment of so many results in legislation and administration by which the party has, after saving the Union, done so much to render its institutions just, equal and beneficent, the safeguard of liberty, and the embodiment of the best thought and highest purposes of our citizens. It has gained its strength by quick and faithful response to the demands of the people for the freedom and equality of all men; for a united nation, assuring the rights of all citizens; for the elevation of labor; for an honest currency; for purity in legislation, and for integrity and accountability in all departments of the government; and it accepts anew the duty of leading in the work of progress and reform. We lament the death of President Garfield.... In the administration of President Arthur we recognize a wise, conservative and patriotic policy.... It is the first duty of a good government to protect the rights and promote the interests of its own people.... We therefore demand that the imposition of duties.... shall be made not for revenue only, but.... to afford security to our diversified industries and protection to the rights and wages of the laborer.... Against the so-called economic system of the Democratic party which would degrade our labor to the foreign standard, we enter our earnest protest.... The Republican party pledges itself to correct the inequalities of the tariff, and to reduce the surplus.... We recognize the importance of the sheep industry.... and respect the demands for a readjustment of duty upon foreign wool.... We have always recommended the best money.... and we urge.... an international standard.... of gold and silver coinage.... Pledge to support such legislation as will fully and efficiently carry out the Constitutional power of Congress over interstate com-

gence.... We favor legislation that shall prevent unjust discrimination and excessive charges for transportation.... A national bureau of labor, the enforcement of the eight-hour law, and a wise and judicious system of general education by adequate appropriation from the national revenues where the same is needed. We believe that everywhere the protection to a citizen of American birth must be secured to citizens of American adoption.... and we favor.... international arbitration.... Unalterably opposed to placing our workingmen in competition with any form of servile labor, whether at home or abroad.... denounce the importation of contract labor.... The reform of the civil service.... should be completed.... The public lands ....should be reserved, so far as possible, for small holdings by actual settlers.... Demand.... speedy forfeiture of all land grants which have lapsed.... Grateful thanks ....are due to the Union soldiers and sailors of the late war.... Favors.... the policy which seeks peace and trade with all powers, but especially with those of the western hemisphere.... Demand the restoration of the navy to its old-time strength and efficiency.... Appointments.... in the Territories should be made from bona fide citizens and residents [of each].... It is the duty of Congress to enact such laws as shall promptly and effectually suppress the system of polygamy.... The people of the United States ....a Nation and not a mere confederacy of States. The National Government is supreme within the sphere of its national duty, but the States have reserved rights which should be faithfully maintained.... The perpetuity of our institutions rests upon the maintenance of a free ballot, an honest count, and correct returns. We denounce the fraud and violence practised by the Democracy in Southern States by which the will of the voter is defeated, as dangerous to.... free institutions, and we solemnly arraign that party as being the guilty recipient of the fruits ....and pledge our.... efforts to promote.... such legislation as will secure to every citizen, of whatever race and color, the full and complete recognition, possession and exercise of all civil and political rights."

NATIONAL, or PEOPLE'S "GREENBACK."

Electoral vote, 0; Popular vote, 133, [illegible]

Benjamin F. Butler, candidate.

Platform—"We, the National party.... declare: That we hold the late decision of the Supreme Court on the legal-tender question to be a full vindication of the theory [of the party].... We demand the issue of such [legal-tender] money in sufficient quantities to supply the actual demands of trade.... The substitution of greenbacks for national bank notes, and the prompt payment of the public debt; we want that money which saved our country in time of war, and which has given it prosperity and happiness in peace. We condemn the retirement of fractional currency and small denominations of greenbacks, and demand their restoration. We demand the issue of the hoards of money now locked up in the U. S. Treasury by applying them to the payment of the public debt now due. We denounce as dangerous to our republican institutions those methods and policies of the Democratic and Republican parties.... the establishment of land, railroad, money, and other.... monopolies, and we demand [the restoration of these powers] to the people.... That policy which has granted to corporations vast tracts of lands, and we demand.... [restoration of] all such.... as have been forfeited.... We demand Congressional regulation of interstate commerce. We denounce "pooling," stock-watering, discrimination in rates and charges.... We demand a government postal telegraph system. All private property, all forms of money and obligations to pay money should bear their just proportion of public taxes.... we demand a graduated income tax.... amelioration of the condition of labor by enforcing sanitary laws in industrial establishments, by the abolition of the convict-labor system, by the rig[id] inspection of mines and factories, by a reduction of the hours of labor.... by abolishing child labor. We condemn importation of contracted labor.... Insist upon a Constitutional amendment reducing the terms of U. S. Senators one-half.... elective directly by the people; also, making the President ineligible to re-election.... [and] to take away from committees [of Congress] a veto power greater than that of President.... While we favor a wise revision of the tariff.... we insist that.... its importance is insignificant as compared with the financial issue.... Give our farmers and manufacturers money as cheap as you now give our bankers, and they can pay high wages to labor and compete with the whole world.... We are in favor of submitting to a vote of the people an amendment ....in favor of suffrage, regardless of sex, and also on the subject of the liquor traffic. All disabled soldiers of the late war should be equitably pensioned.... We are a National party.... having no sectional prejudices.... We appeal to all.... to aid us by voice, and pen, and votes."

PROHIBITION;

Electoral vote, 0; Popular vote, 151, [illegible]

John P. St. John, candidate.

Platform—"The Prohibition party, in national convention assembled, acknowledge Almighty God as the rightful sovereign of all men, from whom the just powers of government are derived, and to whose laws human enactments should conform as an absolute condition of peace, prosperity and happiness. [Here follows an arraignment of the National and State laws maintaining the traffic in alcoholic beverages, and a statement of the evils flowing therefrom.] We therefore call upon our fellow-citizens to aid in the repeal of these laws and in the legal suppression of this baneful liquor traffic. During the twenty-four years in which the Republican party has controlled the general government and many of the States, no effort has been made to change this policy.... Both [Blaine and Logan] virtually recommend the perpetuation of the traffic.... The Democratic party has ....arrayed itself on the side of the drink-makers and sellers, by declaring against.... "sumptuary laws."... That th[ere] can be no greater peril to t[he] Nation than the existing competition of.... [both] parties for the liquor vote.... Patriots.... should.... withdraw from [both].... We favor.... abolition of all sinecures with useless offices, ...and in elections by the people instead.... appointments by the President.... W[e] oppose removal except.... to secure effectiveness in ... issues.... The collection of revenues from alcoholic beverages and tobacco should be abolished.... duties should be levied for the support of the government economically administered, and in such manner as will foster American industries and labor.... Public lands should be held for homes for the people, and not bestowed as gifts to corporations, or sold in large tracts for speculation.... Grateful care and support.... to our soldiers and sailors disabled.... and to their dependent widows and orphans.... We repudiate as un-American.... that any persons.... be excluded from residence or citizenship.... That.... these reforms.... sink into insignificance when compared with the drink traffic, [here follows a repetition of its evils].... endangering the perpetuity of free institutions.... Congress should prohibit it.... in all places over which the government has exclusive jurisdiction; that hereafter no State should be admitted into the Union until its constitution shall expressly and forever prohibit polygamy and the manufacture and sale of intoxicating beverages; and that Congress shall submit to the States [a "prohibitory"] amendment.... Call attention.... to the baneful effects upon labor and industry of the needless liquor business.... No tariff or other legislation can so healthily stimulate production.... as would the suppression of this traffic.... The activity and co-operation of the women of America.... we gratefully acknowledge.... Believing in the civil and political equality of the sexes, and that the ballot in the hands of woman is her right for protection, and would prove a powerful ally ....We commend the principle [of woman suffrage].... We gratefully acknowledge the presence of the Divine Spirit guiding.... temperance reform...."

1889 to 1893—BENJAMIN HARRISON, President.

States voting, 38; total electoral vote, 401.

REPUBLICAN:

Electoral vote, 233; Popular vote, 5,441,123.

Platform—"The Republicans ....pause to honor the memory of.... Lincoln.... Grant, Garfield, Arthur, Logan, Conkling.... recall.... with prayer for his recovery.... the name of.... Sheridan.... Send congratulations to fellow-Americans of Brazil upon their great act of emancipation.... Hope they may soon congratulate.... citizens of Irish birth upon peaceful recovery of Home Rule for Ireland.... Reaffirm unswerving devotion to the Constitution, and the indissoluble union of the States; the autonomy of the States.... the personal rights and liberties of citizens.... especially the supreme.... right.... to cast one free ballot.... and have that ballot duly counted.... Charge that the.... Administration and the.... majority in Congress owe their existence to the suppression of the ballot.... Favor the American system of protection.... protest against its destruction proposed by the President and his party.... The protective system must be maintained.... Denounce the Mills bill.... Condemn the proposition to place wool on the free list.... Would effect all needed reduction of the national revenue by repealing the taxes upon tobacco.... upon spirits used in the arts and for mechanical purposes; and by such revision of tariff as will check imports of articles produced by our people.... and release from import duties those articles (except luxuries) the like of which cannot be produced at home.... Favor the repeal of internal revenue taxes rather than the surrender of any part of our protective system.... Declare hostility to the introduction of foreign contract labor and of Chinese labor.... Opposition to all combinations of capital organized in trusts.... Approve the legislation by Congress to prevent alike unjust burdens and unfair discriminations between the States.... Reaffirm the policy of appropriating the public lands to be homesteads of citizens and settlers.... The restoration of unearned railroad land grants to the public domain for the use of actual settlers.... should be continued.... Deny that the Democratic party has ever restored one acre.... but declare that by the joint action of Republicans and Democrats about fifty millions of acres.... have been restored.... Charge the Administration with failure to execute the laws securing to settlers title to their homesteads.... The government by Congress of the Territories is based upon necessity only to the end that they may become States.... the people of such Territories should be permitted, as a right inherent in them, to form for themselves Constitutions and State governments, and be admitted into the Union.... all officers thereof should be selected from the bona fide residents and citizens.... South Dakota should of right be immediately admitted.... Pledge the party to do all in its power to facilitate the admission of the Territories.... The political power of the Mormon church.... is a menace to free institutions.... therefore we pledge the Republican party to.... legislation stringent enough to divorce the political from the ecclesiastical power, and thus stamp out the attendant wickedness of polygamy ....Favor the use of both gold and silver as money, and condemn the policy of the Administration in its efforts to demonetize silver.... Demand reduction of letter postage to one cent per ounce.... The State or Nation, or both combined, should support free institutions of learning sufficient to afford to every child.... a good common-school education.... Recommend the rehabilitation of our merchant marine, and protest against a Free-Ship bill as calculated to work injustice to labor.... Demand appropriations for the early rebuilding of our navy; the construction of coast fortifications and modern ordnance.... the payment of just pensions to our soldiers.... the improvement of harbors and channels.... the encouragement of the shipping interests.... as well as the payment of the maturing public debt.... far better for our country than the Democratic policy of loaning the Government's money without interest to "pet banks".... The conduct of foreign affairs by the administration has been distinguished by inefficiency and cowardice. Having withdrawn from the Senate all pending treaties.... it has neither effected nor proposed any others.... It has seen with idle complacency the extension of foreign influence in Central America, and of foreign trade everywhere among our neighbors. It has refused to charter, sanction or encourage any American organization for constructing the Nicaragua Canal.... arraign the Administration for its weak and unpatriotic treatment of the fisheries question.... and condemn the policy of the majority in Congress toward our fisheries.... Citizenship is and must be the panoply and safeguard of him who wears it.... it should and must afford him protection at home and follow and protect him abroad.... The men who abandoned the Republican party in 1884.... have deserted the cause of reform in the civil service.... Auspiciously begun under the Republican Administration it should be completed by further extension.... Denounce the spirit shown by President Cleveland in his numerous vetoes of measures for pension relief, and the action of the Democratic House of Representatives in refusing even consideration of general pension legislation.... Invite the co-operation of patriotic men of all parties, and especially of all working men, whose prosperity is seriously threatened by the free-trade policy of the Administration. *Resolution*—The first concern of all good government is the virtue and sobriety of the people and the purity of their homes. The Republican party cordially sympathizes with all wise and well-directed efforts for the promotion of temperance and morality."

DEMOCRATIC:

Electoral vote, 168; Popular vote, 5,536,2[illegible]

Grover Cleveland, candidate.

Platform—"The Democratic party.... reaffirms the platform.... of 1884, and endorses the views expressed by President Cleveland in his last annual message as the correct interpretation of that platform upon tariff reduction, and also endorses the efforts of Representatives to secure a reduction of excessive taxation. Chief among its principles are the maintenance of an indissoluble union of free and indestructible States.... devotion to a plan of government regulated by a written Constitution, strictly specifying every granted power and expressly reserving to the States or people the entire ungranted residue of power, the encouragement of a jealous popular vigilance directed to all classes to enact and execute the laws and charged with the duty of preserving peace, insuring equality and establishing justice.... Welcomes an exacting scrutiny of the Administration.... Challenges the most searching inquiry concerning its fidelity.... During a most critical period of our financial affairs.... it has.... not only averted disaster, but greatly promoted the prosperity of the people. It has reversed the improvident policy of the Republican party touching the public domain, and has ....restored nearly one hundred millions of acres.... to be sacredly held as homesteads.... While carefully guarding the interest of the taxpayers and conforming strictly to the principles of justice and equality, it has paid more for pensions and bounties to the soldiers and sailors than was ever paid before during an equal period.... It has set on foot the reconstruction of the Navy upon a system which forbids the recurrence of scandal and insures successful results. It has adopted and consistently pursued a firm and prudent foreign policy, preserving peace.... while scrupulously maintaining all the rights and interests of government and people at home and abroad. The exclusion of Chinese laborers has been effectually secured.... Honest reform

PROHIBITION:

UNION LABOR:

UNITED LABOR:

AMERICAN:

NOTES.

Alphabetical List of Towns and Counties.

The following is an alphabetical list, by states, of every county, city, town, village and post office in the United States, and shows the population of the same according to the census of 1890. There are some small places whose population was taken together with the civil district in which they are located, and the exact figure being unknown is marked ×. State capitals and large cities are in caps, thus — BOSTON. County towns are in full-faced type, thus — **Buffalo**. Post-offices are in Roman, thus — Boscawen. Places not post offices are in italic, thus — *Aetna*. Express offices are indicated thus — ●. The index letters refer to that portion of the state in which the several counties are located as follows: —

N. .... Northern | E. .... Eastern | N.E. .... North-Eastern | N.W. .... North-Western
S. .... Southern | W. .... Western | S.E. .... South-Eastern | S.W. .... South-Western
C. .... Central

To find any place, first find the county in which it is situated, using the index letters to ascertain its location. The county name being large is quickly seen, as the town will be readily found within its boundaries if on the map. Many small places have been left off the maps owing to lack of space to engrave them, but they will all be found in this list, and their locations can be readily determined by means of the index letters.

ALABAMA.

ALABAMA.—ALASKA.—ARIZONA.

TOWNS.	COUNTIES.	INDEX.	POP.
[illegible]	[illegible]	[illegible]	[illegible]

ALASKA.

[illegible]

ARIZONA.

COUNTIES.	INDEX.	POP.
[illegible]	[illegible]	[illegible]

TOWNS.	COUNTIES.	INDEX.	POP.
[illegible]	[illegible]	[illegible]	[illegible]

ARKANSAS.

ARKANSAS.

[illegible]

CALIFORNIA.

[illegible]

COLORADO.

CONNECTICUT.

DELAWARE.

COUNTIES.	INDEX.	POP.
Kent	C	[illegible]
New Castle	N	[illegible]
Sussex	S	[illegible]
Total		[illegible]

Dist. of Columbia.

FLORIDA.

GEORGIA.

GEORGIA.

GEORGIA.

IDAHO.

ILLINOIS.

TOWNS. COUNTIES. INDEX. POP.

*Population included in Chicago.

*Population included in Chicago.

15

ILLINOIS.

INDIANA

INDIANA.

Indian Territory.

Woodbury
Worth
Wright
Total

IOWA.

IOWA.

KANSAS.

KANSAS.

TOWNS.	COUNTIES.	INDEX.	POP.
[illegible]	[illegible]	[illegible]	[illegible]

KENTUCKY.

KENTUCKY.

KENTUCKY.

[illegible]

LOUISIANA.

[illegible]

MAINE.

Total

MAINE.

MARYLAND.

Massachusetts.

MICHIGAN.

MINNESOTA.

MISSISSIPPI.

MISSISSIPPI.

MISSOURI.

MISSOURI.

TOWNS. COUNTIES. INDEX.	POP.	TOWNS. COUNTIES. INDEX.	POP.	TOWNS. COUNTIES. INDEX.	POP.	TOWNS. COUNTIES. INDEX.	POP.	TOWNS. COUNTIES. INDEX.	POP.	TOWNS. COUNTIES. INDEX.	POP.
[illegible]	[illegible]	[illegible]	[illegible]	[illegible]	[illegible]	[illegible]	[illegible]	[illegible]	[illegible]	[illegible]	[illegible]

42

TOWNS. COUNTIES. INDEX. POP.

[illegible]

MONTANA.

COUNTIES. INDEX. POP.

[illegible]

Total [illegible]

TOWNS. COUNTIES. INDEX. POP.

[illegible]

NEBRASKA

NEBRASKA.

NEVADA.

NEWHAMPSHIRE.

NEW JERSEY.

NEW MEXICO.

NEW YORK.

NEW YORK.

TOWNS. COUNTIES. INDEX.	POP.	TOWNS. COUNTIES. INDEX.	POP.	TOWNS. COUNTIES. INDEX.	POP.	TOWNS. COUNTIES. INDEX.	POP.	TOWNS. COUNTIES. INDEX.	POP.	TOWNS. COUNTIES. INDEX.	POP.
[illegible]	[illegible]	[illegible]	[illegible]	[illegible]	[illegible]	[illegible]	[illegible]	[illegible]	[illegible]	[illegible]	[illegible]

32

NEW YORK.

TOWNS. COUNTIES. INDEX. POP.

[illegible]

64

NORTH CAROLINA

NORTH CAROLINA.

NORTH DAKOTA.

OHIO.

58

OHIO.

62

OKLAHOMA.

OREGON.

PENNSYLVANIA.

PENNSYLVANIA.

TOWNS. COUNTIES. INDEX.	POP.	TOWNS. COUNTIES. INDEX.	POP.	TOWNS. COUNTIES. INDEX.	POP.	TOWNS. COUNTIES. INDEX.	POP.	TOWNS. COUNTIES. INDEX.	POP.	TOWNS. COUNTIES. INDEX.	POP.
[illegible]	[illegible]	[illegible]	[illegible]	[illegible]	[illegible]	[illegible]	[illegible]	[illegible]	[illegible]	[illegible]	[illegible]

PENNSYLVANIA.

PENNSYLVANIA.

TOWNS. COUNTIES. INDEX. POP.

PENNSYLVANIA.

TOWNS. COUNTIES. INDEX.	POP.	TOWNS. COUNTIES. INDEX.	POP.	TOWNS. COUNTIES. INDEX.	POP.	TOWNS. COUNTIES. INDEX.	POP.	TOWNS. COUNTIES. INDEX.	POP.	TOWNS. COUNTIES. INDEX.	POP.
[illegible]	[illegible]	[illegible]	[illegible]	[illegible]	[illegible]	[illegible]	[illegible]	[illegible]	[illegible]	[illegible]	[illegible]

PENNSYLVANIA.

TOWNS.	COUNTIES.	INDEX.	POP.	TOWNS.	COUNTIES.	INDEX.	POP.	TOWNS.	COUNTIES.	INDEX.	POP.	TOWNS.	COUNTIES.	INDEX.	POP.	TOWNS.	COUNTIES.	INDEX.	POP.	TOWNS.	COUNTIES.	INDEX.	POP.
[illegible]	[illegible]	[illegible]	[illegible]	[illegible]	[illegible]	[illegible]	[illegible]	[illegible]	[illegible]	[illegible]	[illegible]	[illegible]	[illegible]	[illegible]	[illegible]	[illegible]	[illegible]	[illegible]	[illegible]	[illegible]	[illegible]	[illegible]	[illegible]

70

RHODE ISLAND.

SOUTH CAROLINA

[illegible]

SOUTH DAKOTA.

[illegible]

TENNESSEE

TENNESSEE.

TENNESSEE.

TOWNS. COUNTIES. INDEX. POP.

TEXAS.

COUNTIES. INDEX. POP.

TEXAS.

TEXAS.

TEXAS.

UTAH.

VERMONT.

VIRGINIA.

VIRGINIA.

VIRGINIA.

WASHINGTON.

WEST VIRGINIA

WEST VIRGINIA.

WISCONSIN.

WISCONSIN.

WYOMING.

WYOMING.

TOWNS. COUNTIES. INDEX.	POP
[illegible], Laramie....SE	×
● Salt Wells, Sweetwater...C	×
● Sanders, Albany....SE	×
Saratoga, Carbon....S	50
Savery, Carbon....S	×
● [illegible] Spur, Laramie...SE	×
[illegible], Carbon....S	42
● [illegible], Converse....E	×
Shell, Big Horn....N	×
Sheridan, Sheridan....N	[illegible]
● Sherman, Albany....SE	45
[illegible], Carbon....S	×
Shoshone Agency, Fremont...W	35
● Siding Number Ten, Weston..E	×
Siding Number Eleven, Weston....E	×
● Siding Number Twelve, Weston....E	×
[illegible], Albany....SE	×
● [illegible], Laramie....SE	56
Silver Crown, Laramie....SE	×
● [illegible], Carbon....S	×
[illegible], Carbon....S	×
● Soda Lake, Albany....SE	×
● Soda Wells, Albany....SE	×
● [illegible], Carbon....S	×
South Bend, Laramie....SE	15
South Pass City, Fremont....W	75
Spring Creek, Big Horn....N	×
Spring Hill, Albany....SE	×
Spring of [illegible], [illegible]....C	×
● [illegible], Natrona....C	×
Sulphur, Carbon....S	×
Sundance, Crook....NE	400
[illegible], Fremont....W	×
[illegible], Carbon....S	60
[illegible], Natrona....C	×
● Table Rock, Sweetwater....C	×
● [illegible], Uinta....W	×
● [illegible], Sweetwater....C	×
[illegible], Converse....E	50
● [illegible], Albany....SE	132
● [illegible], Sweetwater....C	×
● [illegible], Sweetwater....C	×
[illegible], Converse....E	50
[illegible], Big Horn....N	×
[illegible], Laramie....SE	×
[illegible], [illegible]....N	50
● [illegible], Laramie....SE	×
[illegible], Laramie....SE	×
[illegible], Uinta....W	×
[illegible], Laramie....SE	×
112 Mile Post, Sheridan....N	×
113 Mile Post, Sheridan....N	×
● Uva, Laramie....SE	50
● [illegible], Converse....E	×
[illegible], Sweetwater....C	×
[illegible], Laramie....SE	×
[illegible], Converse....E	×
[illegible], Laramie....SE	×
● [illegible], Carbon....S	×
[illegible], Converse....E	×
[illegible], Carbon....S	×
● [illegible], Sweetwater....C	×
Ward, Crook....NE	×

www.ingramcontent.com/pod-product-compliance
Lightning Source LLC
Chambersburg PA
CBHW031358270326
41929CB00010BA/1238

* 9 7 8 3 3 3 7 2 9 3 7 7 2 *